Sustainable Tourism

The Sustainable World

Aims and Objectives

Sustainability is a key concept of 21st century planning in that it broadly determines the ability of the current generation to use resources and live a lifestyle without compromising the ability of future generations to do the same. Sustainability affects our environment, economics, security, resources, health, economics, transport and information decisions strategy. It also encompasses decision making, from the highest administrative office, to the basic community level. It is planned that this Book Series will cover many of these aspects across a range of topical fields for the greater appreciation and understanding of all those involved in researching or implementing sustainability projects in their field of work.

Topics

Data Analysis
Data Mining Methodologies
Risk Management
Brownfield Development
Landscaping and Visual Impact Studies
Public Health Issues
Environmental and Urban Monitoring
Waste Management
Energy Use and Conservation
Institutional, Legal and Economic Issues
Education
Visual Impact
Simulation Systems
Forecasting
Infrastructure and Maintenance
Mobility and Accessibility
Strategy and Development Studies
Environment Pollution and Control
Land Use
Transport, Traffic and Integration
City, Urban and Industrial Planning
The Community and Urban Living
Public Safety and Security
Global Trends

Associate Editors

FIRST INTERNATIONAL CONFERENCE ON SUSTAINABLE TOURISM

Sustainable Tourism 2004

Conference Chairmen

F.D. Pineda
Complutense University, Spain

C.A. Brebbia
Wessex Institute of Technology, UK

International Scientific Advisory Committee

Organised by:

The Wessex Institute of Technology, The Inter-University Department of Ecology of Madrid (involving the Universities Complutense, Autónoma and Alcalá) and EUROPARC España

Sponsored by:

Ministry of Culture and Tourism, Regional Government of Castilla y León, Spain
Municipality of Segovia, Spain

Sustainable Tourism

Editors

F.D. Pineda
Complutense University, Spain

C.A. Brebbia
Wessex Institute of Technology, UK

F.D. Pineda
Complutense University, Spain

C.A. Brebbia
Wessex Institute of Technology, UK

Published by

WIT Press
Ashurst Lodge, Ashurst, Southampton, SO40 7AA, UK
Tel: 44 (0) 238 029 3223; Fax: 44 (0) 238 029 2853
E-Mail: witpress@witpress.com
http://www.witpress.com

For USA, Canada and Mexico

Computational Mechanics Inc
25 Bridge Street, Billerica, MA 01821, USA
Tel: 978 667 5841; Fax: 978 667 7582
E-Mail: infousa@witpress.com
http://www.witpress.com

British Library Cataloguing-in-Publication Data

A Catalogue record for this book is available
from the British Library

ISBN: 1-85312-724-8
ISSN: 1476-9581

The texts of the papers in this volume were set individually by the authors or under their supervision. Only minor corrections to the text may have been carried out by the publisher.

Printed in Great Britain by Athenaeum Press Ltd., Gateshead

Preface

The use of energy not related to feeding and the capacity to transport people and resources over long distances are probably the two essential ecological characteristics that differentiate humans from the remaining biological communities on the planet. Among these characteristics, R. Margalef also includes the use of money and the pollution of the planet.

All of this can be seen in a new phenomenon in the history of humanity – tourism. Indeed, this is an activity typical of *Homo sapiens*. Tourism involves more than anything else the transport of people, but the concentration of these in determined regions and areas requires the transport of considerable amounts of material and energy for their use in these places. This is a lucrative activity and frequently leads to noteworthy changes in the structure of the natural and cultural landscape, as well as a formidable socioeconomic evolution, both in the tourist resorts and, in general, in the society of the State bent on the development of tourism.

Tourism has become tremendously developed in determined regions of the world, and no place is any longer free from curious travelers. Environmental degradation is inexorably accompanied by certain mass manifestations of this activity. The changes that have taken place in many coastal and mountain landscapes, both linked to a high level of seasonal demand, are very evident and serious. At the same time, cultural tourism, until recently practiced by a small number of people, has become more and more established, and involves certain peculiar requirements related to environmental quality. History, reflected in monuments and diverse human works, the traditional agricultural landscape, wildlife and the private life itself of villages and cities have become clear tourist attractions.

In this context, it must be recognized that tourism will not constitute a sustainable activity if we do not carefully study and formalize the demands of a human population that is traveling more and more, along with the characteristics of the sites which attract tourists for multiple reasons.

It is not only the environmental quality of the tourist sites, with a rising number of visitors exercising greater pressure, that is at stake. The cultural landscapes are also being affected, the people who created and maintained them having moved their activities to the tourist sites, attracted by the easy money related to the services required by tourism. The cultural diversity of large areas is therefore related to tourism and sustainability. The organizers of this Conference have therefore kept in mind these problems, gathering together in Segovia a heterogeneous group of experts, attracted by tourism, the common denominator, and motivated by the great variety of circumstances converging therein. The Conference deals with themes which link tourism to the cultural landscape, the protected natural areas, transport, and the economic and social infrastructures and conditioning factors of tourism.

This book is an updated sample of this convergence of interests, which not only involves the professionals, but rather the whole of society.

The Editors,
Segovia, 2004.

Contents

Section 3: Sustainable tourism

Section 4: Ecotourism

Section 5: Cultural tourism

Section 6: Coastal issues

Section 7: Tourism and protected areas

Section 8: Tourism, infrastructure, transport and hotels

Section 9: Surveys and analysis

Section 10: IT in tourism

Section 1
Tourism impact

Assessing tourism's impacts using local communities' attitudes toward the environment

A. Benson[1] & J. Clifton[2]
[1]*Centre for Tourism Policy Studies (CENTOPS), University of Brighton, UK*
[2]*Department of Geography, University of Portsmouth, UK*

Abstract

The presence of ecotourism activities is often cited as a significant benefit in environmental terms owing to the potential for income generation to be linked towards conservation activities. This is of enhanced significance in remote areas of developing countries where opportunities for other forms of economic development may be limited. However, notions of effective conservation are almost exclusively based on Western ideals and principles, with little understanding of local residents attitudes. This research is therefore directed towards examining environmental perceptions held by local residents in a marine protected area in Southeast Sulawesi, Indonesia with a view to assessing the requirements of environmental education programmes initiated by a local ecotourism organisation. Two local indigenous communities were the focus of this work, which used a Modified Thematic Apperception Test to quantify attitudes towards the local environment as represented in a series of illustrations. Statistical analysis indicates that culture and gender characteristics influences environmental preferences. This data indicates the need to recognise the differing environmental perceptions held by the different indigenous groups and therefore, to tailor existing environmental education programmes more directly, in order that the environmental benefits of ecotourism in the region can be appreciated more widely.
Keywords: conservation, ecotourism, environment, indigenous community attitudes, Indonesia.

Sustainable Tourism, F. D. Pineda, C. A. Brebbia & M. Mugica (Editors)
© 2004 WIT Press, www.witpress.com, ISBN 1-85312-724-8

1 Introduction

The presence of ecotourism activities is often cited [1,2,3,4] as a significant benefit in environmental terms, owing to the potential for income generation to be linked towards conservation activities. This is of enhanced significance in remote areas of developing countries where opportunities for other forms of economic development may be limited. However, notions of effective conservation are almost exclusively based on Western ideals and principles, with little understanding of local residents' attitudes. Community perceptions towards conservation programmes and how this is linked to environmental awareness have been well documented in the literature; both positive [5,6,7] and negative attitudes [8,9,10,11]. Successful programmes have similar features; public participation from the beginning, education, collaboration and public participation. Lack of consultation and participation by local communities has fuelled hostilities and loss of trust. Key elements of success in many conservation programmes, has been the implementation of comprehensive education courses or the development of interpretation centres. These assist in raising the whole community's understanding and awareness of the environment and conservation issues. However, these programmes are only successful when the methods of communication are relevant to the specific community where age, gender and literacy levels are considered.

This paper aims to determine whether the two indigenous groups in the study area perceive the environment in similar or different ways. It also focuses on whether gender and age are issues in understanding the environment. The analysis and evaluation of this data is focused towards assessing the requirements of an environmental education programme(s) initiated by a local ecotourism organisation, which meets the needs of the indigenous communities in the study.

2 Background

The two indigenous communities are situated in close proximity to each other within the Wakotabi Marine National park, Southeast Sulawesi, Indonesia. (Figure 1.) Both of these communities have close links to the UK based ecotourism organisation, 'Operation Wallacea' who have operated in the area since 1995. While these communities are located in a remote part of Indonesia, it should be noted that they have access to satellite TV and members of the family often travel to find work in other parts of Asia.

2.1 The Bajau community of Sampela

The 'Bajau' originally lived entirely on the sea, and were commonly called "Sea Gypsies" [12], but due to pressure from the Indonesian government many communities have now settled. Despite this, they still tend to be marginalized and excluded from mainstream society [13]. The Bajau community of Sampela has a total population of 870 and they have settled in a stilt village, which is

Sustainable Tourism, F. D. Pineda, C. A. Brebbia & M. Mugica (Editors)

situated on mudflats and strides out into the sea [14] between Kaledupa and Hoga Islands. Their main sources of food and income come from fishing and 'farming the sea'. The main religion is based on the belief of Spirits and Bajau children finish their formal education at age ten/eleven.

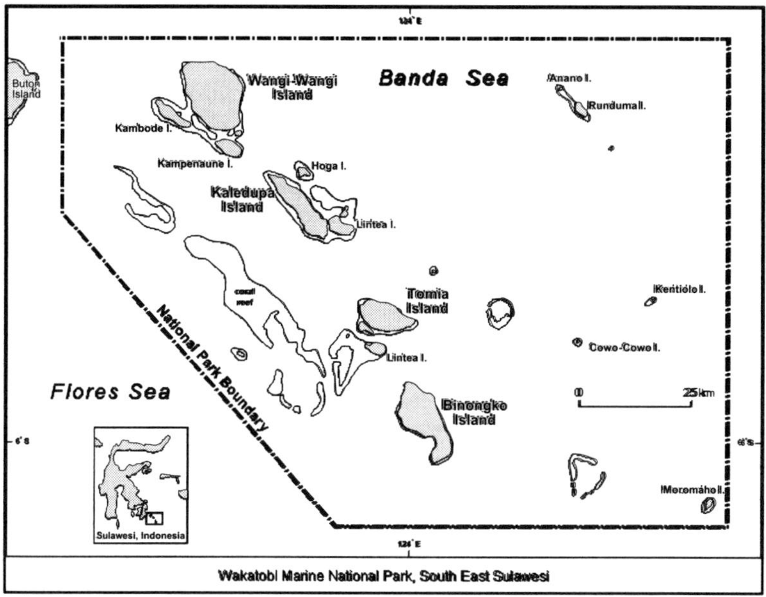

Figure 1: Wakatobi Marine National Park, Indonesia

2.2 The Kaledupan community of Ambeua

This land-based community were established prior to the Bajau settlement and has a population now of just over 2,000. The structure of the community is typical of mainstream Indonesian society including service sector jobs, such as civil servants, doctors, teachers and tradesmen. The Kaledupan community are Muslim and children go to school until the age of sixteen. Traditionally, the main income streams have been agriculture and fishing, however, some of the community members are now employed by Operation Wallacea.

2.3 Operation Wallacea

Operation Wallacea operate from a base site situated on the island of Hoga, a small uninhabited Island within the national park. In addition to this; they have also set up two small satellite camps in Sampela and Ambeua, where international tourists come and stay in a community setting. The organisation conducts a number of scientific wildlife surveys and conservation expeditions [15]. It has also set up various projects to support the environment and encourage the local communities to conserve their resources. Whilst the

Sustainable Tourism, F. D. Pineda, C. A. Brebbia & M. Mugica (Editors)

company believe they have had some success stories; cyanide and bomb fishing have been virtually eradicated and a 'no fishing' zone has been set up; they also recognise that further work with the local communities is necessary to ensure long term sustainability of the national park.

3 Method

In order to quantify attitudes towards the local environment the Thematic Apperception Test, as used by Pollnac [16] was modified. This enabled a visiting artist to sketch a series of six illustrations of local scenes and activities, creating a selection of images that were familiar and identifiable to the local communities. The images were designed to evoke responses about perceptions, either positive or negative, about the everyday environmental surroundings. The images depicted were: a typical Indonesian village of the area, a pristine forest, an area that had suffered deforestation, a mangrove scene, a man net fishing and a woman farming seaweed. The one to one interviews consisted of placing the six images in front of the interviewee in a random order and asking them which image they liked the most and the least, the remaining images were ranked in order of preference. Once the rank order was determined, interviewees were asked to justify why they preferred one image to the next. Forty interviews (10 males, 10 females, 10 boys, 10 girls) were conducted in each of the study villages, Ambuea and Sampela, thus ensuring that the aims of the research could be met with a representative sample in terms of age and gender. In all interviews an interpreter was used to translate between English and Indonesian and in some cases English to Bajau, as some of the older Bajau community did not speak Indonesian. The interpreter was instructed to report what was said and not guide the interviewee or adapt responses in any way.

3.1 Data analysis

Trends were identified in terms of the 'most preferred' and 'least preferred' images. Factor analysis identified certain groups within the whole data set that followed a particular trend in the responses. A series of two tail t-tests identified significant contrasts between categories on ethnicity, culture, gender and age.

4 Research findings

The criteria, in the right hand column of the tables is determined from the illustrations used and outlined in the Method section. Section 4.1 draws comparisons across the whole data set for the Bajau and Kaledupan communities, 4.2 and 4.3 continues on this theme of comparing across the communities and explores the issues of age and gender. The shaded rows in the tables highlight the criteria that are statistically significant, at the $p < 0.05$ level.

Sustainable Tourism, F. D. Pineda, C. A. Brebbia & M. Mugica (Editors)

4.1 Comparison of indigenous communities

As can be seen from Table 1, four of the six criteria show significant differences between the two ethnic communities. If we examine this more closely, it was found that 30% of all Bajau ranked *village* as first (most preferred) compared to 18% of the Kaledupan data set; 18% of Bajau ranked the *forest* as sixth (least preferred) but 0% by Kaledupans; *Logging* was ranked sixth by 38% Bajau and 90% Kaledupans and *mangroves* were ranked as first by 35% Kaledupans and only 3% Bajau.

Table 1: Comparison of Bajau and Kaledupan communities.

Criteria	Bajau Data Set (n=40) Mean	Kaledupan Data Set (n=40) Mean	T Test Statistic
Village	2.6	3.3	0.04
Forest	4.2	3.25	0.00
Deforestation	4.7	5.9	<0.01
Mangroves	3.7	2.3	<0.01
Fishing	2.5	3.1	0.13
Seaweed	3.0	3.1	0.68

4.2 Adults

Table 2 shows that there is only one significant difference between Bajau Adults and Kaledupan Adults. Kaledupan Adults have a higher preference for Mangroves than Bajau Adults.

Table 2: Comparison of Bajau and Kaledupan adults.

Criteria	Bajau Adults (n= 20) Mean	Kaledupan Adults (n= 20) Mean	T Test Statistic
Village	2.95	2.9	0.92
Forest	4.1	3.25	0.08
Deforestation	5.35	5.85	0.07
Mangroves	3.0	2.2	0.01
Fishing	2.45	3.05	0.20
Seaweed	2.7	3.45	0.16

As can be seen in Table 3 and 4, five of the criteria demonstrate significant differences between the men of the different ethnic groups, whilst the women groupings only show one. Table 3 demonstrates that the *village, logging* and *fishing* criteria are ranked higher for Bajau men, meaning these were their preferred scenes. Kaledupan men preferred the *forest* and *mangroves* criteria. Table 4 highlights a lower ranking for *deforestation* amongst Kaledupan women than Bajau women.

Sustainable Tourism, F. D. Pineda, C. A. Brebbia & M. Mugica (Editors)

Table 3: Comparison of Bajau and Kaledupan men.

Criteria	Bajau Men (n=10) Mean	Kaledupan Men (n=10) Mean	T Test Statistic
Village	2.55	3.45	0.04
Forest	4.2	3.15	0.01
Deforestation	4.55	5.75	0.00
Mangroves	4	1.7	<0.01
Fishing	1.7	3.2	0.00
Seaweed	3.35	3.4	0.92

Table 4: Comparison of Bajau and Kaledupan women.

Criteria	Bajau Women (n=10) Mean	Kaledupan Women (n=10) Mean	T Test Statistic
Village	2.65	3.1	0.37
Forest	4.2	3.35	0.07
Deforestation	4.9	5.95	0.00
Mangroves	3.35	2.75	0.15
Fishing	3.3	2.9	0.43
Seaweed	2.55	2.8	0.64

4.3 Children

When examining the test results between Bajau and Kaledupan Children, Table 5, it can seen that Bajau Children showed a higher preference for the *village* and Kaledupan Children a higher preference for *mangroves*, whilst Bajau Children demonstrate a lower preference for the *forest* and Kaledupan Children a lower preference for the *deforestation* scene.

Table 5: Comparison of Bajau and Kaledupan children.

Criteria	Bajau Children (n=20) Mean	Kaledupan Children (n=20) Mean	T Test Statistic
Village	2.25	3.65	0.00
Forest	4.3	3.25	0.01
Deforestation	4.1	5.85	<0.01
Mangroves	4.35	2.25	<0.01
Fishing	2.55	3.05	0.38
Seaweed	3.02	2.75	0.37

The significant differences between Bajau boys and Kaledupan boys as seen in Table 6 are the *deforestation* and *mangrove* scenes. The *deforestation* shows a low preference for Kaledupan boys but a high preference for the Bajau boys. It should be noted that this demonstrates an inverse effect in that, the Bajau boys

Sustainable Tourism, F. D. Pineda, C. A. Brebbia & M. Mugica (Editors)
© 2004 WIT Press, www.witpress.com, ISBN 1-85312-724-8

have no interest in *deforestation* and it is not important for them to give it a low preference value. The *mangrove* scene demonstrates a high preference for the Kaledupan boys but a low preference for the Bajau, this is particularly interesting and will be discussed later.

Table 6: Comparison of Bajau and Kaledupan boys.

Criteria	Bajau Boys (n=10) Mean	Kaledupan Boys (n=10) Mean	T Test Statistic
Village	2.9	3.9	1.87
Forest	4.3	3.2	1.98
Deforestation	3.9	5.8	3.50
Mangroves	5.1	1.7	8.33
Fishing	1.4	3.1	2.64
Seaweed	3.0	3.2	0.30

Table 7, the *village* criteria for the Bajau girls is the highest ranked scene whilst for the Kaledupan girls it ranked fifth out of the six criteria and therefore, is a low preference. The *deforestation* criteria for the girls mirrors the preferences of the boys, as shown above.

Table 7: Comparison of Bajau and Kaledupan girls.

Criteria	Bajau Girls (n=10) Mean	Kaledupan Girls (n=10) Mean	T Test Statistic
Village	1.6	3.4	3.30
Forest	4.3	3.3	1.67
Deforestation	4.3	5.9	3.68
Mangroves	3.6	2.8	1.20
Fishing	3.7	3.0	0.90
Seaweed	3.4	2.3	1.47

5 Discussion

There are significant statistical differences between the responses of the Bajau and Kaledupan communities and, therefore, appear to place different values on their local surroundings. The findings as a whole suggest that the Bajau community are less aware of the consequences of their actions with regard to the environment. It would also seem that gender and to a lesser extent age differences, contribute to environmental preference. However, the general neutral responses in both communities could reflect the lack of experience of being consulted This is particularly so for women and children and the lack of a

Sustainable Tourism, F. D. Pineda, C. A. Brebbia & M. Mugica (Editors)

definite range in the mean results may reflect lack of individual opinions and reflect community values.

Values attributed to the images generally tended to relate to the familiarity, aesthetic and social aspects, as well as the resource and utility functions of what was observed and identified. This is indicative of typical responses in developing countries. The Bajau's strong attachment to marine activities and a lower degree of respect for the land was demonstrated throughout the results, highlighting cultural beliefs and may in part be a consequence of their limited educational background. The Kaledupan's more substantial appreciation of the environment is improved by more formal education and greater access to global media through television.

The sense of community and village life is stronger in the Bajau community and this is demonstrated throughout the data set. It could also be argued that they appear to be more utilitarian in their view of the natural surroundings. Both communities showed a high preference for the fishing scene, which is obviously influenced by the marine location of both communities and is viewed as a source of livelihood by both communities. Seaweed harvesting is also viewed as important by both communities and is a prominent activity in the local area. However, there is little doubt that seaweed harvesting is seen as more important by the women than the men. It is also considered to be the work of women in both communities and this is reflected in the findings.

With the exception of boys, all of the Bajau sub-sets (men, women and girls) put the forest and deforestation as their least preferred criteria. Whilst for the boys the least preferred image was the mangroves, with forest and deforestation ranked the next least favourites. The Bajau discussed not ranking the land-based scenes highly, with fears about the darkness under the canopy and creatures inside the forest and in some cases ancestral stories about spirits influenced their responses. There was, however, a utility value in respect of the natural materials that they readily use to construct their homes and boats, *"the trees can be cut down to make poles for houses"* and *"the wood can be used for many things including firewood or furniture"* indicate this usage. The Bajau do not venture far in-land and collect the resources they require as close to the shoreline as possible. The lower scores for Kaledupan men, could reflect greater environmental consequences of deforestation, as they appear to have a greater awareness of the longer-term conservation issues, although this may be due to its economic value, rather than a strict utilitarian value. Responses from the Kaledupan community showed knowledge of environmental awareness. Comments on carbon dioxide exchange and soil stability were common, one response highlights this *"this activity will cause erosion and flooding and make the soil infertile – all the plants will die"*.

With regard to the mangroves, it is mainly the Bajau boys who collect mangrove wood in their dug-out canoes. Whilst it is viewed as a resource that they use, the fact that the Bajau place their deceased community members in the mangrove undergrowth may highlight why the Bajau boys show this as their least preferred image. Kaledupans have a more positive association with mangroves and are less involved with cutting mangroves than the Bajau. It is

Sustainable Tourism, F. D. Pineda, C. A. Brebbia & M. Mugica (Editors)

also clear to see that the Kaledupans maintain a form of stewardship over the mangroves and have been engaged in replanting schemes in some areas.

One of the reasons the Kaledupan community may be more positive towards the environment is that Operation Wallacea recently gave a presentation to both communities on the significance of mangroves, sea grasses and corals. This was well received, particularly in the Kaledupan community with a high attendance level by Kaledupan men. The presentation to the Bajau was represented by women and children, although it was not well attended. It is unclear why the levels of attendance in the two communities differed and this would be an issue for the ecotourism operator to investigate further.

If the ecotourism operator, Operation Wallacea, is to pursue its educational environmental programme for the local communities, it will need to accept that both communities require a tailored programme of activities that reflects the findings of this paper. Issues such as the level of education being different across the two communities; the Bajau having a more utilitarian approach to resources; the problems of dealing with a community who are superstitious and believe in spirit folklore and in both communities as age increases environmental concerns appear to decrease, which may be associated with familiarity of surroundings; will all need to be part of the evaluation. However, the success of previous educational work by the operator must be acknowledged as this has resulted in positive responses towards the environment and this could be used as a stepping-stone for further work. It is important that the focus of the environmental education programme is to ensure that the indigenous communities are able to manage their resources in a sustainable manner and benefit from ecotourism activities in the area.

6 Conclusions

Statistical analysis indicates that the Bajau and Kaledupan communities are significantly different; it further indicates that culture and gender characteristics influence environmental preferences. Both communities showed high preferences for scenes related to the marine environment, however, the difference between land based scenes demonstrated, the Bajau have little regard for the land except in utilitarian terms, whereas the Kaledupan recognise the importance of land based resources. In general, the Bajau community are less aware of the consequences of their actions on the environment than the Kaledupan community, which may, in part be due to recent educational presentations by the local ecotourism operator. This data indicates the need to recognise the differing environmental perceptions held by the two indigenous groups and therefore, to tailor existing environmental education programmes more directly, in order that the environmental benefits of ecotourism in the region can be appreciated more widely and resources are managed in a sustainable way.

Sustainable Tourism, F. D. Pineda, C. A. Brebbia & M. Mugica (Editors)

References

[1] Boo, E., *Ecotourism: The potentials and pitfalls*, volume 1, World Wildlife Fund: Pennsylvania, 1990.
[2] Weaver, D.B., *Ecotourism in the Less Developed World*, CABI Publishing: New York, 1998
[3] Fennell, D.A., *Ecotourism: An introduction*, Routledge: London and New York,1999.
[4] Wearing, S. & Neil, J., *Ecotourism: impacts, potentials and possibilities*, Butterworth-Heinemann: Oxford, 1999.
[5] Gibson, J., McField, M & Wells, S., Coral reef management in Belize: an approach through integrated Coastal Zone Management, *Ocean and Coastal Management,* 39, pp. 229-244, 1998.
[6] Shafter, C. & Benzaken, D., User perceptions about the marine wilderness on Australia's Great Barrier Reef, *Coastal Management*, 26, pp.79-91, 1998.
[7] Bunce, L., Gustavson, K., Williams, J. & Miller, M., The human side of reef management: a case study analysis of the socio-economic framework of Montego Bay Marine Park, *Coral Reefs*, 18, pp. 369-380, 1999.
[8] Akama, J.S., Lant, C.L., & Burnett, G.W., Conflicting attitudes toward state wildlife conservation programs in Kenya, *Society and Natural Resources*, 8, pp. 133-144, 1994.
[9] Holl, K. D., Daily, G. C. & Ehrlich, P.R., Knowledge and perceptions in Costa Rica regarding environment, population and biodiversity issues, *Conservation Biology*, 9(6), pp. 1548-1558, 1995.
[10] Gillingham, S. & Lee, P.C., The impact of wildlife-related benefits on the conservation attitudes of local people around the Selous Game Reserve, Tanzania. *Environmental Conservation*, 26(3), pp. 218-228, 1999.
[11] Suman, D., Shivlani, M. & Milon, J.W., Perceptions and attitudes regarding marine reserves: a comparison of stakeholder groups in the Florida Keys National marine Sanctuary. *Ocean and Coastal Management*, 42, pp. 1019-1040, 1999.
[12] Djohani R.H., The Bajau: future marine park managers in Indonesia? *Environmental change in South-East Asia: people, Politics and sustainable development,* ed. M.J.G. Parnell and R.L. Bryant, Routledge: London, pp. 260-268, 1995.
[13] Sather, C., *The Bajau laut: adaptation, history and fate in a maritime fishing society of southeastern Sabah*, University Press: Oxford, 1997.
[14] Gregory-Smith, J., *Southeast Sulawesi: Islands of Surprises*, Department of Tourism, Art and Culture: Sulawesi, 2000.
[15] Operation Wallacea , www.opwall.com
[16] Pollnac, R.B., Villagers perceptions of aspects of the natural and human environment of Balikpapan Bay, Indonesia, *Pesisir and Lautan*, 3(2), pp. 19-31, 2000

Sustainable Tourism, F. D. Pineda, C. A. Brebbia & M. Mugica (Editors)

Potential, thresholds and threats of tourism development in Bodrum Peninsula (Turkey)

F. Gezici[1], A. Y. Gül[2] & E. Alkay[1]
[1]Department of Urban and Regional Planning, İstanbul Technical University, Turkey
[2]Department of Urban and Regional Planning, Yildiz Technical University, Turkey

Abstract

Although Turkey has a variety of tourism attractions such as natural, historical and architectural heritage, "sea, sun, sand" factors have been the main components of tourism revenues. Especially after the realization of the problems of mass tourism towards coastal areas in the Mediterranean destination countries, Turkey has also evaluated the tourism development process with its spatial, environmental and socio-economic implications.

The aim of this paper is to discuss the findings of ongoing research and to put forward the thresholds and threats of tourism development in Bodrum Peninsula, which is located on the Aegean coast of Turkey.

In this paper, a three-stage perceptional analysis (scale impact of tourism) is conducted by a pilot survey in order to define the changes on the natural and built environment, socio-cultural development and economic welfare in the Bodrum Peninsula. These changes will be evaluated as thresholds and threats of tourism development. The belief component as an indicator for the level of change and the evaluation component as a level of like are the main components to the essential perceptional analysis. The findings of the research verify the process surpassing thresholds of developments and factors that constitute a threat for the sustainability of tourism. It was revealed that the effects of tourism on the economic environment were positive despite its adverse effects on the natural and social environment.

Keywords: tourism potential, thresholds, perceptional analysis, Bodrum Peninsula.

Sustainable Tourism, F. D. Pineda, C. A. Brebbia & M. Mugica (Editors)

1 Introduction

Sustainability of tourism activities depends on assessing the specific features and values of the destination and presenting them as its unique identity. However, mass tourism and the pressure of economic return of tourism has led to the adverse effects of tourism as well as its positive contributions, which has led to coastal tourism areas that are loosing their unique characteristics and becoming similar to each other.

Especially the countries in the Mediterranean region have become the main attraction areas of holiday tourism with their climate and the trio of see-sun-sand, therefore they have faced unfavorable effects such as intensive constructions in coastal areas because of mass tourism directed to coastal regions, land speculation and environmental pollution. The attempts to prevent speculative growth and come up with alternative solutions have increased after the first Mediterranean Action Plan in 1975. Researches for solutions with the concept of sustainable tourism against all these unfavorable developments have become more important with the 2nd Mediterranean Action Plan held in Barcelona in 1995. Planning coastal regions, transformation and alternative tourism approaches and to increase quality have become more intensive among the solutions.

This paper aims to present the method of a research project that will evaluate the development of tourism in coastal areas of Turkey and to discuss the findings for further stages. However, Turkey increases the share it gets from tourism, it should be derived lessons from the tourism developments in the world. The unique identity and resources of the sample area chosen and how it has been affected from the development process of tourism, thresholds and threats of tourism development will be evaluated, while testing the assumption of the problems faced by coastal areas are more intensive when compared with interior regions. The set of conceptual components of analysis is constituted based on the concept of sustainable tourism and its components. The main feature of the methodology implemented in the survey is that it follows three stages for the perceptional analysis as effect, intensity and evaluation.

The next section will describe the concentration of tourism activities to coastal areas in Turkey. The third section will put forward the general characteristics of the sample area, the development process of tourism and the factors constituting the thresholds. The research methodology and the findings will be presented in the fourth section and the expectations of the research will be evaluated along with the future perspective.

2 Concentration of tourism to coastal areas in Turkey

"Coastal areas" are encountered as areas where tourism activities are intensified due to climatic, geographical and morphological characteristics. Mediterranean basin is the most attractive region for coastal tourism with its intensity. 1/3 of international tourism revenue is in the Mediterranean basin (WTO [1]). 5 Mediterranean countries (Spain, France, Italy, Greece and Turkey) were among

Sustainable Tourism, F. D. Pineda, C. A. Brebbia & M. Mugica (Editors)

the 15 tourism arrival points in year 2001 (WTO [1]; EU Parliamentary Assembly [2]). A decrease in demand for coastal tourism areas have been faced since mid 1980's and functional, environmental, and local/regional restructuring in the sector have become unavoidable for these areas (Marchena Gomez and Rebollo [3]; Robledo and Batle [4]).

According to the estimations of World Wildlife Fund (WWF [5]), Turkey, Greece and Croatia will be the leading tourism areas in the Mediterranean basin in the future. Despite its natural, historical and cultural appeal having tourism potential, Turkey has not been able to get the share it deserves from the Mediterranean basin. Date of year 2000 reveals that while the total number of tourists having visited to Spain corresponds to 125% with 49.5 million tourists, the number of tourists having visited to Turkey is 15% of the population of the country with 9.6 million tourists. When the level of income is compared, it is observed that the tourism income of Spain is 26% of the Mediterranean basin while the tourism income of Turkey corresponds to 7% of the basin.

The tourism activities that are more intensive in coastal areas in the Mediterranean basin display a similar structure in Turkey as well. Among the 17 tourism provinces determined by the Ministry of Tourism in Turkey; 3 provinces (Antalya, Muğla, Aydın) in coastal areas account for %52,55 of the total bed capacity in the country.

Tourism investments and incentives have been directed to coastal areas in precedence during the period of plans since 1963. The seeking of alternatives for coastal tourism, establishment of new tourism centers in the interior regions and attempts to distribute tourism in a more balanced manner within the country were observed in 1990's. However, the development of tourism with emphasis on coastal areas continues.

During the period of 1st Five Year Development Plan covering the years of 1963-67, tourism investments mainly directed on regions having a potential to attract tourists and 11 tourism centers were determined in the Marmara, Aegean and Mediterranean regions as 3 regions with precedence. Within the scope of the Policies of the Transition Period in 1979 the concept of coasts as the driving force of tourism in Turkey was taken up and a comparative tourism research was conducted in the Marmara, Aegean, Mediterranean and Black Sea regions with a "Hypothetical Study on the Spatial Development Model". The centers possessing the characteristics of a tourism province and potential were put in order and 12 Centers with Precedence, which seemed most suitable for tourism investments, were determined (Ministry of Culture and Tourism [6]). These centers were: Bodrum, Marmaris, Kuşadası, Akçay, Çeşme, Alanya, Köyceğiz-Dalyan, Foça, Ayvalık, Side-Manavgat, Kemer and Fethiye. In addition to these, the opportunities and facilities were brought by the Law of Tourism Incentives dated 1982 also led to an increase in the investments focused on the Mediterranean and Aegean coasts.

Besides these studies and decrees to direct the tourism investments throughout the country, the researches have been made and are being made on certain sample areas in the field of determining the potential of tourism in a more detailed manner and evaluate its development (Var *et al.* [7]; Korça [8];

Sustainable Tourism, F. D. Pineda, C. A. Brebbia & M. Mugica (Editors)
© 2004 WIT Press, www.witpress.com, ISBN 1-85312-724-8

Gezici [9]; Gül Yazgan [10]). The contribution of tourism to the economy of the country is an evidence of the fact that it is an effective sector. However, what are the evidences put forward the contribution of tourism to the region where it takes place, its constructive and adverse effects? The best way to evaluate these evidences seems to be the local level. Therefore, the field studies have become more important. The findings of such researches will contribute to the control and sustainability of tourism along with local characteristics- unique features, potentials, thresholds of development.

3 The process of tourism development in the Bodrum peninsula and thresholds of development

The Bodrum peninsula in the province of Muğla is located at the southwestern end of Western Anatolia between the Güllük and Gökova Gulf. Bodrum has an exceptional significance for tourism as a peninsula in the Aegean region. The peninsula displays richness of natural characteristics with its wavy coasts in its gulfs. There are 3 natural harbors and 13 bays along the coasts of the peninsula of length 174 km. The fishermen's village Bodrum, is located one within another with historical Halicarnassos and the peninsula has been transformed into an attractive tourism area with the natural and cultural opportunities that it presents. The total population in the Bodrum Peninsula is 97.826 according to the General Census results for year 2000 and the number of tourists is 167.342 (State Statistics Institute [11], Ministry of Tourism [6]).

Tourism investments that gained a large acceleration in Turkey especially after 1980, were seen in Bodrum as well. Besides the construction of the Dalaman Airport in 1982, the announcement of 5 tourism centers with a total bed capacity of 33.499 in Bodrum by the year of 1985 have accelerated this process (The Bodrum Peninsula Strategic Development Plan [12]). Hence, Bodrum has taken its place in the tourism market as an entertainment holiday center. This image of the settlement has initiated a process of evolution in urban space. The pressure towards the land has increased in the Bodrum peninsula within this process; however the architecture in the region has been able to carry on its unique features to a certain extent. In 1998, the opening of the Bodrum-Milas Airport of 40 km distance to the Bodrum district center, provided easier accessibility to Bodrum. Today, the Bodrum peninsula has 11 municipalities and this constitution is a major threat for future development and integrity of peninsula. Besides the tourism activities (hotels, restaurants, bars) that have been incorporated to the existing settlement, metropolitan urban functions (banks, offices, shopping centers, supermarkets) along the Bodrum–Turgut Reis road as the backbone of Bodrum has been increased rapidly. Although there are various reasons for the claims that Bodrum more intensively faces the adverse effects of tourism and it goes through the stagnation stage according to the tourism life-cycle of Butler [13], the increase of constructions especially as secondary housing pressure in the coastal areas has become the most important factor in this respect. (Bodrum Socio-Economic Spatial Organization Application Report [14]). Bodrum has not been able to utilize its unique features sufficiently.

Sustainable Tourism, F. D. Pineda, C. A. Brebbia & M. Mugica (Editors)

The coastal areas have been opened tourism facilities while especially the sides have been invaded by secondary housing development in accordance with the decisions of the Regional Master Plan. The bed capacity of secondary housing was 57.000 in year 1995, while it is estimated around 158.500 in year 2020 according to feasibility report prepared by the Ministry of Tourism. The plans for 1982, 1998 and 2003 foresee that secondary housing areas spread especially to the northern parts of the peninsula within the process.

Natural values are present in the entire peninsula as thresholds of development. Forest and lands for special cultivation areas, productive agricultural lands, natural and archeological sites are the main thresholds that need to be preserved (see Fig. 1.). Furthermore, areas in which development cannot be foreseen due to geological drawbacks, intensive erosion and lands with slope more than 25% also constitute adverse thresholds of development. At that point, both the existing land-use and the developments due to planning decisions put forward to overcome the thresholds.

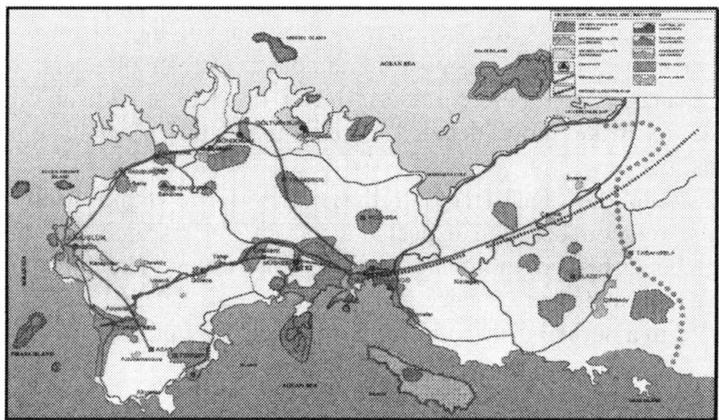

Figure 1: Archeological, natural and urban sites of Bodrum.

The development process and tendencies of tourism in the Bodrum peninsula put forward certain threats on sustainability of tourism. Overcoming thresholds of development in the peninsula, encouraging construction along the coast, the fact that the secondary housing areas compete with tourism facilities and the formation of idle stocks of housing, the insufficiency of infrastructure and especially supply of water and the presence of 11 independent municipalities instead of a local government covering all peninsula impose threats for the future of tourism in Bodrum. Sustainability of being attractive for tourists is important for a tourism destination area. Therefore, the effects of tourism development and the threats for future expectations were dealt with in more detail within the framework of strategies.

Sustainable Tourism, F. D. Pineda, C. A. Brebbia & M. Mugica (Editors)

4 Research methodology and the findings

4.1 Research methodology

Firstly, data set and sampling design were put forward in a framework. The aim of the research is to examine how the concept of sustainability is perceived in coastal tourism areas with the specific example of the Bodrum peninsula, to evaluate the effects of tourism development process on natural, built and the socioeconomic environment, to evaluate the transformation process and to provide direction to future tourism strategies within the framework of the findings.

The sustainable tourism planning criterion are defined as four sub-vectors (identity-originality, tourism planning, effect-transformation and socio-economic structure) and it is emphasised on effect-transformation vector to evaluate the effect of development on tourism within different contexts. At the initial stage of the research, the survey is conducted to the group called as key persons such as taking an effective role in the planning, implementation, administration, investment and operation (deputy mayor, chairman of the chamber of urban planners, chairman of the chamber of architects, urban planners, hotel and restaurant managers and tour operators). Hence, this will provide an opportunity for experts to make more detailed observations and to evaluate neglected dimensions.

Further, both the consistency of the survey form within itself and also whether the relation between expectations from the research and the survey forms will be displayed following to this pilot survey. The total number of surveys are determined as 10 since it is aimed to test a detailed survey form and it is included in a normal distribution and sufficient for a pilot study.

4.2 Findings

When the findings of effect-transformation vector are put forward, at first vector components (natural values–cultural values, built environment, social environment, economic environment), sub-components and the factors constituting them have been displayed (see Fig. 2.). Then, the frequency values of the responses to the components are put forward. The response of each component is obtained in three steps. The first step is about putting forward the effect of the factor by a scale of "yes-no" opposite response. The second step is the definition of the intensity of the effect with a Likert scale of 5 (1: did not protect/increase at all, 2: did not protect/increase, 3: not sure, 4: it protected/increased, 5: it protected/increased a lot). The third step is the definition of how the effect and the intensity have been evaluated as a function of satisfaction with a Likert scale of 5 (1: I am not satisfied at all, 2: I am not satisfied, 3. not sure, 4: I'm satisfied, 5: I'm satisfied very much). Ap and Crompton have adopted this survey implementation that they based on the "tourism effect index" concept of Fishbein (Fishbein [15]) because it provided the opportunity to minimize the deviated results to be obtained from its yes-no

Sustainable Tourism, F. D. Pineda, C. A. Brebbia & M. Mugica (Editors)
© 2004 WIT Press, www.witpress.com, ISBN 1-85312-724-8

opposite response. It helps to see behind the real meaning of the response and helps to get rid of generalizations and provide the opportunity for analytical interpretations (Ap and Crompton [16]).

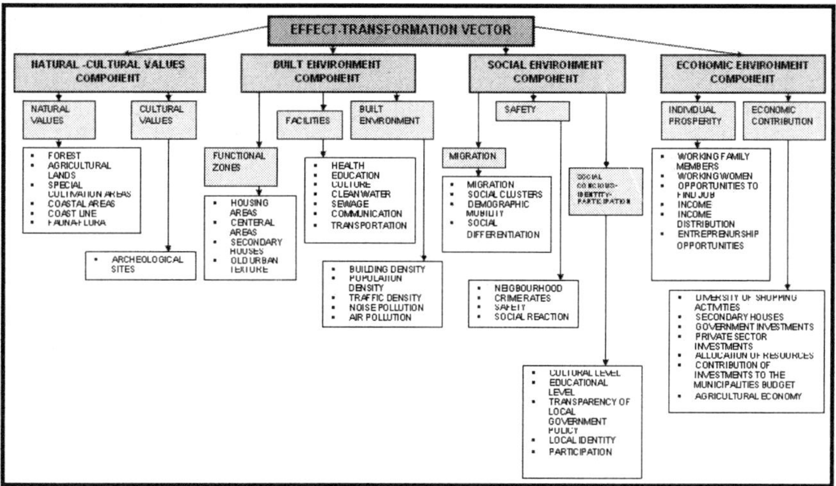

Figure 2: Structure of effect-transformation vector.

The results of the three stages defined in terms of factors are put forward in two phases in the paper. The results of "yes-no" opposite response are reflected in the 1st phase while the responses for the intensity and evaluation are reflected in the 2nd phase.

1st Phase The "yes-no" opposite response: First level findings are reflected both on the basis of factors constituting the components and on the basis of components in the order.

Natural values–cultural values component: It is believed that the forests, productive agricultural lands, special cultivation areas, coastal areas, coastline, fauna and flora constituting the sub-components of the natural values are not protected. On the other hand, they believe that the archaeological areas as sub-component of cultural values are protected.

Built environment component: It is believed that the expansion of residential areas, central areas, secondary houses, distortion of the old urban texture, the transformation of residential areas to the tourism function as the sub-components of functional use of areas, have increased. It is believed that health, education and cultural functions, communication and transportation opportunities have increased as well. On the other hand, the insufficiencies of technical infrastructure opportunities are emphasized. They put forward that the sewerage system did not have any significant extension and that the opportunities for drinking water did not enhanced. Among the factors defining the sub-component of the quality of built environment, it is believed that except for air pollution all other factors, namely density of constructions, population density, traffic density and noise pollution have all increased.

Sustainable Tourism, F. D. Pineda, C. A. Brebbia & M. Mugica (Editors)
 ISBN 1-85312-724-8

Social environment component: It is believed that among the factors constituting the sub-component of migration, except social cluster, all other factors namely, population, migration, social differentiation caused by migration, and volatility of the population within the settlement have increased. They think that tourism did not increase the factors of neighborhood relations and safety that constitute sub-components of safety and that they increased the factors of crime rate and social reaction factors in a manner supporting this opinion. Among the factors defining social conscience-identity-participation sub-component, it is believed that all factors other than development of local identity and transparency of local government policy, namely, cultural level, level of education, and the participation of the local population to the development process of tourism have increased.

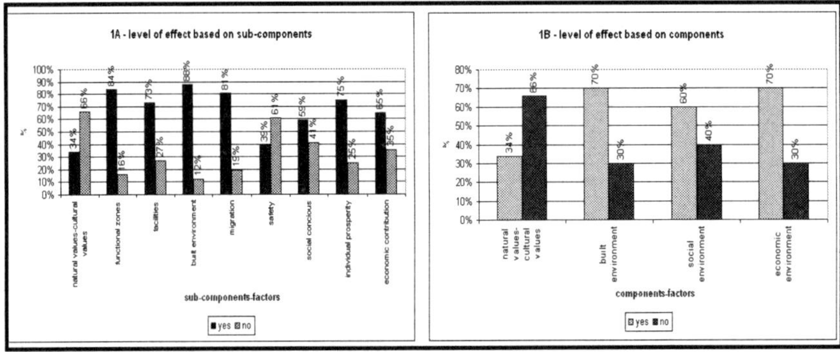

Graphic 1: Level of effect based on sub-components and components.

Economic environment component: It is believed that among the factors constituting individual prosperity sub-component, except for unequal income distribution and the allocation of resources by the local government, all factors such as number of family members working, number of women working, opportunities to find jobs, individual income and entrepreneurship opportunities have increased. While the increase of objective ones among these factors are approved, this clarity is not observed in factors that are more open to interpretation. Among the factors constituting the economic contribution aspect, except for agricultural economy, it is believed that all other factors such as diversity of shopping activities, secondary houses, private sector investments and contribution of investments to the budget of the local government have increased.

The summary of findings of all these factors are put forward on the basis of components can be followed in Graphic 1. In summary, the responses of the key persons have put forward that development of tourism did not contribute to the protection of natural values.

Sustainable Tourism, F. D. Pineda, C. A. Brebbia & M. Mugica (Editors)

2nd Phase: The second and third phase findings reflecting the intensity and evaluation form of the effect displayed in the first phase are put forward on the basis of factors. It is indicated that the factors constituting the natural value sub-component were not protected at all and that they were not satisfied with these conditions and that the factors constituting the cultural values sub-component were protected and that they were satisfied with it (Graphic 2).

It is pointed out that among the factors constituting sub-component of the functional use of land, there was an increase in residential areas, secondary houses in coastal regions and in distortion of old urban texture and that they were not satisfied about it. They indicated that among the factors determining the sub-component of infrastructure areas, increases took place in the areas of health and education, communication and transportation and that they were satisfied about these increases but on the other hand cultural areas, the existing water system and sewerage system did not increase at all and that they were not pleased about it. They revealed that among the factors constituting the sub-component of the quality of built environment, density of constructions, population, traffic and noise pollution increased a lot and that they were not pleased about it at all, but they also indicated that air pollution did not increase at all and that they were pleased with it (Graphic 2).

It is revealed that among the factors constituting the sub-component of migration defining the social environment component, the settled population and in-migration have increased a lot and that they were not pleased with it. Indecisiveness is more common about social differentiation and social clustering. They indicated that among the factors constituting the safety sub-component, neighborhood relations and the feeling of security have decreased while crime rates and social reaction have increased and that they were not pleased about it at all. They noted that among the factors constituting the sub-component of social conscious-identity-participation, the level of culture and education, the transparency of local government policy and local identity values did not increase and that they were not pleased about it. It was noted that indecisiveness was common for topics such as participation to administration, provision of directions by the administration and the participation of the local population to the development process of tourism (Graphic 2).

It is indicated that among the factors constituting the sub-component of individual prosperity defining economic environment component, the number of working women, the opportunities to find jobs and investment opportunities have increased and that they were satisfied about it. They have pointed out that the municipality did not use the income generated from tourism for the inhabitants and that they were not pleased with it. Indecisiveness was observed for topics such as the number of persons working in the family and unequal income distribution. They have pointed out that among the factors constituting sub-component of the economic contribution aspect, diversity of shopping activities, public and private sector investments and contribution to the budget of the municipality have increased and that they were pleased with it. They have indicated that agricultural economy has not become activated and that they were not pleased about it (Graphic 2).

Sustainable Tourism, F. D. Pineda, C. A. Brebbia & M. Mugica (Editors)

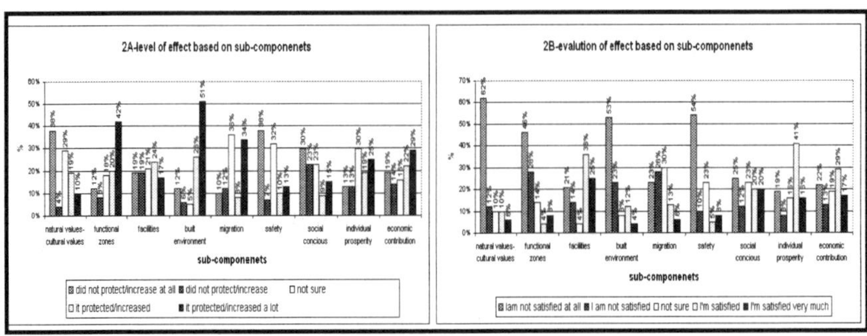

Graphic 2: Level and evaluation of effect based on sub-components.

When the components and sub-components are dealt with the tools of the survey, the general evaluation table in Figure 3 is revealed. This table provides hints that need to be queried in the future steps of the research. Distortion of the natural values and the built environment and decrease in the feeling of safety are features emphasized most as the adverse effects of tourism both in the yes-no opposite response (no), and in the intensity scale (1: not protected at all) and in the level of satisfaction (1: I am not satisfied at all). Indecisiveness is observed only for the sub-component of migration-demographic structure in the social environment component. The fact that tourism increases economic contribution to a high level, it will increase satisfaction to a high level as well. Although the level of satisfaction from infrastructure is at a high level, it is observed that the increase in functional uses of lands or constructions does not lead to satisfaction.

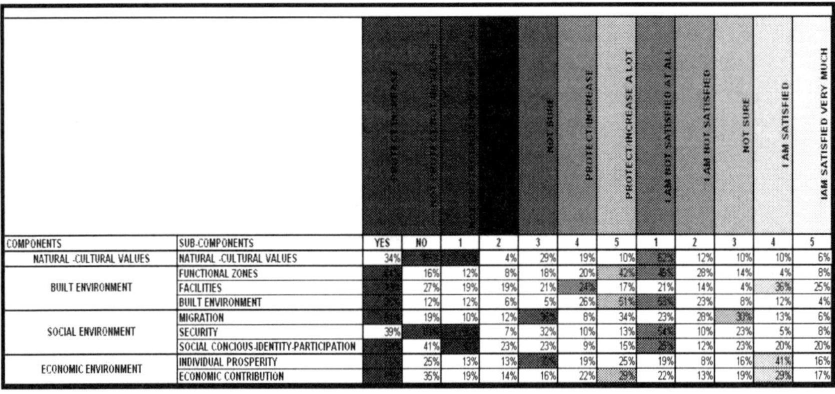

		PROTECT/INCREASE	NOT PROTECT/NOT INCREASE	[illegible]	[illegible]	NOT SURE	PROTECT/INCREASE	PROTECT/INCREASE A LOT	I AM NOT SATISFIED AT ALL	I AM NOT SATISFIED	NOT SURE	I AM SATISFIED	IAM SATISFIED VERY MUCH
COMPONENTS	SUB-COMPONENTS	YES	NO	1	2	3	4	5	1	2	3	4	5
NATURAL -CULTURAL VALUES	NATURAL -CULTURAL VALUES	34%	[illegible]	[illegible]	4%	29%	19%	10%	62%	12%	10%	10%	6%
BUILT ENVIRONMENT	FUNCTIONAL ZONES	[illegible]	16%	12%	8%	18%	20%	42%	45%	28%	14%	4%	8%
	FACILITIES	[illegible]	27%	19%	19%	21%	24%	17%	21%	14%	4%	36%	25%
	BUILT ENVIRONMENT	[illegible]	12%	12%	6%	5%	26%	51%	53%	23%	8%	12%	4%
SOCIAL ENVIRONMENT	MIGRATION	[illegible]	19%	10%	12%	36%	8%	34%	23%	28%	30%	13%	6%
	SECURITY	39%	[illegible]	[illegible]	7%	32%	10%	13%	54%	10%	23%	5%	8%
	SOCIAL CONCIOUS-IDENTITY-PARTICIPATION	[illegible]	41%	[illegible]	23%	23%	9%	15%	25%	12%	23%	20%	20%
ECONOMIC ENVIRONMENT	INDIVIDUAL PROSPERITY	[illegible]	25%	13%	13%	[illegible]	19%	25%	19%	8%	16%	41%	16%
	ECONOMIC CONTRIBUTION	[illegible]	35%	19%	14%	16%	22%	29%	22%	13%	19%	29%	17%

Figure 3: Components and sub-components according to response intensity.

5 Conclusion

Description of sustainable tourism criterion along main vectors in terms of components, sub-components and factors has been effective in achieving an analytical query order. The methodology used in this paper provides the

Sustainable Tourism, F. D. Pineda, C. A. Brebbia & M. Mugica (Editors)

opportunity to test the perception of key actors and verify the responses and hence probability of error has decreased. The "yes-no" type of responses then become stronger with intensity and the evaluation and is finalized by satisfaction from the results achieved. Testing of the survey methodology with three phases and the benefits of it encourages its implementation in other case studies. When the findings of the effect-transformation vector are scrutinized in general, it is put forward that tourism has been maintaining its development process without considering importance of natural values that constitutes the main sources of tourism and its sustainability.

It is a known process that many coastal tourism areas lead to loss of agricultural lands especially in rural or peripheral regions. The development of tourism in the Bodrum peninsula has also followed this trend as well. Especially the transformation of citrus trees known as special agricultural production fields to tourism and secondary housing areas and the fact that fish breeding farms are taking place of fishing as the basis of traditional economy, are consequences of the development process of tourism. The expansion of residential areas, secondary housing areas and shopping facilities display the effects of transformation in the economic structure and land use patterns. It was noted that the level of insufficiencies in terms of technical infrastructure increase especially during the peak tourism season. As a consequence of all these factors, it was revealed that besides the loss of the natural environment, the quality of the built environment has worsened as well. This condition is an inevitable consequence of proceeding with spatial growth and transformation without taking into consideration the thresholds of that region. The findings of the research verify the process surpassing thresholds of developments and factors that constitute threat for the sustainability of tourism.

One of the effective consequences of spatial expansion based on tourism is the transformation in the social environment as well. The social structure has become more heterogeneous caused by in- migration and this has led to problems of social differentiation, communication-interaction, and lack of safety. It was revealed that the effects of tourism on the economic environment were positive despite its adverse effects on the natural and social environment. The effectiveness of tourism was emphasized both for increasing individual prosperity and determination of the economic role and identity of the region. This statement is consistent with the opinion in the literature defending that the adverse effects of development in tourism can be tolerated based on its economic yield.

Sustainability of long term effectiveness and productivity of economic gains constitute the most important topic for economic gains. Within the framework of the consequences determined in essence, there are difficulties in terms of long-term effectiveness and productivity of tourism activities in Bodrum. The fact that natural and historical values can not take part effectively in tourism due to the "coast and entertainment focused marketing" of Bodrum, transforms the peninsula into a tourism region that cannot utilize its unique features on the way of tourism development and imposes the risk of standardization. The losses that take place in the natural values, lack of promotion of historical and cultural values and the

Sustainable Tourism, F. D. Pineda, C. A. Brebbia & M. Mugica (Editors)

transformations in the social environment are significant threats for the sustainability of tourism. At this stage, the development of policies and strategies aimed at especially solving the problems of the two main values and social environment to achieve sustainability.

References

[1] WTO (2002) Tourism Recovery Committee for the Mediterranean Region, Merket Intelligence and Promotion Section, Special Report, No:19, March 2002, Madrid.
[2] EU Parliamentary Assembly (2003) Erosion of the Mediterranean Coastline: Implications for tourism, Doc. 9981, 16 Oct. 2003.
[3] Marchena Gomez, M.J. and F.V. Rebollo (1995) Coastal Areas: Processes, Typologies and Prospects, in European Tourism, Regions, Spaces and Restructuring, Eds. A.Montanari and A.M.Williams, John Wiley&Sons.
[4] Robledo, M.A. and J .Batle (2002) Re-planning for tourism in a Mature Destination: A Note on Mallorca, in Tourism in Western Europe, A Collection of case Histories., ed. By. R.Voase, Un. of Lincoln, CABI Pub.
[5] WWF (2000) Tourism Threats in the Mediterranean.
[6] Ministry of Tourism (2001) Tourism Statistics, Ankara.
[7] Var, T., Kendall, K.W., Tarakçıoğlu, E. (1985) Resident Attitudes Towards Tourists in a Turkish Resort Town, Annals of Tourism Research, C.12, No.4, 652-658.
[8] Korça, P. (1994) Halkın Turizmin Çevresel Etkilerini Algılaması and Değerlendirmesi, TUGEV Yayını, No:31, Istanbul.
[9] Gezici, F. (1998) Sürdürülebilir Bölgesel Kalkınma Amacında Turizm Eylemlerinin Etkisi: Türkiye Üzerine Karşılaştırmalı Bir Araştırma, Doktora Tezi, İTÜ Fen Bilimleri Enstitüsü, Istanbul.
[10] Gül Yazgan, A. (1999) Turizm Alanlarında Kaynak Kulanımı Açısından Risk Faktörü, Doktora Tezi, YTÜ Fen Bilimleri Enstitüsü, Istanbul.
[11] DİE (2001), Genel Nüfus Sayımı, Ankara.
[12] Bodrum Yarımadası Stratejik Gelişme Planı, Hazırlık Çalışmaları-I, Genel Durum Raporu, Akdeniz Ülkeleri Akedemisi Vakfı, Bodrum, Haziran 1998.
[13] Butler, R. (1980) The Concept of a Tourist Cycle of Evolutions Implications for Management of Resources, Canadian Geographer, 24,1.
[14] Bodrum Sosyo-Ekonomik, Mekansal Örgütlenme Başvuru Raporu (1995), Bodrum Gelişme Senaryoları Sempozyumu, 17-18 Mart 1995, Ankara.
[15] Fishbein, M. (1963) An Investigation of the Relationships between Beliefs about an Object and Attitude toward That Object, Human Relations, 16: 233-40.
[16] Ap, J. and Crompton, J.L. (1998) Developing and Testing a Tourism Impact Scale, Journal of Travel Research, Vol.37, 120-130.

Sustainable Tourism, F. D. Pineda, C. A. Brebbia & M. Mugica (Editors)

Impact of residential tourism and the destination life cycle theory

A. Aledo & T. Mazón
Departament of Sociología I y Teoría de la Educación, Alicante University, Spain

Abstract

The goal of this paper is to apply the Tourist Area Life Cycle theory to the analysis of Torrevieja, a tourist town located in Southern Alicante province, which represents a paradigmatic example of a residential tourist destination. We will describe its tourist evolution and its present tourist and environmental state. At Torrevieja, the residential tourists reach more than a half a million in August. We will show that the last stages of the TALC are related to the exhaustion of the main offered resource: urban land. Environmental and landscape degradation, urban infrastructure and social service deficits, lacking of complementary offers, declining urban quality of life, and increasing of urban insecurity are also linked to the decline stage. This research has been financed by the Spanish Ministry of Science and Technology.
Keywords: residential tourism, life cycle, tourist environmental impact, Torrevieja, local development.

1 Introduction

From the 1970s onwards, a new model of town planning centred on the offer of second homes began to be developed on the Spanish Mediterranean coasts. Hundreds of horizontal, low density residential estates were built on large areas of land. A new formula for tourism also appeared: residential tourism Mazón and Aledo [1]. The inhabitability of contemporary towns generates a need for escape in urbanites Omberg [2]. In western Europe, access to this type of residential tourism was opened to many strata of society with the development of the welfare state, more free time, an increase in earlier retirement and better pensions.

Sustainable Tourism, F. D. Pineda, C. A. Brebbia & M. Mugica (Editors)

We understand residential tourism as being the economic activity dedicated to the urbanisation, construction and sale of residential tourist homes that constitute the non-hotel sector. This sector is formed by the total number of properties, which are generally individually owned and offered to the tourist market, nearly always outside conventional channels. The great majority of these properties are located in the coastal area Mazón and Aledo [1]. The purchasers originate from: (a) the property developer's circle (b) from north and central Spain, and (c) other countries of the European Union. Their use may be weekend, holiday and as a semi permanent or permanent residence Warners [3].

Although it is true that there is ample scientific literature that has studied residential tourism, especially Anglo-Saxon and French, on the contrary, and despite the importance attained by the residential tourist sector in Spain, until recent times there have been few researchers who have dedicated their time to the analysis of this sector and the impact it has on the host society and environment. In general, until a few years ago, studies of tourism were looked upon with disdain by Spanish Universities Mazón [4] and, focussing on the analysis of residential tourism by academics, its scarce development might well be related to the interests of the developers, property agents and regional and local politicians in keeping its disproportionate growth obscure.

2 Objectives

The objectives of this study are: first, to describe the characteristics of the residential tourist model developed on the Spanish Mediterranean coasts; secondly, to explain its nature and how it functions, uncovering the environmental, social and economic non-viability of the model, using an adaptation of the destination life cycle model (DLCM). As an example for this analysis, the tourist town of Torrevieja, situated in the southeast of Spain, was chosen as a case study. It will be demonstrated how the lack of planning and rapid growth of residential estates have exhausted the basic resource that sustains residential tourism, land. Consequently, the exclusive focus of the sector on the construction and sale of property has degraded the environment and destroyed the landscape. Parallelly, there has been no development of a hotel offer, or any complementary offer, services or tourist infrastructure that could serve to rechannel (rejuvenate in Butler's terms) the tourist sector of this town towards viable options.

3 Characteristics

We shall now describe the principal characteristics of residential tourism. (1) Despite its seasonality being lower than that of sun and beach hotel tourism, seasonal concentration levels remain high. Therefore, whilst a high percentage of the users of residential tourist homes may establish themselves totally or almost permanently in the host town, the summer residents (understood as the seasonal users of the residential homes) greatly exceed the first group. In Torrevieja, we have counted around 125,000 residents in the winter months, but in the summer

Sustainable Tourism, F. D. Pineda, C. A. Brebbia & M. Mugica (Editors)
© 2004 WIT Press, www.witpress.com, ISBN 1-85312-724-8

high season weeks the figure reaches 500,000. (2) Complementary activities are scarce and of poor quality, which is a frequent problem in the Spanish Mediterranean towns that specialise in this type of tourism. Only the construction of golf courses and marinas improve the level of the complementary services, although these are developed with the aim of increasing the value of the property offer. (3) The appearance of these products is unstructured, the residential tourist properties are not offered to the tourist market. The number of apartments registered in the province of Alicante by the Valencian Tourist Board is only 17,725, whereas in the coastal area alone, we have counted 237,493 residential tourist homes. Therefore, no control mechanisms from the tourist authorities exist and lettings in the rental market are offered clandestinely, defrauding the Spanish revenue. (4) A family that buys a second residence wants to recoup the costs incurred by using or renting the property, which we have found to be much less frequent. For this reason, summer visitors with a second residence are a group who are very loyal to their destination. (5) On the other hand, residential tourism is characterised by a low rotation of tourists and lower spending per tourist/day: This is usually the kind of Spanish tourist who is less given to spending. (6) Spanish town planning legislation leaves a great part of the management and planning of land in the hands of the local authorities. The great majority of coastal councils have based the financing of their budgets on the income generated by urban taxes. This is one of the main reasons behind the lack of planning as, both local authorities and property development businesses have seen urban planning as an obstacle to, or as a brake on, continuous and rapid growth of the economic benefits produced by the construction of these urbanizations Stroud [5]. (7) Finally, the tendency towards the unplanned rapid growth of residential tourism that has taken place in a great number of Spanish Mediterranean towns has had a tremendous environmental impact.

4 Environmental impact of property development tourism

Numerous studies have indicated the environmental impact caused by the expansion of constructed land produced by residential tourist developments Gartner [6]; Grenon [7]; Vera Rebollo [8]. Amongst these negative effects, the following stand out: landscape degradation, reduction of local biodiversity, deforestation and the increase of forest fires, the loss of vegetation, erosion and desertification, the increase of edaphic, acoustic and water pollution, both of superficial and subterranean waters and the eutrophication of the continental waters Almenar et al. [9]. The geographer Vera Rebollo [10] emphasises the battle between agriculture and urban developments for scarce water resources and the abandonment of traditional agriculture for transformation of agricultural land into development land and the cultural loss caused by the disappearance of the agricultural sector.

To understand these impacts, it should be mentioned that whilst ecological flows are mainly vertical, urbanisation and the flows of goods and energy associated with it, together with the development of the built-up area itself, are characterised by being horizontal Bettini [11]. In this way, the vertical flows of

Sustainable Tourism, F. D. Pineda, C. A. Brebbia & M. Mugica (Editors)

the ecological cycles are cut. At the same time, the spatial extent of the residential tourist development increases environmental impact for two reasons: firstly, because it extends the concrete and asphalt covering and activates the processes of waterproofing, erosion and desertification mentioned above Aledo [12]; secondly, because control, management and impact reduction are more difficult and expensive than if the tourist homes were concentrated. For example, in the locality under analysis in this text, Torrevieja (Spain), the population quadruples during periods of maximum occupation. Similarly, domestic waste collection and treatment services and the residual water purifying installations are not prepared for such a high volume of users. The local authorities are unable to justify investment in greater infrastructure that would only be used during a few months of the year. All of these environmental impacts give rise to what Plog [13] calls the destructive tourist cycle: tourism that in the first place is attracted by a quality natural space, ends up by destroying the very thing that is its principal attraction and structural basis.

5 Structural weaknesses of the model

The new residential tourist settlements have been at the heart of the development of many Spanish towns due to the economic benefits that they provide in the short term. However, as we shall demonstrate, this is a model that generates scenarios of high risk and vulnerability due to its structural weaknesses in the long term MUNRES [14]. The wealth generated by tourist residential estates is purely property development when it is not linked to a tourist development strategy. When the building process has concluded, a series of negative consequences appear, caused by using up and bad use of the land, the environmental impact that this generates and the lack of infrastructures and services for tourists. These deficits are worsened by the lack of planning of residential tourist developments Vera Rebollo [10]; Torres Alfonsea [15]; Mazón [4]. Based on these structural problems, a model of tourist offer has been established, with property developers at its centre, who are guided for the most part by interests that are merely speculative. In this way, the sector has destroyed its own base due to the intensive occupation of the land and destruction of the landscape Plog [13]; Sancho [16]. The result is a model with a social and urban morphology that, although it has attracted thousands of tourists-residents to the Spanish coasts and has noticeably raised the standard of living of the local populations thanks to the property development business, it has not created infrastructures, facilities nor services capable of responding to the needs of these tourists, nor to plan any sustainable land use in the medium term Munres [14]. We are, therefore, faced with a socio-economic dilemma that can only be resolved through social consensus and a sustainable development policy.

The demand for this type of residential tourist offer comes on the one hand from the national market, as the socio-economic development undergone by Spanish society over the last two decades has enabled its citizens to purchase a second tourist home Asín and Bayón [17]. On the other hand, they have been joined by mainly retired citizens of the European Union Monreal [18]. The latter

Sustainable Tourism, F. D. Pineda, C. A. Brebbia & M. Mugica (Editors)

are attracted by the mild climate and the difference in the cost of living between Spain and their country of origin. Their stay is mainly during the winter period to escape from the long dark winters of northern Europe. At this point it must be mentioned that foreign demand is increasing, with an inter-annual growth rate of 15.8%. In fact, and according to data from the regional property developers association, the Alicante coast absorbed 90 per cent of foreign property investment in the Valencian Region during the year 2003, with the purchase of 30,000 tourist homes and billing of 3,700 million euros. This offer gives rise to the fact that in the year 2001, in the towns of the Alicante coast, the percentage of second and empty homes whose function is clearly residential tourism, reached 62.9%, whereas in Spain the percentage is 29.5%. But this property development activity is spreading. Foreign demand, and faced with the situation of saturation and collapse of the coastal zone, is provoking a shift of new property development promotions to the towns of the interior, which are adopting the same property development model as the coast.

6 Application of the destination life-cycle model (DLCM)

Butler [19] modified and applied the *product life-cycle* marketing theory to the evolution and development of tourist destinations. This author suggested that destinations experience a cycle of "birth-disappearance", where the number of visitors replaces the sale of the product. Butler divided the life-cycle of a tourist destination into six phases: exploration, involvement, development, consolidation, stagnation and a final phase of rejuvenation or decline. The application of the destination life-cycle model (DLCM) can be grouped into (a) those that emphasise the explicative and descriptive utilities of this theory to better understand the evolution of a determined tourist destination (b) those that indicate that DLCM may serve as a guide for planning and marketing of the resort; and, finally, (c) some authors suggest that it could be a tool to predict the posterior evolution of the destination. However, criticism has emphasised the lack of empirical studies on the final phase of post-stagnation and the non-inclusion of external factors that influence both the dynamics of the demand as well as the evolution of the internal offer Argawal [20] Bianchi [21]. Despite this criticism and the problems presented by any theory that pretends to be nomothetic, DLCM is still widely used by tourologists and planners due to its formulative simplicity and the irrefutability of the expiry of the socio-economic phenomena and processes.

This theory has hardly been used in studies of residential tourism Girard and Gartner [22]. Problems of a methodological order, such as the difficulty in quantifying residential tourists, may explain this gap in the bibliography. Nevertheless, there are important reasons for applying the DLCM to residential tourism: (a) for the social and economic relevance of this model, when related to the explicative potential of this theory and (b) because, in many cases, the development of residential tourism is one of the formulae that tourist destinations use to alter the economic decline predicted by the DLCM. To apply the DLCM to residential tourist destinations, first of all, a series of modifications must be

Sustainable Tourism, F. D. Pineda, C. A. Brebbia & M. Mugica (Editors)

made to the theory. If the classic DLCM, as proposed by Butler, centres on analysis of the demand, taking the arrival of tourists as a dependent variable, and the quality of the offer as an independent variable, then we have to use other variables in the application of the DLCM to residential tourism. The life of a product does not only depend on the strength of demand. The lack or scarcity of one of the resources that forms it may also play a fundamental role. In the case of residential tourism, exhaustion of the land available for development at the destination is a physical limit on the life of the product.

When the object of tourism is not the arrival of tourists but the sale of homes - as is the case of residential tourism, at least in the approach taken by the towns of the Spanish Mediterranean - once the available land for development has been used up, the end of the life-cycle of the product has been reached. The environmental impact of urban development, when it is not undertaken according to sustainable planned formulae, associated with the exhaustion of the land, may accelerate the end of the life of the product. At the same time, if the residential tourist model has not been planned and has developed a poor quality product, the possibilities of restructuring - or rejuvenation using Butler's terms -are directly decreased. In the following pages, we shall apply this theory to a consolidated residential tourist destination, as is the town of Torrevieja, located on the Spanish Mediterranean coast, in the south of the province of Alicante.

Torrevieja: a consolidated residential tourist town.

Torrevieja, situated 48 km to the south of Alicante, covers a surface of 30km^2, 20 km of coast and has a hot dry climate. It has 172 hours of sunshine in winter and 364 in summer, which make it very attractive for tourists who are retired, both Spanish and European. A third of its territory is taken up by a natural lagoon - protected as a Natural Park -, which has been used throughout history for salt extraction. This activity, together with fishing, employed most of its inhabitants until the decade of the 70s in the 20th century. From then on, the decline of fishing, the technification of the salt activity and, in particular, the arrival of tourism transformed the natural and cultural landscape of this town. Since then, the economy of the town has been based on the construction and property business. This is demonstrated by the fact that 28.8% of employment is in these two sectors. Moreover, hotel rooms are scarcely relevant; the hotel offer is a mere 775 rooms, whereas the number of second residences offered is 75,022.

The resident population of Torrevieja has grown considerably, particularly over the past few years, due to immigration Casado-Díaz [23]. If in 1960 - years before the tourist boom - there were 9,564 inhabitants, in 1996 33,521 inhabitants figured on the census, with 82,149 being reached in March 2003. However, calculations based on domestic consumption of water situate the real population at around 150,000 inhabitants in winter, reaching 500,000 in the summer period of maximum occupation.

Immigrants established in Torrevieja are divided into (a) working immigrants attracted by jobs created by the construction and services industries and (b) senior citizens from other Spanish regions as well as from the European Union (especially British) and from other European countries Viruela et al. [24]. According to data from the National Census of the Population and Property of

Sustainable Tourism, F. D. Pineda, C. A. Brebbia & M. Mugica (Editors)

2001, from a total census population of 58,828 inhabitants, foreigners represented 24.06% of the total (14,154). From the latter group, 42.77% are over the age of 55. The numerical importance of this population contingent, together with its special sociodemographic characteristics (elderly population, lack of knowledge of the Spanish language, higher level of income than the local population, etc.) may be a source of conflict with the local population.

Torrevieja is a paradigm of residential tourism. There are 257 non-hotel beds for each hotel bed in the town. The total of non-hotel beds reaches 350,000. The model of development has been based, almost exclusively, on the construction of second residences grouped in residential estates - condominiums of bungalows or semi-detached chalets and detached houses. These residential estates are characterised by being separate and at a distance from the town centre, by having important deficits in all kinds of infrastructures and services, and for their great use of land Barke [25]. They are the result of a complete lack of urban planning. Property developers' interests, purely speculative, are what have guided their growth in the search for cheap land. In the following table, the evolution of the number of houses built in this town in the period between 1985 and 2002 is shown.

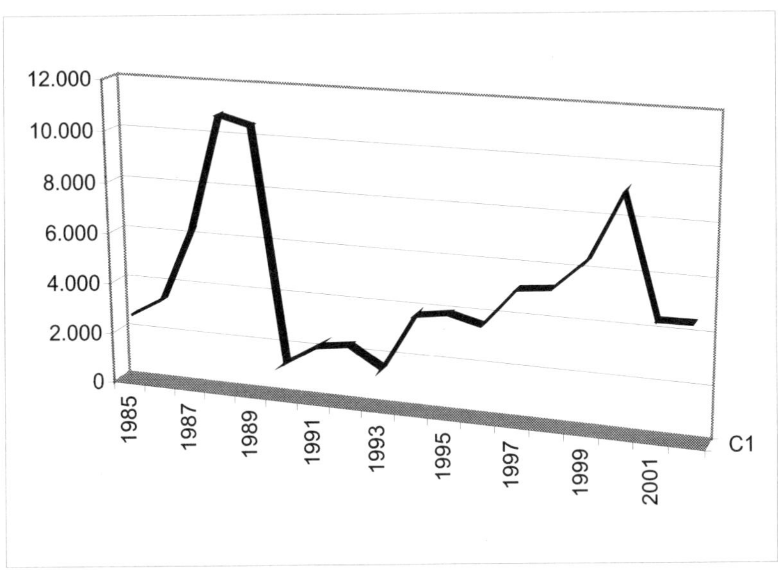

Figure 1: Houses built in Torrevieja (1985-2002).

From 1985 to 2002, 87,259 new homes were built in Torrevieja, with an average of more than 5,000 homes annually. The years of greatest property production are 1988 and 1989 with more than 20,000 homes being built. The economic and tourist crises at the beginning of the decade of the 90s had a serious impact on this sector, which did not recover until 1994, as in 1991 the number of homes built descends 90% in relation to the year before. From 1994

Sustainable Tourism, F. D. Pineda, C. A. Brebbia & M. Mugica (Editors)

onwards, the annual number of properties increases gradually until 1999 when 9,030 units are built. During the two following years, building construction drops by half. The growth of housing, using up urban land as it does, has been such that from the revision of the General Plan for Urban Planning (GPUP) in 2000, it can be seen that a mere 13% of the town's land remains available for urban use and that, in September 2003, only 283 ha. remained free from urbanisation, 8% of the total amount of land that is classified as urban. It is thus evident that the residential tourist sector of Torrevieja has reached the final phase of its life cycle by exhausting its basic resource - land available for development. In a few months, no land will remain in Torrevieja on which to continue building and, therefore, a sector that is based on the construction and sale of properties will cease functioning because there will be no land on which to build new urbanizations.

As in the DLCM proposed by Butler, this final phase could be rechannelled through a process of rejuvenation, a change in the model. This is the aim of the proposal made by the Council Urbanism Office, a change in the town's urban model. The idea is to change from an extensive horizontal model, made up of detached or semi-detached houses, to a denser and higher model. To this end, an amendment to the GPUP of 1988 is foreseen, to enable the construction of buildings with up to 15 storeys in the most central zones of the town centre, with special urbanistic benefits if these new buildings are hotels. The real possibilities of these urbanistic measures attracting hotel chains to situate their new hotels in this town are limited by various factors: a) its poor tourist image MUNRES [14] (b) the lack of tourist services and the scarcity and poor quality of the complementary offer (Baja Segura Tourism Report) and (c) the problems that greater densification would cause in a town centre of old design (it was designed after the earthquake of 1830) with narrow roads and pavements, where greater density of buildings would end up causing greater congestion and a decrease in the quality of life in the town.

These urban dynamics have generated an urban morphology that lacks unity, is isolated and of poor quality. Erroneous and deficient town planning at both touristic and urbanistic levels has led to this situation. The guidelines set out in the GPUPs of 1973 and 1986 have been ignored and 28 partial plans have been drawn up - from the 1986 PGOU up until 2000, which incorporate new land, not included in planning, to the constructed land, without attending to the required development of services. This situation of extensive and unharmonic growth is causing a series of negative effects, amongst which the following stand out: A) the absence of a model for the town, seeing that the current one responds to a collection of disperse and unconnected residential estates, the spectacular increase of its population and total number of properties, the lack of planning in the design of new roads and the situation of the beaches next to the town centre have caused a situation of chaotic traffic, especially in the summer-time. B) The road network infrastructure came after the development of the residential estates, in such a way that the access to and exits from this town are totally insufficient, causing serious traffic delays. C) the sea front is totally occupied by tall buildings, with no kind of reserve on land, which prevents its recuperation or

Sustainable Tourism, F. D. Pineda, C. A. Brebbia & M. Mugica (Editors)
© 2004 WIT Press, www.witpress.com, ISBN 1-85312-724-8

rehabilitation. D) the lack of balance between services and personnel with the demographic profile of the tourists-residents and the notable increase of the population. For example, there are serious deficits in relation to health services, bearing in mind that the national average for the relation of hospital beds for inhabitant is 255 and, in the case of Torrevieja, in the low season, this figure is 700. As for pharmaceutical services, the national average is one chemist shop for 2,093 inhabitants and here it is 12,500 in the winter months and 50,000 in the periods of maximum occupation. In education, the student-class ratio is 38, whereas the national average is 32; the schooling situation is more complex in Torrevieja due to the high number of immigrant students, of various nationalities, who require special educational support programmes that have not been put into action. E) One of the most important problems currently faced by Torrevieja is that of citizens' insecurity, which has been related to the large urban area that makes the strategies and actions of the public security forces more complicated. In 1996 the number of infractions and crimes per 100 inhabitants was 10.45, increasing in the year 2002 to 16, when the Spanish average was 4.5. F) All of these elements end up by forming a local tourist product that offers a bad image, in such a way that the major European tour operators have decided to exclude this town from its selection of tourist destinations.

7 Conclusions

We can define the expansion of property tourism as *phagocytosis of space* Aledo [26], that is to say, the accelerated and unplanned use of urban land for the construction of residential tourist homes until the exhaustion of this structural resource and, therefore, causing the end of the life-cycle of the product. To understand this process, first the perverse dynamics of this type of tourism have to be examined. We have pointed out that the cycle of property development tourism is reduced to the purchase of land, construction of homes and their sale. There is no tourist business as such, we are faced with pure real estate activity. As with any business, it has to keep growing; that is to say, building, because there are no other objectives nor any intentions to create alternative or complementary ones.

The expansion of property development tourism in the region of Torrevieja has been as follows: in the first place, the coastal strip was occupied, a process that began before the decade of the 1930s but it was from the 60s onwards and, in particular, the 80s of the last century when the entire coastline was filled. Once it had been completely built-up with tall blocks of apartments, expansion took place towards the interior, on land at a distance of between 3 to 15 km from the coast, land that is used for dry farming, taking advantage of the lower prices of this land. To obtain greater benefits, thousands of semi-detached houses and chalets have been built in residential estates without services or infrastructures that, latterly, are financed by the town's treasury. The urbanisation of this second zone has been undertaken in a similar way to the occupation of the coastal area, with no minimum criteria for territorial planning. The landscape is unattractive and erodes quickly, due to the lack of water and agricultural activity having been

Sustainable Tourism, F. D. Pineda, C. A. Brebbia & M. Mugica (Editors)

abandoned. Moreover, the poor quality of the buildings and the residential estates is added to this. Over the last few years, the extension of this model to the towns of the interior more than 15km from the coast has been detected. Here, residential tourism competes with the irrigated agricultural land that is more expensive, but the voracity of the model does not seem to have any limits.

It is not only the property development businesses that generate, maintain and benefit this residential tourist circuit, the local political powers also play an important part in the reproduction of the model. The town treasury collects the income that is generated by the process of urbanisation by way of taxes Mazón [27]. In this way, the councils stimulate development of this type of tourism that, in the short term, means significant income. However, in the long term, the costs of maintenance of this enormous urbanisation overtake the income received at the beginning. In the final balance, the cost of the impacts that are not only environmental would have to be entered into the calculation. The costs incurred by the council for the development and maintenance of services and infrastructures that the construction companies and property development businesses do not undertake and which end up coming out of the municipal budget Omberg [2]; McIntyre [28]. Thus, a stage is entered where the councils are obliged to concede more building licences to finance these services and infrastructures that the new tourist-resident population demands. We are dealing with a development spiral with no way back until the town exhausts the land available for development and a crisis point is reached where serious problems of economic viability are faced in the town's finances, due to high indebtedness. In the case of the council of Torrevieja, the individual debt (debt for inhabitant) is 1,105€ compared with 361€ of the Valencian Region – which is added to the environmental unsustainability that the expansion of urbanisation has caused.

These perverse dynamics of tourist-residential development lead to an environmental and socio-economic crisis in the towns centred on this type of offer. To sum up, the exhaustion of the land available for development, the lack of planning, the bad quality of the global product, the destruction of natural resources, the lack of an adequate complementary offer, the scarce hotel development and the bad tourist image of the resort make recovery strategies unworkable. The combination of these elements leads to the exhaustion of the model, at the end of the life-cycle of the tourist product. The sector would need some minimum bases on which to establish the implementation of integrated sustainable tourist development projects McIntyre [28]; Aronsson [29]; Hall and Lew [30] and the sector itself has destroyed the infrastructural basis (environment and land) and has not generated any minimum structures (tourist offer and other services). However, it is very important to indicate that the negative effects are borne by the towns and their inhabitants and not as much by the construction and property development companies; that is to say, the benefits are privatised, whereas the external negatives of the model are socialised García [31]. The real estate businesses and developers have the capacity to move to other zones in their search for new available resources (land and environmental quality) and to initiate a new destructive cycle there. This is what

Sustainable Tourism, F. D. Pineda, C. A. Brebbia & M. Mugica (Editors)

is happening on the southern coast of Alicante. The businesses that have exploited this sector have begun to transfer their field of operations to the coasts of the nearby provinces of Murcia and Almería, where there are still large coastal areas without urbanisation.

References

[1] Mazón, Tomás & Aledo, Antonio, El turismo inmobiliario en la provincia de Alicante: análisis y propuestas, Patronato Provincial de Turismo Costa Blanca, Diputación de Alicante: Alicante, 1996.

[2] Omberg, Ketil, Planificación de zonas recreativas y de tiempo libre: cuestiones locales y regionales. Desarrollos de segunda residencia, MOPT: Madrid, 1991.

[3] Warnes, A. Permanent and seasonal international retirement migration: the prospects for Europe. Population Dynamics in Europe, ed. P. Hooimeijer and R. Woods: Nederlandse Geographische Studies 173, Amsterdam, pp. 66-80, 1994.

[4] Mazón, Tomás, Sociología del Turismo, Editorial Centro de Estudios Ramón Areces: Madrid, 2001.

[5] Stroud, H. Environmental problems associated with large recreational subdivisions, Professional Geographer, 35(3), pp. 303-313, 1983.

[6] Gartner, W.C. Environmental impacts of recreational home development. Annals of Tourism Research, 14, pp. 38-57, 1987.

[7] Grenon, M. El plan azul : el futuro de la Cuenca Mediterránea, Ministerio de Obras Públicas y Transporte: Madrid, 1990.

[8] Vera Rebollo, F. Turismo y urbanización en el litoral alicantino, Instituto Juan Gil Albert: Alicante, 1987.

[9] Almenar, Bono & García, La sostenibilidad del desarrollo: el caso valenciano, Fundación Bancaiuxa, Universidad de Valencia: Valencia, 2000.

[10] Vera Rebollo, F. Turismo y crisis agraria en el litoral alicantino, Los mitos del turismo, ed. Francisco Jurado, Endimión: Madrid, 1992.

[11] Bettini, V. Elementos de ecología urbana, Trotta: Madrid, 1998.

[12] Aledo, A. Desertificación y Urbanismo: el fracaso de la utopía. Ciudades para un futuro más sostenible, 9. http://habitat.aq.upm.es/boletin/n9/lista.html. 1999.

[13] Plog, Stanley, Leisure travel: an extraordinary industry faces superordinary problems. Global tourism. The next decade. Butterworth and Heinemann: Oxford, 1994.

[14] MUNRES, Programa de Revitalización de Municipios con Turismo Residencial, Instituto Universitario de Geografía y Diputación de Alicante: Alicante, 1995.

[15] Torres Alfosea, F.J. Ordenación del litoral en la Costa Blanca, Universidad de Alicante: Alicante, 1997.

[16] Sancho, Amparo, Introducción al Turismo, Organización Mundial de Turismo: Madrid, 1998.

Sustainable Tourism, F. D. Pineda, C. A. Brebbia & M. Mugica (Editors)
 ISBN 1-85312-724-8

[17] Asín, J.M. and Bayón, F. Alojamientos extrahoteleros (chapter 41). 50 años del turismo español. Un análisis histórico y estructural, ed. Fernando Bayón Mariné, Centro de Estudios Ramón Areces: Madrid, pp. 927- 941, 1999.
[18] Monreal, J. El nuevo mercado turístico: jubilados europeos en la región de Murcia, Universidad de Murcia: Murcia, 2001.
[19] Butler, R.W. The Concept of a Tourism Area Cycle of Evolution: Implications for Management of Resources. Canadian Geographer, 24 (1) pp. 5-12, 1980.
[20] Argawal, S. The resort cycle revisited: implications for resorts (Chapter, 11). Progress in tourism recreation and hospitality management. C.P. Cooper and A. Lockwood (eds.), John Wiley: New York, 1994.
[21] Bianchi, R. Tourism development and resorts dynamics: an alternative approach (Chapter 10) Progress in tourism recreation and hospitality management. C.P. Cooper and A. Lockwood (eds.), John Wiley: New York, 1994.
[22] Girard, T.C. & Gartner, W.C. Second home, second view: host community perceptions. Annals of Tourism Research, 20 (4), pp. 685-700, 1993.
[23] Casado-Díaz, M.A. "Socio-demographic impacts of residential tourism: a case study of Torrevieja, Spain", in International Journal of Tourism Research. 1, 223-237, 1999..
[24] Viruela, A.; Martínez, R. & Domingo Pérez, C. Población extranjera en el País Valenciano, Arxius, 5, pp. 147-182, 2001.
[25] Barke, M. The growth and changing pattern of second homes in Spain in the 1970s, Scottish Geographical Magazine 107 (1), pp. 12-21, 1991.
[26] Aledo, A. Turismo inmobiliario y la fagocitación de la naturaleza (Chapter 24). Construçao do saber urbano ambiental: a caminho sa transdisciplinariedad. Ediciones Humanidades: Londrinas-Paraná (Brasil);
[27] Mazón, Tomás, Introducción a la Planificación Urbana, Editorial Aguaclara: Alicante. 1997.
[28] McIntyre, G. Sustainable tourism development: guide for local planners, World Tourism Organization: Madrid, 1993.
[29] Aronsson, L. The Development of sustainable tourism, Continuum: London; New York, 2000.
[30] Hall, W. & Lew, A.A., Sustainable Tourism: A Geographical Perspective, Longman, Harlow: Essex, 1999.
[31] García, E. Medio Ambiente y sociedad, Alianza: Madrid, 2004.

Sustainable Tourism, F. D. Pineda, C. A. Brebbia & M. Mugica (Editors)

Community perspectives on ecotourism carrying capacity: case studies from three bordering villages of Kayan Mentarang National Park, Indonesia

Y. Iiyama[1] & R. Susanti[2]
[1]*School of Forestry and Environmental Studies, Yale University, USA*
[2]*Conservation Agency in East Kalimantan, Indonesia*

Abstract

Too often tourism development adds to the difficulties faced by local people. In particular when the development of tourism exceeds the carrying capacity of the local community, it causes a variety of negative impacts. Upper Pujungan region located in and around Kayan Mentarang National Park (KMNP) which possesses great natural beauty, cultural traditions, and archaeological remains, offers high potential as an eco-tourism destination. Thus far, its difficult accessibility has limited the number of tourists, so that the region's carrying capacity has not yet become a significant issue. However, in a few years time, the District Government of Malinau will complete road construction which, when it reaches the region, will increase accessibility to the National Park. In participatory workshops, the risks and implications of exceeding carrying capacity were discussed and analyzed with community members.
Keywords: carrying capacity, ecotourism, rapid rural appraisal, access road construction, Kayan Mentarang National Park, Dayak, swidden agriculture.

1 Introduction

Lime and Stankey [1] wrote that carrying capacity was among the most controversial topics in recreation management. According to Coccossis [2], early definitions of carrying capacity had a limited perspective, such as biology or sociology. In 1964, Wager defined carrying capacity as a "level of recreational use an area can withstand while providing a sustained quality of recreation" [3].

Sustainable Tourism, F. D. Pineda, C. A. Brebbia & M. Mugica (Editors)

Park management authorities have applied the carrying capacity approach to protect fragile environment from human activities [4]. For example, since the late 1970's, the Environment Agency of Japan has been managing the carrying capacity of the National Parks by restricting traffic to control environmental quality and the quality of recreational experience [5,6].

Discussion of carrying capacity management has been influenced by concepts of sustainable development [7], and more emphasis has been placed on the environmental, social, and economic thresholds of the host community of the tourism [2]. When the development of tourism exceeds the carrying capacity of the local community, it causes a variety of negative impacts. These impacts, such as the displacement of indigenous/local people, local cultural degradation, distortion of local economies, erosion of social structures, environmental degradation, diversion of scarce resources on which local people depend, the outbreak of disease, and so on have been observed around the world [8,9]. Ecotourism can be an alternative form of tourism and may be green business but there are growing debates on the degree of "greenness" [10]. Ceballos-Lascurain defines ecotourism as "environmentally responsible, enlightening travel and visitation to relatively undisturbed natural areas in order to enjoy and appreciate nature (and any accompanying cultural features both past and present) that promotes conservation, has low visitor impact, and provides for beneficially active socio-economic involvement of local populations" [11]. We would argue, however, that the host community of the ecotourism destination itself could have further active participation rights, not limited only to socio-economic benefit but also to their socio-ecological carrying capacity control. We wonder that if these extended participatory rights were applied to the host community, how would they define their carrying capacity and to what extent would they want to develop ecotourism. In this research, through rapid rural appraisal (RRA) at three villages, We sought community perspectives on their carrying capacity as ecotourism destinations.

2 Research site

Kayan Mentarang National Park (KMNP) covers an area of 1.4 million hectares of interior Bornean mountain region, and lies on the border between Sabah and Sarawak, Malaysia. The study sites, 3 villages belong to Upper Pujungan region and are located on the border of the southern part of KMNP (see Figure 1). According to World Wide Fund for Nature - Indonesia (WWF) [12], this region has two main ecotourist destinations: a view point from Batu Ului, a rocky peak by the Pujungan River, and a waterfall on the Melu'ung River, which ends into a deep pool where tourists can swim. These sites are located at the remotest area of the region; the penetralia of Long Jelet village. In addition to these, natural beauty, ethnic cultural traditions of Dayak and natural beauty, ethnic cultural traditions of Dayaks, and archaeological remains of this region offers high potential as an eco-tourism destination [12].

Sustainable Tourism, F. D. Pineda, C. A. Brebbia & M. Mugica (Editors)

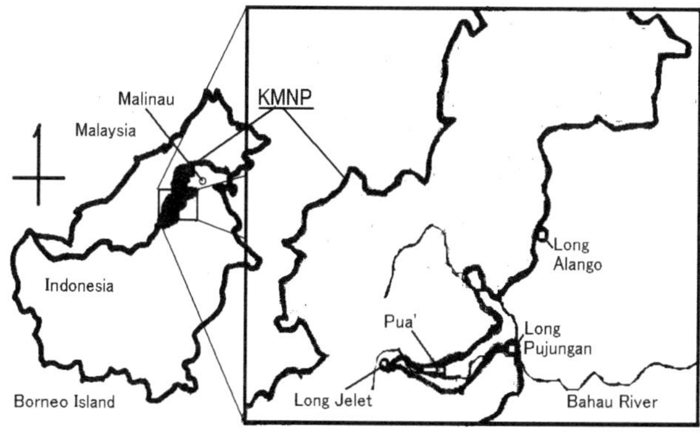

Figure 1: Map.

Community-based ecotourism initiated in cooperation with WWF began in mid-2001, funded by the Danish Agency for Development Assistance (DANIDA) and the International Tropical Timber Organization (ITTO) [13, 14]. Since then, formulation of an ecotourism committee, planning, training, cross visits to other ecotourism destinations, and trans-boundary management coordination have been implemented [13].

According to a KMNP Management Plan [15], the annual arrival of tourists to KMNP is only 25 people, so this National Park is still in a very primitive period of ecotourism development. These 3 villages have received a particularly small number of tourists because of its difficult accessibility; there is no road for car transportation. Therefore, its carrying capacity has not yet become a significant issue. Long Pujungan village has a small airport. From Malinau, the capital of the District, one can reach the Long Pujungan by air in a 5-seat plane with one weekly flight or by small boat in three to five days, depending on the weather conditions. If the condition is bad, it is totally inaccessible. Long Jelet is the most remote village, taking 4 to 6 hours by small boat from Long Pujungan and Pua' is located between Long Jelet and Long Pujungan. The populations of Long Jelet, Pua' and Long Pujungan are 59, 41 and 330 respectively. Because of high demand for ecotourism, there is a huge potential for an explosive increase in tourism development if transportation infrastructure improved.

In a few years' time, the District Government of Malinau will complete the construction of a road that will run between Malinau and Tanjung Nagka, Long Alango, and Long Pujungan according to an official statement of the Malinau District government [16]. The road has the potential to greatly increase accessibility to the National Park. The road construction is financed by selling the logs located in 1 km swaths of the forests along both sides of the planned road and both logging and road construction are implemented by a concessionaire [16]. WWF has been asking the Malinau District Government to conduct an impact assessment (EIA, *AMDAL* in Indonesian) to circumvent negative environmental consequences; however, it has not yet been done, while

Sustainable Tourism, F. D. Pineda, C. A. Brebbia & M. Mugica (Editors)
© 2004 WIT Press, www.witpress.com, ISBN 1-85312-724-8

it was observed that construction had begun and a 100 km of construction from Malinau had already been finished [17].

The main livelihood of this region's villagers is swidden agriculture, hunting, gathering and fishing. The swidden agriculture of these three villages is approximately a 25-year rotation of the fixed village forest area, which has been passed by generation to generation [18]. Thrupp et al. state: "the evolutionary end-result, swidden agriculture, yield[s] high returns per unit of labor; it is the most sustainable agricultural technology ever developed in tropical rain forests" [19]. Villagers produce or collect most of their subsistence needs by themselves, but they have to buy some indispensable goods, such as petrol and salts at shops in Long Pujungan.

3 Research questions

The research objective is to understand the community perspectives on carrying capacity of ecotourism host community at each of the three villages located on the border of the KMNP. "Carrying capacity of ecotourism host community" is defined as:

- how many tourists per month the village are designated to receive,
- to what extent do people in the community desire tourism development
- how do people in the community perceive development generally and think of their society and the environment and their possible vulnerability.

In each community, how and why perspectives differ between genders, experience of tourism activities, and length of commitment to customary tradition (age) are sought.

4 Research methods

The rapid rural appraisal (RRA) is defined as "an approach for developing a preliminary, qualitative understanding of a situation" [20]. Focus group workshops and semi-structured interviews were the core part of this research and the data from discussion at workshops and semi structure interview was triangulated by key informant interviews, secondary data analysis and participant observations.

According to Chambers [21], sensitive issues can be more freely discussed in groups than individuals, and it is more effective to have the group workshops considering social strata. It is reasonable to choose a workshop discussion method divided into genders, ages (divided into two categories: younger than 40 years old and older) and experience of tourism activities where possible, so that discussions induced can address some sensitive issues such as perceptions regarding land and resource use and road construction. In each village, we asked to head of the villages to call all available villagers to participate in one of the workshops, which was fitted to his/her category. However, not all villagers could attend so semi structured interviews were conducted as supplement of the focus groups workshops.

5 Outcomes

5.1 Long Jelet

All of the three categories of villager workshops set the tourism carrying capacity of the village very low: they believe that only 1 to 10 tourists per month would be acceptable and that the number of tourists should be restricted by their time budgets depending on the season of swidden farming. At all workshops, villagers place a premium on swidden farming which they do not want to be disturbed. They will continue with their current lifestyle even though if increasing income from ecotourism may allow them to purchase anything, food they need. In all focus groups, villagers emphasize that "we will continue swidden farming and will never stop it. It should be passed from generation to generation."

Male villagers have become more aware and concerned about the environmental destruction resulting from development activities because they have experienced working for logging companies in Malaysia and WWF project's study tour to Malaysia. They are concerned thefts, logging and mining could deplete resources and destroy their forests. They also are aware of the social-economic consequences of development. Some of the old men participants note from their experience with the WWF's study tour to Malaysia that "In Malaysia, we saw there were already three big hotels so it seemed to be very difficult for other local people to get any benefit from tourists."

Women usually do not travel outside the village, and therefore have less exposure to the potentially negative aspects of development and tourism. Women villagers felt proud of their handicrafts such as bags made of rattan, which they produce for tourists, and their cooperation in promoting the tourism market through the WWF: "We feel very happy that people outside of our village can appreciate our handicrafts and buy them." Although most women villagers have never been outside of the village, their desire to communicate with outsiders is strong. They have experienced small, but tangible benefits from handicraft sales; however, they do not want their tourism-related work to make them too busy to work on swiddens. "To make a rattan bag takes two to three months, because it needs a long process and we make it only little by little when we have spare time that does not disturb our swidden farming."

The head of the village and the head of the ecotourism committee of the village tried to distribute to all villagers the work of guide, transportation, accommodation, and others for us: tourists. We observed at *gotong royong* (mutual help work) that all of men and women villagers and children worked collaboratively for maintenance of the bathroom which was constructed by villagers for ecotourism development in cooperation with WWF. At all workshops villagers inform that all villagers who are in the village share work for tourists. They feel that tourism benefits them although it is still very little since tourists come just twice a year on average. They hope to develop ecotourism a little more; however, they do not want to develop it to the extent that it could be a burden for someone in the village. The community attempts to take advantages of the ecotourism development for mutual rather than individual benefit.

The planned road is not directly connected to Long Jelet village so that their forest area will not be exploited by the road construction. Most women villagers cannot imagine what a road would bring about because they have never seen a road for car transportation: “We don’t know whether we should be for or against it”. The group comprised of old men says, “We are for road construction because it may reduce the price of goods. However, we are concerned that logging companies or any other businesses and resource thieves would come to exploit this village forest more easily than before.”

5.2 Pua’

Pua’ villagers’ workshops also set the carrying capacity low: they will receive 4 to 10 tourists per month. The perceived limiting factor is slightly different between women and men. Women are concerned about their time budgets for swidden farming, whereas men are more concerned about the availability of transportation and accommodation for tourists. One of the male groups argues, “If we become too busy in tourism, we will manage divisions of work in our families.” The old women group notes “If tourism developed, men would concentrate on working with tourism and receive the benefits, and women would become much busier in swidden farming and household but receive no benefits.” Old women groups express their desire to work for tourism because swidden agriculture is quite heavy physical labor, and they found it more difficult as they got older. Most of the both women and men villagers have worked in Malaysia for logging companies. They perceive Malaysia as highly developed but they abhor destruction of their own forests like those of Malaysia. All groups discuss and agree that tourism will not have a negative environmental impact on the village; however, other development such as logging will deplete their environment and resources.

Pua’ is located in between Long Jelet and Long Pujungan. To access the current main ecotourism destinations in Long Jelet, tourists have to pass through Long Pujungan and Pua’ by small boat. Since the current ecotourism benefits are limited to boat transportation for tourists that stay no longer than two days, there is limited tangible benefit for most villagers. The men who have experienced working with tourists think that the village can receive 4 tourists per month maximum because there are only each of four villagers who has a small boat which can be used for tourists transportation from Pua’ to other villages. On the other hand, villagers in the group of men who have not previously worked with tourists think the village could receive 10 tourists per month. If the tourist number is fewer than 10, all tourist jobs are distributed to only the 4 villagers who have the boats. The group of men who have experienced working with tourists says: “We are searching a new tourist destination in this village territory

Sustainable Tourism, F. D. Pineda, C. A. Brebbia & M. Mugica (Editors)
© 2004 WIT Press, www.witpress.com, ISBN 1-85312-724-8

which is accessible on foot. If we can market it as a new ecotourism destination, villagers who do not have small boats can also find tourism jobs as guides and in providing accommodations and more benefits can be distributed among villagers."

Pua' is located two hours distance by boat from Long Pujungan, the end of the planned road. Villagers expect greater mobility and a lowering of the price of the commodities as a result of the easier transportation. The issue about the future possibility of forest exploitation is raised in one of the men's workshops: "We are concerned about a logging company coming to exploit our forests through the constructed road in the future, thinking of our children and grandchildren."

5.3 Long Pujungan

Villagers in Long Pujungan design a larger carrying capacity than that of Long Jelet and Pua' because the population is about six times larger than these villages, and there are infrastructures such as a guest house which can accommodate 20 tourists per night, a small airport, a clinic, and several shops, and therefore they can cope with larger numbers. Male villagers responded with a range varying from 100 to 1,200 tourists per month as acceptable while women with a range varying from 5 to 2,000 per month.

Some young villagers of both genders in Long Pujungan express concern that local tourism development might bring about negative environmental impacts on their village: "I am concerned that a number of outsider tourist-based businesses could intrude in our village and destroy our environment and take away everything." This perspective might be the result of their experience of receiving more visitors because of its location as a capital of Pujungan Sub-District and as a traffic conjuncture.

It is perhaps understandable that more young people seek a larger cash income, more advanced city life, and material convenience as they are more frequently exposed to a cash economy. Some of young men expressed their strong desire to work for a tourism business rather than continue to work with swidden agriculture if the income from tourism becomes reliable, but some young men want to continue swidden agriculture even if tourism becomes highly developed.

Young women do not voice a strong desire to work for the tourism business at the expense of terminating swidden agriculture, and most women say that the seasons when they are busy working for swiddens (January to March), only a limited number of tourists are acceptable. Similar to other villages, a high sense of responsibility to feed all the family and to be workers in traditional gender roles seem to be deeply rooted in women's minds and in the society. Old women villagers hope for more tourism development because of their concern for their health and their desire to do lighter work than swidden agriculture, which is so hard for their aging bodies. Old male villagers tend to not be concerned with high tourism development because they believe that they can control it through customary laws and say, "Tourists should follow our customs such as way of bathing, and have food produced from swidden farms, fishes at rivers, and animals we hunt, because it is too costly if they demand imported food and lifestyle."

Long Pujungan is the planned end of the road under construction. The same as other villages, men villagers are more inclined than women to think that the local development opportunities such as road construction may bring about negative environmental and social impacts, because a larger number of men have traveled and witnessed examples of damage impacts of development and over-exploitation. Villagers want the road because they expect it would lower the purchase prices, simplify transportation means that are currently expensive and dangerous, but they will demand further explanation concerning road construction costs. If it is reasonable and indispensable, they will contribute their forests and ask the district government to keep the forest exploitation area and negative environmental impacts minimal.

6 Conclusions

Living in this capitalist economy, it is difficult to imagine for us the life of the people who live by producing most of their needs by themselves on land and forests that are passed from generation to generation. Our hypothesis stems from general notions such as women are more concern about environment degradation, elder people are more conservative, and tourism experiences give people more impetus to further development. However, other factors such as personal experience also influence an individual's perspective. For example, working at a logging company, visiting a mining location and a tourism developed area, and seeing forest destruction, fishery decline, water pollution, depletion of local economic opportunities by outside businesses, and observing negative social impacts such as prostitution and drugs make people more reluctant to accept uncontrollable development. Most villagers whose day-to-day experience is working in swidden agriculture are determined to conserve their forests and land rather than become embroiled in the cash economy to the extent of giving up the current lifestyle. They perceive their carrying capacity as low level.

Ecotourism development should be carefully planned with particular respect to and participation of the local communities, which could suffer direct threats to their livelihoods. In some communities, consideration of gender is particularly important because ecotourism has a greater potential benefit for most men and greater potential burden for most women if there are no arrangements in the distribution of costs and benefits within the community. Any sort of development project relating to this area should be carefully planned and implemented by the decisions of community members of both genders and of all social strata.

Policy planners should pay attention to the impacts that probably come up on the local community in the future by road construction. That is, on one hand, the community members have a strong desire for transportation development and they therefore decided to allow their forests to be exploited, when they were convinced that it was the only way to construct the road up to their villages.

Sustainable Tourism, F. D. Pineda, C. A. Brebbia & M. Mugica (Editors)
© 2004 WIT Press, www.witpress.com, ISBN 1-85312-724-8

Currently available, limited, slow, expensive and life-threatening means of transportation curtails their mobility and economic development opportunities including ecotourism. On the other hand, they also fear further exploitation of their forests and environmental change, especially the destruction of their swidden lands by other uses.

Tourism carrying capacity has been managed mainly for the protection of the natural environment and for keeping the quality of tourist experience. However, considering local socio-ecological complexity, carrying capacity should be measured and controlled by full participation of the host community.

Acknowledgements

We sincerely thank all villagers in Long Jelet, Pua', Long Pujungan and Long Alango. We received generous support and sponsorship from Ministry of Forestry in Indonesia, Indonesian Institute of Sciences (LIPI), WWF, Japan International Cooperation Agency (JICA), Forestry Agency of Japan, London University and Yale University. I thank Cristina Eghenter for insight comments, and Mubariq Ahmad, Ramon Janis, Ignn Sutedja for cooperation. Iiyama thanks her advisors: Professors Raymond L. Bryant, Michael R. Dove, Pamela McElwee, Stewart Wigglesworth, Sue Prasad, and Cecilia Blasco. All shortcomings of this paper are only our responsibility.

References

[1] Lime, D.W. and Stankey, G.H., Carrying capacity: Maintaining outdoor recreation quality, *Land and leisure: Concepts and methods in outdoor recreation second edition*. eds. Doren, C. S., Priddle, G.B. and Lewis, J.E., Methuen: London, 1979

[2] Coccossis, H., Island tourism development and carrying capacity. *Island tourism and sustainable development: Caribbean, Pacific, and Mediterranean Experiences*. eds. Apostolopoulos, Y. and Gayle, D.J., Praeger Publishers: Westport and London, 2002

[3] p131, Wager, J.A. cited Ceballos-Lascurain, H., *Tourism, ecotourism and protected areas*, IUCN: Gland and Cambridge, 1996

[4] Wilson, G.A. and Bryant, R. L., *Environmental Management: New Directions for the Twenty-First Century*. UCL press: London and Pennsylvania, 1997

[5] Kouyama, M., Yagai Recreation ti no shyuyoryoku ni kannsuru kenkyu-rei. *Shizen kankyo assessment gijyutsu manual*, ed. Shizen Assessment Kenkyu Kai, Shizen kankyo kenkyu kai: Tokyo, 1995

[6] Sayama, H. Personal communication, 30 July 2003, JICA Expert, Advisor on Nature Conservation, Ministry of Forestry in Indonesia

[7] World Commission on Environment and Development, *Our Common Future*, Oxford University Press: Oxford, 1987

[8] Mowforth, M. and Munt, I., *Tourism and sustainability: new tourism in the third world*, Routledge: London and New York, 1998

Sustainable Tourism, F. D. Pineda, C. A. Brebbia & M. Mugica (Editors)

[9] Holden, A., *Environment and tourism*, Routledge: London and New York, 2000
[10] Bryant, R.L. and Bailey, S., *Third World Political Ecology*, Routledge: London, 1997
[11] p20, Ceballos-Lascurain, H., *Tourism, ecotourism and protected areas.* IUCN and WWF: Gland and Cambridge, 1996
[12] WWF-Indonesia, http://www.wwf.or.id/Features/ekoturisme_en1.html
[13] Eghenter, C. Personal Communication, 7 July 2003, Community Empowerment Coordinator, WWF-Indonesia, Tarakan, East Kalimantan, Indonesia
[14] ITTO, *Project Document: Project for Management of Kayan Mentarang National Park to Promote Trans Boundary Conservation along the Border between Indonesia and Malaysian States of Sabah and Sarawak (Phase I)*, ITTO: Yokohama, 2000
[15] Government of Indonesia, *Kayan Mentarang National Park Management Plan 2001-2025 Book I: Management Plan.* Jakarta, WWF-Indonesia, 2002
[16] District Government of Malinau, *Keputusan Bupati Malinau Nomor 318 tahun 2001*, District Government of Malinau: Malinau [Official letter], 2001
[17] Sutdja, I. Personal Communication, 8 July 2003, Project Executant, WWF- Indonesia, Tarakan, East Kalimantan
[18] Ngang Personal Communication, 21 July 2003, the head of Long Jelet village
[19] Dove, M.R. and Kammen, D., The Epistemology of Sustainable Resource Use: Managing Forest Products, Swiddens, and High Yielding Variety Crops. *Human Organization.* 56 (1), pp. 91-101, 1997
[20] p42, Beebe, J., Basic Concepts and Techniques of Rapid Appraisal. *Human Organization* 54 (1) pp. 42-51, 1995
[21] Chambers, R., *Whose Reality Counts? Putting the First Last*, Intermediate Technology Publications: London, 1997

Gravity and the tourism trade: the case for Portugal

Á. Matias
Banco de Portugal, International Relations Department, and Universidade de Évora, Department of Economics, Visiting Professor

Abstract

Tourism economics are still fighting for international academic recognition. This is not surprising considering that the increasingly economic significance of tourism has not yet been accompanied by a parallel development of its theoretical framework. This paper aims to make a further contribution to the theoretical foundations of the emerging subject of tourism economics. Considering the existence of very specific characteristics on tourism goods, tourism analysis requires a non-standardized treatment from economic science, frequently using less usual instruments – as is the case for economic geography. Given the relevance of distance on tourism consumption, we argue that gravitational models can be used to explain tourism flows in general, and the ones towards the Portuguese territory in particular. The estimation of the latter leads to the conclusion that although GDP has an important empirical relevance, the role of (economic) distance is no less relevant in both theoretical and empirical terms. The estimation of this simple model allows us then to confirm empirically the relevance of distance on the determination of annual tourism flows towards Portugal; furthermore, it explains the fact that Spain ranks first among the countries presently supplying tourists to Portugal (with an almost constant 50% ratio over time on the total number of tourists entering Portugal).
Keywords: economic geography, gravity, distance, tourism, tourism flows, tourism goods, externalities, gravitational models.

1 Introduction

Only recently has economic science begun to view tourism in accordance with its growing economic importance. However, this comes without surprise given

Sustainable Tourism, F. D. Pineda, C. A. Brebbia & M. Mugica (Editors)

that tourism has only assumed itself as an organized economic activity during the second half of the 20th century (after World War II). Before that the longer working day and hence the limited leisure time made tourism activity a restricted privilege to a few wealthy segments of society.

With the economic prosperity of the post-war period – closely linked to the role of Breton Woods institutions – and the fast development of transports – namely by air – the distance factor appears generally as a new approach in the study of market opportunities. Nowadays, economic distance is therefore surpassing geographical distance. These events were thus extremely favourable to the tourism business, which rapidly gained considerable significance without a simultaneous development of the due theoretical framework within economic science. As a consequence, a considerable number of specificities of the tourism market vis-à-vis the general economic laws, have so far been ignored by the so-called mainframe economics. This fact had inevitable consequences at various levels, namely as regards the attention that for a long time has (not) been paid to tourism by the economic policy decision-makers and the insufficient basic economic training of qualified human resources for tourism.

This article aims precisely at making a further contribution to the systematisation of the theoretical foundations of the emerging subject of tourism economics. For the purpose, it is divided into two parts: the first one draws the attention to the possible role of economic geography on the study of tourism trade; the second one appeals to the use of some instruments from the new economic geography to study the growing industrialization of the tourism sector, namely gravity models.

This second part stresses in particular the fact that tourism, besides being undoubtedly a service-based economic activity, it is also, to a certain extent, an industry, since the tourism product - to appear as such - undergoes production process that from a theoretical-abstract point of view, is all similar to what happens in traditional industries (from the obtaining of raw materials to the resulting final product). Here, a gravitational model has been used to study the tourism flows towards the Portuguese territory, the estimation of which leads to the finding that, although the economic aggregate (GDP used as a proxy) has an empirical relevance to the explanation of these flows, (economic) distance is the key variable.

Finally, considering distance as a relevant factor to tourism demand, the issue of promoting the national tourism destination (territory-country), and having also in mind the specific characteristics of the tourism good, one must consider that there might be a role for some government regulatory intervention in this sector, namely through thorough public policies duly connected with the remaining national economic policy, with a view to optimising the huge potential of this sector to create wealth.

2 A role for economic geography on the study of tourism trade

Although being undeniably a service-based economic activity, tourism is also, to a certain extent, an industry, once that the tourism product, to be considered as such, must undergo production process similar to the one of traditional industries (from the acquisition of raw materials to the resulting final product).

As this is an industry based on a tradable good, whose sale is intrinsically directed towards external markets, and with the act of consumption depending on the displacement of the consumer to the marketplace, it is important to assess the extent to which the distance variable becomes a determinant one on the explanation of tourism flows.

As economic geography is a subject where distance rises as a relevant element in the decision making process for market agents (whether relating to production or consumption), one can assume that it has potential to make an important contribution to study the main factors determining tourism demand.

2.1 Why studying economic geography within the scope of tourism economics?

Economic geography is concerned with the fact that the economic activity always takes place in a given special location, whose specific characteristics are not at all irrelevant to economic performance. According to Fujita *et al.* [14], this subject studies "where the economic activity takes place and why".

Curiously, although this is not new to economic science, since some classical authors like Adam Smith (1723-1790) and David Ricardo (1772-1823) had already referred to competitive advantages in international trade, with different resources being strongly determined by the geographical variable, it remains something often neglected in economic literature. This happened mainly with texts originally written in the post Bretton-Woods period in particular, when the world economy underwent a primarily protectionist stage, with national economies living in a relatively closed environment and with significant restrictions in terms of monetary conversion.

Nevertheless, at the current time of free trade (and even of advanced economic integration, as it is the case for the European Union), of new information and communication technologies, and of monetary conversion and increased factor mobility, the economic activity always involves aspects related with the optimal location of production. Insofar the location decision process is beginning to be referenced in economic literature as a strategic management decision, once that the competitive advantages arising from the resulting minimization of transaction costs are an unquestionably relevant factor for the strategic profit maximization underlying the rationality imposed on economic agents operating in growingly global and competitive markets [4]. Or, as mentioned by Smith [25, p.150], *"the three most important factors to consider when starting a business are location, location and location"*. Furthermore, the mere empirical observation shows that location can never be considered as an immutable decision, but rather as a variable to be considered at every single moment in the production function of any company.

However, the sole idea of using economic geography to study the tourism activity may seem – at first sight – not to make much sense, since, with natural resources being the fundamental production factor in tourism, the question of the location of tourism activity should not arise, once that it takes place wherever

Sustainable Tourism, F. D. Pineda, C. A. Brebbia & M. Mugica (Editors)
© 2004 WIT Press, www.witpress.com, ISBN 1-85312-724-8

those resources physically exist. A closer analysis leads however to the finding that this is only true for tourism based on natural or historical resources and not for the one based on other resources built by man.

Indeed, as we identify three main types of production factors in tourism: - natural resources (as for instance the famous triple S – *sun, sea & sand*); - historical resources (as it is the case for some types of urban tourism), and; - resources built by man (as special events, museums, theme parks, oceanic aquariums, natural parks, etc.), one can easily conclude that only the first two can be considered as economically fixed production factors, whereas the third one, while being a man's construction can be built at any location chosen by man.

In view of this, and due to the growing importance of tourism flows based on this third factor of tourism production, economic geography will have a word to say, not only as regards the spatial location of tourism supply, but also to explain the reasons underlying some agglomeration effects both on the demand and supply side. Another aspect to be considered is the possibility that some economic geography instruments may be useful for tourism analysis in order to explain certain specific phenomena (an example being the present use of gravitational models to assess the correlation existing in the Portuguese case between tourism flows and the distance vis-à-vis the source country).

After having justified the importance of economic geography to a better understanding of the tourism phenomenon, it is important to attain, even if briefly, how the location theory may contribute to the theoretical framework of tourism economics.

2.2 Location theory and tourism

We know how scarce the production of academic writings on tourism economics in general is. It is therefore no surprise that the same happens with the analysis of spatial location in tourism in particular (an aspect of particular relevance on the case of hotels).

According to Grether [16], the academic researchers interested in questions like marketing and corporate initiative have largely ignored the space and location variables. As the research on tourism (even at university level) has been dominated by the marketing approach, tourism research tends to follow the same pattern. Only very recently has the management school begun to "awaken" to the questions related with location and spatial analysis (see Porter [21]).

Fortunately for tourism researchers, there is already ample literature – both classical, neoclassical and contemporary – on *location economics* (according to Smith's terminology [25]), which simplifies the research on the spatial location determinants in tourism industry.

Naturally the former writings by location theorists do not contain explicit references to tourism, since the tourism industry has only gained momentum during the second half of the 20th century. The first contribution came from the pioneering author of the central location theory – Christaller [10], who in 1964 analyzed the spatial pattern of tourism and observed that it resulted from a process contrary to the one giving rise to central locations, hence to the conclusion that tourism was a "peripheral" activity. Obviously this conclusion no longer holds and has to be considered within the context the author created his theory, a period during which tourism was a luxury good only available to the wealthier classes (note that he wrote mainly in the 30s).

Although no explicit references to tourism are to be found in the writings of the remaining theorists of location, the present economic analysis of tourism benefits a lot from the findings of the so-called *location economics*. The development of a number of basic concepts and theories was of particular use for the scientific analysis of development patterns in industrial and urban areas in general and in the areas of tourism location in particular.

According to Smith [25, p.153], the fundamental contributions of *location economics* to the economic analysis of tourism can be summarized as follows: 1. Spatial location is an important theoretical and practical determinant of the size and success of any given company; 2. The choice of the best location involves trade-offs between transportation costs, availability of resources and market accessibility; 3. The size of the population and the number and location of competing companies may limit the creation of new corporate initiatives; 4. The economic activities too dependent on particularly bulky production factors or on very specific resources (natural or not) tend to choose a localization near those resources; similarly the companies that produce too bulky products tend to be localized as close as possible to their target-market.

If some of these contributions only very recently (namely with the "new geographical economy" in particular) have been duly systematized (as it is the case with the second aspect mentioned above), others (as for instance the first one) can already be found in the writings of the first theorists of location (as Von Thünen, Weber, Moses or Hotelling).

2.3 The origins of gravitational models

After Isaac Newton (1642-1727) has discovered the basic equation of his theory of gravitational attraction between two objects, the use of this equation was not limited to Physics and has spread to other areas of scientific knowledge, including – more recently – economics itself.

A very wise and eclectic man, Newton followed a heterodox line of thought that gave him a strong creative detachment vis-à-vis everything that drew his attention. Although approaching such different areas of knowledge as, for instance, philosophy, mathematics (a subject he taught for many years at Cambridge University) and religion, he got a wider recognition in physics with his *Law of Universal Gravitation"*, originally expressed by his famous gravity equation:

$$F = G\frac{m_1 m_2}{d^2} \tag{1}$$

where F is the gravitational force; m_1 and m_2 are the masses of objects 1 and 2, respectively; d is the distance between the objects; and G is the universal gravitational parameter (thus described by Newton because he believed this parameter to be constant regardless of time or space).

The first application, known so far, of the gravity concept to explain space interactions of human activities was developed by Carey [9], although in his case specifically directed to social-economic aspects. It was then necessary to wait until the 60s of the twentieth century to find the first applications of gravitational models to international trade (independently developed by Tinbergen [26] and Pöyhönen [22], as we shall see below).

Newton's law, widely used by various sciences, was therefore also welcomed by the economic science. Reilly's *Law of Retail Gravitation* [23], although focusing the analysis on urban economics (more precisely on the factors attracting retail trade to larger cities), strongly encouraged other authors after him to use the same concept of gravity to other areas of research, likewise international trade.

Even though, gravity models continue to be considered poor in microeconomic terms. Presently, however, this argument is not very well accepted anymore by some authors. According, to Smith [25, p.133], for example, *"a long standing criticism of gravity models has been that they have no theoretical basis (...); [although] historically correct, this criticism is now irrelevant and no longer valid. Stewart (1948) and Zipf (1946), who independently developed the concept of the gravity model, based their formulations explicitly on an analogy to Newton's law of gravitation."*.

Recently, gravity models are being increasingly used, namely by economic geography (see, for example, Brakman *et al.* [8]), since it's internal logic allows – among other possible applications – for the use of the distance element in the analysis of the economic relations between countries or regions.

2.4 Theoretical framework and applications on gravity and trade

In spite of everything else, one must recognize that within the scope of the theoretical framework of gravitational models, the main aspect derives precisely from the fact that these models have a very strong intuitive basis, instead of relying on duly justified restrictive hypothesis – as usual in the economic science. They are, therefore, simple and intuitive instruments for empirical economic analysis, rather than elegant and formally sophisticated theoretical models very difficult to transpose into reality.

Even so, several attempts of theoretical grounding can be found in the relating literature. As mentioned above, Reilly [23] used the gravitational principle to explain the stronger attraction of larger trade areas in his *retailling models*. For a long time the empirical relevance of gravitational models – see, for instance, Isard [17] and Tinbergen [26] – has outdone its theoretical grounding, which gained momentum when, around the 80s, some authors as Anderson [3] and Bergstrand [6,7] have finally made strong theoretical contributions. The same happened with Anas [2], who demonstrated that gravity models, as *logit* type models alike, can be derived from the maximization of a random utility and succeeded thus in inserting these models in the central theoretical body of economic theory.

More recently, Brakman *et al.* [8], for example, state that the gravitational model was more widely accepted by the international trade theory, precisely

Sustainable Tourism, F. D. Pineda, C. A. Brebbia & M. Mugica (Editors)
© 2004 WIT Press, www.witpress.com, ISBN 1-85312-724-8

because its basic equation – eqn (2) – can be derived from the *new trade theory*. Fujita and Thisse [15, p.220] – apropos the theory of urban center formation under imperfect competition – mention that consumers' incomplete information is an agglomerative (or centripetal) force as *"the expected utility of visiting a cluster of firms increases with its size, which is a reminiscent of the gravity principle"*.

In any case, and despite all the efforts made, it continues notoriously difficult to derive gravitational models from microeconomic principles. One of the most recent attempts was made by Deardorff [11], an author who demonstrated that the gravity equation is consistent with a number of models commonly used by economic science. Note that this author succeeded in deriving a version of the gravity equation that includes transportation costs (using for the purpose the cif and fob measures of trade flows). This was a further step towards a complete theorization of this kind of models.

All the known attempts to establish a theoretical framework for these models have shown some insufficiencies and it is precisely because of the still existing insufficiencies in the theoretical grounding of gravitational models that the option was taken to refer, in this article, to the possible applications of the gravity equation. Now, for the same kind of reasons, tourism economics – also a very recent subject of economic science – is one of the high potential fields for possible estimations of the gravity equation.

As a matter of fact, taking the *Newton's law*, and by doing the necessary adjustments, it is possible to build a theoretical formulation to the intuitive notion that trade flows tend to be larger between neighboring countries. This idea of gravity applied to international trade was early considered attractive from a theoretical point of view, since it permitted to find within the scope of the economic theory of international trade a basis for the statistical fact that geographically adjacent countries or regions had higher trade volumes.

Having in mind the need to search in economic theory a theoretical basis for the observation of trade flows directed to Portugal we propose here an application of the gravity equation to the study of Portuguese tourism market. However, it is important that, before going further into a specific application to a given sub-sector of international trade – as it is the case of tourism – we crosscheck the evolution of the first applications of the gravity principle to international trade.

The first known application of the gravity equation to international trade was, in fact, independently developed by Tinbergen [26] and Pöyhönen [22], who stated that the negative correlation between trade flows and distance (between origin and destination markets) is generally true for all countries, regardless of their differences in terms of wealth, development, culture, political system, history and social organization.

Later, other developments of the same kind were made by Linneman [20], Aitken [1], Leamer [18], and, more recently, Deardorff [12], to mention just a few. All these developments suggested an integration of the gravity equation in economic theory through international trade. Whereas Linneman tries to do it through a Walrasian general equilibrium system, Deardorff succeeds in deriving

Sustainable Tourism, F. D. Pineda, C. A. Brebbia & M. Mugica (Editors)

the gravity equation from the neoclassical Hecksher-Ohlin's factorial endowments.

Aitken and Leamer, in turn, were concerned with more operational aspects of the basic gravity equation. The former suggests that the size of the population must be added to the mass variable (usually expressed by GDP), whereas the latter suggests, when referring to distance, that, despite the major changes of second half of the 20th century, trade continues to exhibit a higher trend volume between neighboring countries, although, as Baptista [5] correctly observes, the concept of "neighbor" used by Leamer must be understood as "in the vicinity" rather then "adjacent to", although this kind of vicinity being not exclusively geographic but also cultural, linguistic, etc. This contribution, refined by Leamer and Storper [19], by referring to the concept of economic distance, gives the location element an important potential as a source of competitiveness.

In short, the gravity equation (in its non-stochastic form), when applied to trade flows, shows as follows:

$$E_{ij} = cY_i^{\theta_1} Y_j^{\theta_2} D_{ij}^{-\theta_3} \tag{2}$$

E_{ij} are the exports between country i and country j; c is a constant; Y_i is the national income on country i, Y_j is the national income on in country j, and D_{ij} is the distance between country i and country j, with θ being the parameter to be estimated, representing the income and distance elasticities of exports. A dummy type variable can be added whenever one identifies possible influences from special factors, such as the cultural proximity between country i and country j, the use of the same language, or any other.

As a result of using logs on eqn (2) it can be now written as follows:

$$\ln E_{ij} = \ln c + \theta_1 \ln Y_i + \theta_2 \ln Y_j + \theta_3 \ln D_{ij} \tag{3}$$

Note that in the above eqns., the estimations for parameters θ_1 and θ_2 are supposed to be positive, whereas for θ_3 the estimation must be negative, as distance is supposed to have a negative effect on trade flows. Fujita *et al.* [14, p.98) even observe that distance has always a high statistical significance in empirical tests, "*typically with the elasticity of trade with respect to distance being of the order – 0,6 to – 1,0*".

This procedure of log-linearization of the gravity equation, followed by an estimation under the usual minimum squares methodology (OLS), depends, as referred by Santos Silva and Tenreyro [24, p.3], on the residuals being statistically independent from regressors. Unfortunately, the variance of residuals is however highly unlikely to be independent from the GDP of countries i and j or from the distance between them (regardless of the concept of distance considered). Under these conditions the OLS estimation must provide inconsistent estimators for the θ parameters in question.

In this article, however, as the empirical application considered below is based on a small sample (N = 12), which by its own nature cannot be extended, the consistency problem does not apply, the results being rather considered as good as it gets for the present purpose. Note however that for larger samples the estimation of gravity models must follow an alternative method to the OLS – as

Sustainable Tourism, F. D. Pineda, C. A. Brebbia & M. Mugica (Editors)

suggested by Santos Silva and Tenreyro [24] – so as to avoid the possible estimation of inconsistent estimators for the θ parameters.

Table 1: Foreign trade intra and extra EU as a percentage of total.

	1960	1970	1980	1990	2000	2001
Exports:						
Intra-EU15	71,3	75,7	79,3	79,3	82,4	80,5
Extra-EU15	28,7	24,3	20,7	20,7	17,6	19,5
Imports:						
Intra-EU15	70,3	74,5	75,1	78,0	81,9	81,0
Extra-EU15	29,7	25,5	24,9	22,0	18,1	19,0

Source: Eurostat Datashop, National Statistics 2003

Although initially used to explain why trade flows were larger between neighboring countries (namely those with terrestrial boundaries), the gravity equation has been also used for other purposes in economic science. Following Dentinho [13], *"gravitational models are used to describe and predict the flows of persons, goods and information through space"*. Among the various possible applications of these models, one must emphasize the study of changes occurred in spatial separation structures (as pay tolls, bridges and new roads), the effects of spatial redistribution of urban activities (for example new residential areas, industrial areas, supermarkets, schools or hospitals), the development of input-output multiregional models, or the space attrition and factors of attraction/rejection present in different places, just to mention a few. This last aspect is of utmost importance in the study of the tourism market as the attraction factor is known as one of the fundamental variables of the tourism demand function.

In general, one can argue that there is a stronger economic motivation for trade to occur between two neighboring countries or regions (at least, due to the fact that the inherent transportation costs are smaller). This argument, also known as *distance deterrence*, implies that the trade flows between two areas is inversely related with the distance between them.

Finally, it is also important to consider that, in the European Union in particular, the vicinity approach gains ground due to the reduction of economic distance resulting from the on ongoing economic integration process.

In this case, as in others, there is an effect of (economic) proximity that surpasses the physical – geographical, which has mostly to do with cultural and linguistic aspects, such ad others of the same nature (besides the obvious reduction on transaction costs deriving from the above mentioned economic integration).

Reality suggests, indeed, that the European Union tends to concentrate more and more its trade flows within the scope of its economic space (see Table 1). In fact, at the beginning of the 21st century, the trade volume of the European Union (EU15) with extra-EU countries accounted for nearly 20%, with 80% of the trade within the European Union taking place between its members (intra-

Sustainable Tourism, F. D. Pineda, C. A. Brebbia & M. Mugica (Editors)

European trade), a fact that clearly fits within the gravitational principle in question.

3 An application of the gravity equation to the Portuguese tourism market

The theoretical concept of gravity is here applied to tourism exports with a double purpose of both helping on the explanation of some reality trends on Portuguese tourism flows, and also to provide an empirical measure of the importance of gravity (distance) in the tourism demand function.

Indeed, the gravity principle is here used not only to find in economic theory an explanation for some statistical observations that can be drawn from the mere observation of reality – as is the case for the strong concentration of Portuguese tourism demand on the Spanish market, which historically accounts for nearly 50% of total tourism demand for Portugal (see Table 2) – but also to determine how much does distance matters as an exogenous variable in the tourism demand function vis-à-vis the remaining demand variables, namely the income (economic mass).

By comparing Table 2 and Table 3 there is one question arising immediately: - if Spain ranks first in terms of number of tourists arriving annually to Portugal, why does it gives place to the UK in terms of annual tourism revenues in that country? A common sense answer to this question would be that probably the higher average income of the British tourists would be enough to overcame (through a higher average expense) their lower number comparing to Spanish tourists. But in this case the hypothesis in question would be that income (purchasing power) matters more than proximity (distance) on the Portuguese tourism demand function. As we will see through the model proposed in the next section that is not really the case. On the contrary, the gravity model proposed will tell us that gravity matters more than income on what respects the main forces behind Portuguese tourism demand.

3.1 A simple gravity model

The simple model we now propose uses then a specific application of economic theory to tourism – a gravitational model – to demonstrate, firstly, that the statistical fact of having half of the tourism demand for Portugal coming from a single adjacent country (Spain) is entirely in accordance with the basic gravitational principle associated with international trade theory. Secondly, it will result simultaneously obvious that the Portuguese tourism demand has a higher degree of dependence on distance rather than on any other exogenous variable, namely income.

Note, for the purpose, that if we consider tourism as an intrinsically export good, eqn (2) can be directly applied to the tourism sector. It is enough, for the purpose, to consider in E_{ij} only the exports of *tourism goods* between country i and country j (in this case j = P = Portugal), the θ parameter being then interpreted as the elasticity of *tourism* exports relating to income and distance.

Sustainable Tourism, F. D. Pineda, C. A. Brebbia & M. Mugica (Editors)

As far as continental tourism is concerned, note also that the means of transportation to be used is not necessarily the airplane – as it is usually the case with insular tourism. This allows for a reduction of transportation costs and will make the distance factor have a significant (negative) impact on tourism flows. Obviously the same will also happen with insular tourism, but with the impact here being smaller, since in this case the consumer has fewer alternatives to reach the place of destination (only by boat), which will diminish the relative weight of the distance factor on the consumer's decision.

Table 2: Portugal: Tourism demand by origin markets in 1998.

	Countries	Tur_i	GDP_i
1	Spain	5756	553
2	United Kingdom	1723	1357
3	Germany	870	1877
4	France	697	1427
5	The Netherlands	435	382
6	Italy	254	1172
7	Belgium*	233	248
8	United States of America	228	8230
9	Sweden	126	226
10	Switzerland	102	264
11	Austria	55	212
12	Japan	41	3783

Notes:
Tur_i = Number of tourists from country i (thousands)
GDP_i = GDP from country i (USD billions)
* includes Luxemburg

Sources: Tur_i - Direcção Geral de Turismo, PT; PIB_i - OECD in Figures 1999.

Thus, the tourism flows directed towards a continental destination, as it is the case with Portugal, must exhibit a negative correlation vis-à-vis the distance from the country of origin, since transportation costs are narrower for shorter distances. Note that if the country of destination has terrestrial boundaries with the country of origin, it is even possible to use transportation by car as an alternative to the airplane. Besides, the car alternative becomes more viable in a unified economic space – with factors and goods moving freely – as it is presently the case with the European Union.

This hypothesis can be tested with a gravity equation derived from eqn (2), where the dependent variable is tourism revenues and the exogenous one is the distance between the countries.

As a result, eqn (2) can now be written as follows:

$$\ln TR_i^P = \ln c + \theta_1 \ln d_{iP} + \theta_2 \ln GDP_i \tag{5}$$

Table 3 shows tourism Portuguese revenues disaggregated by the main origin markets in 1998. The simple observation of these data leads to the conclusion that the main tourism flows take place with European Union countries, with

Sustainable Tourism, F. D. Pineda, C. A. Brebbia & M. Mugica (Editors)

Spain - the only country holding terrestrial boundaries with Portugal - ranking third. This observation suggests at once that, in the case of Portugal, the distance factor has certainly a strong influence on the tourism flows towards the Portuguese market.

Table 3: Portugal: - Tourism demand by origin markets in 1998 measured in terms of tourism revenues.

	Countries	TR_i	GDP_i	d_{iP}
1	United Kingdom	847	1357	2227
2	France	803	1427	1815
3	Spain	793	553	636
4	Germany	577	1877	2887
5	Belgium*	303	248	2114
6	United States of America	254	8230	5733
7	Switzerland	132	264	2230
8	Italy	125	1172	2709
9	The Netherlands	120	382	2485
10	Japan	54	3783	11140
11	Sweden	52	226	3886
12	Austria	33	212	3200

Notas:

TR_i = Portuguese tourism revenues (10^6 €) from country i (demand origin).

GDP_i = GDP from country i (USD billions)

d_{iP} = Distance between country i and Portugal (Km)

* includes Luxemburg

Sources: TR_i - Direcção Geral de Turismo, PT; PIB_i - OECD in Figures 1999;
DiP - Brittanica Atlas and http://www.wcrl.ars.usda.gov to USA and Japan.

Naturally, although distance being only one among various factors determining tourism flows, it impacts on the final price of tourism products due to the aggravation of transportation costs, which does not leave room to many doubts on their negative influence on those flows.

The economic mass (the best proxy being, in this case, GDP), must, on the other hand, impact positively on tourism flows towards Portugal, once that the existence of a high purchasing power level in the country of origin is a basic determinant to the existence of tourism demand itself.

The estimations for the θ_i parameters must therefore be robust so as to allow for their unquestionable estimated negative sign in the case of parameter θ_1 (distance elasticity) and also unquestionable positive sign in the case of parameter θ_2 (mass or income elasticity), a condition for parameters θ_i to be considered structural in this model.

Note again that the results shown below are intended to be mainly illustrative for the Portuguese case, and should hold (with the corresponding elasticity variability applying) for any other continental destinations. This, together with the small size of the sample and the limited ensuing statistical inference, led us to disregard the study of residuals and the stationarity of variables. This option does

Sustainable Tourism, F. D. Pineda, C. A. Brebbia & M. Mugica (Editors)

not affect our conclusions, however, namely because we want to focus primarily on the underlying theoretical logic of the model, bearing in mind that the strict econometric validation of the results could always be achieved with an adequate calibration for the model considered.

3.2 Some results and implications

The OLS estimation produces the following results for this simple model (*t* statistics between round brackets):

$$\boxed{\ln TR_i^P = 13.073 - 1.574 \ln d_{iP} + 0.7 \ln GDP_i} \qquad R^2 = 0.78 \qquad (6)$$

$$(-5.3514) \qquad (4.2026)$$

The reasonable R^2 obtained (apparently explaining 78% of the tourism flows) indicates that the dispersion level of the dependent variable allows for a good adjustment, thus confirming that the Portuguese tourism demand is inversely related with the distance from the country(ies) of origin of the tourism flows directed to the Portugal and directly related with the income of said country(ies). We may then conclude that tourism income depends negatively on the distance and positively from the GDP of country *i*, although the estimation for the parameter representing the distance elasticity (θ_1 = - 1,574) being more significant than the estimation for the parameter representing the mass/income elasticity (θ_2 = 0,7).

It is, however, curious to note that if fully determined by distance, from an analytical point of view it would mean to set $\theta_2 = 1$ (income elasticity equal to one), in which case the following transformation would be valid for the original model:

$$\boxed{\theta_2 = 1} \Rightarrow \ln TR_i^P = \ln C + \theta_1 \ln d_{iP} + 1 \ln GDP_i \Leftrightarrow$$

$$\Leftrightarrow \ln TR_i^P - \ln GDP_i = \ln C + \theta_1 \ln d_{iP} \Leftrightarrow$$

$$\Leftrightarrow \ln\left(\frac{TR_i^P}{GDP_i}\right) = \ln C + \theta_1 \ln d_{iP} \Leftrightarrow$$

$$\Leftrightarrow \boxed{\ln TR_i^{P*} = \ln C + \theta_1 \ln d_{iP}}$$

In other words, if the elasticity of the tourism demand of country *P* relating to the income of country *i* is equal to one, then the equation explaining tourism demand has only one variable – the distance between i and P – and therefore, after making the above transformation for the dependent variable, the model becomes a simple linear regression model.

This particular case of our model explains also tourism demand for $\theta_2 = 1$ and is in line with the work developed by Brakman *et al.* [8, pp.12-15], who suggest to correct trade flows for the demand effect generated by a bigger economic mass (income) in larger countries. This corresponds therefore to a particular case in our model where the income elasticity is equal to one.

Sustainable Tourism, F. D. Pineda, C. A. Brebbia & M. Mugica (Editors)

Under these conditions, the new regression to be estimated would be:

$$\ln TR_i^{P*} = \ln C^* + \theta^* \ln d_{iP} \qquad (7)$$

With the following corresponding new regression results adjusted by income (*t* statistic between round brackets):

$$\ln TR_i^{P*} = 12.9667 - 1.8142 \ln d_{iP} \quad R^2 = 0.80 \qquad (8)$$

$$(-6.242)$$

As can be seen, the negative estimation for θ^*, together with a significant absolute value (≈1,8), shows a high elasticity of TR_i^{P*} relating to d_{iP}, all this for a considerable quality adjustment ($R^2 = 0{,}8$).

Comparing these results with the ones obtained with the non-adjusted simple regression, $\ln TR_i^P = \ln C + \theta \ln d_{iP}$, we shall easily conclude that the results of the estimation would not be very satisfactory. Indeed, in this case, the estimation by the OLS would produce a much lower distance-elasticity ($\theta^* - 1{,}018$) and also a much worse R^2 (0.36). The lower R^2 obtained in this case (accounting only for 36% of tourism flows) would indicate that the level of dispersion of the dependent variable does not allow for a better adjustment.

It shows then as appropriate a methodology as the one proposed by Brakman *et al.* (2001), which provides better results both from an econometric point of view (a significantly higher R^2 hence the same happening with the *t* statistics), and as regards the estimation of the θ^* parameter, which has a higher value, thus conferring a steeper inclination to the adjustment function and expressing a stronger (negative) impact from distance on tourism flows.

It can thus be concluded that this application of the gravity equation shows distance prevailing on economic mass to explain the Portuguese tourism income. Moreover, this result can be inferred either on the basis of the model as a multiple linear regression [eqn (5)], with the estimator for parameter θ_2 tending to equal one; or by having the model as a simple linear regression [eqn (7)], without the correction of tourism revenues by income, resulting on a non satisfactory econometric result.

Note also that – by comparing it with eqn (6) – the estimator for parameter θ_1^* is now more representative (-1,8 against -1,5), which is not a surprise, as by withdrawing the GDP variable from the base equation we also withdraw the wealth element, hence gaining the distance variable full preponderance on the decision to travel.

The similarity of this estimation (constant term, *θ* coefficient and also R^2) vis-à-vis those obtained with the original multiple regression model (with $\theta_2 \neq 1$), also confirm the argument of Brakman *et al.* [8], according to whom, although the economic mass is important in the gravitational model, the most relevant

Sustainable Tourism, F. D. Pineda, C. A. Brebbia & M. Mugica (Editors)
© 2004 WIT Press, www.witpress.com, ISBN 1-85312-724-8

element to determine the trade flows between two countries is the distance between them.

Besides, this similarity of results with $\hat{\theta}_2 = 0,7$ indicates that the simple regression works for values of θ_2 close to one, but not necessarily equalling one. As to the quality of the statistical inference, the observations made over the estimation of the multiple regression model above remain valid.

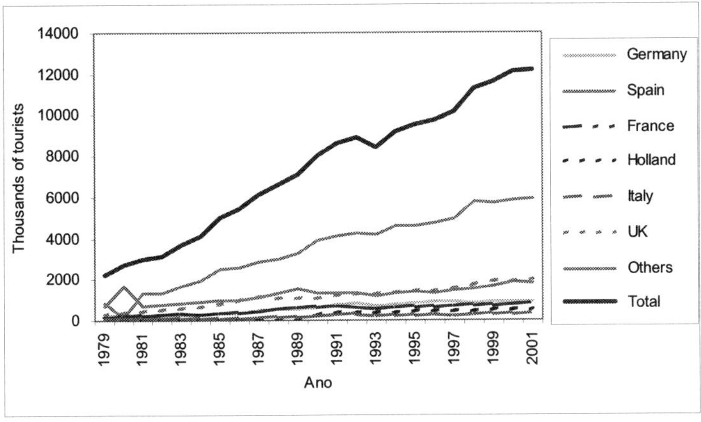

Source: Own (data: ICEP).

Figure 1: Portugal: - Evolution of the 6 main tourism origin markets 1979-2001.

At this point, our conclusion is that the Portuguese geographical proximity to the Spanish territory is determinant to the attraction of tourism flows into Portugal, being even of a higher importance than the income level (which is lower in Spain than in the UK, in particular).

Generalising, and bearing in mind what has been said above about the characteristics of continental tourism, one can even state that this statistical relevance of the gravitational principle must appear as a rule in any type of continental tourism. The same cannot however be said about insular tourism for the reasons discussed.

Moreover, Figure 1 shows that, for the Portuguese case in particular, the Spanish market has been growing since the 70s at a faster pace than the remaining markets, being presently the first main supplier of tourists to Portugal (Table 2) and the third in terms of the total tourism revenues generated (Table 3).

4 Conclusions

Having in mind that tourism has only recently assumed itself as an organized economic activity, the time has come to the establishment of an according development of its theoretical framework. While being aware that the specific characteristics of tourism goods require, when considered as a whole, a non-

Sustainable Tourism, F. D. Pineda, C. A. Brebbia & M. Mugica (Editors)

standardized treatment from economic science, one must consider a tailored approach for the study of tourism economics, frequently using less usual instruments of economic analysis – as is the case for economic geography as suggested here.

Using a simple gravity model, we have shown that distance matters more than income on the determination of tourism flows in continental destinations in general and in Portugal in particular.

Once that distance is accepted as a relevant factor to tourism demand, and mostly when it matters more than income of the origin country, one must then consider the implications of this result on the issue of promoting a national tourism destination. Namely when considered together with the specific characteristics of the tourism good, the empirical importance of distance in this context suggests that there may be a role for some Government regulatory intervention in the tourism sector, notably with a tourism policy duly connected with the remaining national economic policies, with a view to optimizing the huge potential of this sector to create economic wealth.

In terms of normative policy implications, on one hand the statistical relevance of distance on the explanation of tourism flows implies that efforts (namely financial ones) should focus firstly on marketing the home destination in the closest countries (economic distance), and, on the other hand, whenever the tourism demand is highly country-concentrated (as is the case for Portugal, with 90% of total demand concentrated in just 5 countries – SP, UK, DE, FR and NL) it matters not only to keep those markets under control but also to put in place some diversification in order to reduce the dependence degree on the markets in question.

References

[1] Aitken, N. D. (1973) – "The Effect of the EEC and EFTA on European Trade: A Temporal Cross-Section Analysis", American Economic Review, 63, December 1973, pp. 881-892

[2] Anas (1983) – "Discrete choice theory, information theory, and the multinomial logit and gravity models", Transportation Research B, 17, pp. 13-23

[3] Anderson, J. (1979) - "A Theoretical Foundation for the Gravity Equation", American Economic Review, 69, 106-116

[4] Baker, M.; Hayzelden; Sussmann (1996) – "Can Destination Management Systems Provide Competitive Advantage? A Discussion of the Factors Affecting the Survival and Success of Destination Management Systems", Progress in Tourism and Hospitality Research, 2, (1), pp. 1-13

[5] Baptista, Paulo (2003) – Um Modelo Input-Output Inter-Regional: A Abordagem Gravitacional, PhD Thesis (unpublished), Faculdade de Economia da Universidade do Algarve, Portugal, March 2003

[6] Bergstrand, J. (1985) – "The Gravity Equation in International Trade: Some Microeconomic Foundations and Empirical Evidence", Review of Economics and Statistics, Vol. 67, No. 3 (Aug., 1985), pp. 474-481

Sustainable Tourism, F. D. Pineda, C. A. Brebbia & M. Mugica (Editors)

[7] Bergstrand, J. (1989) – "The Generalized Gravity Equation, Monopolistic Competition, and the Factor-Proportions Theory in International Trade", The Review of Economics & Statistics, 1989, vol. 71, issue 1, pages 143-53

[8] Brakman, S.; H. Garretsen, C. van Marrewijk (2001) – An Introduction to Geographical Economics, Cambridge University Press

[9] Carey, Henry Charles (1865) - The Principles of Social Science, Philadelphia: Lippincott & Co. 1858–9 (3 Volumes.)

[10] Christaller, W. (1964) – Central Places in Southern Germany, translation by C. W. Baskin of the original work of 1933, Prentice-Hall, Englewood-Cliffs

[11] Deardorff, A. V. (1998) – "Determinants of bilateral trade: does gravity work in a neo-classical world?", in J. Frankel (ed.), Regionalization of the World Economy, University of Chicago Press and NBER, Chicago, 7-22

[12] Deardorff, A. V. (1995) – "Determinants of Bilateral Trade: Does Gravity Work in a Neoclassical World?, National Bureau of Economic Research, Working Paper nº 5377, December 1995

[13] Dentinho, T. Ponce (2002) – "Modelos Gravitacionais", in José Silva Costa (coordenador), Compêndio de Economia Regional, Capítulo 22, Colecção APDR, Associação Portuguesa para o Desenvolvimento Regional

[14] Fujita, Krugman, Venables (1999) – The Spatial Economy, MIT Press, Cambridge, Massachusetts

[15] Fujita, M.; Thisse, J. F. (2002) – Economics of Aglomeration – Cities, Industrial Location, and Regional Growth, Cambridge, Cambridge University Press

[16] Grether, E. T. (1983) – "Regional-spatial analysis in marketing", Journal of Marketing, nº 47, pp. 36 - 43

[17] Isard, W. (1956) – Location and the Space Economy, John Wiley, New York

[18] Leamer, E. E. (1974) – "The Commodity Composition of International Trade in Manufactures: An Empirical Analysis", Oxford Economic Papers, 26, pp. 350-374

[19] Leamer, E. E. and M. Storper (2001) – "The Economic Geography of the Internet Age", Journal of International Business Studies

[20] Linneman, H. (1966) – An Econometric Study of International Trade Flows, Amsterdam, North-Holland Publishing Company

[21] Porter, M. (2000) – "Locations, Clusters, and Company Strategy", in Clark et al., The Oxford Handbook of Economic Geography, Capítulo 13, Oxford University Press

[22] Pöyhönen, Pentti (1963) – "A Tentative Model for the Volume of Trade Between Countries," Weltwirtschaftliches Archiv 90 (1), pp. 93-99

[23] Reilly (1931) – The Law of Retail Gravitation, New York, Pilsbury

[24] Santos Silva, J. C. and Silvana Tenreyro (2003) – "Gravity-defying trade", No 03-1 in Working Papers from Federal Reserve Bank of Boston

Sustainable Tourism, F. D. Pineda, C. A. Brebbia & M. Mugica (Editors)

[25] Smith, Stephen L. J. (1995) – Tourism Analysis – A Handbook, second edition, Pearson Education (print on demand edition)
[26] Tinbergen (1962) – Shaping the World Economy: Suggestions for an International Economic Policy, New York, Twentieth Century Fund

Sustainable Tourism, F. D. Pineda, C. A. Brebbia & M. Mugica (Editors)

Section 2
Tourism strategies

Destination management and strategic market planning: a strategic planning technique of the total tourism product with the assistance of section elevation diagrams

G. Siomkos[1], Ch. Vassiliadis[2] & Th. Fotiadis[2]
[1]*Athens University of Economics and Business*
[2]*University of Macedonia*

Abstract

Herein, a methodology for analysing an area's broad tourism product is presented. In particular, after theoretically approaching the issue of Destination Management, and the issues of marketing and planning geographical sections, the use of a Destination Card is proposed for applications relevant to areas' strategic analyses. The aforementioned card is a result of the combination of tools for landscape architectural design (landscape planning/section elevation diagrams) and particularly face analysis sections, with the presentation of both practical evaluation criteria and area categorisation criteria from the theory of Destination Management. Destination analysis through the Card may facilitate the procedures of Strategic Planning and tourism development-elevation for destinations. Furthermore, the Destination Card is based on the application of marketing concepts, since it makes use of data and information related to the demand and to the opinions of residents/professionals within each community.
Keywords: destination management, strategic market planning, destination card, section elevation diagrams, tourism product analysis, SWOT analysis.

1 Marketing places and tourism destination management – tools for planning development strategies

Kotler et al. [19, pp.99-138] constructed a table for identifying an area's strategic development potentialities. The audit instrument for infrastructure, attractions and people includes measurements regarding the current situation, the audit potential, and the effect potential on the issues of infrastructure, attractions and

Sustainable Tourism, F. D. Pineda, C. A. Brebbia & M. Mugica (Editors)

people as well as on basic services and area planning. According to the aforementioned writers, there are five processes on the subject of the area development philosophy. Those are the following [19, pp.72-98]:

- Community development. This process's positive issues centre upon infrastructure development plans regarding a community's neighbourhoods or subsections. Infrastructure features contribute to the development of sectors like health, education, public safety, residency, and transport. This process has a major disadvantage; it does not provide for future community development. Deficiencies centre upon financial weaknesses and lack of provision regarding the systematic integration of the community into a competitive prefectorial, regional, national and international environment. In addition, it does not take into account new economic circumstances since planning is made from inside towards outside. Community is regarded a good product and since it sells, it also attracts people. In this case, we do not take into account that also somebody else may copy or develop similar or better products, communities. Also, development discordances are frequently observed between residents and organisations.

- Urban design. This philosophy follows the community development philosophy which in turn will assist to the development of a qualitative environment within which residents live and work. It is differentiated in the sense that it is particularly concerned with issues relevant to the areas' design quality. The architecture, the aesthetics of city areas and of environment, the quality in the use of public services by people (with or without special needs), the transportation network, the sanitation, and the environmental pollution, are all study fields of the area development design. Designers believe that changes in those issues cause changes in the perceptions and behaviours of residents. A main disadvantage of this philosophy, taking into account that also this process is affected by the disadvantages of the previous process, is the inadequate attention given to the economic viability of both the designs and the area in general.

- Urban planning. Often this process is directed by qualified departments for urban planning. Committees evaluate the best possible studies (from developmental companies-consultants and government agencies) based on the cost/benefit relationship, taking into account the limitations posed by the available budget. Often here, the largest part of the total time is devoted to evaluating studies and protecting public interest.

- Economic development. This particular process is the subject issue of economic development departments (committees and consultancies). It enfolds the creation of employment and the attraction of people through new industries, investment growth, and productive use of resources. In particular, economic planning enfolds activities that encourage destination competitiveness regarding economic, social, educational and cultural issues. Community competitiveness is based upon the four factors aforementioned. More analytically, these factors are the life quality of the local community, the positive image and marketing, the potential for economic development, the natural structure of the community, tenable technology, the skilful, adequate, motivated workforce, and the available funds. During the process of planning, SWOT analyses (see also Mc Donald, [23, p.34]) determine both the internal and external factors influencing local

Sustainable Tourism, F. D. Pineda, C. A. Brebbia & M. Mugica (Editors)

economy and community. Based on the philosophy of the development procedure herein, local economies should be capable of producing income in order to repay imported commodities. This process should examine and include also planning activities of previous processes. Planning in view of economic growth looks forward to the future. Continuously coordinated and planned activities target the community's viability. Often herein, during the strategic planning of structure, industry, attractions and skilful workforce, the participation of a wide range of representative community populations is required.

- Strategic market planning. The reinforcement of local communities regarding decision-making issues, the bureaucracy and the weakness of authorities to encourage economic activities in districts as well as the intensive pressure from competition during the 1980's caused the adoption, development and establishment of business philosophy or Market Concept by authorities that are known as public authorities. It is worth mentioning that anymore European development programmes stress the contribution also of private authorities broadening in this manner the financial features of investment activities [40, pp.187-207] and [9, ss. 9-34, 56-67]. This necessity is understood if one examines the planning procedures adopted by the European Union during the 1980's. In this manner, marketing activities appear to contribute to the strategic planning of areas by helping to illuminate-elevate a destination's competitive advantages, also to develop new activities-products for the destination and to encourage economic, community, cultural, educational activities regarding the identification of market opportunities. In particular, strategic market planning follows the following steps:

a. Area evaluation. Situation and SWOT Analysis
b. Future visions and objectives. Preferences of interested parties (Market Research).
c. Formulation of strategy (Strategic planning)
d. Actions and Tactics-plan.
e. Application and feedback.

Next are briefly presented some Marketing Strategic Design instruments regarding the broad tourism product-potential of areas.

According to Inskeep [16, pp.95] tourism destination planning improves by using the Evaluation Matrix for Tourist Attractions technique. The evaluation of attractions (Attraction Feature) (natural, cultural, and special characteristics) is part of the wider geographic area planning and is an inextricable part of an area's tourism development plans. The attractions' evaluation procedure is done in scales of 1 to 5 or of 1 to 10 and is concerned with the following factors (Evaluation Factors):

- Accessibility
- Economic potential for development
- Environmental impact of development
- Sociocultural impact of development
- National / regional significance
- International significance

 Sustainable Tourism, F. D. Pineda, C. A. Brebbia & M. Mugica (Editors)
© 2004 WIT Press, www.witpress.com, ISBN 1-85312-724-8

Moreover, roughly the last couple of decades, practice adopted the use of double dimension maps. In 1973, Belt, Collins & Associates made use of the aforementioned maps aiming for the tourism development of the Fiji Honolulu, Hawaii islands [16, p.103-106]. The map's two dimensions included the following attraction features:

- Landscape, natural features and leisure features
- Cultural, historical features and archaeological features of attractions

The aforementioned attractions are categorised based on the dimensions in space; then specific development areas are identified. Gunn [35, p.188-191] made use of the zone identification technique for the state of Texas U.S.A. (Gunn [13, p.115-121]). During that particular process, six criteria were identified concerning the categorisation of a geographical area into specific zones of tourism destinations. The research criteria were:

- the regional identity
- the infrastructure of the region
- the size of the region
- the attractions
- the existence of authorities that shall develop activities in the region
- the accessibility potential

Identified zones that were recognised through technique analyses such as the aforementioned destination area-zone identification or the nearest neighbour analysis ([35, p.219-226] and [38]), may thereafter be analysed in selected destination areas so as to enrich the decision-making process. Subjects of research may be the specific points of nearest neighbour analysis or also sections elevations with total points more than 1.

More than one points of the previous analysis methodology are incorporated in the sections. Moreover, points in sections may be identified in the resultant broader areas that were identified after the end of the destination area-zone identification process. Next, the use of functional diagrams improves the visual presentation of the functions in the geographical space (zoning, access, places of interest, help centres). At the same time, apart from the aforementioned technical analyses, section elevation diagrams are used as strategic instruments for identifying the adequacy of area characteristics with the preferences and interests of various groups of Demand (Segments), taking also into consideration competition and the visitors' interests as indicators of the current situation [38]. This analysis approaches the modern philosophy of destination development through a strategic marketing process.

Next, an improved tool for enhancing tourism destination development strategies is presented based on the marketing concept (see also [19, pp. 72-98]). The tool comprises a practical card for analysing the current situation and market research information. Namely, it includes analyses of:

- the geographical areas
- the total tourism product to be integrated from the aspects of natural-cultural places of interest and wider tourism offer (see also [16, pp.95])
- the development potential of those areas
- the target groups of visitors

Sustainable Tourism, F. D. Pineda, C. A. Brebbia & M. Mugica (Editors)

- the level of organisation of the community's authorities and lastly
- the competition [1, pp. 58-59]

2 Planning procedures – strengths and opportunities

The strategic tool of Planning – Analysis should inform about the following issues-questions (see also [29, p.232-234]:

- Organisation-Environment (OE): What are our strengths – weaknesses with regard to the integration of both the internal and the external Image of the destination (coordination between residents-authorities-professionals and creation of Image for potential visitors)?

- Demand-Visitors (DV): What do visitors want and what is their attitude towards us regarding competition?

- Market/Competition-Product (MP): Is there a potential for an increase in the activities within the current market or is it possible to open out in new markets (fashions in preference of lucrative sectors)? Should the product stay as it is or should new lines be developed in order to exploit the unique advantages of the destination?

2.1 Strengths and opportunities

Based on the aforementioned, destinations should organise tourism development activities starting from the OE features. Ere market segments are analysed and strategies regarding the whole tourism product offer of an area are determined, significant importance should be given on the coordination of authorities [29, pp.229-243]. Therefore, e.g. the coordination between communities, municipalities, districts, regions, national, international and professional authorities is considered essential for the accomplishment of the strategic objectives (see also [19, p.34]. Coordination is simplified through the enhancement of communication networks between the authorities for cooperation and the authorities for realising strategic plans (see also [14, 33]). The unity of actions for the coordination of authorities also includes the coordination of authorities and the community [17, p.3-11]. The establishment of sustainable tourism conscience by residents also contributes to the creation of a better climate for cooperation between local community and the governing bodies. In practice, the expression of that essential commission is met in the form of sustainable regional development plans, also known as SAM (Special Area Management plans) [41, pp.335-344]. The quality of the services offered, depends greatly on the human workforce employed in the tourism industry or residing in the local community [18, p.1545]. The success of residents in the Kozaki community in Japan, regarding the unchangeable conservation of their traditions and the development of tourism activities in parallel, is owed to the coordinated activation of community members and supportive authorities (public authorities and retailers) that were located in Tokyo [7, pp.239-254]. Generally, residents' participation in Planning contributes to the creation of a destination image with internal and external clarity ([34, p.3-7] [36, ss.31-66]). Often we

Sustainable Tourism, F. D. Pineda, C. A. Brebbia & M. Mugica (Editors)

ignore the participation of residents in decision making. Often also, being carriers of Supply, we do not take into consideration the desirable life quality of the average resident and of the temporary visitor. Here, authorities should not apply research techniques that simply analyse the data from a routine collection through assessment instruments. The experience of daily routine, in-depth research and resident role-playing by researchers- authorities in order to understand the local needs of small communities, is a research methodology often disregarded. Quality research of that type supplements the quantitative data and provides information about the structure design, the implementation of marketing strategies, and the particularities in need of attention during the participation of local community residents ([32, p.3-11], see also [11, pp.479-488]). Both local and social development contracts include reports for the creation of common tourism conscience of the participants. The creation of uncompetitive primary education, the strengthening of education in issues of local developmental needs, the expansion of know-how into broader groups of local communities through training, as well as the potential for exploitation in funding issues, comprise features of sustainable development with a strategic marketing character. Also in this stage of Design, the destination features regarding accessibility, the existence of banks and retail shops, the existence of public authorities' information offices, the existence of local tourism offices and travel organisers, entertainment services, leisure, gastronomy, culture and education are taken into account (see also [20]). The evaluation of local and of wide tourism infrastructure and the simultaneous coordination of authorities conduce to the improvement of services and strengthen the efforts for development of tourism activities in areas of interest.

Once the aforementioned analysis of OE features is achieved, further actions should focus on the analysis of target groups (DV). Apart from the capabilities for investigating the adequacy of the product potential regarding the preferences of consumer groups, fashions and the preferences of specific groups of visitors often involve market opportunities worth investigating [21,pp.48-55]. In 1970, Gray specified two groups of visitors based on their interests, namely the sun – lust tourists and the wander – lust travellers. The former prefer warm beaches and destinations with water and sun. The latter prefer destinations with unique natural and human constructions [3, p.296]. At the same time, opportunities may emerge from knowing the behaviour of tourists regarding competitive destinations (CD) as well as from restructuring their clientele about available product lines, e.g. information regarding the demographic characteristics and the activities of potential tourists for product lines such as the long term tourism – mild -alternative tourism, and the short term tourism –holidays-mass tourism. In addition, the motivation for coming characteristics may constitute a basis for classifying alternative categories of tourists [10, p.746, 760].

The analysis of the features of pre-selected groups of tourists helps the evaluation process of the total offered tourism product per geographical area and predetermines the adequate Demand groups that shall yield profits for the geographical destination (CD). The identification of adequate Demand groups for the geographical area's destinations contributes to a more economic

Sustainable Tourism, F. D. Pineda, C. A. Brebbia & M. Mugica (Editors)

formulation of marketing strategies, because of the more rational use of resources for marketing activities. Often the climate, the landscape, the mode of life, the level of tourism services offered, as well as the wider tourism infrastructure comprise features for illuminating tourism areas. From the side of tourists, these features represent push and pull motivation factors for travelling ([2, pp.46-53] [13, p.123] [15, pp.29-34] [42, p.42]). These features have both a natural and an artificial character and once they are organisationally coordinated and are accompanied by services of high quality, then they facilitate the process of illumination of the unique characteristics of the relevant destinations ([12, pp.2-9] [35, p.164]). Subsequently, the aforementioned features contribute to the formulation of a differentiated destination image that offers distinctiveness to tourists (e.g. unique sightseeing and services) and are connected to the residents' living quality.

A relevant example of assimilation of Canada's all-season resorts product features with the characteristics of European market segments is the following: According to Owens [28, p.41], Canadian tourism attractions assimilate the preferences of Europeans regarding the following features: snow ski, golf, authentic culture, and cultural activities, high level of hygiene, warm welcoming of visitors, friendly residents. Namely, Canadian attractions are associated with two main market segments in Europe:

- Sports-and-outdoors, and
- Culture-and-nature groups.

The first segment of approximately 8 million people is composed mainly of young people, single men seeking adventure products. The second segment of approximately 6 million people is mainly composed of people of various demographic characteristics for each European country under examination. Thus in England, the culture-and-nature group consists of women between 45 and 54 years of age, while in Germany it consists of people of 25-34 years of age. Their main interests include beforehand organised travels based on informational material, looking for different cultural experiences, and looking for impressive landscapes.

The analysis of the aforementioned factors regarding the destination's strengths and opportunities facilitates the subsequence of the Design process, i.e. the process of the determination of objectives [19, pp.90-98]. However, what needs great attention is the structure of the broader environmental factors of SWOT Analysis. Generally, the following should be analysed:

- Natural-social factors (e.g. area distance, residents' hospitality, climate, seismic areas, or areas with a lot of natural disasters) ([24, pp.222-231] [26, pp.36-39]). Political factors and facts (such as Design policies harming local particularities (the balearisation case: [39, pp. 193-195), general image of the country, travelling instructions, areas of war conflict or of social crises-terrorism, as well as the general image exposed by the media or by opinion makers [6, pp. 56,60] [37, p.36]). Economic factors (such as increase in cost of equipment, energy, funds, available natural resources and forecasts) (see also [8, p.194] [27, pp.41-65]).

Sustainable Tourism, F. D. Pineda, C. A. Brebbia & M. Mugica (Editors)

- Marketing factors (e.g. intensity of competitors' exposure and distribution networks- influence of travel agents in destination development) ([5, pp.425-431))

- Substitution factors (e.g. entertainment parks, teleconferencing (see also [28, p.29, 31-34]) and technological factors (e.g. transportation, communication [25, pp.39-47]), as external or uncontrollable factors may lead a destination to an economic crisis, and may also strengthen the efforts of competitive destinations to maintain or expand the market segments they already have. Thus, while in 1986 European destinations held 63.5% of the total arrivals worldwide (World Tourism Organisation's Europe region), only after a decade in 1996 the same destinations held the 59.2% of the total arrivals worldwide. The investigation of the rates in competitive geographical areas shows a clear tendency of an increase in arrivals (more than 8% per year during the decade 1986-1996) within the regions of East Asia and the Pacific, Africa and the Middle East. The region East Asia and the Pacific also showed during the decade 1986-1996 a unique tendency to increase income exchange compared to all other worldwide destination [4, pp.290,293].

Often, there are coordination and control weaknesses regarding the process of the centrally directed tourism Planning and Management to monitor the quality of the services and to restrict both the uncontrolled development and reduction in the quality of the tourism sites in regional destinations. Usually, the impacts of the aforementioned weaknesses in known destinations are described through the complaints of traditional categories of visitors. Among others, complaints concentrate on the issues of high prices compared to offered value, differences in the exchange value, low level of services, and overdevelopment-saturation of tourism areas [6, p.59].

3 Analysis Card of a tourism product of an area (Destination Card)

The following strategic planning instrument is a Destination Card. The Card's concept is based on the presentation of neighbour geographical areas in the form of section elevation diagrams [30, pp.112-127]. The diagrams are presented on the card in sequence based on the faces that are pre-selected in the area to be analysed (see also [38]). The following graph presents a lake area of a hypothetical architectural design. The area includes six view sites (a, b, c, d, e, f). The view sites correspond to the related analysis sections regarding each one of the faces of the aforementioned Card. For each one of the geographical points of the sections presented, follows an analysis of the following features-criteria (see Fig. 1, 2):

- Organisation-cooperation level of community authorities (e.g. state in every possible community of the relevant to last sections).
- Natural, cultural, special, technical service based on each area of each section analysis.
- Market Segment Analysis. In this level, the most important characteristics and the preferences of potential visitor groups are presented and are cross-checked with the Supply potential of the areas of each section. The data are collected

Sustainable Tourism, F. D. Pineda, C. A. Brebbia & M. Mugica (Editors)

through primary research by market research companies-institutes-foundations and may be about market segments of countries or areas of visitors' origin (e.g. countries exporting flows of visitors). Data and information may also be collected from local community research e.g. research regarding the analysis of the visitors' profile.
- Access potential, economic potential for development, socio-political impact of the development, national significance, international significance of sections.
- Competition is evaluated based on the above criteria. The evaluation is done on the last right column of the Card. Specifically; it includes the Country, the destination, and the evaluation of each criterion. In the Card column there may also be presented other important reports-information for activities and other issues relevant to each criterion e.g. competitors' product features and relevant target groups.

The evaluation of areas is done subjectively by responsible specialists-consultants-researchers based on three categorisation levels (see Fig. 2). The evaluation scale includes three levels: a. bad/low (white/ light colour), b. average (dark colour/ grey/ darker grey than the previous evaluation level), c. very good/high (very dark colour/black/ the darkest grey relative to the previous evaluation levels). In the analysis graph of the creation procedure of the Destination Card, the evaluation of sections based on selected criteria is done on the basis of white, black and grey colours. Colouring is done on the rod - bars, when it is about the evaluation of the adequacy of the areas regarding the unique features and the preferences of the target groups of Demand (e.g. vibrant colour=high i.e. adequate area-Supply). In addition, in the evaluation of areas based on pre-selected criteria, the colourings of the circles show by the first criterion e.g. dark colour=very good organisation of the community's authorities.

Lastly, a total evaluation of the areas of each section is performed based on the aforementioned evaluation levels. The total score-value of a View Site's areas or in other words a Section's areas determines next the place of each section of the analysis area and therefore the most significant development and elevation areas of a destination's Tourism Product.

Evaluation of areas based on the aforementioned criteria contributes to determine the objectives of a specific geographical area's strategic development plan. As it was already made clear in the introduction, destination card analyses are part of the broad SWOT analysis and contribute to the rational selection procedure of objectives and determination of strategies.

4 Example application of destination card, and possible limitations

In the following example, a destination card is developed for the geographical area between Xanthi and Alexandroupolis, Greece (see Fig. 1, 3, and 4). For a better demonstration of the strengths, weaknesses – opportunities and threats of the card's section areas, the following snake plot was created. Sections were evaluated on the snake plot based on the average mean of the evaluations for each of the twelve criteria of the card (see Fig. 1).

Sustainable Tourism, F. D. Pineda, C. A. Brebbia & M. Mugica (Editors)

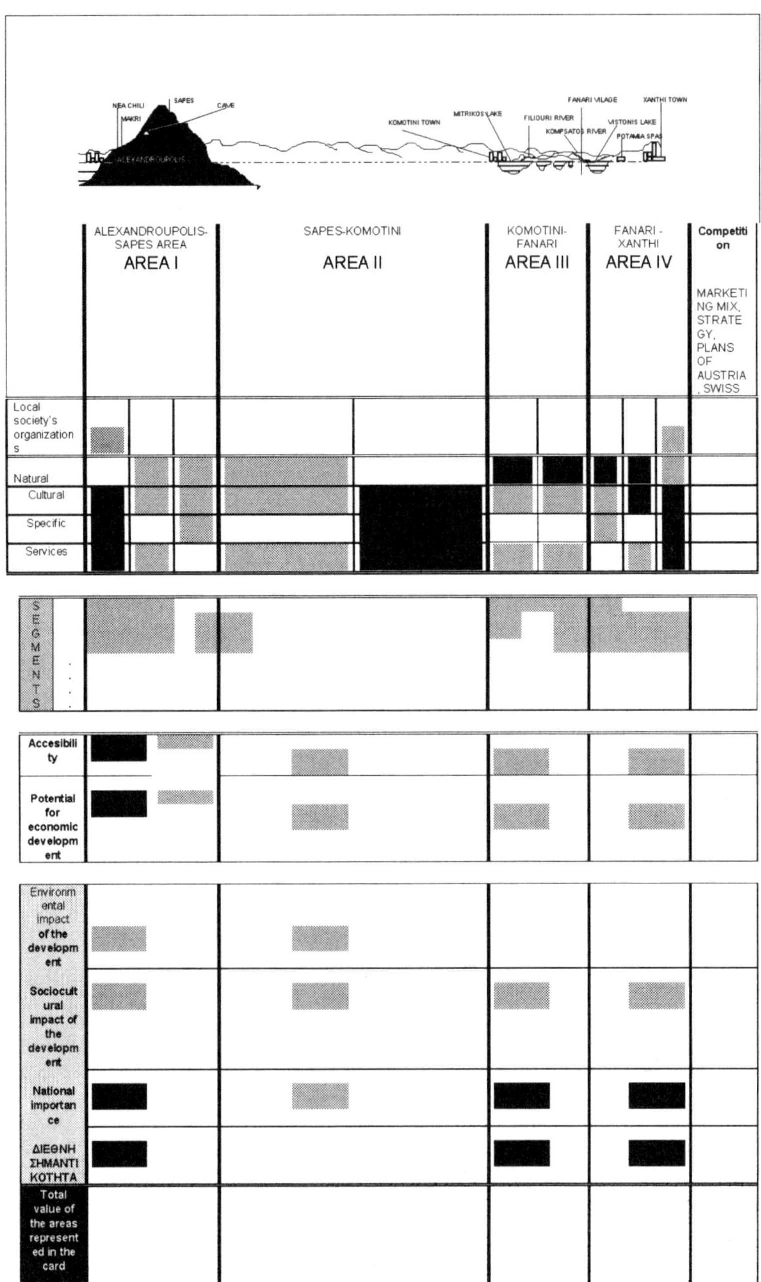

Figure 1: Destination card – Analysis of the tourist product of geographic area. (Four-folded card – each fold stands for a specific area.)

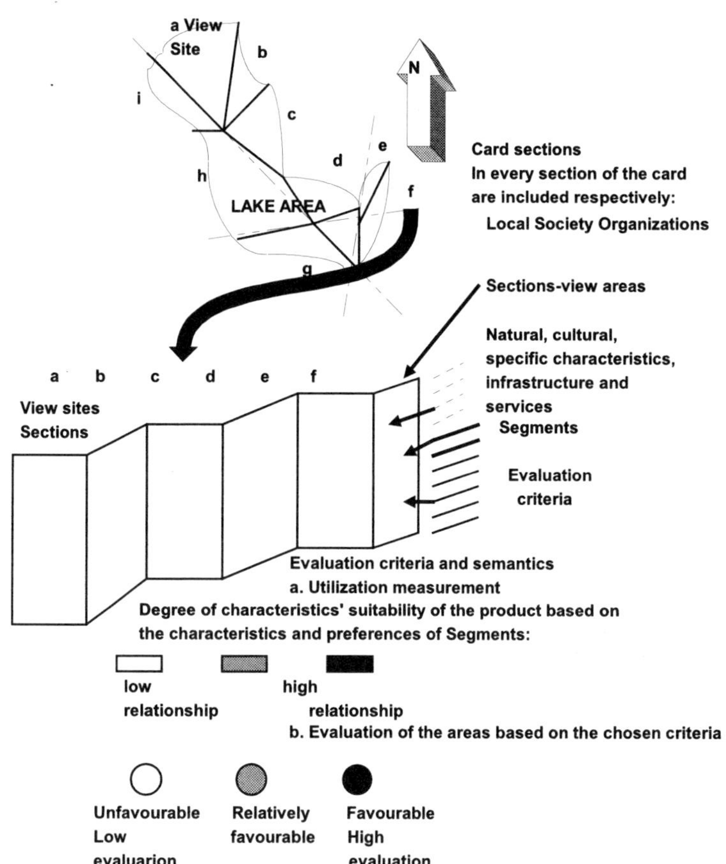

Figure 2: Analysis of the procedure of the development of the destination card concerning the evaluation of the infrastructure and its matching with the visitors' needs and the local society.

The difficulty of applying the Card in practice regarding the evaluation of criteria is owed to weaknesses in finding primary data from the designer-consultant researcher. Incoherent collection of necessary data for the criteria will consequently influence the quality of findings. According to Sahlberg ([31, p.21]), in the next decades we expect in Tourism, apart from the already existing and under development automated reservation systems, the development of destination information systems which directly concern consumers. The systems' success shall depend on the professional research on the fields of Consumer Behaviour and the Mode of Life of consumers (see also [22, pp. 99-164]). This progress in research and information transmission is a point for further development by the responsible destination authorities (e.g. departments for area planning and development), since it additionally contributes to the analysis of

Sustainable Tourism, F. D. Pineda, C. A. Brebbia & M. Mugica (Editors)
© 2004 WIT Press, www.witpress.com, ISBN 1-85312-724-8

co-operators and residents of the area, apart from the visitors (Image and creation of common tourism conscience analyses).

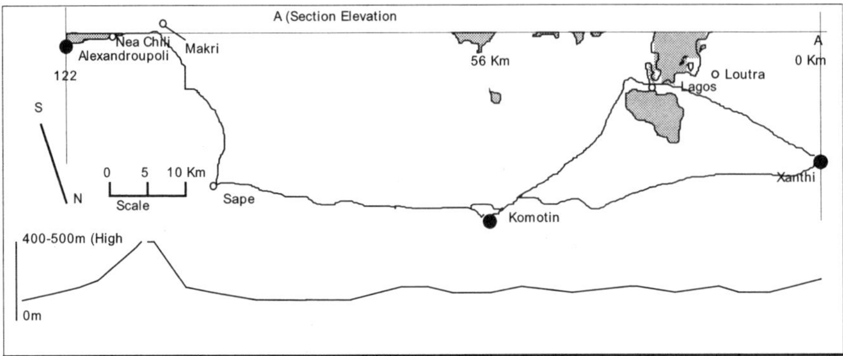

Figure 3: The study area and the position of the section.

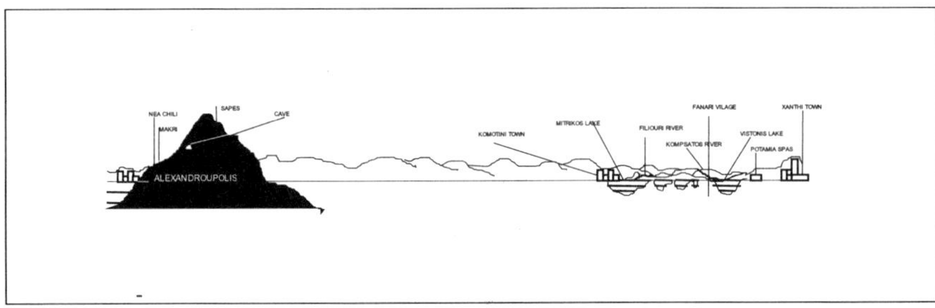

Figure 4: The Section Elevation diagram AA of the road scenic area from Xanthi to Alexandroupolis (Thrace/GR). – View site from the Sea to the North East Country.

5 Conclusions-recommendations

Based on the above snake plot we approach the sections that may exhibit threats or weaknesses. In our example, four sections need attention in terms of:
- AREA I, Organisation of community authorities
- AREA II, Inadequate Segments, Organisation of community authorities, International significance of the area
- AREA III, Special services-places of interest/ infrastructure, Organisation of community authorities, Environmental impact
- AREA IV, Environmental impact

Respectively, opportunities/strengths and therefore the advantages of the areas are the following:
- AREA I, Adequate Segments, Accesses, Economic potential for development, National and International significance of the area

Sustainable Tourism, F. D. Pineda, C. A. Brebbia & M. Mugica (Editors)

- AREA II, Cultural, Technical service (more effort to elevate and develop the section)
- AREA III, Natural places of interest, National and International significance of the area
- AREA IV, Economic potential for development, National and International significance of the area

The aforementioned procedure for data collection on the criteria for the Card development, and the drawing of a snake plot, facilitate area planners in the strategic planning of the activities for the area's development. In our example, a check point for the areas' Supply may be the competitive destinations (Austria and Switzerland) that attract segments of foreign tourists who compile our focal point. An easy approach to the data of the competitive product can be done through the Internet.

The aforementioned analysis can initiate examinations and adjustments in the wider tourism potential of the research areas. Based on the adjustments to be made, the objectives will be easily approached, and alternative strategies as well as a more adequate marketing mix for every section will be developed.

References

[1] Aaker D. A. and Shansby G. (1982), *Positioning Your Product*, Business Horizon, May-June, pp.56-62

[2] Ayala H. (1996), *Resort Ecotourism: A Paradigm for the 21st Century*, Cornell Hotel & Restaurant Administration Quarterly, 37 (5), pp.46-53

[3] Bakkal I. (1996), *Characteristics of West German demand for international tourism in the northern Mediterranean region,* Applied Economics, 1991, 23, pp.295-304

[4] Bar-On R. R. (1997), *Global tourism trends - to 1996,* Tourism Economics, 3 (3), pp. 289-300

[5] Carey S., Gountas Y. and Gilbert D. (1997), *Tour operators and destination sustainability,* Tourism Management, Vol. 18, No. 7, pp.425-431

[6] Clements M. (1998), *Planning to Tourism Capacity in a Crisis,* Journal of Travel Research, August, pp.56-62

[7] Creighton M. (1997), *Consuming Rural Japan: The Marketing of Tradition and Nostalgia in the Japanese Travel Industry,* Ethnology, Vol. 36 no 3, Summer, pp.239-254

[8] Dicken P. (1992), *Global Shift: The Internationalization of Economic Activity,* London Paul Chapman, in: Verdaquer C. C. i (1995), *Mega - Events, Local Strategies and Global Tourist Attractions*, in: Montanari A. and Williams A. M., *European Tourism-Regions, Spaces and Restructuring,* John Wiley & Sons, UK, pp.193-195

[9] Europaische Kommission, (1994) Generaldirektion XXIII- Referat Tourismus, *Studienprogramm im Bereich Fremdenverkehr-Zusammenfassung der allgemeinen Ergebnisse, Schlussfolgerungen und Empfehlungen aus den Berichten,* (D) April DE PC

Sustainable Tourism, F. D. Pineda, C. A. Brebbia & M. Mugica (Editors)

[10] Eymann A. and Ronning G. (1997), *Microeconomic models of tourists` destination choice*, Regional Science and Urban Economics, 27, pp.735-761
[11] Fetterman D. M. (1998), *Ethnography* in: Bickman L. and Rog D. J. (edits), *Handbook of Applied Social Research Methods,* SAGE Public., USA, pp. 473-504
[12] Fick, G. R. and Richie, J. R. B. (1991), *Measuring service quality in the travel and tourism industry,* Journal of Travel Research, 30, pp.2-9
[13] Gunn C. A. (1988), *Vacationscape: the design of travel environments,* 2nd ed.,VNR, USA
[14] Haramis G. E. (1994), *General Aspects of an Information System (IS) for Financial Justification of Investments in Tourism Marketing Information Systems (TMIS`s) Development -Proceedings of the International Conference in Innsbruck*, Austria, Springer-Verlag Wien New York
[15] Hu Y. and Ritchie R. B. (1993), *Measuring Destination Attractiveness: A Contextual Approach,* Journal of Travel Research, Fall, pp.29-34
[16] Inskeep E. (1991), *Tourism Planning*, John Wiley & Sons, Inc., Canada
[17] Jurowski C., Uysal M., and Williams D. R. (1997), *A Theoretical Analysis of Host Community Resident Reactions to Tourism,* Journal of Travel Research, Fall, pp.3-11
[18] Keane M. J. (1996), *Sustaining quality in tourism destinations: an economic model with an application,* Applied Economics, Vol. 28 pp.1545-1553
[19] Kotler P., Heider D. H., and Rein I. (1993) *Marketing Places,* The Free Press, USA
[20] Lew A. A. (1987), *A Framework of Tourist Attractions Research,* Annals of Tourism Research, 14 (4), pp. 553-575
[21] Luzar E. J., Diagne A., Gan C. E., and Henning B. R. (1988), *Profiling the Nature-Based Tourist: A Multinomial Logit Approach,* Journal of Travel Research, Vol. 37, August 1998, pp.48-55
[22] Mazanec J. A. (1994), *Segmenting Travel Markets* in: Teare R., Mazanec J.A., Welch S. C., and Calver S., *Marketing in Hospitality and Tourism-A Consumer Focus,* Cassell, Great Britain
[23] Mc Donald M. H. B. (1996) *Marketing Plans (Third Edition),* Butterworth-Heinemann, Great Britain
[24] McIntosh R. W., Goeldner C. R. and Richie J. R. B. (1995), *Tourism - Principles, Practices, Philosophies (7th ed.)* , John Wiley & Sons, Inc. USA
[25] McKercher B. (1998), *The Effect of Market Access on Destination Choice,* Journal of Travel Research, August, pp.39-47
[26] Milo K. J. and Yoder S. L. (1991), *Recovery From Natural Disaster: Travel Writers And Tourist Destinations,* Journal of Travel Research, Summer, pp.36-39
[27] Montanari A. (1995), *The Mediterranean Region: Europe`s Summer Leisure Space,* in: Montanari A. and Williams A. M., *European Tourism-Regions, Spaces and Restructuring,* John Wiley & Sons, UK, pp.41-65

Sustainable Tourism, F. D. Pineda, C. A. Brebbia & M. Mugica (Editors)
© 2004 WIT Press, www.witpress.com, ISBN 1-85312-724-8

[28] Owens D. J. (1994), *The All-Season Opportunity for Canada`s Resorts,* The Cornell H.R.A. Quarterly, October, pp.28-41

[29] Pearce D. (1995), *Planning for tourism in the 1990s* in: Butler R. and Pearce D. (1995), Routledge, London, pp.229-244

[30] Reid G. W. (1987), *Landscape Graphics,* Witney Library of Design, New York

[31] Sahlberg B. (1993), *The Demand for new Information Systems in Travel and Tourism,* Revue de Tourisme-The Tourist Review-Zeitschrift fur Fremdenverkehr, 2/1993, pp.20-23

[32] Sandiford P. J. and Ap J., (1998), *The Role of Ethnographic Techniques in Tourism Planning,* Journal of Travel Research, Vol. 37, August, pp.3-11

[33] Shertler W., Schmid B., Tjoa A M., and Werthner H. (eds) (1994), *Information and Communications Technologies in Tourism-Proceedings of the International Conference in Innsbruck*, Austria, Springer-Verlag Wien New York

[34] Simpson R. (1993), *Sustainable Tourism for Europe`s Protected Areas - Guidelines and ways forward,* Revue de Tourisme, 3/1993, p.3-7,

[35] Smith S. L. J. (1993), *Tourism Analysis,* Longman Scientific & Technical, Singapore

[36] Sovis W. (1993), *Die Entwicklung von Leitbildern als strategische Analyse - und Planungsmethode des touristischen Managements* (D) in: Zins A. (Hrsg.) Strategisches Management im Tourismus: Planungsinstrumente fur Tourismusorganisationen, Springer, Austria, ss. 31-66

[37] THE ECONOMIST (1991), *Package holidays-Crash landing,* 16TH, p.36

[38] Vasiliadis Ch. A. and Kobotis A. (1999), Spatial analysis-an application of nearest neighbour analysis to tourism locations in Macedonia, *Tourism Management*, Vol. 20, No. 1, pp.141-148

[39] Verdaquer C. C. i (1995), *Mega - Events, Local Strategies and Global Tourist Attractions*, in: Montanari A. and Williams A. M., *European Tourism-Regions, Spaces and Restructuring,* John Wiley & Sons, UK, pp.193-195

[40] Wanhill S. (1995),*The economic evaluation of publicly assisted tourism projects,* in: Butler R. and Pearce D. (1995), Routledge, London, pp.187-207

[41] White A. T., Barker V., and Tantrigama G. (1997), *Using Integrated Coastal Management and Economics to Conserve Coastal Tourism Resources in Sri Lanka,* Ambio Vol. 26 No.6, Sept., Royal Swedish Academy of Sciences, pp.335-344

[42] Yuan S. and McDonald C. (1990), *Motivational Determinates Of International Pleasure Time,* Journal of Travel Research, Summer, pp.42-44

Sustainable Tourism, F. D. Pineda, C. A. Brebbia & M. Mugica (Editors)

Policy-making for sustainable tourism

C. Pforr
School of Management, Curtin University of Technology, Australia

Abstract

In the tourism context the sustainability paradigm can be seen as a key driver for public policy development. Indeed, governments have become extremely canny in making all the right noises without, however, at the same time actually effecting major fundamental policy shifts in the direction of sustainable development. But there is a strong argument in favour of fundamental reforms based on the frequently discussed characteristics of the tourism system and its inherent manifolded shortcomings such as its highly fragmented and little co-ordinated nature, a lack in information exchange and often unclear responsibilities. These are major obstacles that the machinery of government must address, impediments that demand of the political system a high degree of adaptability and flexibility, combined with an ability to accommodate far-reaching reforms in its own processes and structures. In this context, it is therefore important to discuss the role of government involvement in tourism, since it has major implications for more sustainable outcomes. The paper begins with an overview of government's role in the industry, noting the shifts in policy directions as a response to the changing environment of the tourism system. This is then followed by a more detailed account on the conditions for a successful sustainable tourism policy, focusing in particular on collaboration and co-ordination, participation, decentralisation and information as well as strategic planning. These policy instruments are seen as crucial to facilitate sustainable tourism development.
Keywords: sustainable tourism, tourism policy and planning, collaboration, co-ordination, decentralisation, participation, information.

1 Introduction

Notwithstanding the debate about diverse interpretations, sustainable development reflects an international political process, which established "a new standard for political action and change" [1, p. 190] and has become a guiding

Sustainable Tourism, F. D. Pineda, C. A. Brebbia & M. Mugica (Editors)

principle for public policy [2,3]. One hundred and seventy countries committed themselves to the principles of sustainable development at the Rio Earth Summit (1992) and agreed *via Agenda 21* to implement sustainable development in their jurisdictions through the development of national strategies. However, this does not mean that the process of re-thinking society and development in terms of sustainability is thereby any closer to becoming reality. Most of the national commitments are marginal and introduce only minor modifications to the *status quo*. There has been little commitment to the policy changes needed to initiate a national sustainable development process [4,5,6]. More than ten years further on it appears as an opportunity missed and demonstrates the difficulties experienced in translating the sustainability agenda into action [7]. On the other side it can, however, also be argued that the rapid policy developments in the 1990s at national and regional levels have been an encouraging first step. Governments have at least accepted the principles of sustainable development and are aware of a necessary long-term shift in the current pattern of production and consumption within all parts of society [1,3]. But no matter how this process might be evaluated and assessed, the conceptualisation of sustainable development demands clearly set-out, unambiguous, long-term and integrative aims and objectives. These together constitute the strategic policy approaches that are the crucial prerequisites for the successful implementation of sustainable development [3. 7, 8, 9]. Since "sustainable problems are significantly different than [*sic*] most other policy problems, fields or foci (e.g. taxation, education, health, service delivery, etc.)" [10, p. 309], it is argued that existing political processes and structures have to be analysed if they are capable to manage the demands created by the challenging sustainability paradigm. Consequently, as Christie [3, p. 5] argues, "the culture of policy-making ... may need to be rethought in many ways".

In the tourism context the sustainability paradigm can be seen as a key driver for public policy development. Indeed, governments have become extremely canny in making all the right noises without, however, at the same time actually effecting major fundamental policy shifts in the direction of sustainable development [6, 11, 12]. But there is a strong argument in favour of fundamental reforms based on the frequently discussed characteristics of the tourism system and its inherent manifolded shortcomings. Petermann [13, p. 173], for instance, comments that "[c]omplexity, insufficient communication, a lack in co-ordination, duplication, blockades and inefficiency are in short the central topics in the criticism of a fragmented and interlaced, but at the same time little co-ordinated tourism policy". These are major obstacles that the machinery of government must address, impediments that demand of the political system a high degree of adaptability and flexibility, combined with an ability to accommodate far-reaching reforms in its own processes and structures. In this context, it is therefore important to discuss the role of government involvement in tourism, since as Jenkins and Hall [14, p. 43] outline, it "has significant implications for the sustainability of tourism development". The paper begins with a brief overview of government's role in the industry, noting the shifts in policy directions as a response to the changing environment of the

Sustainable Tourism, F. D. Pineda, C. A. Brebbia & M. Mugica (Editors)

tourism system. This is then followed by a more detailed account on the conditions for a successful sustainable tourism policy, focusing in particular on collaboration and co-ordination, participation, decentralisation and information as well as strategic planning. These policy instruments are seen as crucial to achieve more sustainable outcomes.

2 The nature of government involvement in tourism

In a climate of economic uncertainty, re-structuring processes, globalisation of the economy and deregulation, tourism has come to be seen in many countries around the world as a guarantor for economic growth and employment. Hence, it has seen increased government involvement since the 1980s. It is not surprising that governments' main interest in tourism has remained within the traditional bounds of an industry focused economic perspective. However, this approach has been increasingly criticised in recent years. It is doubted that this economic emphasis adequately recognises tourism's status in modern societies, not just its economic significance but also its ecological and socio-cultural importance. While governments have been keen to exploit the economic benefits of tourism, tourism policy has generally failed to address adequately the negative impacts of tourism. Ecological and social costs, if considered at all, have been acknowledged only very reluctantly and then again, often only from an economic perspective [15]. Although issues beyond this pre-dominant economic framework have had, at least to a certain degree, their place in tourism public policy, it has to be kept in mind that "it is not just the range of objectives that needs to be considered but the relative priority attached to objectives" [16, p. 114]. Thus, economic issues continue to dominate the framing of tourism policies. This is partly a reaction to an increased competition and partly to greater globalisation of the market, generating shifts towards pro-active destination marketing [17, 18]. In this context, government's role in tourism has emphasised a financial commitment to promotion and marketing, a streamlining of government organisations and, in line with the tendency of convergence between the public and private sectors, a greater focus on strategic partnerships with the industry, all of which have aimed to achieve a more commercial orientation through corporate governance [16, 17, 19, 20, 21].

The concept of sustainable tourism implies the need to depart from the *status quo*, which also means a fundamental re-thinking of current policy priorities and directions. To incorporate the concept into the tourism system, development must combine and balance ecological, economic and social aspects. Despite being manifested as a leading motif for future tourism development in many tourism policies around the world, the implementation of sustainable tourism appears, however, to be a long and difficult process [4, 22, 23, 24]. Since there is still a deficiency in its transformation into positive political action more than ten years after Rio, it can be argued that the traditional machinery of government lacks capacity and motivation to respond adequately to the challenges of the complex and dynamic sustainability agenda. A lack of a clear political direction and an inability to achieve sustainability often characterise current deficiencies in

Sustainable Tourism, F. D. Pineda, C. A. Brebbia & M. Mugica (Editors)
© 2004 WIT Press, www.witpress.com, ISBN 1-85312-724-8

tourism politics [5, 13, 21, 25, 26]. In contrast, the conceptualisation of sustainable development demands clearly set-out, unambiguous, long-term and integrative aims and objectives. These together constitute the strategic policy approaches that are the crucial prerequisites to assist in the implementation of the sustainability agenda into the tourism system [23].

3 A strategic policy approach

Through *Agenda 21* governments were urged to develop national strategies for sustainable development (UN 1992). This call was again emphasised during the UN follow-up conference (Rio + 5) in New York in 1997 with the pronouncement that "[b]y the year 2002, the formation and elaboration of national strategies for sustainable development that reflect the contributions and responsibilities of all interested parties should be completed in all countries" (UNGASS 1997 in [27, p. 2]). The demand to implement the concept of sustainable development into national jurisdictions received a positive response and resulted in rapid policy developments with the formulation of many plans, policies and strategies for sustainable development world-wide.

In the context of tourism, such a strategic approach is seen as a suitable tool to achieve more sustainable outcomes [23]. With long-term, strategically formulated goals and objectives for sustainable tourism development it gives clear directions of how tourism should develop in the medium and long-term future. It provides therefore an effective, efficient and predictable framework to guide and direct the actors in the tourism system. It has, however, to be pointed out that the existence of a strategy for sustainable tourism by itself does not necessarily imply more sustainable tourism development. It refers more to a directed socio-political process of getting closer to the paradigm of sustainability [22]. To be able to implement established goals and objectives, they must be linked to clearly defined instruments and measures. A crucial question here is, which instrument or combination of instruments should be selected as the most appropriate to achieve sustainable tourism development. It is argued that only a mix of command and control, market adjustments and collaboration between the various stakeholders will be able to achieve more sustainable outcomes [25]. In the following, some of those complementary policy imperatives are discussed as important instruments to implement the sustainability agenda into the tourism system, namely improved mechanisms of collaboration and co-ordination as well as greater democratisation and decentralisation of policy processes and also the establishment of a better information and knowledge base.

4 Collaboration

A socio-political goal like sustainability relies particularly on the support and the commitment of all affected parties. This entails a process of transparent collaboration involving all relevant stakeholders, which will not only create greater acceptance of the consensually established policy goals but will also

Sustainable Tourism, F. D. Pineda, C. A. Brebbia & M. Mugica (Editors)

assist their implementation [2, 25, 28]. Collaborative and partnership approaches have been frequently discussed in tourism analysis in recent years [16, 20, 22, 29, 30, 31]. Bramwell and Lane [32, p. 180], for instance, argue that "collaborative arrangements for sustainable tourism are part of the conflict resolution, problem solving and capacity building processes that are central to sustainable development". The literature on collaborative arrangements is also characterised by a great diversity in its terminology encompassing everything from coalitions, alliances, task forces and networks to public-private partnerships [33]. Here the term collaboration is used to refer to a mechanism, which involves all relevant stakeholders in dialogue structures and information networks to negotiate a binding strategic plan through consensual agreements on common objectives [22].

Despite the acknowledgement of the benefits of collaborative arrangements in tourism policy and planning, a successful collaboration of all relevant stakeholders is rarely found. There are certain problems associated with a collaborative approach, which often result from existing conventional power structures and political processes [34]. For example, the common business-government alliance can impact negatively on the inclusiveness of policy networks. This often neglects stakeholders representing socio-cultural and environmental community-needs [19, 20, 30]. The appropriate inclusion of all relevant stakeholders in the policy-making process forms, however, the basis for consensus and shared decision-making, which in turn leads to a greater legitimacy of political decisions, democratic empowerment as well as equity and therefore fulfils aspects of the social dimension of sustainability [22]. Collaboration is therefore an important mechanism "for achieving sustainable outcomes and as symbolic of new ways of working" [35, p. 393]. However, some questions still remain unanswered [19, 20, 36]: How can the process of consensus-building be organised best? Who is allowed to participate and who gives that permission? What happens to those who are not? How is the process entrenched in existing political structures? Thus, the debate about collaboration in tourism policy and planning is inherently political and shows again the political nature, in particular the distribution of power, that shapes the approach to tourism development.

5 Co-ordination

Co-ordination is next to collaboration another significant, closely associated political mechanism. As Ladkin and Bertramini [34, p. 72] note, "coordination can be seen as the first step towards a collaborative process". It aims to bring together the core actors in the tourism system to organise their communication effectively through appropriate structures and processes, encompassing "the formal institutionalised relationship among existing networks of organizations, interests and/or individuals" [22, p. 83].

The highly fragmented nature of the tourism system with its complex network of actors, diverse political structures and processes, disjointed and divided political competencies and the unclear political allocation of responsibilities

Sustainable Tourism, F. D. Pineda, C. A. Brebbia & M. Mugica (Editors)

warrants the establishment of an effective and efficient co-ordination regime [16, 21, 37]. Since "there is no other industry in the economy that is linked to so many diverse and different kinds of products and services as is the tourism industry" [37, p. 7], a unique role emerges for government to oversee and develop opportunities, to provide leadership, to establish mechanisms to co-ordinate the tourism industry, to reduce uncertainty and confusion in tourism policy and to plan as well as to enhance the relationships among the key stakeholders from the private and the public sector [22]. Co-ordination is a complex political activity of consensus-building [22] and, at the same time, can establish important dialogue structures and information networks. In particular hierarchical policy and decision-making processes and structures (e.g. federal political system, subsidiarity principle) demand a co-ordinated approach to tourism policy and planning, horizontally as well as vertically [22, 38]. Such an approach embraces administrative and policy co-ordination between and within the national, regional and local political tiers, appropriate industry co-ordination, the co-ordination of responsibilities between government and the private sector as well as the management of a wide range of organised and unorganised community interests [21, 22].

6 Decentralisation and community participation

Like collaboration, decentralisation and participation are also core elements of socio-political sustainability [22, 30, 32, 33]. In the discussion about co-ordination and collaboration the subsidiarity principle is often mentioned [38]. It is based on the view that higher levels in the decision-making hierarchy should take over only such functions and responsibilities that cannot be handled effectively or adequately at lower levels. Adhering to this principle not only relieves the pressure on higher levels in the decision-making hierarchy, it aims to generate local solutions that may well be more closely connected to the problems. It therefore emphasises the role of local or community level organisations in the sense that the community is seen as the most adequate level at which dialogue and collaboration can bring about conflict resolution and consensual decision. Such an approach has the potential to be more democratic, it provides greater opportunities for participation and influence on the policy and decision-making process [22, 32, 33]. Thus, it is argued that the subsidiarity principle is an additional important aspect for the implementation of the concept of sustainable tourism.

At the Rio Conference (1992) greater participation in the policy-making process and a decentralisation of political decisions have been recognised as core elements in the discussion about sustainable development. With the resolution of *Agenda 21* all signatory countries committed themselves to an extensive public consultation process in which great emphasis was placed on working at a community level. This renewal of politics from the bottom means that the regions and communities are positioned to play an important part as pacemaker and impulse generator in the implementation process of sustainable tourism. The concept of 'social capital' [39] also highlights the importance of community

Sustainable Tourism, F. D. Pineda, C. A. Brebbia & M. Mugica (Editors)
 ISBN 1-85312-724-8

participation in the policy process. It emphasises the potential and capacities of regions and their communities to facilitate the implementation of economically, socially and environmentally sustainable development. One aim is to encourage democratic processes at these levels and to allocate greater autonomy, based on social network structures, trust, collaboration and self-determination. The existence of social capital within communities is regarded as a 'soft infrastructure' for collaboration and consensus among stakeholders [40]. Even if the local level by now plays an important role in many countries as a political actor, the kind and extent of its authority for political decisions has, however, to be seen against the background of the respective political tradition and culture. Hall [22, p. 61] argues further that "[t]he capacity of individuals and groups to participate … is not just the result of cultural and democratic values, it is also a product of the structures of public governance and the extent to which such structures are genuinely open to participation and debate".

With the call for the inclusion of the community in the tourism policy and planning process the need to understand community views on tourism has been increasingly recognised in recent years as one foundation for tourism's sustainability in the future. A strong focus is often set on the merits of specific techniques of different forms of participation, ranging from non-participation to citizen power [22, 33]. However, there are often distinct problems associated with a more democratic, participatory approach especially in terms of the scope and degree of participation [29]. Indeed, Hall [22, p. 32] argues that "the level of public involvement in tourism planning throughout most of the world can be more accurately described as a form of tokenism in which decisions or, just as importantly, the direction of decisions has already been prescribed by government. Communities rarely have the opportunity to say no". While collaboration and participation can positively support sustainable tourism and must therefore be seen as important constituents of the tourism policy-making process, these mechanisms do not automatically lead to sustainable outcomes. The focus and extent of collaboration and participation may vary between different contexts and functions and can therefore not be assessed equally positive under all circumstances. Part of the problem involves difficulties faced by the wider community in dealing with complex issues and to gain an insight into and also access to the decision-making process. These problems often coincide with limited community interest as well as a lack of resources and sufficient information. Such a participatory process has also been criticised as being too costly and time-consuming, which in turn might negatively affect the effectiveness and efficiency of how decisions are made [28].

7 Information

A sustainable tourism policy addresses very complex issues and contributes to the process of re-thinking society and development, thus it affects all parts of society. To be successful it needs to ensure an adequate knowledge base and a sufficient exchange of information between the relevant stakeholders. In this context, information is understood broadly, to encompass "monitoring, research,

Sustainable Tourism, F. D. Pineda, C. A. Brebbia & M. Mugica (Editors)

data bases and information systems, communication, dissemination and ownership of information describing natural systems and human interactions with them" [41, p. 142]. In order to achieve effective policies on sustainability, governments rely on the expertise and knowledge of the relevant actors from the public and the private sector, community groups and academia and their willingness to collaborate; governments must initiate and guide such complex processes actively [13, 22, 25, 32, 33, 41, 42]. Further, the establishment of communication networks and an adequate exchange of information will improve the limited information and knowledge base required to ensure more adequate policy responses to sustainability issues. Currently, however, it would appear that despite the widespread acceptance of the importance of sustainable development "the information systems to support its achievements are in general myopic, under-resourced, uncoordinated, and constantly buffeted by the winds of political fashion and expediency" [41, p. 156].

Information can never be complete in the sense of covering every aspect of every issue. Policy and decision-makers will always be confronted by new and unforeseen developments for which information is lacking or patchy, hence it follows that policies will emerge in contexts of some degree of uncertainty [42]. The lack of information impacts on the entire policy process, from policy initiation to evaluation and review. Nevertheless, this deficit must be continually addressed to improve the available information systems to support the policy and decision-making process more effectively and efficiently and to develop an adequate policy monitoring system. The so-called precautionary principle is a prominent approach to reduce and compensate for the unavoidable uncertainties and information deficits, which are part of the policy-making process [13, 41, 42]. Derived from environmental policy, the precautionary principle has been widely accepted internationally in many policies and strategies, such as the *Rio Declaration* (1992). Although it is still contested, particularly in regard to its implementation, it is another important feature of the concept of sustainable development [41]. To overcome uncertainty and the lack of information, research activities are, furthermore, crucial in the attempt to implement the concept of sustainable development. Communication and co-operation between academic researchers and policy communities must therefore be re-defined.

The provision of adequate information to the public to create greater awareness for the issues of sustainability and as a means to change its behaviour is a further perspective, which requires consideration. Education and training can create a better understanding and acceptance for the changes needed to implement the concept and therefore highlight the need to understand sustainable tourism policy as a form of information policy. Dovers [41, p. 152] summarises the core concerns and issues that are an essential part of developing the information dimension of the sustainability agenda. He states "that uncertainty is unavoidable; that, this aside, our information base is less adequate than it needs to be; that the menu of policy instruments generally used and criteria from choosing from this menu are often too narrow; and that policy and information are inextricably linked".

Sustainable Tourism, F. D. Pineda, C. A. Brebbia & M. Mugica (Editors)

8 Conclusion

In this paper sustainable tourism as a relatively novel public policy area has been discussed with reference to the concept of sustainable development. Its demands on policy and the greatest obstacles to its successful implementation were briefly outlined. Collaboration and co-ordination, decentralisation and participation as well as information are regarded as important parameters for a successful sustainable tourism policy. Such a process should lead to a comprehensive, integrative and long-term strategy for sustainable tourism. It has been argued that these mechanisms require a high degree of political adaptability and flexibility, combined with the willingness to introduce far-reaching reforms in political processes and structures.

The question remains, however, if the traditional policy processes and structures in place are able to cope with those demands; Dovers [10, p. 308-309], for instance, argues that they "may 'handle' the problem and the greater part of the policy community be satisfied, for a time, across a series of conflicts, but environmental degradation, or poverty for that matter, may well continue or increase". A greater role of the civil society in the search for sustainable tourism requires a political modernisation from the 'bottom' and therefore the willingness to introduce far-reaching reforms at the 'top' to complement the existing hierarchical processes and structures of the political-administrative system. In summary, Hall [22, p. 5] argues: "Clearly, meeting such conditions for sustainability is a major political, economic and environmental issue as it requires new ways of thinking about the nature and purpose of development and growth, and the role of individuals, government and the private sector in developing sustainable futures, a concern which is increasingly at the forefront of the analysis of tourism".

References

[1] Lafferty, W.M., The politics of sustainable development: Global norms for national implementation. Environmental Politics, 5(2), pp. 185-208, 1996.

[2] Stabler, M.J., Tourism and Sustainability. Principles to Practice, CABI: New York, 1997.

[3] Christie, I., Britain's sustainable development strategy. Environmental quality and policy change. Policy Studies, 15(3), pp. 4-20, 1994.

[4] Fritz, G., Ausgangsbedingungen und konzeptionelle Ansatzpunkte einer Politik für nachhaltigen Tourismus. Tourismuspolitik der Zukunft. Perspektiven, Handlungsfelder, Strategien, ed. Evangelische Akademie Loccum, Evangelische Akademie Loccum: Rehburg-Loccum, pp. 88-106, 1999.

[5] Kahlenborn, W., Kraack, M. & Carius, A., Tourismus- und Umweltpolitik. Ein politisches Spannungsfeld, Springer Verlag: Berlin, 1999.

Sustainable Tourism, F. D. Pineda, C. A. Brebbia & M. Mugica (Editors)

[6] MacLellan, R., The effectiveness of sustainable tourism policies in Scotland. Tourism and Sustainability. Principles to Practice, ed. M.J. Stabler, CABI: Wallingford, pp. 305-322, 1997.
[7] Lafferty, W.M. & Meadowcroft, J., (eds). Implementing Sustainable Development, Oxford University Press: Oxford, 2000.
[8] Jörgensen, K., Ökologisch nachhaltige Entwicklung im föderativen Staat, FU Berlin (Forschungsstelle für Umweltpolitik): Berlin, 2002.
[9] Jänicke, M., Strategien der Nachhaltigkeit - Eine Einführung. Umweltplanung im internationalen Vergleich. Strategien der Nachhaltigkeit, eds M. Jänicke & H. Jörgens, Springer Verlag: Berlin, pp. 1-14, 2000.
[10] Dovers, S.R., Sustainability: Demands on policy. Journal of Public Policy, 16(3), pp. 303-318, 1996.
[11] Hunter, C.J., Aspects of the sustainable tourism debate from a natural resources perspective. Sustainable Tourism. A Global Perspective, eds R. Harris, T. Griffin & P. Williams, Butterworth-Heinemann: Oxford, pp. 3-23, 2002.
[12] Hunter-Jones, P.A., Hughes, H.L., Eastwood, I.W. & Morrison, A.A., Practical approaches to sustainability: A Spanish perspective. Tourism and Sustainability. Principles to Practice, ed. M.J. Stabler, CABI: Wallingford, pp. 263-274, 1997.
[13] Petermann, T., Entwicklung und Folgen des Tourismus. Gesellschaftliche, ökologische und technische Dimensionen (Band 1) (Studien des Büros für Technikfolgen-Abschätzung beim deutschen Bundestag 52), TAB: Bonn, 1997.
[14] Jenkins, J. & Hall, C.M., Tourism planning and policy in Australia. Tourism Planning and Policy in Australia and New Zealand: Cases, Issues and Practice, eds. C.M. Hall, J. Jenkins & G. Kearsley, Irwin Publishers: Sydney, pp. 37-48, 1997.
[15] Kramer, D., Aus der Region – für die Region. Konzepte für einen Tourismus mit menschlichem Maß, Deuticke: Wien, 1997.
[16] Hall, C.M., Tourism and Politics: Policy, Power and Place, John Wiley: Chichester, 1994.
[17] Greuter, F., Bausteine der schweizerischen Tourismuspolitik. Grundlagen, Beschreibungen und Empfehlungen für die Praxis, Haupt: Bern, 2000.
[18] Fayos-Sola, E., Tourism policy: A midsummer night's dream. Tourism Management, 17(6), pp. 405-412, 1996.
[19] Jenkins, J.M., Statutory authorities in whose interests? The case of Tourism New South Wales, the Bed Tax, and "The Games". Pacific Tourism Review, 4, pp. 201-218, 2001.
[20] Hall, C.M., Rethinking collaboration and partnership: a public policy perspective. Journal of Sustainable Tourism, 7(3 & 4), pp. 274-288, 1999.
[21] Hall, C.M., Introduction to Tourism. Development, Dimensions and Issues (3rd ed.), Longman: South Melbourne, 1998.

Sustainable Tourism, F. D. Pineda, C. A. Brebbia & M. Mugica (Editors)

[22] Hall, C.M., Tourism Planning. Policies, Processes and Relationships, Prentice Hall: Harlow, 2000.

[23] Pforr, C., On the road to sustainable tourism? Policy diffusion of sustainable development principles. Creating Tourism Knowledge, C. Cooper, C. Arcodia, D. Solnet & M. Whitford (eds), University of Queensland: Brisbane, pp. 566-576, 2004.

[24] Pforr, C., Ökotourismus in Australien: Echte Alternative oder nur Alibi? Eine tourismuspolitische Perspektive. ÖKOZIDjournal, 19(1), pp. 11-18, 2000.

[25] Brendle, U. & Müller, V., Für eine Wende in der Tourismuspolitik, Bundestagsfraktion Bündnis 90/Die Grünen: Bonn, 1996.

[26] Pridham, G., Tourism Policy in Mediterranean Europe: Towards Sustainable Development, University of Bristol (Centre for Mediterranean Studies): Bristol, 1996.

[27] Nordbeck, R., Nachhaltigkeitsstrategien als politische Langfriststrategien: Innovationswirkungen und Restriktionen, Forschungsstelle für Umweltpolitik: Berlin, 2002.

[28] Jenkins, J.M., Tourism policy in rural New South Wales - policy and research priorities. GeoJournal, 29(3), pp. 281-290, 1993.

[29] Bramwell, B. & Sharman, A., Collaboration in local tourism policy making. Annals of Tourism Research, 26(2), pp. 312-328, 1999.

[30] Selin, S., Developing a typology of sustainable tourism partnerships. Journal of Sustainable Tourism, 7(3-4), pp. 260-273, 1999.

[31] Jamal, T.B. & Getz, D., Collaboration theory and community tourism planning. Annals of Tourism Research, 22, pp. 186-204, 1995.

[32] Bramwell, B. & Lane, B., Editorial. Journal of Sustainable Tourism, 7(3-4), pp. 179-181, 1999.

[33] Bramwell, B. & Lane, B., (eds). Tourism Collaboration and Partnerships: Policy, Practice and Sustainability, Channel View Publications: Clevedon, 2000.

[34] Ladkin, A. & Bertramini, A.M., Collaborative tourism planning: A case study of Cusco, Peru. Current Issues in Tourism, 5(2), pp. 71-93, 2002.

[35] Robinson, M., Collaboration and cultural consent: Refocusing sustainable tourism. Journal of Sustainable Tourism, 7(3-4), pp. 379- 397, 1999.

[36] Ryan, C., Equity, management, power sharing and sustainability – issues of the 'new tourism'. Tourism Management, 23, pp. 17-26, 2002.

[37] Edgell, D.L., International Tourism Policy, Van Nostrand Reinhold: New York, 1990.

[38] Mundt, J.W., Einführung in den Tourismus, Oldenburg Verlag: München, 1998.

[39] Putnam, R. , Making Democracy Work: Civic Traditions in Modern Italy, Princeton University Press: Princeton, 1993.

[40] Ritchey-Vance, M., Social capital, sustainability and working democracy: New yardsticks for grassroots development. Grassroots Development, 20(1), pp. 3-9, 1996.

Sustainable Tourism, F. D. Pineda, C. A. Brebbia & M. Mugica (Editors)

[41] Dovers, S.R., Information, sustainability and policy. Australian Journal of Environmental Management, 2, pp. 142-156, 1995.
[42] Dovers, S.R., Norton, T.W. & Handmer, J.W., Uncertainty, ecology, sustainability, and policy. Biodiversity and Conservation, 5, pp. 1143-1167, 1996.

Sustainable Tourism, F. D. Pineda, C. A. Brebbia & M. Mugica (Editors)

Section 3
Sustainable tourism

Identifying tourism stakeholder groups based on support for sustainable tourism development and participation in tourism activities

E. T. Byrd[1] & L. D. Gustke[2]
[1]*The University of North Carolina at Greensboro, USA*
[2]*North Carolina State University, USA*

Abstract

The purpose of the study was to explore and identify stakeholder groups in tourism development based on a stakeholder's support for or against sustainable tourism development and a stakeholder's participation in tourism and political activities. To assist in identifying the stakeholders an instrument was developed and administered to two rural North Carolina counties, Johnston County and Martin County. The analysis of the data was conducted employing SPSS and developing decision trees for support for sustainable tourism and participation in tourism and political activities using the Exhaustive CHAID method in SPSS Answer Tree. Based on the results of the study evidence was found that allowed for the identification of twelve stakeholder groups. The stakeholder groups identified by the decision trees can be described as high participant/high supporters, high participant/moderate supporters, high participant/low supporters, high-moderate participant/high supporters, high-moderate participant/moderate supporters, high participant/low supporters, low-moderate participant/high supporters, low-moderate participant/moderate supporters, low-moderate participant/low supporters, low participant/high supporters, low participant/moderate supporters, and low participant/low supporters. From the results of this study a better understanding of the social dimension of sustainable tourism was developed.

1 Introduction

The decline of traditional rural industries such as agriculture, mining and forestry over the past three decades has required many rural communities to explore

Sustainable Tourism, F. D. Pineda, C. A. Brebbia & M. Mugica (Editors)

alternative industries to strengthen their economic base [1, 2]. Tourism has become one of the main industries identified as having the potential to assist local communities in developing stronger economic diversity [1, 2, 3]. However, for tourism development to be successful and sustainable it must be planned and managed responsibly [4, 5, 6]. Inskeep [5] furthered the concept of responsible management, stating, "ill-conceived and poorly planned tourism development can erode the very qualities of the natural and [social] environments that attract visitors in the first place" (p. 460). Similarly, communities that use or plan to use tourism as an economic development tool to diversify their economy must develop policies for the sustainable development of the community [4, 6]. Gunn [7] also suggests that the success and implementation of a tourism development plan is often based on the support of stakeholders, which include: citizens, entrepreneurs and community leaders.

Freeman [8] defined a stakeholder as any individual or identifiable group affected by or that can affect the achievement of given objectives. Conflict can arise in the tourism development process from stakeholder groups with different interests and ideas about the cost and benefits of the development [9, 10, 11]. One aspect of stakeholder management that needs to be understood is the type of involvement the stakeholders will have in the tourism development process.

The differing interests of each stakeholder group must be understood for stakeholder involvement to have the greatest chance of success. Based on this understanding, planners can then find indicators of where groups stand and how they feel about an issue [6, 11, 12]. Identifying stakeholders and their interests is only the first step in the process that can lead to sustainable development. This identification alone does not resolve conflicts; it simply assists planners in identifying conflicts that need resolution.

2 Method

The study of tourism stakeholders described in this paper was conducted in two rural North Carolina counties in 2003. The counties selected for the study were Johnston County and Martin County. Stakeholders, which included the county residents and visitors, were mailed a questionnaire inquiring about their attitudes and perceptions of tourism development, their participation in local political and tourism activities, and their view of the impacts of tourism. The responses were collected and analyzed to identify stakeholder groups in the area based on their support for sustainable development and participation in tourism development.

A questionnaire was developed based on previous research and variables identified by the literature review [17, 18, 19, 20, 21]. Questions included perceptions about tourism development and the environment, perceptions of tourism impact in the community, types and amount of community participation, the individual's participation in recreational activities, and basic demographics. The questionnaire consisted of 56 items that included nominal, categorical, and interval measures. The total response rate for the study was 23.50% The responses for both counties were similar. For Johnston County the response rate was 23% and for Martin County it was 25%.

Sustainable Tourism, F. D. Pineda, C. A. Brebbia & M. Mugica (Editors)

Analysis of the responses was conducted using SPSS Answer Tree. This facilitated the identification of stakeholder groups based on support for sustainable tourism development and stakeholder participation in tourism and political activities.

To identify stakeholder groups decision trees were developed for support for sustainable tourism and participation in tourism and political activities using the Exhaustive CHAID method in SPSS Answer Tree using the indexes and variables. Support for sustainable tourism and participation in tourism and political activities were the dependent variables and other variables in the study were independent variables.

SPSS Answer Tree 3.1 is a statistical application that uses algorithms to develop decision trees. A decision tree is a model that can be used to classify or predict variables [23]. It is an exploratory method used to study the relationship between a dependent variable and independent variables [24]. Decision trees indicate how groups develop by dividing the dependent variable by the independent variables. The specific statistics that are used in a decision tree are based on the algorithm that is employed. This study used the Exhaustive Chi-square Automatic Interaction Detection (CHAID).

The Exhaustive CHAID is a second-generation CHAID algorithm used in SPSS Answer Tree [24]. The Exhaustive CHAID method was selected for the study because it is a more comprehensive method and yields more accurate results than CHAID and the other decision tree methods within SPSS Answer Tree [24]. CHIAD splits the data into subsets that best describe the dependent variable [23]. For nominal and ordinal variables, chi-square analyses and for interval variables an analysis of variance is used [24]. The split is based on which variable had the lowest p value. If a tie occurs between two or more variables the variable that has the highest F value is selected as the predictor.

3 Results

The decision trees were created using the Exhaustive CHAID method. Two answer trees were developed for the total sample. The first tree included the dependent variable, support for sustainable tourism development. The second decision tree included the dependent variable, participation in tourism and political activities.

3.1 Support for Sustainable Tourism Development Decision Tree

The Support for Sustainable Tourism Development Decision Tree (SSTDDT) can be divided into three main branches and 8 levels. The root node for the SSTDDT was the individuals score on the support for sustainable tourism index. The index ranged from 17 to 85, with 17 indicating strong disagreement with sustainable tourism, and 85 representing strong agreement with sustainable tourism. The respondents in this study had a mean score of 64.98 and a standard deviation of 6.89 on the support for sustainable tourism index. These respondents can be differentiated based on five variables (see Table 1). Perceived impact was

Sustainable Tourism, F. D. Pineda, C. A. Brebbia & M. Mugica (Editors)

selected as the variable for prediction in the decision tree because it had the smallest p value (p<.05). The respondents were divided into three groups represented by Branch 1, Branch 2, and Branch 3 based on the individual stakeholder's perceptions of the tourism impact.

Table 1: Predictors for Node 0 root split.

Predictor	F	DF	P value
Perceived Impact	24.78	2, 477	p<.05
Bird Watch/Did Not Bird Watch	19.81	1, 478	p<.05
Attend a Festival/Did Not Attend a Festival	12.33	1, 478	p<.05
Photography/Did Not Take Photographs	8.12	1, 478	p<.05
Gender (Male/Female)	9.36	1, 478	p<.05

The split of node 0 results in three groups on level 2 of the SSTDDT. These three groups are represented by node 1; individuals that moderately to neutrally perceived that tourism had a negative impact on the community (Score of <=36 on the Impact Index); node 2 individuals that neutrally to moderately perceived that tourism had a positive impact (Score of 36-45 on the Impact Index); and node 3 individuals that moderately to strongly perceived that tourism had a positive impact (Score of >45 on the Impact Index). These three nodes are the parent nodes for branches 1, 2, and 3. Node 1 is located on branch 1, node 2 is located on branch 2, and node 3 is located on branch 3. Respondents in the first group (node 1) indicate a lower level of support (62.31), based on the support index, than those in the second group (node 2) (64.60). Those in the second group (node 2) were less supportive (64.60) than those in the third group (node 3) (69.19).

Node 1, individuals that moderately to neutrally perceived that tourism had a negative impact on the community, represented 18.33% of the respondents in this study. These respondents can be further differentiated by three other variables. The respondent's age was found to be the most significant predictor of the level of support for sustainable tourism development based on a p value <.05 (see Table 2).

Table 2: Predictors for Node 1 individuals that moderately to neutrally perceived that tourism had a negative impact on the community.

Predictor	F	DF	P value
Age	16.20	1, 86	p<.05
Visited/Did not Visit the Visitors Center	4.05	1, 86	p<.05
Area (Town/Outside of Town)	4.00	1, 86	p<.05

Node 2 begins the second branch of the SSTDDT. Node 2, individuals that neutrally to moderately perceive that tourism had a positive impact represented 64.17% of the respondents. The respondents can be further split by three other variables (see Table 3). Participation or lack of participation in bird watching was selected as the most significant indicator of their support for sustainable tourism development, based on a p value <.05.

Sustainable Tourism, F. D. Pineda, C. A. Brebbia & M. Mugica (Editors)

Table 3: Predictors for Node 2 individuals that neutrally to moderately perceived that tourism had a positive impact.

Predictor	F	DF	P value
Bird Watching	13.92	1, 306	p<.05
Gender	16.44	1, 306	p<.05
Hiking	5.96	1, 306	p<.05

Node 3, individuals that moderately to strongly perceived that tourism had a positive impact, represented 17.50% of the respondents. These respondents can be further divided by three other variables (see Table 4). Participation or lack of participation in bird watching was the most significant indicator of support for sustainable tourism development, based on a p value <.05, for this group and used for the split.

Table 4: Predictors for Node 3 individuals that moderately to strongly perceived that tourism had a positive impact.

Predictor	F	DF	P value
Bird Watching	7.39	182	p<.05
Attend a Festival	5.85	182	p<.05
Hunting	3.82	182	p=.05

3.2 Participation in Tourism and Political Activities Decision Tree

The Participation in Tourism and Political Activities Decision Tree (PTPADT) can be divided into four main branches and 9 levels. The root node for PTPADT was the individual's score on the participation index. The index ranged from 0 to 19, with 0 indication no participation and 19 representing high participation.

The respondents in this study had a mean score of 4.11 and a standard deviation of 3.09 on the participation index. This indicates participation by individuals varies. These respondents can be differentiated based on five variables (Table 5). The individual stakeholder's perspective was selected as the variable for prediction in the tree because it had the smallest p value (p<.05) and largest F value (125.71). The respondents were divided into four groups represented by Branch 1, Branch 2, Branch 3, and Branch 4 based on the individual stakeholder's perspective about tourism.

Table 5: Predictors for Node 0 root split.

Predictor	F	DF	P value
Perspective	125.71	4, 491	p<.05
Impact	30.87	2, 493	p<.05
Education	27.47	2, 493	p<.05
Length of Residency	17.67	2, 493	p<.05
Attend a Sports Event	25.74	2, 493	p<.05

Sustainable Tourism, F. D. Pineda, C. A. Brebbia & M. Mugica (Editors)

The split of node 0 results in four groups on level 2 of the PTPADT. The split contains 100% of the respondents of this study. Node 1 represents governmental officials. Node 2 represents local residents. Node 3 represents visitors to the county. Node 4 represents local business owners. These nodes are the parent nodes for branches 1, 2, 3 and 4. Node 1 is located on branch 1, node 2 is located on branch 2, node 3 is located on branch 3 and node 4 on branch 4.

Respondents who were government officials (node 1) participated more (10.55) than any other group. The next highest participators were the business owners (node 4) (5.03) followed by the residents (node 2) (3.17) and the visitors (node 3) (2.35). This supports the first and third hypotheses of the study. Understanding the stakeholder's perspective is extremely important but does not tell the entire story. Other variables need to be investigated.

Node 1, government officials, represents 9.07% of the respondents in this study. These respondents can be further differentiated by two other variables (see Table 6). The most significant predictor of government officials participation in tourism and political activities was how long the respondent had lived in the county, based on a p value <.05.

Table 6: Node 1 predictors for individuals that were government officials.

Predictor	F	DF	P value
Length of Residency	17.3784	1, 43	p<.05
Gender	8.5122	1, 43	p<.05

Node 2

Node 2, local residents, represents 60.08% of the respondents in this study. These respondents can be further differentiated by three other variables (see Table 7). The most significant predictor of residents participation in tourism and political activities was the individual's perception of the impact tourism has on the community, based on a p value <.05.

Table 7: Predictors for Node 2 individuals that were residents.

Predictor	F	DF	P value
Perceived Impact	22.36	2, 295	p<.05
Attend a Sports Event	16.90	1, 296	p<.05
Education	10.09	2, 295	p<.05

Node 3, visitors to the county, represents 11.49% of the respondents in this study. Node 3 is a terminal node. These respondents cannot be further divided by any other variables. There were no variables that were statistically significant enough (p value = .05) to justify the division.

Node 4, local business owners, represents 18.15% of the respondents in this study. These respondents can be further divided by two other variables (see Table 8). The most significant predictor of business owners participation in tourism and political activities was the individual's perception of the impact tourism has on the community, based on a p value <.05.

Sustainable Tourism, F. D. Pineda, C. A. Brebbia & M. Mugica (Editors)
© 2004 WIT Press, www.witpress.com, ISBN 1-85312-724-8

Table 8: Predictors for Node 4 individuals that were business owners.

Predictor	F	DF	P value
Perceived Impact	12.05	2, 87	p<.05
County	4.81	1, 88	p<.05

Node 5 consists of respondents that could not be identified as a specific perspective due to missing data. The data was missing due to a conscious effort by the respondents to remove the identification marker form the questionnaire.

The second level of the PTPADT differentiates that respondents into four groups based on their perspectives related to tourism. These groups can be further divided based on other variables, length of residency and perceived impact.

4 Conclusion and discussion

This study explored the different stakeholder groups in a given community. Using decision trees the study was able to identify stakeholder groups based on multiple variables. The variable that were found to be statistically significant at the .05 or lower level of significance were perception of tourism impact, general demographics, participation or lack of participation in recreational activities. Twelve stakeholder groups can be inferred based on the results of the two decision trees. These twelve groups are the result of combining the groups identified in the SSTDT with the groups identified in the PTPADT. The twelve groups are described below under a sub heading that depicts the group.

High participant/high supporters (HPHS) can be generalized as stakeholders who are government officials or are in governmental positions, perceive that tourism has a very positive impact on the community, and did not participate in natural resource based activities in 2002, but did attend festivals and events in 2002. This group can be assumed to be familiar with tourism opportunities by their participation in tourism activities such as attending festivals. It can be speculated that the HPHS familiarity with a tourism product, such as festivals, gives them a better appreciation of how tourism positively impacts the community and this in turn influences them to be more supportive of sustainable tourism development. HPHS will be involved in most major decisions in the county in which they live or work, including those related to sustainable tourism development. HPHS would support most sustainable tourism activities and be active in getting them initiated and developed. Just as important, this group will be in a position to block any tourism plan and product development that they might perceive as being non-sustainable.

High participant/moderate supporters (HPMS) can be generalized as stakeholders who are government officials or are in governmental positions, perceive that tourism has a positive impact on the community and did not participate in natural resource based activities in 2002. The main difference between the HPMS and the HPHS was their perception of the impact tourism has on the community. HPMS perceived that the impact tourism has on the

Sustainable Tourism, F. D. Pineda, C. A. Brebbia & M. Mugica (Editors)

community is less positive than the HPHS. The HPMS may be skeptical of radical changes in the tourism industry. They may require convincing if there are not obvious benefits from the development and if they do not perceive the tourism plan to be sustainable.

High participant/low supporters (HPLS) can be generalized as stakeholders who are government officials or are in governmental positions, perceive tourism does not have a positive impact on the community, lived in a town or urban area, and had not visited the local visitor's center nor attended any motor sports events in 2002. It can be inferred from the results that HPLS were not familiar with tourism opportunities in their community. HPLS may be a group that would support non-sustainable tourism activities as well as sustainable tourism activities. Also, there may be some sustainable tourism activities that this group would not support, such as the preservation of a natural area that the HPLS may perceive as being a good location for industrial development. HPLS may indicate the strongest opposition for any sustainable tourism development. They need to be assured of the benefits of any type of tourism development on the community and the costs that are associated with development that could be considered unsustainable. It is important that there concerns be addressed and that the HPLS be informed of the contributions to the community that sustainable tourism makes and will continue to make in the future.

High-moderate participant/high supporters (HMPHS) can be generalized as stakeholders who are business owners, perceive tourism has a major positive impact on the community, did not participate in natural resource based activities in 2002, but did attend festivals and events in 2002. It can be inferred from the results that this group was familiar with tourism opportunities and participate in some tourist activities such as attending a festival. Similar to the HPMS, HMPHS familiarity with a festival which is a tourism product gives them a better appreciation of how tourism positively impacts the community and this in turn influences them to be supportive of sustainable tourism development. This group would support most sustainable tourism activities. HMPHS need to be informed about any tourism policies or plans that will be developed. This group will be involved in sustainable tourism development as long as they are aware and are given an opportunity to participate. Therefore communication is vital for this group. Communication with HMPHS as well as the other groups discussed can be conducted in multiple ways. These include email, newsletters, newspapers, and public meetings. Whatever type of communication strategy employed there must be a way for the stakeholders to respond back to the planners.

High-moderate participant/moderate supporters (HMPMS) can be generalized as stakeholders who are business owners that perceive tourism had a positive impact on the community and did not participate in natural resource based activities in 2002. They will be involved in the process as long as they perceive positive benefits to themselves, but will not take a leadership position in the development of sustainable tourism. This group needs to be kept aware of the benefits tourism for them and their business, so that they will support sustainable tourism development. HMPMS need to be made aware of the long-term benefits of sustainable tourism development.

Sustainable Tourism, F. D. Pineda, C. A. Brebbia & M. Mugica (Editors)

High-moderate participant/low supporters (HMPLS) can be generalized as stakeholders who are business owners, perceive tourism does not have a positive impact on the community, lived in an urban area, and did not visit the local visitor's center. Inferences can be made from the results that this group may not be as familiar with tourism opportunities in their community as other groups. HMPLS may be a group that would support non-sustainable tourism activities as well as sustainable tourism activities. Also, there may be some sustainable tourism activities that this group would oppose. HMPLS should be identified and contacted to discover the reasons for their negative perceptions of tourism's impacts. Once their interests are understood they should be addressed. Addressing the interests may came in the form of attempting to lessen negative impacts that affect this group and informing the stakeholders to resolve any misconceptions about tourism. For HMPLS to support sustainable tourism they would have to be shown that the development benefited them directly.

Low-moderate participant/high supporters (LMPHS) can be generalized as stakeholders who are residents, perceive that tourism has a major positive impact on the community, did not participate in natural resource based activities in 2002, but did attend festivals and events in 2002. LMPHS should be encouraged to participate more in both tourism and political activities. Unless they become more active this group will have little influence on what type of tourism development policies are implemented. LMPHS will, however, always influence the success of these policies and will be affected by them. Impacts form non-sustainable developments that can affect the residents include, traffic congestion, increases in property values, and pollution.

Low-moderate participant/moderate supporters (LMPMS) can be described as stakeholders who are residents, perceive that tourism has a positive impact on the community and did not participate in natural resource based activities in 2002. This group should be encouraged to participate more in both tourism activities and political activities. Similar to LMPHS, LMPMS will have little influence on the type of tourism policies are implemented unless they become more involved, but they will influence the success of these policies and will be affected by them. LMPMS, as well as other host community stakeholders, will interact with visitors to the community. If this interaction is positive, than tourism in the community becomes more sustainable..

Low-moderate participant/low supporters (LMPLS) can be identified as stakeholders who are residents, perceive tourism does not have a positive impact on the community, lived in an urban area, have not visited the local visitor's center nor participated in motor sport events in 2002. Due to not visiting the visitor's bureau, it can be inferred from the results that LMPLS were not familiar with tourism opportunities in their community. LMPLS will have limited participation in sustainable tourism development and only on issues that they perceive directly affecting them. They will view any tourism development initiatives with skepticism. LMPLS will need to be made aware of tourism's benefits before they will support the tourism plan or development. In addition they may have little influence on tourism policy development, but as with every

Sustainable Tourism, F. D. Pineda, C. A. Brebbia & M. Mugica (Editors)

other group will influence the success of these policies and will be affected by them.

Low participant/high supporters (LPHS) can be described as stakeholders who are visitors to the county, perceive that tourism has a major positive impact on the community, did not participate in natural resource based activities in 2002, but did attend festivals and events in 2002. LPHS will have limited participation in sustainable tourism policy development, because they do not live in the area. It is important to understand that even though the visitors are considered low participants, they will, like the residents, be impacted by the policy and will be extremely influential in the success of any sustainable tourism process. Therefore it is important to be aware of their concerns and wants, and account for them in the tourism development process. If they perceive that a tourism development in the area is not sustainable they may decide not to visit the area in the future. For example if development of a new lodging facility degrades the natural environment the LPHS may decide to travel to another area.

Low participant/moderate supporters (LPMS) can be described as stakeholders who are visitors to the local community, perceive that tourism has a positive impact on the community and did not participate in natural resource based activities in 2002. It is important to understand that even though the visitors are considered LPMS and they will have limited to no influence on policy development, they will be impacted by the policy and will be extremely influential in the success of any sustainable tourism process. Therefore, it is important to understand their concerns and wants and account for them in the tourism development process.

Low participant/low supporters (LPLS) can be identified as stakeholders who are visitors to the local community, perceive tourism does not have a positive impact on the community, reside in an urban area, they have not visited the local visitor's center and have not participated in any motor sports in 2002. It can be inferred from the results that LPLS were not as familiar with tourism opportunities in the county. As with the LPMS, it is important to be aware of LPLS concerns and wants and account for them in the tourism development process.

References

[1] Gustke, L. Improving rural tourism extension and research in the south, 1993.

[2] Long, P.T., Perdue, R.R., & Allen, L. Rural residents' perceptions and attitudes by community level of tourism. *Journal of Travel Research*, 28 (3), 3-9, 1990.

[3] Hassan, S.S. Determinants of market competitiveness in an environmentally sustainable tourism industry. *Journal of Travel Research*, 38 (3), 239-245, 2000.

[4] De Oliveira, JAP. Governmental responses to tourism development: three Brazilian case studies. *Tourism Management, 24,* 97-110, 2003

Sustainable Tourism, F. D. Pineda, C. A. Brebbia & M. Mugica (Editors)

[5] Inskeep, E. Tourism planning: An integrated and sustainable development approach, New York: Van Nostrand Reinhold, 1991.

[6] Yuksel, F., Bramwell, B. & Yuksel, A. Stakeholder interviews and tourism planning at Pamukkale, Turkey. *Tourism Management, 20,* 351-360, 1991.

[7] Gunn, C.A. *Tourism planning: Basic concepts cases (3rd ed).* Washington, D.C.: Taylor and Francis, 1994.

[8] Freeman, R.E. Strategic management: A stakeholder approach. Boston: Pitman, 1984

[9] Byrd, E.T. *Barriers to rural tourism: A comparison of the perceptions of the* host community, local business owners, and tourists. Unpublished master's thesis, North Carolina State University, Raleigh, NC., 1997

[10] Ioannides, D. A flawed implementation of sustainable tourism; the experience of Akamas, Cyprus. Tourism Management 16(8), 583-592, 1995.

[11] Markwick, M.C. Golf tourism development, stakeholders, differing discourses, and alternative agendas: the case of Malta. Tourism Management, 21, 515-524, 2000.

[12] De Lopez, T.T. Stakeholder management for conservation projects: A case study of Ream National Park, Cambodia. Environmental Management, 28 (1), 47-60, 2001.

[13] Goeldner, C.R. & Ritchie, J.R.B. (2003). Tourism: Principles, practices, philosophies (9th ed.). New Jersey: John Wiley & Sons, Inc, 2003.

[14] Allen, L., Hafer, H., Long, P., & Perdue, R. Rural residents' attitudes toward recreation and tourism development. Journal of Travel Research, 31 (4), 27-33, 1993.

[15] Murphy, P.E. Perceptions and attitudes of decision making groups in tourism centers. Journal of Travel Research, 21 (3), 8-12, 1983.

[16] Pizam, A. Tourism's impacts: The social costs to the destination community as perceived by its residents. Journal of Travel Research, 16(4), 8-12, 1978.

[17] Mason, P. & Cheyne, J. Resident's attitudes to proposed tourism development. Annals of Tourism Research, 27 (2), 391-411, 2000.

[18] McFarlane, B.L. & Boxall, P.C. (2000). Factors influencing forest values and attitudes of two stakeholder groups: The case of the Foothills Model Forest, Alberta, Canada. Society and Natural Resources, 13, 649-661, 2000.

[19] Perdue, R. Long, P. & Allen, L. Resident support for sustainable tourism development. Annals of Tourism Research, 17, 586-599, 1990.

[20] Stein, T.V., Anderson, D.H., & Kelly, T. Using stakeholders' values to apply ecosystem management in an upper Midwest landscape. Environmental Management, 24(3), 399-413, 1999.

[21] Vincent, V.C. & Thompson, W.T. Assessing community support and sustainability for ecotourism development. Journal of Travel Research, 41, 153-160, 2002.

Sustainable Tourism, F. D. Pineda, C. A. Brebbia & M. Mugica (Editors)
© 2004 WIT Press, www.witpress.com, ISBN 1-85312-724-8

[22] Babbie, E. The practice of social research (7th ed). Belmont: Wadsworth Publishing Company, 1995.
[23] Kass, G.V. An exploratory technique for investigating large quantities of categorical data. Applied Statistics, 29 (2), 119-127, 1980.
[24] Huba, G.J. CHAID. The Measurement Group. Retrieved May 30, 2003, from http://www.themeasurementgroup.com/Definitions/CHAID.htm, 2003.

Sustainable Tourism, F. D. Pineda, C. A. Brebbia & M. Mugica (Editors)
© 2004 WIT Press, www.witpress.com, ISBN 1-85312-724-8

Indicators for sustainable tourism development: crossing the divide from definitions to actions

J. M. Bloyer, L. D. Gustke & Y. Leung
North Carolina State University

Abstract

Once the Brundtland Report on sustainable development was published in 1987, and "sustainable tourism" was accepted into the lexicon of tourism discourse, a substantial amount of so-called "sustainable tourism development planning" has occurred in a number of destinations. The use of indicators to monitor development and maintain sustainability were included in these plans, but rarely operationalized effectively. This problem was the result of a lack of agreement over what, exactly, "sustainable tourism development" means, and the resulting confusion over creating indicators for an undefined concept [1, 4, 13, 14, 18]. The purpose of this paper is to examine the current state of research in sustainable tourism development as it pertains to these indicators that point toward the sustainability of a destination. A substantial amount of literature exists regarding the problems involved in operationalizing the concepts of sustainable development and sustainable tourism [4, 2, 6, 15]. There is, however, evidence suggesting a positive movement toward not only an operational definition of sustainable tourism development, but feasible indicators as well. Several indicator frameworks have been developed by tourism researchers, some based on existing frameworks, such as the Limits of Acceptable Change [1], while others have been constructed according to the site-specific needs of a destination [18]. Research on indicators for sustainable tourism development can help tourism managers translate destination needs (areas in need of rehabilitation, protection, etc) into management actions. This paper will explore these differing indicators for sustainable tourism development, how managers and tourism developers can use these indicators to reach their sustainability goals, and determine the "next step" in the process of achieving sustainable tourism.
Keywords: sustainable tourism development, indicators.

Sustainable Tourism, F. D. Pineda, C. A. Brebbia & M. Mugica (Editors)

1 Introduction

Since the Bruntdland Report on sustainable development was published in 1987, and the concept of "sustainable tourism" was subsequently accepted into the lexicon of tourism dialogue, destinations and tour operators have hailed their movement toward sustainable plans for the future. Sustainable tourism has joined terms such as 'ecotourism,' 'nature-based tourism,' and 'alternative tourism' as an environmentally-friendly, culturally-friendly, and economically competitive alternative to mass tourism. Over the past decade, a substantial amount of so-called "sustainable tourism development planning" has occurred in a number of destinations. As these plans were penned, ideas of using *indicators* to monitor development and maintain sustainability were included, but rarely operationalized effectively. This problem was the result of a lack of agreement over what, exactly, "sustainable tourism development" means, and the resulting confusion over creating indicators for an undefined concept [1, 4, 13, 14, 18]. The purpose of this paper is to examine the current state of research in sustainable tourism development as it pertains to these indicators that point toward the sustainability of a destination.

2 Sustainable development and tourism

Sustainable development became a catch phrase among conservationists, environmentalists, and community developers as a concept that would, at its heart, allow us to "have our cake and eat it, too" [21]. Ideally, development would occur in such a way that "meets the needs of the present without compromising the ability of future generations to meet their own needs" [20]. According to Swarbrooke [17], sustainable development "was based on the idea that economic growth had to take place in a more ecologically sound and socially equitable manner." Hardy and Beeton [9] claim that sustainable development's origins are found in the convergence of economic development theory and environmentalism. As the concept evolved, there was a realization that sustainable development can be thought of as existing along a spectrum, from very weak to very strong, rather than as a rigid framework [10, 12]. While this evolution of thought on sustainable development has influenced the concept of sustainable tourism, researchers in the tourism field have been theorizing on the potential impacts of tourism on the environment and on host societies for decades [17]. It was not until 1997, when Agenda 21 saw its five-year review with the United Nations that the term "sustainable tourism" saw wider usage as a descriptive term for tourism that adhered to the principles of sustainable development [5, 19]. The two concepts appeared to fit well together, and the subsequent popularity of "sustainable tourism" followed closely behind that of "sustainable development."

Recently, authors in the tourism field have started to point out some fairly significant problems concerning the operational definitions of sustainable development and sustainable tourism. The concept of sustainability is criticized by many as vague and confusing. Berke and Conroy [2] conducted a comparative

Sustainable Tourism, F. D. Pineda, C. A. Brebbia & M. Mugica (Editors)

study of communities who actively use "sustainability" language in their strategic plans (using terms such as equity, equality, environmental protection, etc), and communities who do not include "sustainability" language. They found no significant differences over time between them. Cohen [6] points to certain dangers involved in the vagueness of the definitions of sustainable development and sustainable tourism. He contends that the imprecision of the term lends to its misuse by tourism entrepreneurs. This concern is echoed by Sirakaya et al. [15], who worry that the negative impacts of so-called sustainable tourism "seem to indicate business-as-usual, confirming the concerns raised by some tourism scholars." A second concern of Cohen's is that "the concept of sustainable tourism is frequently couched in apparently neutral, technical language of planning and management" [6]. Butler claims that a rigid look at the terms "sustainable" and "tourism" results in a relatively obvious definition: "tourism which is in a form which can maintain its viability for an indefinite period of time" [4].

Without a clear definition or conceptualization of sustainable tourism, there is only confusion regarding how to monitor the success of instituting a plan for sustainable tourism development [4, 14, 18]. Monitoring, according to Twining-Ward and Butler is:

> "...crucial to all sustainable development strategies as it provides the opportunity to assess the effectiveness of policies and actions, identifies the most successful and appropriate ones, and draws attention to most successful and appropriate ones, and draws attention to problem areas so that appropriate management responses are activated."

In a similar tone, Butler [4] claims that an absence of indicators (for residential impact, environmental quality, etc) renders the term "sustainability" meaningless. The question of "what is sustainability" is accompanied by questions of "what should tourism sustain" and "how do we measure sustainability." McCool et al. [14] in a 2001 study of tourism industry perceptions of indicators, found that there is wide-ranging inconsistency in the industry regarding what should be sustained, and even more of a "disconnect between preferences for what should be sustained by tourism and indicators that might measure progress toward this goal."

A standard, widely agreed upon definition of sustainability as it pertains to tourism may be unattainable for the time being. Hunter [12] reasoned that the concept of sustainability "is malleable and can be shaped to fit a spectrum of world views." He contends that this is not a disadvantage. While our definitions of sustainability may be broad and dynamic, a measurement of local definitions for the concept of sustainable tourism can be site specific and operationalized.

3 Indicators for sustainable tourism development

While the previous sections outline a somewhat pessimistic outlook in the literature regarding the success of sustainable tourism development, there is also

Sustainable Tourism, F. D. Pineda, C. A. Brebbia & M. Mugica (Editors)

evidence of hope regarding indicators of sustainability. Several studies suggest a movement toward not only finding operational definitions of sustainable tourism development, but feasible indicators as well. This section will explore current research being conducted in formulating indicators for sustainable tourism development, and provide examples of these efforts.

Some preliminary attempts at planning and monitoring sustainable tourism development were devised from concepts derived specifically for sustainable development. The Bellagio Principles – a set of sustainable development principles developed by the Rockefeller Foundation in 1996 – deal with four primary aspects of assessing progress toward sustainable development: enumerating clear goals for sustainability and practical definitions of those terms; merging a sense of an overarching system with specific, small scale issues; assessment of processes; and monitoring [8]. Other criteria for indicators were penned specifically for sustainable tourism development (see Table 1).

Table 1: Conditions for an ideal indicator [7,11].

- Be easy to identify and measure.
- Be functionally important in the ecosystem.
- Have a high imputed value.
- Be relatively sedentary.
- Have modest technological requirements.
- Be sensitive to the stress in question.
- Have mechanisms whose response should be understood.
- Be quick to respond.
- Be low in ambiguity.

A recent study conducted by Twining-Ward and Butler [18] utilizes the Bellagio Principles in an examination of the implementation of sustainable tourism development in the island nation of Samoa. The authors broke the process of indicator creation into one of first determining development themes, then objectives within each theme, followed by sub-objectives, and finally one or more indicators for each sub-objective. They derived 10 technical criteria from the literature (relevant, reliable, feasible, stable, trend, scope, historical, secondary, participatory, and simple) to screen indicators for their technical feasibility. If an indicator passed this process, it was screened additionally by an expert panel for relevancy. An example of this process is included in Table 2.

Following this process of indicator selection, study participants (expert panel and stakeholder groups) selected acceptable ranges for change in a process analogous to that of the Limits of Acceptable Change framework [16]. However, the authors applied the LAC process to this tourism setting in a manner similar to that used by Ahn, Lee, and Shafer [1]. Indicators were then taken into the field and used to measure current conditions against preferred conditions. The most critical step of the monitoring process, according to the authors, is "to establish a system whereby indicator results can actually be converted into management action." The monitoring process for Samoa resulted

Sustainable Tourism, F. D. Pineda, C. A. Brebbia & M. Mugica (Editors)

in 10 "priority areas" for action that required attention from tourism managers. A status report was another result of the process, and this document is being actively utilized, according to the authors, by the Samoan government to monitor tourism and determine management strategies.

Table 2: Example of technical screening table [18].

Theme	***Environment***				
OBJECTIVE	Encourage the sustainable management of land and in particular forest resources.				
Sub-objectives	Encourage the participation of village communities in conservation programs.		Promote the careful use of tourism as an income generating activity for conservation areas and other natural areas under protection.		
Indicator	Number of villages participating in land and forest conservation programs.	Amount of forest listed as 'critical' that is protected by law.	Proportion of protected areas gaining income from tourism.	Number of ecotourism activities in conser-vation areas.	Tourist visits to conserv-ation areas.
Criteria					
1. Relevant	✓	✓	✓	✓	✓
2. Reliable	✓	✓	✓	×	✓
3. Feasible	✓	✓	✓	✓	✓
4. Stable	✓	✓	×	✓	✓
5. Trend	✓	✓	✓	✓	✓
6. Scope	✓	✓	✓	✓	✓
7. RESULT	PASS	PASS	FAIL	FAIL	PASS
8. Historical	✓	✓			×
9. Secondary	✓	✓			✓
10. Participatory	✓	✓			✓
11. Simple	✓	✓			✓
TOTAL SCORE	4	3			3
RESULT	PASS	PASS			PASS

This study brought together a panel of experts (in ecology, visitor impacts, tourism management, etc), stakeholders, and the Samoan government to devise monitoring strategies based on site-specific indicators for tourism development. This process resulted in a status report on tourism in Samoa, as well as a set of guidelines for monitoring and management. This research can aid in the process of translating special needs (areas in need of rehabilitation, protection, development, etc.) into management actions. While the concept of sustainability may be difficult to translate into an operational definition, a broad definition of the term coupled with site-specific indicators may enable some sort of long-term, sustainable tourism product.

Sustainable Tourism, F. D. Pineda, C. A. Brebbia & M. Mugica (Editors)

References

[1] Ahn, B., Lee, B., & Shafer, C.S. Operationalizing sustainability in regional tourism planning: an application of the limits of acceptable change framework. *Tourism Management*, **23**, pp. 1 – 15, 2002.

[2] Berke, P., Conroy, M. Are we planning for sustainable development? *Journal of the American Planning Association*, **66(1)**, pp. 21-33, 2000.

[3] Butler, R.W. Tourism, environment, and sustainable development. *Environmental Conservation*, **18(3),** pp. 201 – 209, 1991.

[4] Butler, R.W. Sustainable tourism: A state-of-the-art review. *Tourism Geographies*, **1(1)**, pp. 7-25, 1999.

[5] Clarke, J. A framework of approaches to sustainable tourism. *Journal of Sustainable Tourism*, **5**, pp. 224 – 233, 1997.

[6] Cohen, E. Authenticity, equity, and sustainability in tourism. *Journal of Sustainable Tourism*, **10(4)**, pp. 267-276, 2002.

[7] Furley, P. Hughes, G. & Thomas, D. *Threshold, carrying capacity, and sustainable tourism: monitoring environmental change in the coastal zone of Belize*. Dept. of Geography, University of Edinburgh: Edinburgh, 1996.

[8] Hardi, P. Measurement and indicators program of the International Institute for Sustainable Development. *Sustainability Indicators: Report of the Project on Indicators of Sustainable Development*: *SCOPE Report No. 58,* eds. Moldan, B. and Billharz, B. John Wiley: Chichester, pp. 28 – 32, 1997.

[9] Hardy, A.L. & Beeton, R.J.S. Sustainable tourism or maintainable tourism: managing resources for more than average outcomes. *Journal of Sustainable Tourism*, **9(3)**, pp. 168 – 192, 2001.

[10] Hediger, W. Sustainable development and social welfare. *Ecological Economics*, **32**, pp. 481-492, 2000.

[11] Hughes, G. Environmental indicators. *Annals of Tourism Research*, **29(2)**, pp. 457 – 477, 2002.

[12] Hunter, C. Sustainable tourism as an adaptive paradigm. *Annals of Tourism Research*, **24(4)**, pp. 850-867, 1997.

[13] Ko, J.T.G. Assessing the progress of tourism sustainability. *Annals of Tourism Research*, **28(3)**, pp. 817 – 820. 2001.

[14] McCool, S.F., Moisey, R.N., & Nickerson, N.P. What should tourism sustain? The disconnect with industry perceptions of useful indicators. *Journal of Travel Research*, **40**, pp. 124 – 131, 2001.

[15] Sirakaya, E., Sasidharan, V., & Sonmez, S. Redefining ecotourism: the need for a supply side view. *Journal of Travel Research*, **38**, pp. 168 - 172, 1999.

[16] Stankey, G.H., Cole, D.N., Lucas, R. C. Peterson, M.E., & Frissell, S.S. *The limits of acceptable change (LAC) system for wilderness planning.* USDA, 1985.

[17] Swarbrooke, J. *Sustainable Tourism Management.* CAB International: New York, 1998.

Sustainable Tourism, F. D. Pineda, C. A. Brebbia & M. Mugica (Editors)

[18] Twining-Ward, L. & Butler, R. Implementing STD on a small island: development and use of sustainable tourism development indicators in Samoa. *Journal of Sustainable Tourism*, **10(5)**, pp. 363 – 387, 2002.
[19] United Nations. *Sustainable Development Issues, In United Nations Division for Sustainable Development.* Online. http://www.un.org /esa/sustdev/sdissues/tourism/tourism.htm.
[20] WCED. *Our Common Future.* Oxford University Press, 1987.
[21] Weaver, D.B. Introduction to Ecotourism (Chapter 1). *Ecotourism in the Less Developed World*, pp. 1-33. CAB International: New York, 1998.

Sustainable Tourism, F. D. Pineda, C. A. Brebbia & M. Mugica (Editors)

Theme trails and sustainable rural tourism – opportunities and threats

K. Meyer-Cech
Department of Spatial, Landscape and Infrastructure Sciences, Institute of Spatial Planning and Rural Development, University of Natural Resources and Applied Life Sciences, Vienna

Abstract

Theme trails are networks of attractions which are typical for a region and which are marketed together under a certain theme. In Austria the implementation of theme trails has become a popular means of sustainable tourism development in rural areas, for public authorities as well as for cultural and agricultural regional initiatives. The main objective of theme trails is to attract potential visitors into the region to raise the regional added value. At the same time they contribute to the preservation of the cultural heritage of the region - be it the diversified farm landscape, historic monuments or traditional handicrafts - and they are considerate to the natural environment, because they hardly call for the construction of any new facilities or infra-structures.

Based on the examination of Austrian case studies this paper identifies the conditions under which the implementation of theme trails can contribute to the development of sustainable tourism and where respective insufficiencies lie. Most theme trails represent a form of tourism that complies with the concept of sustainable development concerning social aspects as well as the natural environment. Yet great shortcomings can be found on the economic and organisational level: the development of theme trails in Austria must be called inflationary, in many cases the input of financial resources is inefficient and the quality of the tourist product is inadequate. This paper ends with a list of necessary measures on the national and regional levels to improve the implementation practise of theme trails, e.g. the need for national coordination of theme trails or the establishment of a seal of approval for theme trails which may only be awarded to initiatives that fulfil certain quality standards.
Keywords: theme trails, rural tourism, regional networks and co-operations.

Sustainable Tourism, F. D. Pineda, C. A. Brebbia & M. Mugica (Editors)

1 Introduction

Sustainable tourism aims at increasing the economic welfare of the inhabitants as well as contributing to their subjective well-being and cultural identity. It also wants to fulfil the needs of the tourists and to preserve the natural resources while at the same time maintaining the options of action of future generations (Müller et al. [1]). Theme trails seem to comply with several characteristics of sustainable tourism. They are networks of attractions which are typical for a region and which are marketed together under a certain theme. The main objective of theme trails is to attract potential visitors into the region to raise the regional added value. At the same time they contribute to the preservation of the cultural heritage of the region and they are regardful of the natural environment, because they hardly call for the construction of any new facilities or infra-structures.

In the last 20 years theme trails have become a popular means of promoting sustainable tourism for public authorities and regional initiatives in Austria, especially in economically less favoured rural areas. Since the end of the 1980s about three theme trails per year have been established in Austria. Today there are about 70 theme trails – be it heritage trails like the Iron Trail, be it trails based on products of the region like the famous Austrian wine roads – and still their number keeps on growing. But only a few actually are effective means of sustainable tourism development, because many theme trail initiatives find themselves in economically adverse circumstances. Reasons for this lie in the fierce contention of theme trails among each other and in shortcomings on the level of business management.

This paper identifies the conditions under which the implementation of theme trails can contribute to the development of sustainable tourism and where respective insufficiencies lie.

2 Methodology

The clarification of the terms sustainable tourism and theme trail is followed by an overview of theme trail networks in Austria concerning organisational structure, size and topics dealt with by the initiatives. The overview was sought through undertaking telephone interviews with tourist boards and regional development corporations. Five case studies were chosen for deeper examination, because they appeared to be the most economically promising, and according to the following criteria: being of average size for an Austrian theme trail (i.e. concerning an area of approximately 25 municipalities), having different themes, and presenting inter-sectoral networks (i.e. that stakeholders come from different economic branches and the cultural sector) (Meyer-Cech [2]). The focus of the examination lay on organisational and socio-economic matters. Aspects of tourist demand and ecological issues were not explicitly dealt with. The main sources of information were explorative interviews based on structured questions posed to managers or project leaders of the five case study theme trails. In addition to literature on sustainable tourism and regional

Sustainable Tourism, F. D. Pineda, C. A. Brebbia & M. Mugica (Editors)

development as well as regional co-operations and regional marketing, a further source of information was statistical data on the socio-economic situation of the five regions where the theme trail initiatives operate.

The listing of the results that theme trail initiatives strive for - to a large extent these comply with the requirements of sustainable tourism - is followed by an assessment of the strengths and weaknesses of theme trails concerning the sustainable regional development of tourism. The paper ends with suggestions for measures on the national and regional level to improve the implementation practise of theme trails.

3 Clarification of terms

3.1 Theme trail

Theme trails are regional initiatives that come into being around typical regional features. The implementation of a theme trail should contribute to valorising special regional assets, to increasing appreciation for them and to their preservation while making use of them commercially at the same time. From the organisational perspective theme trails are inter-sectoral networks of regional actors such as cultural initiatives, enterprises, semi-public and public authorities. According to the viewpoint of the tourism industry theme trails mainly are marketing instruments that should help to brand a region and to increase the number of potential guests. From the viewpoint of regional development theme trails should also have positive impacts on other economic sectors aside from tourism and should help to increase the regional added value. Further it is hoped that the implementation of theme trails contributes to immaterial goals such as strengthening the regional culture and identity (Meyer-Cech [2]).

3.2 Sustainable tourism

The question of tourism and sustainable development is closely linked to the concept of sustainable development that became part of international politics with the Brundtland report in 1987. Further milestones were the United Nations Conference for the Environment and Development in 1992, the World Conference on Sustainable Tourism in 1995 and the statement of international tourism organisations on how to apply the Agenda 21 to the travel and tourism industry in 1997. In 1999 the United Nations Conference on the Environment and Development also dealt with the issue of tourism and sustainable development.

Sustainable tourism is a form of tourism that strives to realise the principles of sustainable development. (The term *sustainable tourism* is used in this paper even though strictly speaking it is a confusing term, because tourism is just one branch of economy whereas the concept of sustainable development emphasises the fact that it encompasses all sectors of economy and all spheres of life.) (see Baumgartner and Röhrer [3])

Sustainable tourism aims at increasing the economic welfare of the

Sustainable Tourism, F. D. Pineda, C. A. Brebbia & M. Mugica (Editors)

inhabitants as well as contributing to their subjective well-being and cultural identity. It also wants to fulfil the needs of the tourists and to preserve the natural resources while at the same time maintaining the options of action of future generations (Müller et al. [1]). Murphy [4] specifically stresses the fact that tourism development needs to contribute to the well-being of the host community and that it is just one of several options of self-determined community development.

Baumgartner and Roehrer [3] follow these definitions in general, but they explicitly address issues of sustainable tourism on the regional level (this is relevant concerning theme trails, which are defined as regional initiatives in this paper), such as strengthening the cultural identity of the region, increasing the rate of people employed in the region, embedding tourism in the regional economic structure and creating new institutional structures for different forms of collaboration.

4 Theme trails in Austria

4.1 Dimensions

The term "trail" cannot be taken literally, as many theme trails are a network of attractions rather than a linear route. A theme trail symbolically connects tourist attractions, municipalities and other actors, and it helps to brand and market a region. Due to the netlike structure of theme trails in Austria it is hard to tell their average length. If one takes the greatest distance between two tourist attractions or two involved municipalities the average length lies between 20 and 100 kilometres. Of the approximately 70 theme trails in Austria 90% cover a region of up to 30 municipalities. The remaining 10% are either national trails that spread over the whole country or even cross national trails.

The five case studies cover an area of approximately 25 municipalities and 60.000 inhabitants. The administrational units theme trails have to work with are small, which adds to the challenge of managing them. The level of local government is organised on a small scale in Austria: there are 2,355 municipalities, 97% of them have less than 10,000 inhabitants. Almost 40% of municipalities have only 1.000 to 2.000 inhabitants.

4.2 Covered themes

The themes covered by Austrian theme trails can be divided into two main categories. Almost two thirds of theme trails are food trails. The remaining third are trails that deal with aspects of cultural history. Food trails focus on such aspects as an agricultural product with its typical cultural landscape including regional architecture, on special methods of cultivating agricultural products and processing them into foods and drinks, as well as on regional traditions that are connected to the agricultural product, e.g. the festive cattle drive from the alpine pastures into the valley in September. The most prominent sub-group of food trails in Austria are wine roads. Other agricultural products dealt with by food trails are apples, cider, pumpkins, milk and cheese.

Sustainable Tourism, F. D. Pineda, C. A. Brebbia & M. Mugica (Editors)
© 2004 WIT Press, www.witpress.com, ISBN 1-85312-724-8

The cultural history trails may focus on castles, historic trade routes, such as the Amber or the Iron Road, or on traditional industries as is the case in the wood or textile trails.

In some cases the classification of food and cultural history trails is not clear. Some cultural history trails for instance feature associations of restaurants that offer regionally typical dishes, e.g. the Iron Trail restaurants or the restaurants of the Weavers' Road.

Summing up one can say that the eponymous theme is the uniting bracket for a set of tourist attractions and it helps to improve the marketing efforts and the successful positioning of a region. Yet the uniting effects of a common theme will not manifest if the theme is occupied too often on the over-regional level due to imitators or if it does not fulfil the expectations it arouses, i.e. when the theme cannot be experienced by the tourist due to a lack of visibility and entertaining elements.

4.3 Theme trail networks

Theme trails are networks of actors that come from different sectors of the economy as well as from the cultural sector. The analysis of those organisations that are in charge of the theme trail lead to the following results:

Cultural initiatives are often the main actors in cultural history theme trails. For example the origin of the Austrian Iron Trail, an initiative that interprets the history of mining the ore and processing iron, can be traced to local historians who prevented the demolition of old forges in the course of a construction project. Another important factor in cultural history theme trails are *museums*, whose efforts in preserving and interpreting the cultural heritage coincide with the goals of the theme trail.

Farm enterprises are strongly involved in food trails. Many theme trails, such as the Cheese Trail Bregenzerwald (Bregenzerwald is the name of a region in the West of Austria) or most wine roads, originated from producer and marketing associations for agricultural products that established a link to the tourism sector.

Potentially *tourism enterprises* are important partners in theme trail networks. Gastronomic enterprises usually are among the members of the network. In many cases they are not just a complement to the thematic tourist offer but rather an integrated part of the theme trail concept, e.g. they process the name giving product to special dishes, often according to historic and regionally typical recipes, and market them effectively. Surprisingly accommodation is involved in theme trail networks only in exceptional cases, e.g. when a theme restaurant rents out rooms. Usually the point of contact between theme trail members and accommodation is limited to the membership of accommodation in the tourist board, one of whose tasks it is to support the marketing efforts of the theme trail. This fact disagrees with the aim of theme trail initiatives to prolong the length of stay of the visitors and to increase the amount of overnight stays.

Trade and industrial enterprises are the main actors in theme trails that focus on a regionally important industry or trade, such as the textile industry or wood processing.

In some cases a *regional development association*, i.e. an association of

Sustainable Tourism, F. D. Pineda, C. A. Brebbia & M. Mugica (Editors)
© 2004 WIT Press, www.witpress.com, ISBN 1-85312-724-8

municipalities on a voluntary basis with the goal to improve the quality of life in the region, is the organisation in charge of a theme trail initiative. This usually is the case when the reason for tourist development is more a matter of public concern rather than of managerial economics, for example because it is an economically less favoured area and tourist infrastructure is lacking.

Regional tourist boards play an important part in the marketing of theme trails, as their main responsibilities lie in communicating the image of the region, in stimulating a positive attitude towards tourism among the inhabitants and in developing a tourist offer. Regional tourist boards are formed according to the provincial tourism legislation, they are financed by contributions of the municipalities of the respective region. In some theme trails the regional tourist board is the main contact for potential guests, other trails have a clear division of tasks between the tourist board, which hands out information, especially about accommodation, and the organisation in charge of the theme trail, which looks after the guests as regards content.

5 Target results

The great variety of actors in theme trail networks reflects in the different results that they wish to achieve by their involvement. The main target results that theme trails are hoped to contribute to are listed below. They correspond to the above mentioned criteria of sustainable tourism.

Economic welfare of the inhabitants: The thematic offer of theme trails should help to create a marketable image for the region, induce visitor flows and create economic impacts in the region due to expenditures of the tourists. The underlying concept of theme trails is to enable benefits for a large range of actors, of municipalities, enterprises and individuals. From the viewpoint of business economics a concentration of tourist attractions would make more sense than spreading them along a route, but theme trails should help to develop a whole region and thereby contribute to reducing regional disparities.

The extent of economic impact induced by theme trails may vary. The distance visitors come from and their length of stay vary, often depending on the dimensions of the theme trail and the budget available for marketing activities. Some theme trails try to position themselves on the international market and aim at increasing the number of overnight stays whereas others merely focus on day tourism and local recreation.

Most theme trails in Austria can be found in economically less favoured areas, where it is hoped that they will have positive effects on the employment situation, not just in the tourist sector. Tourism helps to secure existing jobs, perhaps even create new ones. Promotional money for theme trail initiatives, e.g. for the renovation of historic buildings, and private investments lead to an increase of economic activity in the regional hospitality and accommodation sector as well as in other sectors.

As yet hardly any research has been done concerning the economic effects of theme trails. Some insight can be gained by the evaluation of a provincial exhibition on the topic of iron that was organised in 1998 by an association

Sustainable Tourism, F. D. Pineda, C. A. Brebbia & M. Mugica (Editors)

belonging to the Austrian Iron Trail (Baaske et al. [5]). The authors of this survey found out that the employment effects of the exhibition were about 1,300 person-years excluding honorary work. Further they could prove that the two obvious sectors tourism and the construction trade (many historic buildings were renovated) benefited a lot (these sectors contributed 15 to 20% each to the regional value added), but that also other sectors had economic benefits.

Strengthening the cultural identity of the region: Cultural history theme trails aim at preserving precious cultural heritage, be it the diversified farm landscape, historic monuments or traditional handicrafts, and to increase the appreciation for it among inhabitants and visitors. Leaders of theme trails state that often the special regional feature which later becomes the centre of marketing activities is viewed as something quite normal or even of minor value by the inhabitants. The attention regional assets receive through tourist activities and the efforts in interpretation can enormously improve their public image and thereby foster the self-confidence of the inhabitants of the region and develop an appreciation of sense of place. Two examples for the initial disregard and later pride can be found concerning the hard cheese in the Cheese Trail Bregenzerwald as well as concerning iron and the history of mining in the Austrian Iron Trail.

Creating new institutional structures for different forms of collaboration: Theme trail networks are examples of new structures that enable collaboration between actors of different economic sectors, cultural institutions and public authorities. Heintel et al. ([6] p.6) states that cooperation or non-cooperation on location are signs of the functioning or non-functioning of regional development. Those theme trails that actively contribute to the social and economic life of a region and that hold entertaining experiences for the potential visitors, are usually based on networks of various actors. In contrast there are many tourist routes that are promoted as theme trails, but that are in fact only route descriptions in a brochure or a sign posted trail of attractions without an underlying network of actors. In general these routes do not contribute to the tourism development of a region.

Another finding is that inter-sectoral theme trail networks seem to have more impact on the socio-economic regional development than theme trails whose actors come from only one economic sector or from only one field, such as monument conservation.

Preserving natural resources: The ecological dimension of sustainable tourism is not prominent with theme trails, but food trails do contribute to the preservation of special cultural landscapes with their scenic and biological diversity, for example alpine pastures like in the Cheese Trail Bregenzerwald or orchards like in the Cider Trail. Theme trails usually are small scale forms of rural tourism with scarce visitor flows, and which make use of already existing resources and infrastructure. That is why the impacts of theme trails on the ecosystem are comparatively low. From an economic point of view this fact may represent a disadvantage, e.g. if the length of stay cannot be increased due to lacking accommodation capacities.

Sustainable Tourism, F. D. Pineda, C. A. Brebbia & M. Mugica (Editors)

6 Conclusions

Theme trails can contribute to the development of sustainable tourism in rural areas, but not all theme trails do so automatically. Austrian theme trails comply with the criteria of a sustainable tourism development in varying degrees, one of the reasons being strong differences in the quality of the offered tourist product. The evaluation of Austrian theme trails lead to the following results.

6.1 Strengths

Bundling of existing regional resources: Theme trails make use of endogenous resources and activate them. Regional resources can mean the cultural landscape with its agricultural products, cultural assets or special skills of the regional populace. Theme trails bundle them and give them a direction of impact by providing a common theme.

Imaging of a region: Theme trails contribute to the positioning of a region, helping the region to distinguish itself from other regions and to create a unique tourist offer.

Increasing the regional value added: The thematic offers of theme trails bring many day and weekend tourists into the region, which has positive effects on the tourism industry. Consumption of services in the area of the theme trail leads to direct and indirect impacts on the regional value added and employment situation.

Compensation of competitive disadvantages: Theme trail cooperations help to compensate the competitive disadvantages that result from the ownership structure of the Austrian (tourism) economy, in which small and medium sized enterprises dominate - for example 70% of the accommodation facilities are privately run, 70% of the farms are smaller than 30 hectares. By collaborating actors reach the critical mass that is necessary for the theme trail to be noticed by potential guests and to become attractive for longer stays. Working together in a network also makes marketing activities more effective.

6.2 Weaknesses

Inflationary appearance of theme trails: Too many regions have “discovered” theme trails as an instrument of sustainable tourism development. Since the end of the 1980ies about three theme trails per year are being implemented per year in Austria. This extremely dynamic development can only be called inflationary. The range of theme trails has become quite unclear for potential guests, decision-makers and entrepreneurs. As a result there is increased competition among municipalities and regions, because the competitive advantage a branding of the region usually brings compared to other rural areas has been lost due to the oversupply of theme trail initiatives. Another result of this development is a levelling of the tourist offer.

Lacking minimum standards: Quite differing tourist products are offered under the term “theme trail”. Almost 25% of Austrian theme trails are just route descriptions in a brochure and of these not even all have been sign posted. Aside

Sustainable Tourism, F. D. Pineda, C. A. Brebbia & M. Mugica (Editors)

from very few exceptions theme trail initiatives do not follow any common quality standards. Therefore many theme trails lack professionalism concerning the components of the tourist offer as well as concerning the interpretation of the theme.

Inefficient use of resources: There are two main reasons why public authorities and entrepreneurs do not use financial as well as human resources efficiently. Firstly, the life span of theme trails is often closely linked to the duration of the public subsidies. When the public support measure ends relevant activities of the theme trail often cannot be kept up anymore. Secondly, each theme trail initiative, metaphorically speaking, reinvents the wheel. An organised exchange of experience does not take place between the theme trail regions.

Tension and conflict: Collaboration in a theme trail network brings along tension and conflict among the network actors that impair the quality of the tourist offer. Difficulties in collaboration may result from economic competition, personal conflicts and political or administrational barriers.

6.3 Recommendations

Especially for rural areas the implementation of theme trails could be an opportunity to develop a sustainable form of tourism. Yet the following points have to be taken into consideration and implemented, otherwise the theme trail boom might backfire resulting in a wasteful and therefore unsustainable use of resources and in dashed hopes.

Nationwide coordination – establishment of a round table for theme trails: There is an urgent call for action concerning the development and implementation of a national strategy and general normative guidelines for theme trails. The establishment of a round table for theme trails is recommended at this point, which should host experts from the economy, the environmental sector, culture, politics, administration and science on the one hand and from the theme trail regions on the other hand. Further it has to be clarified which public authority or which institution - e.g. ministry of the environment, ministry of commerce, national tourism organisation - should take the leading responsibility concerning support and coordination of theme trails.

Formulating minimum standards: Theme trails should meet a minimum standard concerning the quality of the offered products and services and concerning entertaining and educational elements. The criteria defining the minimum standard should pertain to the concept of sustainable tourism, which means that aside from aspects of business economics also those of environmental and social compatibility have to be taken into consideration. There must be a superordinate institution, such as the above mentioned round table, that is in charge of developing a set of minimum standards and checking if these standards are abided by.

Defining eligibility - bundling of resources: Parallel to the formulation of a set of minimum standards criteria for the eligibility of theme trails concerning public support measures have to be defined in order to guarantee an efficient use of resources. Aside from criteria relating to quality it is important to name spatial criteria. It does not make sense to implement a theme trail in every region. In

Sustainable Tourism, F. D. Pineda, C. A. Brebbia & M. Mugica (Editors)

accordance with the integrative approach of sustainable development inter-sectoral theme trail networks should be favoured.

Making the management more professional: Conflicts and tension in collaboration can only be alleviated by a more professional management of the theme trail, e.g. establishing a permanently operating and adequately staffed head office.

Establishing the term "theme trail" as a seal of approval: If theme trails are supposed to contribute to the development of sustainable tourism the term "theme trail" must become a seal of approval, that will only be awarded to those regional initiatives that meet a minimum set of quality standards. Awarding the theme trail title must follow strict rules and a scheme that has been harmonised nationwide. Establishing an umbrella brand name, such as "theme trail Austria", could also help small initiatives with limited budgets to position themselves on the international tourism market. But similar theme trails have to look for different thematic focus points under this umbrella brand name, so as not to harm each other by too fierce competition.

References

[1] Müller, H., Krippendorf J., & Kramer B., *Freizeit und Tourismus: Eine Einführung in Theorie und Politik.* 8th ed. Berner Studien zu Freizeit und Tourismus, ed. Forschungsinstitut für Freizeit und Tourismus Univ. Bern, FIF: Bern, 1999.

[2] Meyer-Cech, K., *Themenstraßen als regionale Kooperationen und Mittel zur touristischen Entwicklung - fünf österreichische Beispiele*, thesis at the Institut für Raumplanung und Ländliche Neuordnung, Universität für Bodenkultur Wien: Wien, 2003.

[3] Baumgartner, C. & Röhrer C., *Nachhaltigkeit im Tourismus: Umsetzungsperspektiven auf regionaler Ebene*, Manz: Wien, 1998.

[4] Murphy, P.E., *Tourism: A Community Approach.* 4th ed., International Thomson Business Press: Oxford, 1997.

[5] Baaske, W., Moshammer, M., Sulzbacher, R. & Edelbauer, B., *LA 98 Evaluation der OÖ Landesausstellung 1998 - Studie i.A. der OÖ Landesregierung.* ed. STUDIA-Studienzentrum für interantionale Analysen: Schlierbach, 2000.

[6] Heintel, M., Perspektive 2000: Von einer eigenständigen zu einer professionalisierten Regionalentwicklung. *Pro Regio Lokale Agenda 21 im ländlichen Raum - zwischen Nachhaltigkeit und Modernisierung - Zeitschrift für Eigenständige Regionalentwicklung*, **24-25(14)**, p. 7-12, 2000.

Sustainable Tourism, F. D. Pineda, C. A. Brebbia & M. Mugica (Editors)

Section 4
Ecotourism

Challenges for balancing conservation and development through ecotourism: insights and implications from two Belizean case studies

S. E. Alexander & J. L. Whitehouse
Department of Environmental Studies, Baylor University, USA

Abstract

As an idealized alternative to mass tourism, ecotourism seeks balance between economic benefits for resident hosts and protection of the natural resource base against environmental costs. Yet these ambiguous descriptors fail to consider what is to be sustained, at what levels, and for whom. Nor is the fundamental contradiction resolved between the demand for economic growth to ameliorate poverty-induced ecological destruction and environmental conservation that inhibits economic growth. If ecotourism is to induce sustainable development, it must be ecologically sound, culturally sensitive, and economically viable. Using data from two Belizean case studies, this paper challenges optimistic assessments concerning the impacts of ecotourism and points to the leakage of profits back to tourist-source countries, high emigration rates, and a tourism industry that is likely more "brown" than "green" Even though ecotourists in Belize tend to be affluent and spend more money than "mass tourists" leakages persist, local multipliers are low, and some natural resources are continuously threatened. If ecotourism is to support appropriate development, it should accelerate economic growth but also promote sound livelihood opportunities for local populations while simultaneously braking against environmental costs. How one defines these relationships and how communities work to achieve a balance between seemingly disparate goals is critically important to the process of using ecotourism as a development strategy. Given its recent commitment to ecotourism, Belize offers a unique opportunity to study local models and explore sustainable human-ecosystems in the context of this newly-developing industry.
Keywords: ecotourism development, economic benefits, environmental costs, social impacts, Belize.

Sustainable Tourism, F. D. Pineda, C. A. Brebbia & M. Mugica (Editors)

1 Introduction

Ecotourism is rapidly expanding and becoming increasingly more popular Weinberg *et al* [1]. In 1999, 652 million tourists travelled to other countries accumulating over $550 billion in global tourism receipts. Accounting for approximately eight percent of total export earnings of goods and services worldwide, the industry has great potential to generate foreign exchange for development, thereby explaining developing countries' aggressive pursuit of economic growth through tourism Schlevkov [2].

As an idealized alternative to mass tourism, ecotourism seeks balance between economic benefits for resident hosts and environmental costs so that the natural resource base is sustained for the future. However, such ambiguous descriptors fail to consider what is to be sustained, at what levels, and for whom Wall [3]. Nor is the fundamental contradiction resolved between the demand for economic growth to ameliorate poverty-induced ecological destruction and environmental conservation that inhibits economic growth Redclift [4]. If ecotourism can induce sustainable development, it must be ecologically sustainable, culturally sensitive, and economically viable Wall [3,5].

Ecotourism can contribute to positive changes in local communities: increases in jobs Weinberg *et al* [1]; ecosystem preservation Stem *et al* [6]; protection of indigenous cultures and peoples Kerr [7]; and social, political, economic, and psychological empowerment of local communities Scheyvens [8]. In contrast, many businesses consider the promotion of tourism participation and the minimization of visitation impacts to be potentially conflicting objectives Farrell and Marion [9]. In order for such businesses to maintain profitability, it is essential to incorporate a balance between economic benefits, environmental costs, and social and cultural appropriateness Wall [3,5].

Ecotourism is usually tied to protected areas Wall [5], and in principle, reconciles the contradiction between economic development and environmental conservation Wallace and Pierce [10]. Yet local populations near or within protected areas frequently bear the cost of protection through denied resource access while receiving few benefits in return Durbin and Ralambo [11]. Indeed, host populations, tourists, the tourism industry, and environmentalists have mutual interests in ensuring that tourism development is sustainable Cater [12].

Using data from two Belizean case studies, this paper identifies challenges faced by local communities as they struggle to seek balance between conservation principles and economic development policies centred on ecotourism. The Tourism Impact Assessment (TIA) method, by Alexander and Gibson [13], was used in this research to evaluate the social and economic benefits of tourism at the household level and community and environmental well-being over the long term.

2 Ecotourism as sustainable development

2.1 Economic viability

The basic premise of ecotourism is to strive for sustainable community development Weinberg *et al* [1]. Researchers have found that ecotourism

Sustainable Tourism, F. D. Pineda, C. A. Brebbia & M. Mugica (Editors)

facilitates economic growth, minimizes leakage by relying on local labour and commodities, increases employment opportunities, and generates more income in remote areas Cater [12] where ideally, it operates on a small-scale around locally-owned businesses and activities Weaver [14]. Foreign investment in ecotourism businesses and sites in the developing countries is becoming highly lucrative Cater [15].

Conversely, some researchers question such optimistic assessments of ecotourism and point to the leakage of profits back to tourists' countries of origin Brown [16]; the tendency to benefit only large tourism firms and corporations Cater [15]; inflated food prices; local communities' adjusting to a world that is based on monetary terms Dearden [17]; and visitor dissatisfaction which equates to little economic gain Inskeep [18]. In Belize, it is estimated that 90 percent of all coastal developments are foreign owned. As a result, prices of land, property, and food are oftentimes too inflated for local residents Cater [15].

Boo [19] expresses a concern for local economic dependency on ecotourism, because it is an unstable source of income susceptible to factors outside of their control, such as fluctuating politics, weather conditions, and volatile currency exchange rates. Furthermore, once a destination is established and highly profitable, it attracts more developers Tisdell [20]. As the area becomes saturated with ecotourism businesses, the profits of the original operators decline. Also, if the airline and hotel accommodations are foreign-owned, Britton [21] estimates that a mere 22 to 25 percent of an all-inclusive tour price goes to the local economy.

2.2 Environmental consequences

There are two major approaches in measuring environmental protection through tourism: protecting the environment *for* the tourism industry and protecting the environment *from* the tourism industry Cohen [22]. Ecotourism challenges the mass tourism industry by potentially supporting conservation of the natural environment with funding for management of the area, education of the protected area for tourists and local communities, limiting number of visitors, and construction of facilities that minimize impact Tisdell [20]. In western Sichuan, China, Fang [23] found ecotourism to be successful in protecting the natural environment. Managers of the area took measures to effectively control logging, encourage sound energy use, and enforce visitor rationing policies, all of which in turn resulted in a 6.7 million hectare increase of forested area with a vegetation cover of nearly 90 percent.

Despite its motives of resource conservation and sustainability, ecotourism persists in raising environmental challenges, including: contamination in terms of waste, traffic, and noise Weinberg *et al* [1]; loss of "ecological integrity" of highly visited areas Obua [24]; and increased unsustainable pressure on resources Tabatchnaia-Tamarisa *et al* [25]. These challenges exist because oftentimes ecotourism destinations are unusually sensitive places that have limited ability to withstand excessive use; travel is likely to occur at critical times (e.g., during mating or breeding season); unknown and unexplored relationships between volumes of use and multi-layered environmental impacts;

Sustainable Tourism, F. D. Pineda, C. A. Brebbia & M. Mugica (Editors)

and "en route impact" from traveling to the site (e.g., consuming resources for planes) contributes to global climate change Wall [3].

2.3 Social appropriateness

Sociocultural impacts of ecotourism development include: the “demonstration effect” Dearden [17]; encouragement of drugs NDACC [26]; increases in crime rates van der Borg *et al* [27]; and local aggression toward tourists and managers of protected areas Farrell and Marion [9]. Dearden [17] identified environmental and sociocultural consequences of trekkers in northern Thailand. Bamboo stands, used to construct rafts, were depleted; there were inadequate facilities for disposal of human waste; and the “demonstration effect” was in full force where tribes learned that their traditional dress was worth cash and sold it in the tourist good markets.

Another sociocultural impact is the unfair acquisition of land to develop national park systems and ecotourism sites Kirkpatrick [28]. Local and indigenous people are dispossessed of land they have inhabited for generations. The Aboriginal people of Tasmania lost their land that was eventually protected as a national park system. They recently regained some of the land after intense public debate and escalated media attention.

Though clearly in the minority, some researchers have found positive social impacts of tourism. Today, in the Amazon rainforest of Ecuador, visitors hike in the rainforest with members of the Huaorani group and are taught about aspects of life in the area Kerr [7]. In return, the Huaorani ask that visitors raise awareness at home about their fight to protect their forestland and culture from the oil industry.

3 Ecotourism development in Belize

Belize’s tourism industry began in the mid-1960s when the world’s second largest barrier reef came to the attention of scuba divers. Today, roughly 43% of Belize’s land and marine resources have protected status CSO [29]. After 20 years as a diving destination, Belize entered a golden period of tourism growth in the late 1980s [30]. Arrivals grew from 77,542 in 1991 to 195,995 in 2000 BTB [31]. In 1996, Belize’s tourism industry accounted for $125.4 million, or 17.5% of total GDP CSO [32]. In the early to mid-1990s, the government chose to focus on the development of what was called “eco-cultural” tourism at that time, promoting the country’s natural and archaeological resources.

In 1999, the Belizean government passed the National Tourism Development Policy which acknowledged *responsible tourism* as the key guiding principle for tourism development. The ethical practices defining responsible tourism include: a proactive approach by stakeholders and partners in the sector to develop, market, and manage the industry; environmental stewardship; environmentally-based tourism activities; local participation in decision-making processes about tourism; and respect for guests and between guests and hosts [30].

Sustainable Tourism, F. D. Pineda, C. A. Brebbia & M. Mugica (Editors)

One noteworthy initiative, viewed as a model for other developing countries, is the Protected Area Conservation Trust (PACT) which oversees management of revenue generated by a conservation fee added to the airport departure tax charged to all foreign tourists. The fund is used for projects related to biodiversity protection, cultural heritage preservation, and community-based ecotourism ventures Honey [33]. As part of this initiative, the Ministry of Tourism supports development of community-based ecotourism projects Alexander [34,35].

4 Research design and methods

The data presented in this paper were collected as part of a larger research project conducted in Belize and Costa Rica from June 2001 through May 2002. This research examined the impacts of ecotourism on household livelihood security and vulnerability in four tourism-based communities paired with four non-tourism based communities.

Using participant observation, key informant interviews, and household surveys, the results presented in this paper include qualitative and quantitative data whose interpretations rely heavily on direct participation of informants. Key informant interviews were conducted with community leaders and individuals involved in various tourism industries. This information was used to finalize the Household Survey comprised of two parts: Part 1 was administered during the low tourist season in 2001 and collected information on household composition, basic demographics, migration, and employment histories. A total of 68 Part One Surveys were completed in Placencia and 188 in San Ignacio.

Part Two of the Survey was conducted during the high tourist season in 2002 (January-April). Part Two elicited information on the various components of household livelihood security, including nutritional status of children, health conditions of household members, food availability and access issues, school enrollment rates, adult education levels, employment opportunities, economic security issues, and participation in various types of social networks. Specific data were also collected on household members' perceptions of the impacts tourism is having on themselves, their families, their community, and their immediate physical environs. Fifty-seven Part Two Surveys were completed in Placencia and 163 in San Ignacio.

4.1 Site selection

Located at the top of an 11-mile peninsula and approximately 40 miles south of Dangriga along the coast, *Placencia* is one of the oldest continuously inhabited villages in Belize. Legends purport that English buccaneers founded the village in the early 1600s; artifacts discovered in the area suggest Placencia was the location of several intense battles between Spanish and British sailors Mahler and Wotkyns [36].

In this century, Placencia has been a fishing village and today's permanent population consists mostly of Creoles but the numbers of North Americans,

Sustainable Tourism, F. D. Pineda, C. A. Brebbia & M. Mugica (Editors)

Garifunas, and Hispanics are on the rise. Average household size is 3.95 people; average age of the head of the household is 45 and the average adult level of education/household is approximately 11 years (equivalent of "some high school"). The most prevalent household type is the nuclear family (52.6%).

A variety of tourism opportunities are available from Placencia. The South Water Cayes, Laughing Bird Caye, the Sapodilla Cayes, and Glovers Reef are all easily accessible for diving and snorkeling, and inland day trips to the Cockscomb Jaguar Sanctuary and the Monkey River area are also available. Consequently, a variety of types of tourists visit the area – ranging from those who prefer the exclusive resort to the low budget backpacker. Regardless, the social atmosphere is relatively relaxed and villagers report little conflict between hosts and guests.

San Ignacio town, the administrative center for Cayo District, lies on the west side of the Macal River approximately 72 miles southwest of Belize City. At the turn of the 20th century, San Ignacio was established as a logging centre. Today, the town relies on cattle ranching, tourism, and small retail businesses Hoffman [37]. Average household size is 4.48 people; the average age of the head of the household is roughly 43 and the mean level of education for all adults in the household is 9.49 years. Approximately 70% of households are comprised of nuclear families.

Over the last decade, ecotourism has come to be San Ignacio's primary industry. The main attractions luring tourists to the area include the Mountain Pine Ridge Forest Reserve and a number of significant Maya ruins – Xunantunich, Cahal Pech, El Pilar and Caracol in Belize, and Tikal in the eastern Petén of Guatemala. Canoeing, tubing, caving, hiking and horseback riding along the Belize River, are all readily accessible from San Ignacio.

5 Data presentation

As reported by the residents of both study communities, the impacts tourism has had on their lives have been diverse and intense in nature. The following discussion provides a summary of critical responses made by residents when asked to comment on the various ways tourism has impacted their families and their communities.

5.1 Economic impacts

The most cited economic benefits of tourism are that it provides jobs, additional income, and opportunities for entrepreneurs, as shown in table 1. One longstanding concern in Belize has been that tourism mainly benefits foreign investors while local Belizeans are burdened by inflated land and consumer prices. With few domestic industries, a limited arts and crafts tradition, and with most of its investment in foreign hands, the tourism industry has been plagued by the lack of multiplier effects Barry [38].

Placencia is following in the footsteps of San Pedro (Ambergris Caye) where the tourism industry was birthed in the 1960s. While the population may be

Sustainable Tourism, F. D. Pineda, C. A. Brebbia & M. Mugica (Editors)
 ISBN 1-85312-724-8

better off than it was several decades ago, the encroachment of foreigners into the tourism sector has caused land and property values to skyrocket. Even though there are still family-owned businesses, much of the upper-end tourism dollar is controlled by American, Canadian and European investors.

Table 1: Local Perceptions of Tourism Impacts (all figures indicate the percent of affirmative responses).

Variable	Placencia	San Ignacio
Has tourism changed…		
…family life?	63.2	37.4
…your community?	91.8	90.2
…the environment?	75.4	58.9
How has tourism changed…		
…family life?		
• Employment	53.5	80.3
• No time for family	8.8	0
• Don't want to have anything to do with tourists	0	27.9
…your community?		
• More job opportunities	15.4	51.0
• More money	19.2	34.0
• More businesses	19.2	36.1
• Better economy	0	9.5
• More people	11.5	0
…the environment?		
• Destruction of natural resources	34.9	2.1
• Overcrowding	25.6	4.2
• More buildings	25.6	8.3
• Villages are cleaner	23.3	55.2
• Increases in air and water pollution	18.6	2.1

The lack of multiplier effects in San Ignacio is not as pronounced. Belizeans resent the all-inclusive tour, booked through the foreign-owned agency, while little money is spent in San Ignacio. Complicating this feeling is the fact that the government does not support local involvement in tourism and foreigners are able to secure permits for tourism-based businesses with greater ease than Belizeans.

There is no doubt that tourism has brought more businesses, and in turn, more employment and economic security to residents of Placencia. In this community, 59.7% have an occupation they would directly link to tourism. Roughly 64% of households report they are always able to pay their monthly expenses while 7% report they are never able to do so. In Placencia, approximately 58% of households report they have savings and 54% indicate they have given money to other family members over the course of the last year. Fifty-six percent of households report they have secured credit within the last year, most typically from a credit union; 21 % were borrowing to help rebuild homes and businesses after Hurricane Iris.

Sustainable Tourism, F. D. Pineda, C. A. Brebbia & M. Mugica (Editors)

Beyond these benefits, people cite an array of problems, from not benefiting at all to a destruction of family, community, the environment, and a loss of privacy. Many also feel that tourism has destroyed the fishing industry. Few young men want to fish; most want to be tour guides or dive masters. Older residents blame the protected status of the marine reserves for helping to destroy the livelihood of the older fishermen who are physically unable to make the transition to tour guide or dive master.

A similar trend is occurring in San Ignacio but Belizeans are not being shut out of the industry to the same extent. While ecotourism is the mainstay of the economy, the economic base is more diversified. The most significant change has been the transition from agriculture and timber to tourism. Only 19% of sampled households have an occupation they would directly link to tourism. Roughly 39% of households report they are always able to pay their monthly expenses while almost 16% report they are never able to do so. Almost 59% of households report they have savings but only 32.5% indicate they have given money to other family members over the course of the last year. As well, 13.5% of households report they have secured credit within the last year, most typically from a bank or credit union. The purpose for the loan ranged from building a house to paying bills or schooling costs, to borrowing for food and/or medical expenses.

5.2 Environmental impacts

Tourism has definitely contributed to more environmental awareness and division of responsibility to address environmental problems. The Belizean government was skeptical about conservation five years ago, but today, they strongly support conservation efforts. Both communities are located near a number of significant protected areas – terrestrial, riparian and marine.

Garbage disposal, disposal of raw sewage, the disappearing mangroves, the explosive growth in population and building, and the proliferation of marinas and charter boats are all environmental issues of concern to residents of Placencia, as shown in table 1.

The village is located at the end of a long but narrow peninsula and has to manage its own garbage, including the garbage that charter boats and tourists leave behind. Residents are most concerned that the septic system is over-taxed and no longer practical for a village with a growing population. There are no laws to regulate the current practice of dumping raw sewage in the lagoon.

Mangroves are also disappearing as a result of the proliferation of marinas on the peninsula. Several full service marinas have been built recently and one of the newer and larger resorts has secured a permit to build a canal separating the peninsula from the mainland completely, creating an island.

In San Ignacio, residents have commented on increased congestion, increases in water and air pollution, and increases in noise pollution. They are concerned that more land is being cleared for business construction as well as roads. Tourism is also cited in San Ignacio as a contributing cause to increased levels of air pollution. Increases in demands for transportation services have meant more vehicles. Given fuel prices, more people use vehicles that burn diesel. Increases

Sustainable Tourism, F. D. Pineda, C. A. Brebbia & M. Mugica (Editors)

in demands for electricity necessitated building the hydroelectric dam located upriver from San Ignacio. Parallel to the growing tourism industry, population size has increased – the two trends combined have increased demands for air conditioning and electricity.

5.3 Social and cultural impacts

Ecotourism has changed social life in these communities significantly. More people are more highly educated. Educated women are working, and most people have more money than they did a decade ago. At the same time, people are abandoning their culture. The traditional Creole language has changed since the growth of tourism. It is spoken everyday but they utilize more American English words. Tourism has impacted the way people dress. People are eating different foods, watching cable television, and abandoning their traditional Belizean music for rap and rock and roll. The movement to processed packaged foods is of particular concern considering the high rate of Type-II diabetes among both men and women in Placencia.

In Placencia, the tourism-based society is centred around the activities of its male members. With the exception of a few expatriate women, licensed tour guides are invariably men. While women may own and operate guesthouses and restaurants, men have the most contact with the largely female tourists. Women and the work that they do are invisible.

Young men in Placencia pursue white women tourists and then go back to their Creole girls when the tourist season is over. Heterosexual Creole women have few choices unless they leave the village. If they frequent the clubs they quickly acquire a reputation as women with loose morals. Consequently, women socialize among themselves at home or at their places of employment.

Social life in Placencia is strongly influenced by the economy of tourism which is also blamed for attracting drug dealers and other "scamps." There are few people in the village who have not benefited in some way from the drug economy. Those who are not active participants tolerate the sale of cocaine and marijuana to tourists. Today, many villagers who were productive members of the community are now addicted to crack. The street level sellers are young men conducting their business for the most fashionable name brand clothes, sunglasses, cell phones, or other consumer electronic goods.

In both communities tourism is also blamed for rising crime rates. Most people blame crack addicts for the rash of thefts and burglaries. Others are quick to point the finger at the "Spanish" who have become scapegoats for the ills of the village. However, most people contend that the "thieving" is done by people with long roots in the community. Tourism only impacts crime rates when the rate of tourism activity declines. When people are not making money crime rates escalate.

Many locals in San Ignacio report that one of the main reasons the foreign-owned hotels bother them is that they try to influence policies associated with tourism development, and do so to the exclusion of Belizeans. Many Belizeans are no longer involved in tourism organizations because they feel they are not empowered and receive little benefits from membership.

Sustainable Tourism, F. D. Pineda, C. A. Brebbia & M. Mugica (Editors)

According to many, tourism has destroyed the sense of family in this community. Many say when Placencia was a small fishing village the community was more like a family. They say that of course there were competitions and rivalries, but not sustained vendettas. Now that land has become so valuable, personal rivalries have reached a dangerous level. Property values have soared, so the stakes are very high. The competition is threatening social network security.

6 Discussion

As related by a prominent community leader who was one of the earlier promoters of an ecotourism sector in Belize:

> Without tourism, we would have been less developed. We would have had a smaller population, not just because of reproduction but because the knowledge of Belize because of tourism has led to more tourists living here. It depends on where you want the country to go. Without tourism, I can't imagine what people would do for an income. We started with woodcutting…agriculture…chicle…. Belize is better now with tourism. We need it as a means to survive. Without tourism people would be leaving to go abroad. It provides a way of life and a way of surviving.

Placencia has significant potential as an ecotourism destination where development could be sustained in sound ways. The resource base is still largely in its pristine state and much of it is in protected status. Unfortunately, protective status has brought higher visitation rates causing resource degradation and threats to recreational and ecological carrying capacities.

Environmental problems in town also affect the area's attractiveness. Waste management is of paramount concern. Placencia is the second largest contributor of foreign exchange through tourism, yet it receives no assistance from the government for waste disposal. Villages cannot lay and collect taxes, so they have no financial resources to manage this problem.

The fast buck associated with tourism is definitely influencing policy and management decisions regarding critical natural resources. Dredging the lagoon to create more land for real estate is a good case in point. Many feign concern about the lagoon, when in fact there are few people in the village who have not applied for a dredging permit to create new land. The reasons are simple economics and the scarcity of land.

Few people in the tourism trade see an intrinsic benefit to preserving wildlife. Most people explain that the main advantage of the marine reserves is they provide tour guides easy access to areas that can be exploited for the tourist dollar. A local cafe owner wonders why fishermen cannot fish at places like Goff Cay because it is the breeding area for whale sharks, but tourists are allowed to spend thousands of dollars to swim with the same sharks.

Although Placencia has a friendly and relaxed attitude about tourism, in many ways its' advent has disrupted community life. Local culture is definitely losing out to tourism, particularly in reference to women's status. The male

Sustainable Tourism, F. D. Pineda, C. A. Brebbia & M. Mugica (Editors)

patterns of sexual behaviour (with white female tourists) has resulted in low self-esteem among young women in the village, who in turn, suffer psychological and emotional abuse.

The economic impacts of ecotourism on local residents in San Ignacio parallels that of Placencia – pronounced foreign ownership, lower end service jobs but increased incomes. Tourism brings in much needed foreign exchange and the businesses provide employment for local residents, but many still comment about the "role of servitude" for Belizeans. The people who are profiting the most are the foreigners. "Foreigners shouldn't control everything. I hate the idea of foreigners coming in and exploiting us," complains one tour guide from Cayo District.

In essence, tourism has been good for the economy and for local residents with some exceptions. Tourism provides numerous employment opportunities. Everyone benefits whether or not they are directly involved with tourism, even the farmers and vegetable sellers at the market. At the same time, locals are being denied access to resources they have always been able to use and enjoy. Mountain Pine Ridge "...used to be for everyone. Now it's an exclusive area. Average Belizeans can't afford to even have a cup of coffee there. The resorts are not made for average Belizeans. Belizeans are not encouraged to go year round, only in the low season. It's created a class consciousness that didn't used to be here."

On a more positive note, a Belizean hotelier from San Ignacio made the following comment:

> Tourism shows Belizeans that is doesn't have to be all work. Husbands can take their wives out to dinner or take their families to the swimming pool. They learn that they should do things with their family and not just hang out with their friends. They see that tourism isn't just for foreigners. It also benefits how we look at our cultural and natural resources. We learn to respect and preserve them since these are what people are coming to see.

7 Conclusions

Tourist destinations and the people in them change in response to tourism. If ecotourism promotes development and conservation, it should accelerate economic growth while simultaneously braking against its environmental costs. In documented cases of successful ecotourism projects, compromise is always part of the process. The central question comes to be the means by which compromises are sought and the direction these decisions take local residents and the natural resources upon which they depend.

Belize is at a critical point in its ecotourism development. The government has placed a significant amount of the country's natural resources in protective status, but in doing so, they have also raised the dilemma of whether they are protecting these resources *for* tourism or whether they want to protect them *from* the tourism industry. Current policies surrounding cruise-ship development would suggest the former, whereas in reality their own responsible tourism

Sustainable Tourism, F. D. Pineda, C. A. Brebbia & M. Mugica (Editors)

policy mandates the promotion of environmental stewardship as well as a proactive approach toward environmentally-based tourism activities. The intent for conservation is clear; the enforcement of policy is less clear.

The question of foreign ownership and local participation in decision-making about tourism is most serious. The issue of Belizean ownership of tourism businesses persists and will escalate if the leakage trend intensifies as it most certainly will. Local populations already feel alienated and are resentful of the high incidence of foreign investors. Many have lost any sense of empowerment, and in turn, their feelings of apathy have translated into little or no participation in tourism organizations.

Tourism is changing many aspects of social life and cultural traditions. One older resident from Placencia claims that people in the village are "killing themselves." He argues that the promise of fast money in tourism, coupled with global media images of conspicuous consumer consumption, has destroyed people's lives. He points to the escalation of drug dealing and drug use in recent years.

The key to whether any tourism development is sustainable lies in one of the basic premises of Belize's responsible tourism mandate, that is, the promotion of local participation in decision-making processes. In the data that have been presented here, evidence that this mandate is being upheld is scant. While there are local tourism-related non-governmental organizations in both of these communities, with some local membership, many residents comment that their feelings of apathy about their own empowerment and influence in the political process prevents their participation even at this level.

A lifetime resident of Placencia asks, "With this hope of tourism, is there danger for our community?" While hoping that tourism can provide Placencia the secure economic future it needs as the fishing cooperatives have struggled, he fears the foreign investors, he fears the influx of multitudes of tourists, he fears the environmental degradation, and he fears the lifestyle changes. All of these impacts have occurred in his community and the changes will continue.

How one defines the relationships between economic growth, promotion of sound livelihood opportunities for local populations, and environmental conservation, and how communities work to achieve a balance between seemingly disparate goals is critically important to the process of using ecotourism as a development strategy.

References

[1] Weinberg, A., Bellows, S., & Ekster, D., Sustaining ecotourism: insights and implications from two successful case studies. *Society and Natural Resources*, **15**, pp. 371-380, 2002.

[2] Schlevkov, A., Global trends and prospects for central and eastern European countries. *Proc. Of the World Tourism Organization,* 2002

[3] Wall, G., Is ecotourism sustainable?, *Environmental Management*, **21(4)**, pp. 483-491, 1997.

Sustainable Tourism, F. D. Pineda, C. A. Brebbia & M. Mugica (Editors)

[4] Redclift, M., The meaning of sustainable development. *Geoforum* **23(3)**, pp. 395-403, 1992.

[5] Wall, G., Ecotourism: old wine in new bottles?. *Trends*, **31(2)**, pp. 4-9, 1994.

[6] Stem, C., Lassoie, J.P., & Lee, D.R., Community participation in ecotourism benefits: the link to conservation practices and perspectives. *Society & Natural Resources*, **16(5)**, pp. 387-413, 2003.

[7] Kerr, M., Ecotourism: alleviating the negative effects of deforestation on indigenous peoples in Latin America. *Colorado Journal of International Environmental Law & Policy*, **14(2)**, pp. 335-364, 2003.

[8] Scheyvens, R., Case study - ecotourism and the empowerment of local communities. *Tourism Management*, **20(2)**, pp. 245-251, 1999.

[9] Farrell, T.A., & Marion, J.L., Identifying and assessing ecotourism visitor impacts at eight protected areas in Costa Rica and Belize. *Environmental Conservation*, **28(3)**, pp. 215-225, 2001.

[10] Wallace, G.N., & Pierce, S., An evaluation of ecotourism in Amazonas, Brazil. *Annals of Tourism Research* **23(4)** pp. 843-873, 1996.

[11] Durbin, J.D. & Ralambo, J.A., The role of local people in the successful maintenance of protected areas in Madagascar. *Environmental Conservation*, **21**, pp. 115-120, 1994.

[12] Cater, E., Environmental contradictions in sustainable tourism. *The Geographical Journal*, 161(1), pp. 21-28, 1995.

[13] Alexander, S.E. & Gibson, J.W., Tourism Impact Assessment (TIA): participatory empiricism in the measurement of ecotourism. *Proc. of the Society for Applied Anthropology*, 2000.

[14] Weaver, D., Alternative to mass tourism in Dominica. *Annals of Tourism Research*, **18**, pp. 414-432, 1991.

[15] Cater, E., Ecotourism in the third world—problems and prospects for sustainability (Chapter 5). *Ecotourism: a sustainable option?*, eds. Erlet Cater & Gwen Lowman, John Wiley & Sons: New York, pp. 69-86, 1994.

[16] Brown, F., *Tourism reassessed*, Butterworth Heinemann: Oxford and Boston, 1998.

[17] Dearden, P., Tourism and sustainable development in northern Thailand. *Geographical Review*, **Oct.**, pp. 400-13, 1991.

[18] Inskeep, E., *Tourism planning: an integrated and sustainable development approach*, Van Nostrand Reinhold: New York, 1991.

[19] Boo, E., *Ecotourism: the potentials and pitfalls.* Washington, D.C.: World Wildlife Fund, 1990.

[20] Tisdell, C., Ecotourism: aspects of its sustainability and compatibility with conservation, social and other objectives. *Australian Journal of Hospitality Management*, **5(2)**, pp.11-21, 1998.

[21] Britton, R.A., The political economy of tourism in the third world. *Annals of Tourism Research*, **9**, pp. 331-558, 1982.

[22] Cohen, E., The impact of tourism on the physical environment. *Annals of Tourism Research*, **Apr./Jun.**, pp. 215-230, 1978.

Sustainable Tourism, F. D. Pineda, C. A. Brebbia & M. Mugica (Editors)

[23] Fang, Y., Ecotourism in western Sichuan, China. *Mountain Research and Development*, **22(2)**, pp. 113-115, 2002.
[24] Obua, J., The potential, development and ecological impact of ecotourism in Kibale National Park, Uganda. *Journal of Environmental Management*, **50**, pp. 27-38, 1997.
[25] Tabatchnaia-Tamirisa, N., Loke, M.K., Leung, P., & Tucker, K., Energy and tourism in Hawaii. *Annals of Tourism Research*, **24(2)**, pp. 390-401, 1997.
[26] National Drug Abuse Control Council, *National anti-drug strategy 2000-2004*. Belize: NDACC, 1999.
[27] van der Borg, J., Paolo Costa, P., & Gotti, G., Tourism in European heritage cities. *Annals of Tourism Research*, **23(2)**, pp. 306-21, 1996.
[28] Kirkpatrick, J.B., Ecotourism, local and indigenous people, and the conservation of the Tasmanian Wilderness World Heritage Area. *Journal of the Royal Society of New Zealand*, **31(4)**, pp. 819-829, 2001.
[29] CSO (Central Statistical Office), *Environmental statistics for Belize*. Central Statistical Office, Ministry of Finance: Belmopan, 1999.
[30] Blackstone Corporation and HELP for Progress Ltd. *A tourism strategy plan for Belize*. The Ministry of Tourism and the Environment: Belmopan, 1998.
[31] BTB (Belize Tourism Board), *Belize Travel & Tourism Statistics*, BTB: Belize City, 2001.
[32] CSO (Central Statistical Office), *Belize abstract of statistics*. Belmopan: Central Statistical Office, Ministry of Finance, 1997.
[33] Honey, M., *Ecotourism and sustainable development: who owns paradise?*, Island Press: Washington D.C., 1999.
[34] Alexander, S.E., The role of Belize residents in the struggle to define ecotourism opportunities in monkey sanctuaries. *Cultural Survival Quarterly*, **23(2)**, 1999.
[35] Alexander, S.E., Resident attitudes towards conservation and black howler monkeys in Belize: the Community Baboon Sanctuary. *Environmental Conservation*, **Oct.**, 2000.
[36] Mahler, R., & Wotkyns, S., *Belize: a natural destination*. John Muir Publications: Santa Fe, 1992.
[37] Hoffman, E., *Adventuring in Belize*. Sierra Club Books: San Francisco, 1994.
[38] Barry, T., *Inside Belize*. Resource Centre Press: Albuquerque, 1995.

Sustainable Tourism, F. D. Pineda, C. A. Brebbia & M. Mugica (Editors)

Ecolabelling at lodges in South Africa

G. H. Pieterse
Tourism Consultant, South Africa

Abstract

The development of ecolabels has been unbalanced and in large parts of the developing world there are no operating ecolabels although studies have shown that it is likely that ecolabelling can be implemented successfully in these areas. In Pieterse [1], research focused on lodges in South Africa and it was concluded that it would be useful and relevant to develop an ecolabel based on the experience offered and not based on the form of accommodation as is traditional. There are a number of issues and trends that have an influence on the development and operations of ecolabels. This paper considers how an ecolabel based on the lodge experience would impact on these trends and developments.
Keywords: ecolabel, lodge, lodge experience, ecolabel trends and developments, ecological certification, South Africa tourism, sustainable tourism.

1 Introduction

Tourism ecolabelling has been in existence since the 1980's and there are a large number of schemes operating in various parts of the world [2]. Ecolabels have developed in a very haphazard fashion and in large parts of the developing world there is no ecolabelling scheme in operation. In 2002 South Africa was the fastest-growing tourism destination in the world [3]. Lodges form an integral part of the country's wildlife ecotourism product. In 1997 it was estimated that 34% of visitors wanted to stay in a lodge/guest house during their vacation in South Africa. Despite this, there are however no established ecolabelling schemes operating at lodges in South Africa.

For the purpose of this paper, Dooley and Kirkpatrick's definition of an ecolabel in Synergy [4] will be used: "a term used to describe an officially sanctioned scheme in which a product may be awarded an ecological label on the basis of its 'acceptable' level of environmental impact. The acceptable level of environmental impact may be determined by consideration of a single

Sustainable Tourism, F. D. Pineda, C. A. Brebbia & M. Mugica (Editors)

environmental hurdle, which is deemed to be particularly important, or after undertaking an assessment of its overall impacts." (p. vii).

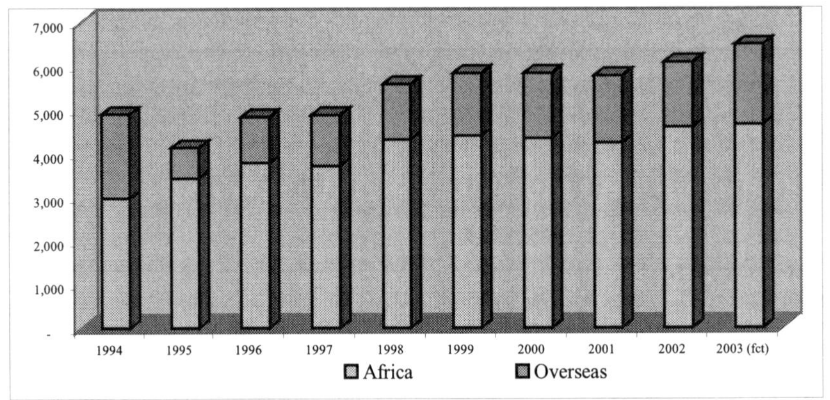

Figure 1: Growth in arrivals to South Africa 1994 – 2003 [5].

Research done in Pieterse [1] found that there is significant potential for ecolabelling at lodges in South Africa. It also specifically pointed out that such potential would best be served when an ecolabel is developed based on overall experience offered at lodges, not just based on its accommodation classification. This paper draws directly from that research. The South African lodge experience is examined as well as current trends and developments in the ecolabelling industry and the objective of this paper is to assess what impact the development of an ecolabel, based on the 'lodge experience', would have on issues and trends that currently influence new and established developments.

2 South African lodge environment

2.1 South African tourism

From 1994 to 2002, since the start of the new South Africa, overseas arrivals grew by an incredible 89%! In 2002 South Africa was the world's fastest growing tourism region [3] and overseas arrivals grew by a staggering 23% [5]. Although official figures have not been released, despite war in Iraq, SARS and weaker economies in most main source markets, and compared to a decline in global tourism of –1,2%, South Africa's preliminary overseas arrivals figures seem to have grown by 3% in 2003 [5]. Studies have repeatedly shown that South Africa's scenic beauty, sunny climate, abundant wildlife and varied cultures are its main attractions, basically all of which are offered at lodges in one form or another [6].

Sustainable Tourism, F. D. Pineda, C. A. Brebbia & M. Mugica (Editors)
© 2004 WIT Press, www.witpress.com, ISBN 1-85312-724-8

2.2 Lodges

The Tourismgrading Council of South Africa defines a lodge as "an accommodation facility located in natural surroundings. The rates charged are usually inclusive of an experience offered at the lodges, viz. game drives, battlefield tours etc. In general, food and beverage services are provided for all meals" [7, Lodge section 1]. It is estimated at present that there are about 300 lodges operating throughout the country [8]. There is however no official number. The majority of lodges are found in the Lowveld region in the northeastern part of South Africa. Average prices for up market lodges range from R2500 – R4500 p.p.p.n. It is a very intense market and competitive advantage stems mainly from two aspects: the quality of game viewing, especially the Big Five, and standards of service [9].

A typical visit to a lodge would involve a stay in surroundings as close to nature as possible to experience nature to the full, and all activities are focused on learning and feeling nature first-hand, with game rangers and trackers as personal tutors. A traditional day spent at a lodge will offer an early morning game drive, a late morning brunch, a guided walk in the bush or game-watching from the patio, a late afternoon game drive, sundowners along the way and then a meal served in a boma under the stars [10].

2.3 Sustainable actions at lodges

Lodges' operations and existence are so closely linked to their direct environment that often they have no option but to act sustainable. For many lodges acting in a sustainable way, i.e. recycling, being involved in the community, caring for their land, just "makes business sense" [1].

Although differing in scale and extent, there is a great deal of overlapping in terms of the type of actions taking place. For example, all of the lodges recycle tins, glass and bottles, but only at one lodge has this been turned into a further initiative where an employee takes responsibility for collection and transportation and can therefore collect on revenue gained from the effort. It is also important to note that in many instances the parameters of their surroundings compel lodges to go beyond what would normally be considered as sustainable actions. Many lodges are forced to build waste cages in order to keep trash away from hyenas and other scavengers, a problem not likely to be encountered by a hotel in the Johannesburg city center![1].

2.4 Lodges as an experience

It was a conclusion in Pieterse [1] that rather than establishing and considering ecolabelling schemes and criteria in terms of the type of accommodation offered, there should be a classification of accommodations in terms of the experience offered. Across the world, it seems that ecolabels have attempted to rate establishments according to the same classification used by service grading schemes, that is, different segments within accommodation or facilities or locations. Although Blue Flag's official classification is in terms of facilities, the

Sustainable Tourism, F. D. Pineda, C. A. Brebbia & M. Mugica (Editors)

success of their label could be attributed to the fact that their label conveys information relevant to an experience, that of going to the beach. Different from hotels in cities, which are focused on providing only accommodation, lodges are not just "hotels in the bush", they offer a total experience (see section 2.2). Different lodges offer different nature-based scenery and activities (dessert landscapes in Namibia or Big Five safaris in Mpmulanga, etc.) but these all boil down to the experience of guests feeling and learning from nature. Therefore, although lodges can offer and operate as five star hotels in the bush, they should not be regarded and judged in the same way as a five star hotel in the city centre because their approach, operations and focus, in order to bring about a desired five star experience, differ radically.

3 Current trends and developments

3.1 Background to ecolabelling

Ecolabelling has been used for about three decades. The first official ecolabel was the German "Blue Angel" in 1978, which labelled everyday household products [11]. Since then a number of industries worldwide have joined the effort to promote sustainable business through ecolabelling [12]. Ecolabelling was introduced to the tourism industry around 1985 when the Foundation for Environmental Education in Europe (FEEE) awarded its first Blue Flag label for beaches and marinas [13]. Currently, there are over 100 tourism ecolabels functioning throughout the world [13, 14]. Because of this significant growth and resultant confusion, there has been increasing interest in, as well as concern over, the future development of ecolabelling, and a number of issues and trends are currently receiving attention on the tourism ecolabel scene.

3.2 Demand

Discussions by Synergy [4], Honey and Rome [14] and, Font and Buckley [15] identify a lack of clear, and often contradictory demand, as one of the major issues in terms of ecolabelling.

Both Honey and Rome [14] and Font and Buckley [15] argue that although interest and support for "green" actions is increasing and becoming stronger, there is no clear indication that this translates into actual green behaviour in the tourism industry. As maintained by Honey and Rome [14], whenever demand is verified, surveys indicate that as soon as consumers need to give something up to obtain an environmentally friendly product, for example having to pay additional costs, they tend not to choose that product. Key factors influencing the choice of a destination still seem to be price, accommodation and the activities offered [4, 13]. The only exception to this appears to be when the environmental state of the product or service is fundamental to the enjoyment of the whole experience [4, 14, 15]. The relative success of the Blue Flag label and its focus on sanitation and safety facilities can be traced back to this principle.

Sustainable Tourism, F. D. Pineda, C. A. Brebbia & M. Mugica (Editors)

There seems to be agreement among stakeholders that the overabundance of ecolabels has also created confusion among tourists. In Costa Rica, Green Globe, New Key, CST and ECOTEL have all certified different accommodations within the same region, leaving consumers confused and sceptical over the meaning of a logo and the credibility of a certified hotel [14]. Consequently, Font [13] and Sasidharan et al. [16] concluded that tourists then tend to ignore labels, further diminishing demand.

3.3 Mass tourism, sustainable tourism and ecotourism certification

The decision regarding the type, focus and scope of an ecolabel is a complex and important consideration in its establishment. Honey and Rome [14] identified and discussed three umbrella-like types of certification programmes, namely mass tourism, sustainable tourism and ecotourism.

Mass tourism certification focuses on accommodation in the mass tourism segment, for example hotels and resorts. They cater for a diverse global mass market and consequently their criteria and frameworks are more vague. These schemes tend, however, to be the most well known, marketed and funded [14].

Sustainable Tourism Certification is focused on aspects of the "triple baseline". These schemes invariably have much more detailed criteria [14].

Ecotourism certification programmes are a more specialised form of a sustainable tourism programme. They look beyond the business to its impact on its surroundings and how it fulfils the characteristics of an ecotourism establishment [14].

According to Amos Bien in Honey and Rome [14], the major problem with this kind of distinction among programmes is that a lodge might be environmentally green according to "mass tourism" criteria while, due to the more stringent criteria of "ecotourism" standards it might not be considered "green", again influencing the credibility of both the ecolabel and establishment [14].

3.4 Focus of ecolabels

Once the type of certification programme, mass tourism, sustainable tourism or ecotourism, has been established, the actual scope and focus of an ecolabel should be considered.

In the UNEP study conducted in 1998 [2], four different scopes of ecolabels were identified. These were international, regional, national and sub-national schemes. Although most of the established schemes still operate on only a regional or national level, a lot of attention is currently paid to the feasibility and development of international schemes (section 3.6). Regional schemes operate across the borders of several countries and their focus is based on defined features, for example, Blue Flag that operates at beaches [2].

The focus area of a scheme normally deals with one particular segment in the industry. According to UNEP [2], focus areas include accommodation, such as hotels or campsites; services, such as tour operators; and locations, such as golf courses. Based on the segment it focuses on, a scheme will then formulate its

Sustainable Tourism, F. D. Pineda, C. A. Brebbia & M. Mugica (Editors)
© 2004 WIT Press, www.witpress.com, ISBN 1-85312-724-8

criteria and methods of assessment. The mainstream accommodation segment is the most popular.

3.5 The big business vs. small and medium enterprises (SME's) divide

In a comparison of papers written by Synergy [4], Honey and Rome [14], and Sasidharan et al. [16], it becomes clear that developing countries and SMEs often share common problems when compared with developed countries and bigger businesses, respectively. Developing countries and SMEs form the basis of the ecotourism sector and stand to gain the most from ecolabelling schemes, but are often not able to stand their ground against bigger players due to a lack of resources. Eco-protectionism is increasingly identified as a major obstacle curbing the development of ecolabels. (Sasidharan et al. [16] explain eco-protectionism as something that happens when larger companies, often originating in developed countries and because of their resources, are able to be eco-certified, and they then use this certification to attract foreign "green" tourists at the cost of many smaller, locally-owned enterprises not able to join such schemes.)

According to Honey and Rome [14], SMEs comprise some 97% of the tourism industry and according to Sasidharan et al. [16] it is likely that bigger corporations who have more time, funding and human resources will have a larger influence on the formulation of criteria and the ability to enforce their viewpoints. Both Sasidharan et al. [16] and Font and Buckley [15] consequently warn against criteria unintentionally established at levels, which would make it impossible for SMEs to comply.

3.6 Towards a global overseeing structure

International tourism is increasing throughout the world and tourists want to know what ecolabels at their destinations mean [16]. In an attempt to curb this problem the tourism industry has engaged in a number of discussions. Two possible solutions have been proposed. The Rainforest Alliance has undertaken to determine the feasibility of a Global Sustainable Tourism Stewardship Council (STSC), which will act as an international accreditation body that will verify the credibility of all operating ecolabels through affiliation with such a scheme [17]. At the World Ecotourism Summit in Quebec in 2002, representatives from the Ecotourism Association of Australia and Green Globe 21 (Asia Pacific) tabled a second option, that of an International Ecotourism Standard [18]. This solution instead proposes the establishment of generic standards for tourism businesses within a specific segment, in each case adapted to take into account site-specific issues.

4 The lodge experience and ecolabelling issues and trends

In South Africa, it seems most lodges support a compulsory scheme and they support the fundamentals of such an effort. In addition, the government is very

Sustainable Tourism, F. D. Pineda, C. A. Brebbia & M. Mugica (Editors)
© 2004 WIT Press, www.witpress.com, ISBN 1-85312-724-8

much for, and involved in, actions towards responsible tourism. It is, therefore, possible that a scheme can be made compulsory or at least be regulated through some official body within the South African context, and this would greatly increase its potential. However, across the world, schemes are voluntary and there is no guarantee that a scheme could be made compulsory. It is for this reason that Pieterse [1] found formulating criteria in terms of the experiences offered at lodges a more plausible solution. In this way, only one scheme's criteria would be applicable to lodges and credibility can be maintained and confusion avoided. Assuming this as a possible scenario and based on the discussion above, the following inferences can be drawn regarding the impact of the 'lodge experience', as a basis for an ecolabel, on current trends and developments in the ecolabelling industry.

When it comes to actual demand from tourists for an ecolabel, it seems lodges' sustainable actions, as in the rest of the world, more often than not are not a determining factor when guests choose a destination. Actual interest of lodge guests in environmental aspects at their destination seem to stretch only as far as it concerns their own safety and the quality of their experience. In the case of lodges such questions relate for example to whether malaria is a threat at the lodge or whether it offers the Big Five (lion, leopard, elephant, rhino, buffalo) or not. However, because lodges are so small and remote there is much more interaction of guests with the milieu of the lodges. Guests interact with ground level personnel as well as with all levels of management, while the nature of their visit allows them to intimately experience the natural environment through the interpretations of a ranger. Lodges can therefore play a huge role in sensitising guests to responsible environmental behaviour. Also, of the total foreign leisure tourists to South Africa in the first quarter of 2002 only 30% were first-time visitors while some 26% have been to the country ten or more times [19]. As such, the lodge experience itself can play a significant role in "creating" demand among guests for environmentally responsible establishments.

Lodges are a rather small, but distinct and significant segment of the South African tourism industry. By their very existence, situated in nature and offering wildlife, lodges have to act more "green" than other normal accommodation establishments. A mass tourism scheme would therefore not help or enable them to act more sustainable but as Sasidharan et al [16] argue, chances are lodges will join such an ecolabel simply for the "green" marketing tool it would provide. If criteria were however developed based on the experience offered at the establishment, only one scheme's would be applicable and relevant, avoiding erroneous certifications by other irrelevant schemes.

The same also applies for the focus of ecolabels. If criteria and procedures are based on the experience offered at lodges, categorization of businesses as per the traditional alternatives becomes obsolete and there would be no confusion as to which category would best apply to the lodge.

As for the scope of ecolabels, lodges, as defined in this study, are a unique experience of the African continent, specifically Southern and Eastern Africa. They share common site-specific issues and if an ecolabel were to focus on the

Sustainable Tourism, F. D. Pineda, C. A. Brebbia & M. Mugica (Editors)

experience offered at an establishment it would be quite possible to operate it across borders without any major adjustments necessary. This would allow a label to gain broader market acceptance as well as exposure and this would be beneficial to the credibility of that ecolabel. Because this 'lodge experience' is so unique to the African continent, and because an ecolabel based on such experience would only be suitable for Africa, the possible problem of eco-protectionism by developing countries could not become one. All of southern Africa, where the label will operate, is considered developing countries. This is also the case with eco-protectionism by bigger companies. Although no official study has been done, the majority of lodges are SME's and an ecolabel based on the 'lodge experience' would therefore effectively avoid this problem.

As pointed out earlier, an ecolabel would have no impact if its meaning is not known to its patrons. As the majority of visitors to lodges come from outside the country's borders, up to 90% at some, participation in or accreditation by an international scheme would increase the credibility and recognition of such an ecolabel. As per the argument in this paper, lodges in South Africa work under unique circumstances in comparison with for example, hotels in Johannesburg or eco-lodges in Costa Rica, and although there will always be generic standards applicable in any scheme (such as recycling), there are many issues that can only be understood and explained in a South African or African lodge context. In light of this it would seem that the Rainforest Alliance's STSC holds more promise for an ecolabelling scheme at lodges than an international ecotourism standard. Under the auspices of such a body, a scheme will be able to operate autonomously, allowing it to determine its own 'lodge experience'-based criteria and operating procedures while maintaining credibility through accreditation.

5 Conclusion

The classification that forms the basis for any ecolabel will always result in specific issues and trends relating to that specific basis. This then also has an influence on the further development and existence of new ecolabels. As discussed above, currently all ecolabels are classified on the traditional segmentation of the tourism sector. It is to be expected that any new classifications for ecolabels would deliver their own issues and trends. However, the aim of this paper was not to identify possible new issues when an experience-based ecolabel were to be developed. Rather, it was to assess in what way a 'lodge experience'-based ecolabel would impact current issues and trends. Although demand might not increase only because a different classification is used, the 'lodge experience' as such seems able to actually create demand for its ecolabel. Focusing only on lodges, such an ecolabel would be able to avoid potential problems that may arise regarding the question of an applicable type and focus of an ecolabel scheme for the particular establishment. As the industry market for this specific market is much more homogenic, the problem of ecoprotectionism can be avoided, both in terms of the fact that lodges basically only operate in developing countries and that most lodges are SME's. This homogeneity will also allow lodges to operate on a regional level which will add

Sustainable Tourism, F. D. Pineda, C. A. Brebbia & M. Mugica (Editors)

exposure and credibility to their label. Also on a global level, basing an ecolabel on the 'lodge experience' will duly fit in with the suggestion for an international accreditation body, allowing it to operate within the global scene. It is the conclusion of this paper that a 'lodge experience'-based ecolabel would positively impact on current issues and trends and that it would add value and credibility to ecolabelling.

References

[1] Pieterse, G.H., Ecolabelling at lodges in South Africa. *Unpublished M.Sc. Dissertation*. University Center "Cesar Ritz", Brig, Switzerland, 2003.

[2] UNEP (United Nations Environmental Programme). *Ecolabels in the tourism industry*. Paris: United Nations Environment Programme, Industry and Environment, 1998.

[3] Keppler, V., *SA toerisme groei vinnigste ter wereld* [SA tourism growth fastest globally]. *Rapport*. p. 3, 2003, March 3.

[4] Synergy, *Tourism Certification: An analysis of Green Globe 21 and other tourism certification programmes*. http://www.wwf.org.uk/filelibrary/pdf /tcr.pdf. 2000.

[5] Horwath Tourism and Leisure Consulting, Personal communication, 21 February 2003, Cape Town, South Africa.

[6] Jordan, Z.P., Address delivered at the International Conference on Sustainable Tourism, Berlin. http://www.environment.gov.za. 1997.

[7] Tourismgrading. Tourismgrading Council of South Africa. http://www.tourismgrading.co.za

[8] Weaver, D.B. (Ed.)., *The Encyclopedia of Ecotourism*. Wallingford, UK.:CABI Publishing. 2001.

[9] P Shorten, Personal communication, Jan 29, 2003, Managing Director, Sabi Sabi, Johannesburg, Cape Town.

[10] Ulusaba. *Ulusaba Game Reserve*. http://www.ulusaba.com /atypicalday.html

[11] Salzhauer, A.L., Obstacles and opportunities for a consumer ecolabel. *Environment* Vol 33(9), p. 10, 1991.

[12] Parris, T.M., Seals of approval: Environmental labelling on the net. *Environment* 40(2), 3-4, 1998.

[13] Font, X., Environmental certification in tourism and hospitality: Progress, process and prospects. *Tourism Management* 23(3), 197-205, 2002.

[14] Honey, M., & Rome, A., *Protecting paradise: certification programs for sustainable tourism and ecotourism*. http://www.ips-dc.org /ecotourism/protectingparadise. 2001.

[15] Font, X. & Buckley, R.C. (Eds.)., *Tourism Ecolabelling: Certification and Promotion of Sustainable Management*. Wallingford, UK.: CABI Publishing. 2001.

[16] Sasidharan, V., Siarakya, E., & Kerstetter, D., Developing countries and tourism ecolabels. *Tourism Management* 23(2), 161-174, 2002.

Sustainable Tourism, F. D. Pineda, C. A. Brebbia & M. Mugica (Editors)

[17] Rainforest Alliance., *An accreditation body for sustainable tourism certifiers: STSC project summary.* Retrieved September 18, 2002, from http://www.rainforest-alliance.org/programs/sv/stsc-summary.html, 2001.
[18] Crabtree, A., O'Reilly, P. & Worboys, G., Setting a worldwide standard for ecotourism: Sharing expertise in ecotourism certification: Developing an international ecotourism standard. Paper presented to World Ecotourism Summit, Quebec, Canada. Retrieved January 30, 2003, from http://www.ecotourism.org.au/ies/ies.cfm, 2002.
[19] SATOUR, South African tourism index: Quarterly report January-March 2002. South African Tourism, 2002.

Sustainable Tourism, F. D. Pineda, C. A. Brebbia & M. Mugica (Editors)

Ecological understanding: a prerequisite of sustainable ecotourism

S. Zahedi
Department of Management, Allameh Tabataba'i University, Iran

Abstract

Sustainable ecotourism is a nature-oriented tourism that maintains a sound relationship with the environment, and contributes to its conservation. Ecological understanding is a prerequisite of sustainable ecotourism. Nature conservation and ecotourism are interdependent. There should be a symbiotic relationship between the two, in which both derive sustainable benefits in a lengthy period of time. In order to decrease natural deterioration, the present ecotourism economic and financial assessment should be challenged. Sustainable ecotourism demands new managerial methods that can estimate both environmental inputs and outputs in every single ecotourism venture and meets the required criteria of both. A triple-bottom-line accounting approach provides a foundation for the assessment of environmental, social, and financial costs and benefits of ecotourism ventures. Ecotourism companies can allocate some of their resources to nature conservation and the education of people. This is how they can obtain a positive triple bottom line. Developing environmental management strategies, programs and procedures with measurable objectives, and allocating adequate funds for their effective implementation is recommended in this article. An effective financial management system with capable accounting mechanisms would provide ecotourism organizations with the necessary foundations for transition towards sustainability.

1 Introduction

Ecotourism constitutes a viable economic activity within tourism section in many developing countries. While it can stimulate the economy and generate crucially needed foreign exchange earnings, it might be harmful to the natural environment of the host countries. The purpose of this article is to discuss the

Sustainable Tourism, F. D. Pineda, C. A. Brebbia & M. Mugica (Editors)
 ISBN 1-85312-724-8

relationship between ecotourism and ecology, and to address issues that are relevant to ecotourism financial management and accounting mechanism. Following an overall review of the tourism typology, an emphasis is placed upon sustainable development and ecotourism management.

2 Sustainable tourism

Tourism may be defined as the sum of phenomena and relationships arising from the interaction of tourists, host governments, origin governments and host communities in the process of attracting and hosting these tourists and other visitors [13, p. 10]. There appears to be direct relationship between the emergence of paradigm of sustainable development and sustainable tourism. Sustainable development advocates that people at present time meet their present needs without compromising the ability of future generations to meet their own needs in the future [15]. Thus sustainable tourism is tourism which is developed and maintained in an area in such a manner and at such a scale that it remains viable over an indefinite period and does not degrade or alter the environment in which it exists to such a degree that it prohibits the successful development and well being of other activities and processes [3, p. 29].

3 Tourism and typology

There are different categorizations for tourism from different perspectives. In this article tourism is divided into two main categories:
1) Ordinary tourism, and
2) Nature-oriented tourism.

3.1 Ordinary tourism

Ordinary tourism is large-scale, highly commercialized tourism, which is mostly based on packaged tours, concentrated in dominant markets throughout the world.

3.2 Nature oriented tourism

Nature oriented tourism is forms of tourism that maintain a relationship with the natural environment for their attractions. Nature oriented tourism may be divided into six sub-categories: 3S tourism, adventure tourism, consumptive tourism, captive tourism, health tourism, and ecotourism.

3.2.1 3S tourism
This type of tourism is related to sun, sea, and sand (3S) and is associated with the emergence of a leisure-dominated pleasure periphery occupying a significant portion of the Mediterranean and Caribbean basins, along with the parts of the South-Pacific, South-eastern Asia and Indian Ocean basin [9, p. 36]. 3S tourism has become symbolic of the negative economic, environmental and sociocultural

Sustainable Tourism, F. D. Pineda, C. A. Brebbia & M. Mugica (Editors)

impacts. Although it is more in harmony with unsustainable paradigm, it is very popular and demanded throughout the world (ibid.).

3.2.2 Adventure tourism

This form of tourism contains elements of risk, skill, physical exertion and is associated with natural environment which provides challenge and excitement. Related activities include white-water rafting, skydiving, wilderness hiking, sea kayaking, mountain climbing, caving and orienteering [12, p. 47].

3.2.3 Captive tourism

In this form of tourism some elements of the natural environment are presented under controlled conditions, such as zoological gardens, aquariums, aviaries and botanical gardens. There has been an argument accompanied by accusations that captive tourism is unethical, and this is why in most countries there is a growing tendency to change zoos and the like to national parks with almost similar conditions to the natural settings.

3.2.4 Health tourism

This kind of tourism is related to therapeutic and hygiene activities and is mostly demanded by tourists who seek nature-based methods of therapy. Related activities include medical plants, therapeutic water and mud.

3.2.5 Consumptive tourism

There is element of consumption in all forms of tourism, but consumptive tourism refers to the activities, which emphasize to attempt to seek out, kill, and remove an organism from its environment, such as hunting and fishing. This form of tourism is often environmentally unsustainable and it has been declining in recent years [4, p. 35].

3.2.6 Ecotourism

Word "ecotourism" is derived from two other words: ecology and tourism, and ecotourism is supposedly a sustainable form of natural resource-based tourism that focuses primarily on experiencing and learning about nature, and which is ethically managed to be low-impact, non-consumptive, and locally oriented (control, benefits, and scale). It typically occurs in natural areas, and should contribute to the conservation of such areas [5, p. 43].

This article focuses on ecotourism and the problems related to it from financial management perspective.

4 Ecotourism and sustainability

Responsible ecotourism can offer an alternative form of tourism, which is based on the principles of sustainable development and can be viable over time. But although ecotourism is a relatively young industry, there are already well-documented cases of negative impacts or mismanagements [1, 10]. The main cause of the problem is that the principles of financial management and

Sustainable Tourism, F. D. Pineda, C. A. Brebbia & M. Mugica (Editors)

accounting are not incorporated into the practice of ecotourism. Prior to elaborating more on this subject, a brief description of ecology is required.

5 Ecology

The word ecology is taken from the Greek "Oikos" meaning "house", and thus refers to our environment [11, p. 2]. In 1870 the German zoologist Ernst Hackel, described ecology as the body of knowledge concerning the economy of nature-the investigation of the total relations of the animal both to its organic and to its inorganic environment: including above all, its friendly and inimical relation with those animals and plants which it comes directly or indirectly into contact. Thus, ecology is the science by which we study how organisms (animals, plants, and microbes) interact in and with the natural world (ibid.).

5.1 Ecological hierarchy

Ecological hierarchy consists of different ecological systems with progressively more complex entities:

- An organism (the fundamental unit of ecology)
- A population (consisting of organisms)
- A community (different populations living together)
- Ecosystems (assemblages of different organisms with their physical and chemical environment)
- Biosphere (all the organisms and environments of the earth)

In the ecological hierarchy every single entity plays a particular role in the functioning of the whole and is related to the other entities by exchanging energy and materials. Plants and algae fix the energy of sunlight: animals and protozoa consume biological forms of energy, fungi are able to penetrate soil and dead plant material and so play an important role in breaking down biological materials and regenerating nutrients in the ecosystem (ibid.). Bacteria are biochemical specialists, able to accomplish such transformations as the biological assimilation of nitrogen and the use of hydrogen sulfide as an energy source, both of which are essential components of ecosystem function (ibid., p. 21). These exchanges contribute to the environment, and cycling of elements in the environment, from the smallest dimension (organism) to the largest (biosphere). Ecological understanding is a prerequisite of sustainable ecotourism. In order to create new managerial techniques to support our immediate surroundings and oikos- our vulnerable environment- we should have ecological knowledge and insight. Understanding ecological principles and rational application of those would prevent environmental harming and protect our limited resources for the present and future generations.

5.2 Ecological principles

Ecological principles are as follows:

Sustainable Tourism, F. D. Pineda, C. A. Brebbia & M. Mugica (Editors)

- Ecological systems are physical entities; life builds upon the physical properties and chemical reactions of matter (ibid., p. 14).
- Ecological systems exist in a homeostasis situation. Homeostasis implies the exchange of energy or material with the surroundings and yet maintaining a dynamic steady state [16, p. 14].
- The maintenance of living systems requires expenditure of energy.
- Ecological systems undergo evolutionary change overtime [11, p. 15].

5.3 Diversity and extinction

Biological diversity is fundamental to ecological sustainability, and the survival of human being depends upon maintaining the existing biodiversity. Biodiversity is often considered at three levels: genetic, species and ecosystems. Genetic diversity is the viability of generic materials within the species. Species diversity refers to the number and range of different species. Ecosystem diversity relates to the variety of habitats, biotic communities and ecological process [7, p. 54].

Diversity has a vital role in stabilizing ecosystem function. The diversity decreases when species extinct. Extinction is a natural phenomenon and is a normal characteristic of natural systems. It represents the disappearance of evolutionary lineages that never can be recovered [11, p. 486]. There are three types of extinction: 1) Background extinction, 2) Mass extinction, 3) Anthropogenic extinction (ibid., p. 487). As ecosystems change, some species disappear and others take their place. This turnover at a relatively low rate is background extinction. Mass extinction refers to the dying off of large numbers of species because of natural catastrophes such as volcanoes, hurricanes, and meteor impacts happen occasionally, and species that are in their way disappear. Anthropogenic extinction is caused by the human and is similar to mass extinction in the number of taxa affected and its global dimensions and catastrophic nature. But this one can be under control (ibid.). So far humans usurp more than 40% of biological productivity of biosphere and have caused extinctions by irrational use of energy and resources. They have reproduced too much of wastes, far excess of needs dictated by biological dimensions. This has caused few problems: 1) Disruption the ecological processes; 2) Extinction of some of the species; 3) Decreasing biodiversity; 4) Increasing environmental stresses and deteriorating environmental well-being; 5) Threatening human life on the earth.

These problems are crying for urgent remedial strategies. In the context of this article, nature conservation and sustainable ecotourism are of important priorities.

5.4 Nature conservation

Conservation is managing the resources of the environment- air, water, soil, mineral resources and living species including human- so as to achieve the highest sustainable quality of life [7, p. 103]. Nature conservation and ecotourism are interdependent. Responsible ecotourism must conserve natural areas and decreases risk to the natural environment. This leads to protecting

Sustainable Tourism, F. D. Pineda, C. A. Brebbia & M. Mugica (Editors)

natural areas and thus contributing to the growth of the ecotourism. Ecotourism can either stimulate measurements to protect natural environment or provide basis for detrimental and harmful damages to it. There should be a symbiotic relationship between ecotourism and conservation of natural environment in which both derive sustainable benefits in a lengthy period of time. This requires an ecoethic, which recognizes the importance of nature preservation, and values the physical and biological natural environment. Moral principles are necessary to deal with those human behaviors that have environmental impact.

6 New mechanisms

In order to decrease natural deterioration and environmental exploitation, the present ecotourism economic and financial assessment should be challenged immediately and seriously.

Sustainable ecotourism demands new managerial methods that can estimate both environmental inputs and outputs in every single ecotourism venture, and meets the required criteria of both. According to Buckley, the environmental input is the geographical factor, which has led the tourist to a particular destination. The environmental output is the overall net global cost or benefit of the tour operation to the natural environment. This is an accounting question, which requires the identification, quantification and summation of all costs and benefits through all potential mechanisms [2, p. 2].

The most promising approach in which environmental, social, and financial costs and benefits are assessed independently is triple bottom line accounting. In this approach, the company is not in credit unless all three bottom lines are positive. Buckley believes that this is a useful step, which recognizes that sustainability can only be achieved through major changes to human social structure and behavior, and that social and environmental accounting may be one tool to promote such changes. .

The social and environmental reports, if not more than financial reports, at least should be attract the same attention, and must demonstrate detailed information regarding their impact.

Every ecotourism venture and activity, in addition to the financial information should have an environmental bottom line. In order to have a positive social or environmental bottom line in any meaningful accounting sense, Buckley believes that ecotourism ventures should identify and quantify all the direct environmental and social costs and benefits of its entire operations and calculate the difference between the benefits and the costs (ibid., p. 4).

A positive triple bottom line means a net improvement in conservation of the natural environment and net social benefits for local communities as well as a net profit for shareholders and/or a net gain for national or regional economies (ibid.).

Thus sustainable ecotourism requires a departure from the present financial management and accounting systems to a precise and accurate system that provides valid information about the triple bottom line for ecotourism ventures.

Sustainable Tourism, F. D. Pineda, C. A. Brebbia & M. Mugica (Editors)

Ecotourism companies can allocate some of their resources to the nature and to the people, nature conservation and people education. They can do this through establishing funds for the conservation and spending generously on the cultural and social activities. This is how they can obtain a positive triple bottom line and develop a proper accounting system. Through this system they can demonstrate their contribution to the components of ecosystem.

7 Conclusion

As mentioned earlier, humans are damaging the natural environment in a speed far more than nature can tolerate. They impose on nature far excess of needs dictated by ecological and biological dimensions. According to chaos theory and the role of uncertainty and the butterfly effect, there can be no precise knowledge about the expected results of any action [8, p. 52]. A harmful behavior in a particular place and a particular time can have many unknown unexpected results in other places and other times. This implies, damaging the life of the next generations and negating the principles of sustainable development.

Human behavior often violates the principles of sustainability. Developing environmental management strategies, programs and procedures, with measurable objectives, and allocating adequate funds for their effective implementation, is strongly recommended. The author believes that the environmental considerations should be incorporated into financial management and accounting system of every single organization in general and ecotourism organizations in particular.

Effective financial management system with capable accounting tools and mechanisms would provide the ecotourism organizations with the necessary foundations for transition toward sustainability.

References

[1] Boo, Elizabeth (1991) "Ecotourism: The potentials and pitfalls", World Wild Life Fund, Washington D.C.

[2] Buckley, Ralf, "Environmental inputs and outputs in ecotourism: geotourism with a positive triple bottom line?", Unpublished paper, International Center for Ecotourism Research, Griffith University, Southport, Australia, 2002.

[3] Butler, R.W. (1993) Tourism- an evolutionary perspective In: Nelson, J. G., Butler, R. W. and Wall, G. (eds), "Tourism and sustainable development: monitoring, planning, managing" Department of Geography Publication Series 37, University of Waterloo, Waterloo, Canada.

[4] Cordell, H. K., Lewis, B. and McDonald, B. L (1995) Long term outdoor recreation participation trends, In: J.L. Thompson, D.W. Lime, B. Gartner, and W. M. Sames (eds) "Proceedings of the Fourth International Outdoor Recreation and Tourism Symposium and the National Recreation Resource Planning Conference", St. Paul, MN, USA, University of Minnesota.

Sustainable Tourism, F. D. Pineda, C. A. Brebbia & M. Mugica (Editors)

[5] Fennell, David A., (2000) "Ecotourism, an introduction", Routledge, London and New York.

[6] Faulkner, Gianna Moscardo and Eric Laws (2000), "Tourism in the 21st century, lessons from experience", Continuum, London & New York.

[7] Jafari, Jafar, (2000) "Encyclopedia of tourism", Routledge, London.

[8] Knil, G, (1991) Towards the green paradigm, "South African Geographical Journal", 73.

[9] Lawton, Laura and David Weaver, In: Bill Faulkner Gianna Moscardo and Eric Laws (2000), "Tourism in the 21st century, lessons from experience", Continuum, London & New York.

[10] Lindenberg, K. (1991) "Policies for maximizing nature tourisms ecological and economic benefits", Washington D.C., World Resources Institute.

[11] Ricklefs, Robert E. (2001) "The Economy of Nature", fifth edition. W. H. Freeman and Company, New York.

[12] Sung, H., Morrison A. and O'Leary, L. (1996/97) Definition of adventure-travel: conceptual framework for empirical application from the providers perspective, "Asia Pacific Journal of Tourism and Research", 1(2).

[13] McIntosh, R. Geoldner, C. and Ritchie, J. (1995) "Tourism: principles, practices and philosophies", 7th edition, John Wiley, New York.

[14] Weaver, David B., (1998) "Ecotourism in the less developed world", CAB International, Wallingford, Oxon, U.K.

[15] World Commission on Environment and Development (1987).

[16] Zahedi, Shamsosadat (2000) "Systems Analysis and Design", Allameh Tabataba'i University, Tehran, Iran.

Sustainable Tourism, F. D. Pineda, C. A. Brebbia & M. Mugica (Editors)
© 2004 WIT Press, www.witpress.com, ISBN 1-85312-724-8

Ecotourism: it's good for your health

B. MacKenzie
Tai Poutini Polytechnic, New Zealand

Abstract

The parameters of ecotourism require inclusion of local communities in the development and operation of ventures. This requirement resonates with the literature on health improvement, which shows that enabling individuals and communities to increase control over their lives – and the change in power relationships that is entailed – is health enhancing. An implication of this approach is that the successful development of ecotourism ventures will need to replicate the approach set out in the WHO's Ottawa Charter for Health Promotion: ensuring a supportive policy environment; community action in developing activities; creating supportive, sustainable environments for tourist activity; increasing the personal knowledge and skills of those involved; and reorienting resources from the 'curative' end of the environmental perspective (i.e. fixing the damage done) to the preventive (not doing the damage in the first place). This approach has been successful in improving health, and it is therefore posited that the approach would lead to sustainable ecotourism development.

This paper explores the relationship between ecotourism development and health. It then outlines current moves on the West Coast of New Zealand's Southern Alps to strengthen and develop ecotourism, including the provision of education and training, as the first step towards creating a Centre for Sustainable Development.
Keywords: ecotourism, health improvement, sustainable development, New Zealand.

1 Ecotourism

In the past thirty years, world tourism flows have trebled, and international tourist arrivals now total around 700 million annually (WTO [1]). The impact on popular destinations has caused some to re-evaluate the benefits. For example,

Sustainable Tourism, F. D. Pineda, C. A. Brebbia & M. Mugica (Editors)

Majorca, whose tourist numbers grew from around 400,000 in 1960 to around 10 million by the turn of the century, introduced in 2002 an 'eco-tax' to pay for improvements to the infrastructure, and repair some of the damage caused.

The term 'ecotourism' was coined by Hector Ceballos-Lascaurain at a conference in Mexico City in July 1983:

> "Ecotourism…involves travelling to relatively undisturbed natural areas with the specific object of studying, admiring and enjoying the scenery and its wild plants and animals, as well as any existing cultural aspects….Ecotourism implies a scientific, aesthetic or philosophical approach…..the person who practices ecotourism has the opportunity of immersing him or herself in nature in a way that most people cannot enjoy in their routine, urban existences…..(and) that will convert him into somebody keenly involved in conservation issues." (Mader [2]).

The concept is growing and developing, and ecotourism is now being promoted as a sustainable alternative to mass tourism. Although there is some contest over detail, its components are generally held to include interaction with relatively unmodified physical environments; conservation; and environmental interpretation and/or education (see, e.g, the definition offered by the Ecotourism Association of Australia [3]).

An extended articulation of the definition of ecotourism was adopted by the 2002 World Ecotourism Summit. It distinguishes ecotourism from sustainable tourism by the addition of specific principles in relation to

> "conservation of the natural and cultural heritage, inclusion of local and indigenous communities in the planning, development and operation of ventures, thus contributing to their well-being; interpretation of the natural and cultural heritage of the destination to visitors; and preferring independent travellers and small groups." (World Ecotourism Summit [4]).

It is not enough that tourist operators develop ecotourism ventures that conform to these principles; multi-sectoral approaches are required – including the various levels of government – in order that developments occur as part of balanced strategies (SDE Web-Conference [5]).

In summary, then, ecotourism is currently held to sit within four parameters:

- it involves interaction with the natural environment
- it has an educational component (i.e. is designed to increase understanding of the environment and how it works)
- it is done with a light ecological footprint
- it is managed by businesses that are developed and run by local communities

Each of the parameters creates tension. First, there is a continuum of views on the degree to which people are regarded as part of – or threats to - the environment. On one hand, we share the planet with its waterways, flora and fauna; it is important to our mental and spiritual health that we do so; but there is an issue about the extent to which we exploit those interactions. On the other, the ecology of (certainly some of) our physical environment is so fragile that it needs a degree of protection that can only be offered by completely excluding humans.

Sustainable Tourism, F. D. Pineda, C. A. Brebbia & M. Mugica (Editors)

Secondly, there is debate about the extent to which the educational component should be specifically designed to change the behaviour of people. Some say this should always be an explicit aim of ecotourism ventures; others say that telling the stories of an environment and how it operates is enough. Some believe that there is a particular class of tourist – ecotourist – made up of people who have values and beliefs about where tourists should go and how they should behave (see, e.g., Duffy [6]); others, that the legitimacy of the term 'ecotourism' resides in the experience itself, and not in who is having the experience (MacKenzie [7]).

Thirdly, there is the debate about what constitutes a light footprint – and how 'light' is enough. Some argue that almost any intercontinental tourism is unlikely to qualify because of the amount of energy expended in getting to the destination; others believe that ameliorating the energy expended by increasing the length of visitor stay is acceptable. (The Friends of Nature Quality Criteria for Ecological Travel [8], for example, include the suggestion that air travel should be made only for distances of more than 800 kilometres involving stays of more than 12 days). This 'light footprint' debate is often the place where general discussions about ecotourism start and stop; and where those discussions get confused with the broader discourse on the 'greening' of business

Finally, there is a divergence of views between those who accept (ethically-run) large companies owning and operating ecotourism businesses as long as the employment is generated locally, and those who say that the businesses must be owned and operated locally. This is a key debate, because it is here that we intersect with the discussions on the determinants of health.

2 Health and its determinants

There is wide recognition that health cannot be defined in terms of its relationship to states of disease or illness: witness, for example, the World Health Organisation's 1946 definition of health as "a state of complete physical, mental and social well-being, and not merely the absence of disease or infirmity" (WHO [9]). Health, in this construct, is seen as a basic human right (WHO [10]) that is a resource for living, not an end in itself (WHO [11]). Prerequisites for health include peace, shelter, education, social security, social relations, food, income, the empowerment of women, a stable eco-system, sustainable resource use, social justice, respect for human rights, and equity (WHO [10]).

Once the pre-requisites for health are in place, health status is determined by a number of factors, including age, sex and heredity; social and community influences; living and working conditions; individual lifestyle; gender and culture; and socio-economic and environmental conditions. Many of the most powerful factors act primarily at the level of whole communities and population groups, rather than individuals (MoH [12]). For example, in Britain, death rates at all ages are two to three times higher among disadvantaged social groups than the more affluent groups (Benzeval and Judge [13]; DoH [14]). In New Zealand, while life expectancy has improved dramatically for the majority ethnic group over the past 20 years, for Mäori and Pacific ethnic groups it has remained

Sustainable Tourism, F. D. Pineda, C. A. Brebbia & M. Mugica (Editors)

static (Ajwani et al. [15]). Recent estimates are that 23% of years of life lost because of mortality prior to age 75 in Canada can be attributed to income differences (Raphael [16]).

The evidence, then, is clear enough to support the view that there is a causal link between low socio-economic status and poor health, even if there is contest about the mechanism(s) through which causation occurs. Where the differences between high and low incomes are small, infant mortality rates are lower - and life expectancy at age one is higher - than countries where there are large differences in income levels (Wilkinson [17]; Putnam et al. [18]; Kawachi et al. [19]; Raphael [16]). There is a strong argument that key factors are (a) the degree of income inequality within communities, and (b) the degree to which, inter alia, community members feel included in decision-making processes and trust both the people around them and the institutions that serve them.

As the Ottawa Charter for Health Promotion notes:

> "Health is created by caring for oneself and others, by being able to take decisions and have control over one's life circumstances, and by ensuring that the society one lives in creates conditions that allow the attainment of health by all its members" (WHO [11]).

The focus on the importance of personal control and social contribution supports Wilkinson and Marmot [20] when they argue that the income inequalities are important because they reflect social inequality and the existence of social hierarchies; and that the power differentials that hierarchies represent impact adversely on health status.

In my view, this construction of the concept of health is in harmony with the understandings of health shared by many indigenous peoples - understandings that articulate a complex of factors similar to those outlined by New Zealand Maori, who see good health as being dependent on a balance of factors that affect well-being:

> **Te taha wairua:** spiritual health, including the practice of tikanga Maori (Maori customs and culture) in general
>
> **Te taha hinengaro:** the emotional and psychological well-being of the whanau (extended family) and of each individual within it
>
> **Te taha tinana:** the physical aspects of health.
>
> **Te taha whanau:** the social environment in which individuals live – the whanau of family, the communities in which whanau live and act.
>
> **Te ao turoa:** the environment: the relationship between Maori and te ao turoa is one of tiakitanga (stewardship). It is the continuous flow of life source. Without the natural environment, the people cease to exist as Maori. (MoH [21])

The notion of environmental stewardship contributing to well-being has current resonance, not only in its echoing of the 19th century focus on curbing the transmission of highly communicable diseases, but in the late 20th century concerns with ability of the natural environment to sustain the current rate of resource depletion. "A new public health has emerged in which healthy environments that include a healthy social and economic milieu are seen as the way forward to improve population health" (Taylor and Guest [22]). Labonté

Sustainable Tourism, F. D. Pineda, C. A. Brebbia & M. Mugica (Editors)

has argued that the public health paradigm has changed. Whereas the imperatives were once to protect people from the ravages of the environment (with the consequences of failure being that people died, sometimes in huge numbers), the imperative now is to protect the environment from the ravages of people (with the consequence of failure being that the planet dies) (Labonté [23]).

3 Ecotourism as health improvement

There is no current evidence on which to base an absolute assertion that development of ecotourism will lead to improved health within the communities in which it takes place. However, ecotourism developments, as defined, are developed and operated by and with the communities in which the developments are based, and what we already know about the impact on health of changing power structures – of increasing the extent to which individuals and communities feel in control of their lives – supports the view that the development of ecotourism has the potential to increase this sense of control.

Ottawa Charter s	Applied to Ecotourism
Build healthy public policy Health promotion goes beyond health care. It puts health on the agenda of policy makers in all sectors and at all levels, directing them to be aware of the health consequences of their decisions and to accept their responsibilities for health. Health promotion policy combines diverse but complementary approaches including legislation, fiscal measures, taxation and organisational change. It is co-ordinated action that leads to health, income and social policies that foster greater equity. Joint action contributes to ensuring safer and healthier goods and services, healthier public services, and cleaner, more enjoyable environments.	A supportive policy environment at all levels of government, so that policies encourage processes that support the development of ecotourism opportunities, and that explicitly do not support activities that would threaten the viability of ecotourism ventures For example, the policy environment could • require an assessment of the economic, social and environmental impact of a venture • offer financial incentives to local businesses starting up • encourage the 'greening' of businesses and so on
Create supportive environments. Our societies are complex and interrelated. Health cannot be separated from other goals. The inextricable links between people and their environment constitutes the basis for a socio-ecological approach to health. The overall guiding principle for the world nations, regions and communities alike, is the need to encourage reciprocal maintenance - to take care of each other, our communities and our natural environment. The conservation of natural resources throughout the world should be emphasised as a global responsibility……	There is, arguably, an exact fit here: a supportive environment for ecotourism development would equal that for health promotion.

Sustainable Tourism, F. D. Pineda, C. A. Brebbia & M. Mugica (Editors)
© 2004 WIT Press, www.witpress.com, ISBN 1-85312-724-8

Strengthen community action Health promotion works through concrete and effective community action in setting priorities, making decisions, planning strategies and implementing them to achieve better health. At the heart of this process is the empowerment of communities, their ownership and control of their own endeavours and destinies.	The development of community-owned local enterprises, including tourist ventures, is at the heart of a community's ability to improve its well-being. The educative component in ecotourism also allows the local ventures to reach people in other communities, because visitors take their learning with them.
Develop personal skills Health promotion supports personal and social development through providing information, education for health and enhancing life skills. By so doing, it increases the options available to people to exercise more control over their own health and over their environments, and to make choices conducive to health. .	Enabling people to gain the skills to run ecotourism ventures in their community gives them more control over their destiny, thereby increasing their options.
Reorient health services The responsibility for health promotion in health services is shared among individuals, community groups, health professionals, health service institutions and governments. They must work together towards a health care system which contributes to the pursuit of health. The role of the health sector must move increasingly in a health promotion direction, beyond its responsibility for providing clinical and curative services	Reorientation of resources from the 'curative' end of the environmental perspective (i.e. fixing the damage done) to the preventive (not doing the damage in the first place) is a key theme in ecotourism ventures. Arguably, all businesses – including mainstream tourist ventures – will need to move in this direction.

This principle of local ownership and shared power is in complete accordance with the Ottawa Charter for Health Promotion, which argues that health improvement requires action and support in five domains.

There is every reason to expect, then, that developing ecotourism has the potential to improve the levels of well-being within local communities, and that this might well translate into lower levels of premature morbidity and mortality

4 Developing ecotourism on the West Coast of the Southern Alps

The West Coast has 8% of New Zealand's land mass and 1% of its population. 87% of its land mass is conservation estate (compared to 40% for the rest of New Zealand). Physically isolated by an alpine fault, it stretches a distance of some 550 kilometres.

The West Coast economy has historically been based on the utilisation of the region's natural resources, notably gold, timber and coal. Early in the 20th century, farming came to prominence in the regional economy. Tourism - long

Sustainable Tourism, F. D. Pineda, C. A. Brebbia & M. Mugica (Editors)
© 2004 WIT Press, www.witpress.com, ISBN 1-85312-724-8

established at the region's two glaciers, but now developing rapidly elsewhere - has recently begun to rival agriculture in economic importance. In 1990-91 tourist expenditure on the West Coast was in the order of $117m, and this has since grown to almost $130m (WCRC [24]).

The combination of a small (circa 30,000) and dispersed population, together with a high proportion of elderly and others reliant on income support, means that a high standard of health and social services are essential, but difficult and expensive to deliver (WCRC [24]). In 1996, GDP per capita was 5% below the national average, but by 2000 this had slipped to 12% below. Seven of the 31 census areas were in the most deprived 20% in New Zealand. The West Coast as a whole has the lowest median household and per capita income in New Zealand, and a higher rate of benefit (income support) usage, for a longer duration. Educational attainment levels are amongst the lowest in New Zealand (WCDHB [25]).

The region's Economic Development Strategic Plan includes an aspiration to be recognised as a centre of excellence for ecotourism, and specific targets relating to the increase of visitor numbers for 'eco-experiences' (WCRC [26]). This will require coherence in the planning and resource-use policies of the four local authorities and the Department of Conservation. Growing this coherence will require the support of public sector leaders, both politicians and officers.

Tai Poutini Polytechnic - the region's main tertiary education provider – has committed to establishing a national centre of excellence for ecotourism. The Centre for Ecotourism is likely to have four related arms:

1. *A research and development centre* that would develop and implement methodology to:
    - research opportunities for ecotourism ventures
    - develop the business case(s), in conjunction with local communities
    - support the business development during the first 2-5 years.
    - assist existing ecotourism operators to improve their businesses
    - assess and monitor the links between ecotourism development and population health; and the impact of ecotourism development on the local and regional infrastructure
    - develop and disseminate methods for sustainable management of visitors.
2. *An education centre* that would
    - initially provide vocational education and skills training, both in ecotourism and in business management
    - develop as a centre of educational excellence in ecotourism – and its impact on health improvement and infrastructure - and, by linking with appropriate University partners, have the capacity to offer under-graduate and post-graduate education programmes.
3. *A marketing centre* that would:
    - develop expertise in marketing ecotourism
    - offer assistance to ecotourism businesses - whether developed by the R&D centre or not - in the ongoing marketing of their ventures

Sustainable Tourism, F. D. Pineda, C. A. Brebbia & M. Mugica (Editors)
© 2004 WIT Press, www.witpress.com, ISBN 1-85312-724-8

4. *An accreditation centre* that could contribute to the development of accreditation for New Zealand ecotourism operations that meet agreed standards

A number of significant steps have been taken:

- in 2003, a Certificate in Ecotourism programme was offered; a Diploma has been added this year.
- We have an agreement with Lincoln University to work with us on the development of ecotourism, and on a broader education and training agenda around issues of sustainable development
- funding has been made available by the Polytechnic Regional Development Fund to support the initial stages of establishing of the Centre, as well as building capacity within both Polytechnic staff and operators.

5 Conclusion

The development of ecotourism ventures on the West Coast of the Southern Alps in New Zealand has the potential to act as a force for the development of local communities in an area of the country that is sparsely populated and ranks highly on indices of deprivation. Done well, the communities will experience a greater degree of control over their affairs. The perceptions of increase in power that result could well lead to an improvement in well-being, measured at both the community and individual levels.

References:

[1] WTO 2002. Press release to mark the launch of International Year of Eco-tourism. World Tourism Organisation. Available at http://www.worldtourism.org/newsroom/Releases/more_releases/january2002 /launch_ecotourism.htm Accessed 15/7/02

[2] Mader R 2000 Ecotourism Champion: A Conversation with Hector Ceballos-Lascurain http://www.planeta.com/planeta/00/0005qahectorceballos.html. Accessed 7/1/2004

[3] Ecotourism Association of Australia. http://www.ecotourism.org.au/

[4] World Ecotourism Summit 2002 Quebec Declaration on Eco-tourism. Available at http://www.world-tourism.org/sustainable/ecotourism2002.htm. Accessed 5/8/02

[5] SDE Web-Conference 2002 Final Report United Nations Environmental Programme and World Tourism Organisation Available at http://www.world-tourism.org/sustainable/2002ecotourism/eng.htm. Accessed 30/7/02

[6] Duffy Rosaleen 2002. A Trip Too Far: Ecotourism, Politics and Exploitation. London. Earthspan

[7] MacKenzie B 2003 A trip too far: ecotourism, politics and exploitation. Review. Community Development Journal 38:1 pp 168-70

Sustainable Tourism, F. D. Pineda, C. A. Brebbia & M. Mugica (Editors)

[8] Friends of Nature Quality Criteria for Ecological Travel. Available at http://www.nfi.at/english/Arbeitsbereiche/tourism/EcoTour/documents/iversionkrit_enw.pdf. Accessed 31/03/2003
[9] WHO 1946 Available at http://www.whoint/aboutwho/en/definition.html Accessed 3/12/00
[10] WHO 1997 - The Jakarta Declaration on leading health promotion into the 21st century World Health Organisation http://who.int/hpr/docs/jakarta.html Accessed 3/12/00
[11] WHO 1986. The Ottawa Charter for Health Promotion World Health Organisation Available at http://who.int/hpr/docs/ottawa.html Accessed 3/12/00
[12] MoH 2001. Preparing the New Zealand Strategic and Action Plan for Public Health: Discussion document for consultation. Wellington. NZ Ministry of Health
[13] Benzeval M and Judge K 2001 Income and health: the time dimension. Social Science & Medicine vol 52 pp1371-1390
[14] DoH 1998 Report of the Independent Inquiry into Inequalities in Health. London. Department of Health
[15] Ajwani S, Blakely T, Robson B, Tobias M, Bonne M. 2003. Decades of Disparity: Ethnic mortality trends in New Zealand 1980-1999. Wellington: Ministry of Health and University of Otago.
[16] Raphael D 2001. Inequality is Bad for Our Hearts: Why Low Income and Social Exclusion are Major Causes of Heart Disease in Canada. Toronto: North York Heart Health Network. Available at http://www.yorku.ca/wellness/heart.pdf. Accessed 2/9/02
[17] Wilkinson R 1996 Unhealthy societies: the afflictions of inequality. London. Routledge
[18] Putnam D, Leonardi R & Nanetti R 1993 Making democracy work: civic traditions in modern Italy. Princeton University Press
[19] Kawachi I, Kennedy B, Lochner K and Prothrow-Stith D 1997. Social capital, income inequality and mortality. American Journal of Public Health 87, pp1491-8
[20] Wilkinson R and Marmot M (eds) 1998 Social Determinants of Health: The Solid Facts. Copenhagen. World Health Organisation Regional Office for Europe
[21] MoH 2002 Te pai me te oranga o nga iwi: Health for all people. An Overview of Public Health Wellington. NZ Ministry of Health.
[22] Taylor R & Guest C 2001 Protecting health, sustaining the environment. in Pencon D et al Oxford Handbook of Public Health Practice, pp 206-217. Oxford. OUP
[23] Labonté R 1991 Health Promotion and Empowerment: Practice Frameworks. Toronto. Centre for Health Promotion/ParticipACTION
[24] WCRC 2002. About Our Region. West Coast Regional Council. Available at http://www.wcrc.govt.nz/environment/about.htm. Accessed 30/7/02

[25] WCDHB 2001 An Assessment of Health Needs in the West Coast District Health Board Region: Te Tirohanga Hauora o Tai Poutini. Greymouth. West Coast District Health Board. Available at http://www.westcoastdhb.org.nz/reports/WestCoastSummaryReport.pdf

[26] WCRC 2002 Regional Economic Development Strategy. West Coast Regional Council. Available at http://www.wcrc.govt.nz/council/publications/Regional%20Economic%20Development%20Strategy.htm. Accessed 30/7/02

Sustainable Tourism, F. D. Pineda, C. A. Brebbia & M. Mugica (Editors)
© 2004 WIT Press, www.witpress.com, ISBN 1-85312-724-8

A survey on Afghanistan and Iraq wars effects on the eco–tourism industry in Iran: pilot study in northern Iran

M. Sakari[1] & A. Vahabi[2]
[1]*Tonekabon Islamic Azad University, Iran*
[2]*Ministry of Interior, Iran*

Abstract

The Afghanistan and Iraq wars effects on the eco-tourism industry were studied during a 4 year survey, in northern Iran, Guilan province. In this study, the number and volume of applications for traveling to Iran for sport birds hunting like woodcock from European countries was the main factor in the study. After the year of 1999, which the first group of hunters entered into Iran, in the year of 2000-2001 the number increased and after this year, decreased again. In late 2000 and early 2001, 84 people entered into Iran for hunting. In late 2001 and early 2002, although 200 people registered for bird hunting tours, finally only 9 persons traveled to Iran. The next hunting years, 2002–2003, it raised again and the number reached to 30. The results of survey, conversation with hunters and agencies owners show us that the Middle East conflicts are the main factors.
Keywords: war, Afghanistan, Iraq, eco–tourism, woodcock, Guilan.

1 Introduction

The tourism is one of the important economic activities in all around the world. According to World Tourism Organization (WTO) report, there were 449 million tourists in the world in 1991. Tourism industry for under development countries had US$ 62.5 billion income in 1990.

Eco-tourism or the tourists for the nature, is a part of tourism activities and a new phenomenon in the world. Main subject for eco-tourism activity is nature enjoyment for several different reasons like studies, hunting, fishing, landscapes, and birds watching Pourvakhshoori [2].

Sustainable Tourism, F. D. Pineda, C. A. Brebbia & M. Mugica (Editors)

This type of tourism activity has basic differences by others, because of its low harmful effects on the environment. Hunting, itself, is not an eco-tourism activity, but if the goal of hunting is a part of nature conservation, this can include as an eco-tourism industry. One of activities, which can conserve the nature, is harvesting of wildlife's over population because of their bad ecological effects on habitats. Every year, in many countries like Iran, the governments decide to balance the population of the wildlife stocks Majnonian [1].

Iran, a country with different geographic and weather conditions, has high attractions for tourism activities including eco-tourism. In recent years, new changes in political and social views of the government happened and there are opportunities for development of these activities now. Although to reach to optimal conditions, the country has a long way. Conditions that the authors believe that the country need are infrastructures like culture, legislations, and harmony between governmental parts, locals, and political situation in the region, international awareness and right news.

Tourists hunting application return to past decades in Iran. It was a way for apart of DOE and guardsmen income and locals as well. After revolution in 1979 and many political limitations from western countries, demand decreased until 1997, when some changes happened in political atmosphere in Iran. During the recent years, there are ongoing increases on application for hunting.

In this study, the authors try to have a survey on hunting eco-tourism activity in a province in Iran and show how it damaged by political conflicts in Middle East region. Also we would like to suggest some sort of solutions for the problems, which is addressed in this study.

2 General topics of the study

In this part some of introductions and descriptions explain in details for further sections.

2.1 Study area

The study area, Guilan province, describes as a small province in North West part of Iran, with 14711 km^2 surface, fig. 1.

The province is located in geographical features of 36 34 N to 38 27N and 48 53 E to 50 34 E. The population in the province according to 1996's census was 2,224,000. Most of them live in towns and the rest are in villages and their jobs are rice farming. In winter they catch fish from the Caspian and hunt in the lagoons and irrigation ponds. Tourists are their new incomes in recent years. At least 5 million people visit Guilan per year and most of then are locals and domestic. There are many opportunities for tourist attraction in cultural heritage subjects but because of central part of Iran's values, there are not huge applications on it in Guilan. Lands of Guilan are bounded between Alborz Mountain in west and south and the Caspian in north and east. Also some provinces surrounded it and Azerbaijan Rep. is only foreign neighbor country.

The weather is moderate and wet. The humidity is very high and in some cases it meet 100%.

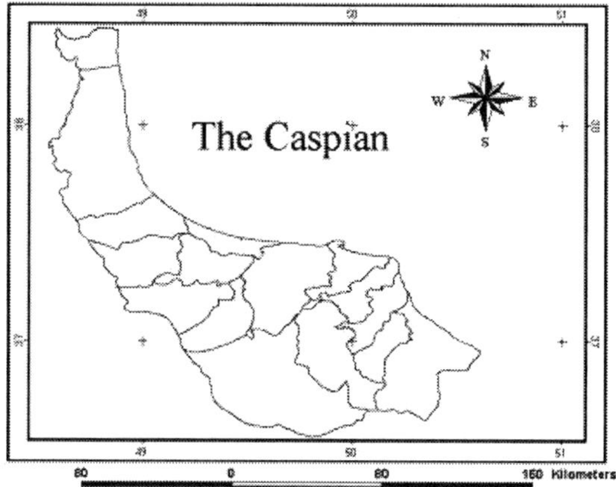

Figure 1: Map of Guilan.

The differences of land's height are more than 3000 m and it has a wide range of the precipitation. It starts from some parts of south with 150 mm to more than 2000 mm in Anzali city.

The various kinds of ecosystems like rangelands; forests, hills, seaside, sea, wetland, alpines and rivers are its potential for the wonderful environment.

2.2 Birds and hunters

The main subject of tourist attraction in the study area was sport bird of Woodcock.

Woodcock, *Scolopox rusticulum*, is a Migratory bird. Every year, from early autumn till middle of winter, these birds migrate to north of Iran from European countries, fig. 2. Iran is not only destination for migratory groups of the bird but they also can select Azerbaijan Rep. and Ukraine by their ecological needs, priority and criteria. The birds flying are too fast and into a coverage area of small and tall trees.

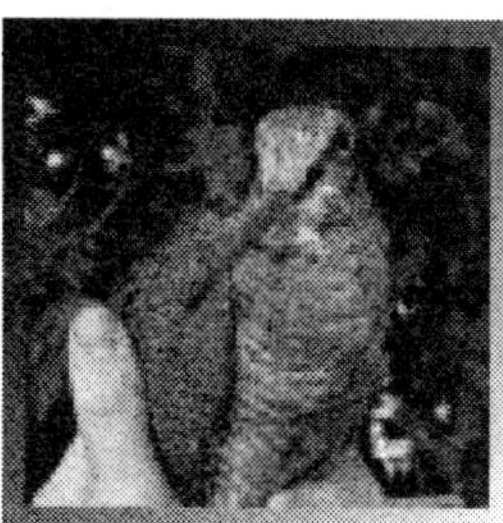

Figure 2: Woodcock, *Scolopox rusticulum*.

Sustainable Tourism, F. D. Pineda, C. A. Brebbia & M. Mugica (Editors)

The birds can hide at moments and also hunting in this situation is not too easy. According to this situation many of hunters would like to demonstrate their ability in hunting skills. Woodcock eats under ground worms and its brain has informal position in the head skeleton. Every day in sunset and sunshine times, birds have their daily flight to high and low level lands.

The first part of the bird's wing is very suitable for ink writing and many people know that as a French pen. Annual estimation of bird's population is more than 15,000. Birds breeding area is not in Iran and returns to their home countries in late winter. In Iran, hunters prefer to hunt it in night by light, but this is illegal. This activity is not very common in the locals' communities and people prefer to hunt bigger size of the birds like ducks, geese and coots.

2.3 Game areas

The habitats, which the bird prefers to stay in migratory routs, are low land forest with low slope and low-medium density of trees. According to these criteria the best and available area is located in north of Iran in Guilan and Mazandaran provinces. These provinces are located in the Caspian coastal line of Iran where the sea meets land. In the beginning stage of birds' arrival, they select top area of mountains and in colder weather, birds settle in lower habitats. In all around Guilan province every body can find Woodcock, but main density and population are located in specific parts like Gisum Forest, Nahalestan area, Radarposhteh region, Saravan Park, shanderman area and Doostlat hills, fig. 3,4.

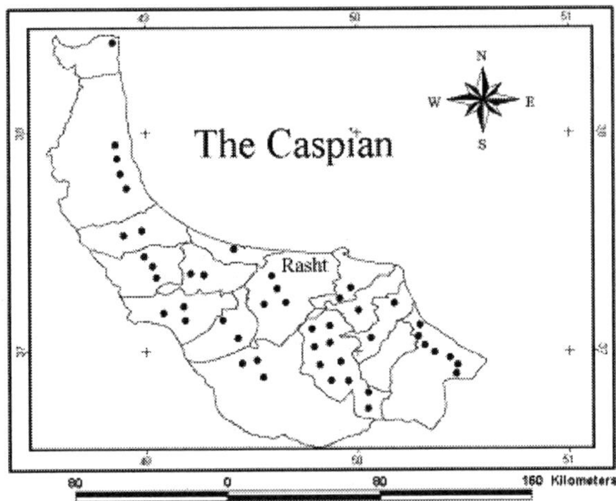

Figure 3: The distribution of Woodcock habitats in Guilan.

Land ownership in many areas is for government and very small area of orchards are owned by private sectors. The game area is located in west and central part of the province.

Sustainable Tourism, F. D. Pineda, C. A. Brebbia & M. Mugica (Editors)

2.4 Activity

Woodcock hunting group are include of hunters, local guide, translator, car driver, and a representative of DOE. In the game area only local guide and DOE people are with hunters. Hunting starts at one hour after sunshine and finishes one hour before sunset. These activities according to their permission can extent up to 6 days. The hunters also have dogs and other hunting facilities for their need.

Figure 4: A sample of game area.

DOE representative has a survey with a distance to hunters and in the end of daily activity measures the biometric characters of hunted birds.

Hunters allow hunt birds up to 6 birds per day. Hunter and DOE guardsmen register their investigation in specific sheets for their records. This program started in 1998-1999 by informal planning for tourism agencies surveying in capacity recognition. In 2000-2001, 84 people from Italy traveled to the study area for hunting.

3 Methods

Many of forms and information sheets provided for the study, from beginning years. In hunting programs, many of data collected, including of birds biometric records, weather conditions, observed birds, number of hunted birds and by hunt species. Data organized in several information sheets and surveyed by simple statistics program in computer software of Excel. Also some kind of graphs prepared for the results & discussion parts by same software. According to many interviews with tour agencies owners and hunters, meantime, the recent history of Middle East conflicts compared with the travels rate.

Sustainable Tourism, F. D. Pineda, C. A. Brebbia & M. Mugica (Editors)

4 Results

Results of the study show that in the years of 2000-2001, the rate of application was very high, because of stable political situation in neighbor countries around Iran. In these years, 1284 Woodcock hunted by hunters, meantime we permit them to hunt up to 1500. For 2001-2002 at least 200 people nominated to be in a part of Iran's eco-tour. After the September the 11th and terrorist attach to United States and US decision for the Afghanistan war only 9 people in 2 groups traveled for hunting including 2 Asian. The table 1 shows more details. After the Afghanistan war the application rate started to increase, but Iraq's conflicts had some effects on it again. During the diplomatic dialogue for Iraq's Weapons of Mass Destruction (WMD) solution ways finding, decision for travel to Iran had a low increasing rate. Many of tourists did not know that the war against Iraq will start or not and when it will start. In the other hand, from the basic year of 2000-2001, there are 89.29% decreases for the activity and it reached to 10.71%. In 2002-2003 these rates met 35.71%. In conflict years because of low demand for travel to Iran, the prices decreased. In good years for each person in average 5.2 persons-days stayed in hunting areas and in conflict years it met 5.4. In other hand, because of low pressure on stocks, observation of the birds and its hunting increased in conflict years and the number of hunted birds reached to 17.55 in average. In stable years it reached only to 15.4 in average.

Table 1: Years of study, hunters and hunting information.

Years of study	2000-2001 Base year	2001-2002	2002-2003
Number of people	84	9	30
Average days staying	5.2	5.4	5
Total days for groups	438	49	150
No. Of birds (hunted)	1294	264	810
Average hunted birds per day	5.2	5.4	5.4
Increasing rates (%)	100	- 89.29	- 64.29
Conflicts history	Nothing	Afghanistan War	Threat of war on Iraq

5 Discussions

The results show that wars and international conflicts in the Middle East region effected eco-tourism industry in north of Iran in the negative way, fig 5.

Sustainable Tourism, F. D. Pineda, C. A. Brebbia & M. Mugica (Editors)

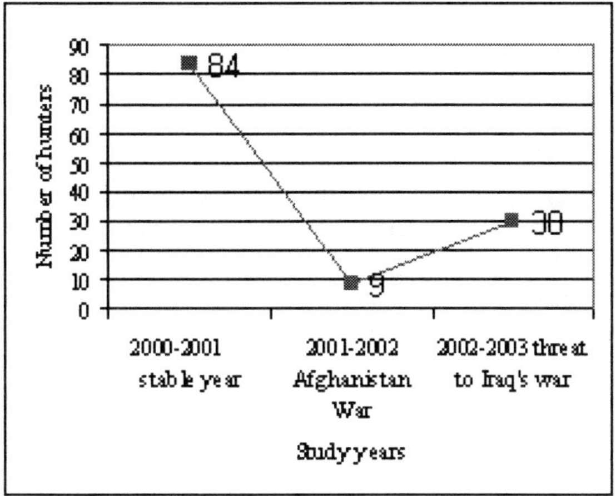

Figure 5: Rates of hunter arrival to Iran.

If we look at the map of the region, we can recognize between 600-1500 kilometers distances between hunting area and wars point. It means that there is not any threat on tourists in the destinations. From 1999 when the first groups of hunters entered in study area, some jobs have been supported like handy crafts making, translation, driving, local guiding & hotel managing. One of the hotel owners in the area in an interview told that, after first year of the activity from pure income, he bought new facilities and furniture for his hotel. The tourists for their each travel spent $US 4000. It includes travel expenses, accommodation, food cost, guides and gifts buying. According to Iran's special legislation and laws, which prevent western style enjoyment, this is a good opportunity for money making in bad economical situation in the country. At least the potential for this activity in the study area can make more than $US 1 million per year and it is sustainable for each year without negative impacts on the environment. It can include 300 people every year and there is much possibility to invite other interested groups for other species of birds. Hunters and visitors say if there is possibility for their travel to Iran for hunting they will come several times as possible. In our records there are a few persons who traveled to Iran for 3 times in one year. Also it could be a successful pattern for other eco-tourism activity like birds watching groups. It seems that public awareness is under harmful and effective news attack in comparison with first line of the war. News broadcasting agencies, televisions, radios, newspapers and other kind of media has effectiveness negative effects on people's brains washing.

Most of visitors and hunters are worried about security things in Iran. They think that travel to Iran is not too safe as a right choice. After their travel all of them could find that the imagination was wrong. Most of people in communities and groups for services and guide are very kind and helpful. Although, most of them believe DOE cost for bird's rates is too expensive exactly in comparison by

Sustainable Tourism, F. D. Pineda, C. A. Brebbia & M. Mugica (Editors)
© 2004 WIT Press, www.witpress.com, ISBN 1-85312-724-8

other countries. The facilitator company on behalf of the hunters charge $US 20 for one bird and they should pay at least for 15 birds in advance.

6 Suggestions

In the last part of the documents, the authors would like to suggest some solutions for prevention of negative effects on eco-tourism activity in conflicts situation.

It is too clear that we cannot prevent governments to war, easily, but there are some simple way to reduce the negative effects and making a capacity building for better using from opportunities.

1- Introducing the eco-tour activities for the governments and NGOs for investments in good livelihood for local community's life.
2- Establishment of an eco-tour agencies news network for right news.
3- Having several correspondents in destinations for final coordination.
4- Establishment of some conventions for the government commitments in eco-tours atmosphere saving.
5- Books publication for introduction of eco-tours capacities.
6- Having an annual conference between the country members for using of their experiences.
7- Protection of countries environmental potentials and landscapes.
8- Real cost charge for the eco-tour activity. It should not to be low or high.

Acknowledgements

The authors would like to have thanks to all people who help them in this report in different stages. Also, special thanks to Mr. Esmaeel Hasani, DOE expert in Guilan province for his big efforts in data management and information gathering. Thanks to Mr. Hooshmand and Mr. Zamani DOE experts in Guilan province for their efforts to provide final needed information. Finally thanks to Mr. Ramazanipour, the GIS expert of DOE Guilan for maps and GIS supporting.

References

[1] Majnonian, H., The guide to national parks and conserved areas preparation for tourism, Published by Department of the Environment of Iran, 1998.
[2] Pourvakhshoori, Z., Environmental development solutions for shoreline tourism, published by Department of the Environment of Iran, pp. 1-51, 2001.
[3] Makhdoom, M., Fundamental of land uses planning, Tehran University Press, 1993.
[4] DOE Guilan reports archives, 2003.

Sustainable Tourism, F. D. Pineda, C. A. Brebbia & M. Mugica (Editors)

Section 5
Cultural tourism

Preserving Najaf's heritage

G. Abraham
Research Triangle Institute, USA

Abstract

The holy city of Najaf and its neighboring holy cities of Karbala and Kufa have tremendous significance for the Shi'i. These cities with tombs of Imman Ali, Imam Hussein, Imam Abbas, and Muslim Bin Akil are significant stewards and learning centers for Shi'i. The Shrines of these great men, immediate family of The Prophet Mohammad draw Shi'i from many countries in the region. With a majority of Shi'i in Iraq and Iran, and a significant number in Pakistan and India the number of visitors expected in any given year exceed several million. In May 2003 alone, over 1.5 million visitors came to the shrine of Imam Hussein in Karbala[1]. While visitors come throughout the year, the city of Najaf has 38 official religious holidays. In Egypt, a major tourism attraction in the region, the Ministry of Tourism boasted 5 million visitors in its peak year 2002[2]. Najaf as a center of religious pilgrimage competes with these figures. With the development of local governments throughout Iraq, and specifically the growth of the cities, the heritage of Najaf must be a priority in considering its future.
Keywords: Najaf, Heritage, Shi'a, Shi'I, urban development, heritage, tourism, pilgrim.

1 Background

This religious and cultural heritage of Najaf is replenishable and unlike the pyramids will not erode over time or from more visitors. As such, it is the most sustainable form of tourism. However, the city in its present state is unable to capitalize from this rich resource. Moreover, with the large number of visitors the existing resources of the city are being strained to limit. Traffic congestion and circulation is choking the city, pollution has exponentially increased, sewerage and water treatment plants are short of capacity.

The city planning office has not produced a master plan since 1982, and even then, it was created by the Ministry of Planning in Baghdad, the existing map of

Sustainable Tourism, F. D. Pineda, C. A. Brebbia & M. Mugica (Editors)

the city was made by the Soviet Union in 1976. The city has since grown in an ad-hoc manner at best.

The need for the program is prompted by increasing numbers of Pilgrim visitors from all over the world to Najaf, especially as the borders become more porous and the country stabilizes. The dedication of pilgrims in viewing the shrines is a threat. Their very presence is becoming detrimental to the quality and preservation of the Shrines and other religious facilities. In the city and in the shrine, their increasing number and the virtual lack of any effective crowd management creates an uncontrollable environment. At the same time, the virtual absence of facilities for other pilgrim activities means very short stays in the area, skewed economies, lessening the long term benefits to the local infrastructure and economy, and less flexibility in scheduling visits for religious festivals. Even so, the increasing number of Pilgrims visiting Najaf has provided the impetus for accelerated growth in Najaf and its surrounding areas. Growth pressures in turn have resulted in encroachments and urban sprawl, thereby jeopardizing the religious heritage and impairing their value. Additionally, regional growth pressures now risk loss of potentially productive agricultural lands, as an expanding population seeks space for living in a constrained environment.

In developing a Master Plan for the city of Najaf, it is proposed to create a Program that is inclusive of existing and future grants. **The Comprehensive Development Plan for the city of Najaf Program** (CDCN) proposes a strategy for Najaf that would address, in a coordinated manner:

Preservation and protection of the unique antiquity settings, cultural resources, and heritage of Najaf region, while expanding opportunities for pilgrim and visitor activities;

Planned city and subsequently, regional growth strategy that would promote sustainable economic development, by preventing further urban sprawl and the deleterious effects of unplanned development on Najaf's cultural heritage and on the living conditions; and

A regional development strategy that would create new economic opportunities for the citizens of the region.

The CDCN Program is conceived to have four distinct types of products that would combine both long-range planning and immediate actions:

- Institutional capacity building
- Structure Plan
- Investment Projects
- Heritage Plan

2 Institutional capacity building

The city needs to be able to plan for the growth of Najaf. This will mean developing the capacity of key departments in the governorate and municipality including the department of planning, water and sewerage, construction, environmental protection, tourism, while assisting in the strengthening of the of relevant civil society organizations, such the chamber of tourism, the hotel

Sustainable Tourism, F. D. Pineda, C. A. Brebbia & M. Mugica (Editors)
© 2004 WIT Press, www.witpress.com, ISBN 1-85312-724-8

associations, marketing and tour operators association, engineers unions and other professional associations (syndicates). Multinational grants can be utilized to:

- Train relevant government departments in budgeting and strategic planning
- Assist with organizational structure and parliamentary process in the professional associations
- Provide study tour/s to regional tourism centers.

3 Structure plan

Clearly, all of the products of the CDCN are closely intertwined and should be reviewed jointly for a full understanding of their total scope. The Structure Plan provides the overall framework to which the other elements relate.

The Structure Plan will present an overall strategy for the twenty-year growth of the Najaf region, focusing upon planned growth within Najaf city and several target development areas across the region.

Figure 1: City Center Najaf.

The plan must recognize that Najaf is a changing, dynamic city. Historic resources must be protected in a way which allows growth and change of the city and its surroundings. The challenge is to accommodate contemporary development in a living, historic city and to achieve a qualitative understanding of the important values and priorities which should guide such development. Equally, the Plan should define a clear implementation agenda of actions which

Sustainable Tourism, F. D. Pineda, C. A. Brebbia & M. Mugica (Editors)

can enable the development and refinement of the Plan; their sequence, approximate scale, and required resource commitments. In this manner, appropriate priorities can be developed to scope and identify the required public and private investment programs that will be the ultimate product of the work.

This Plan will encompass strategies for how the region should grow, where population should be concentrated, and how growth opportunities can be addressed to meet the CDCN Program objectives. Multinational grants can be utilized to:

- Develop baseline studies to document existing physical condition of city, including topography, built environment, road networks, city and district boundaries, municipal services
- Develop a mapping facility in the Planning office
- Organize international competition for preservation and restoration projects
- Prepare an international competition for a Democracy Monument to proclaim the rebirth of a great city
- Design and implement a program for urban renewal and beautification
- Restore basic services and upgrading circulations
- Landscape the city center
- Reforest the denuded green zones and forests in and around the city
- Design and build transportation termini
- Develop a master plan with a 20-year horizon with review and recommendations on primary circulation, intercity transportation termini, pilgrimage facilities, zoning and land use for city and residential communities.

The structure plan will necessitate an active program advisory committee to decide on short and long term objectives. Its engagement will reinforce through an iterative process organization, parliamentary process, debate and dialogue, consensus building and most importantly an end result that can showcase transparency in governance.

4 Investment projects

The structure plan to be completed under the CDCN with priorities set by the governing council, civil society organizations and Program Advisory Committee, will provide a framework for identifying the investment projects to be developed into full proposals for donor and private sector funding. The investment project could cover a wide-range of development needs. A listing of some of the prospective investment projects is indicative of the range of needs in Najaf.

4.1 Transportation

- Airport to accommodate growing international air travel and a management/financing plan for operations and maintenance.

Sustainable Tourism, F. D. Pineda, C. A. Brebbia & M. Mugica (Editors)

- A greatly expanded road network to relieve congestion and make the sites accessible, and a major highway to connect Najaf to the major cities and the holy corridor of Najaf-Kufa and Karbala.
- Bus depot for inter and intra city transportation.
- Linking Najaf to national rail network.
- A pedestrian crossings at key intersections.

4.2 Utilities

- Water/sewerage treatment and solid waste disposal; expand serviced land to provide for unserviced areas and new planned settlements; possible public/private partnership to build and operate water and wastewater treatment plants, and solid waste management. Use of secondary treated wastewater can be considered for irrigating greenbelts and new golf courses and other recreational areas to be developed.
- Develop water and other resource conservation programs in hotels and resident areas to include such measures as water saving devices and recycling of grey water for toilet use and landscape irrigation and beautification.
- Expand electric and telephone service and placement of electric and telephone cable underground to correct service interruptions.
- Develop large open area cooling systems to make tourism more comfortable in tourist areas outside the monuments, e.g., the old market areas and proposed new theme villages, and thus expand opportunities for tourist outside activities.

4.3 Economic development

- Develop a Heritage Plan for better management of tourism and make Najaf a world-class managed tourism destination, comparable to Mecca, Medina, and the Vatican.
- Complete antiquities museum and cultural tourism management.
- Develop Centers for research and education for both scholars and tourists.
- Develop new recreational opportunities to increase stop-over touristic nights; new recreation includes golf courses, thematic parks, horseback and camel riding trails, exhibition and tournament areas, sport stadiums, game halls and theaters.
- Develop new hotel zones nearer shrine to replace informal settlements and with the financial proceeds from hotel land sales pay for relocation of the informal settlements.
- Develop theme hotels to serve different cultural requirements of tourists from many nations.
- Develop financing and technical assistance for small and micro-enterprise expansion to improve economy and expand job opportunities.

Sustainable Tourism, F. D. Pineda, C. A. Brebbia & M. Mugica (Editors)

- Develop the dormant and ad-hoc cottage industries for religious tourism products and tours to see how products are made.
- Expand agricultural lands to replace lands taken for urban growth and to create new economic enterprises; especially for import substitution to service tourism needs for fresh foods.

3.4 Social development

- Improve the administrative capability of Najaf city government and identify opportunities to privatize selected public services where the private sector can better finance/manage.
- Identify revenue and financing strategies to fund administrative and development requirements of the Najaf city and governorate.
- Relocate informal villages negatively affecting the monuments with provisions for housing, sanitation, health, education and market services to provide incentives for relocation.
- Develop adequate health care facilities for urban and rural residents and tourists.
- Develop higher education institutions to improve opportunities for residents, e.g., completion of universities.
- Develop new primary, secondary, and technical schools to serve growing population.
- Develop scientific waste management and pollution control programs.

3.5 Critical Considerations in Developing Investment Projects for Najaf

Public Finance in Iraq: There are no mechanisms for longer term financing such as bond issues to amortize by user-fees; nor does a financing institution exist which specializes in financing infrastructure costs. Users are often asked to pay for infrastructure costs up front. Consideration should be given to the introduction of mechanisms to finance both public capital costs and user connections fees, ranging from bond financing to specialized municipal banks. Capturing the increases in property values resulting from public investments is also an important consideration. Loan Development Fund financing is available for local units providing financing for private "productive" purposes, although legally these could also be used for infrastructure.

Proactive Environmental Management by implementing ISO 14000: The International Standards Organization (ISO) in Geneva is in process of formulating a generic series of environmental management standards which will become a framework for international approval for products and services. In Najaf, tourism may be impacted by ISO 14000 as European and North American tourism associations begin assessing tourist destinations based on compliance with ISO 14000. Already a number of European states have adopted environmental management standards and the ISO 14000 is but a means to integrate and standardize formats. Compliance with ISO 14000 has positive environmental benefits and will promote Najaf as a desirable tourist destination.

Sustainable Tourism, F. D. Pineda, C. A. Brebbia & M. Mugica (Editors)
© 2004 WIT Press, www.witpress.com, ISBN 1-85312-724-8

ISO 14000 is implemented by individual companies and does not require a public regulatory structure. It is a voluntary management program that assists companies to become environmentally conscious in their operations. A private certification program in Iraq would be constructive in assisting local industry and tourist facilities to comply with ISO 14000. A proactive ISO 14000 program in Najaf would give the area a competitive advantage over other international destinations that have not adopted a program.

Small and Micro Enterprises (SME): Creating large industrial complexes in Najaf, which is geographically remote from the centers of commerce and industry, will be difficult to accomplish. High unemployment and under-employment in both the urban and rural areas is a priority concern As tourism expands in Najaf, enhancing small business will be a productive means to increase employment and with less investment than required in an attempt to attract a large-scale industrial enterprise. SME programs serve both urban and rural populations and can bring jobs to locations away from the monuments.

Public/Private Partnership for Area Management: The local private sector can be involved in augmenting public services and enhancing the management of key areas in Najaf. There is a growing movement in cities for the private sector to organize and establish commercial and residential area management districts, referred to in the U.S. as Business Improvement Districts (now numbering over 2,000 nationwide)[3] and homeowner associations. These private districts raise funds, primarily through a self-adopted assessments and fees-for-services, to provide auxiliary services such as additional street cleaning, garbage removal and security. With sanitation and security issues in Najaf being of primary concern to the residents and tourists alike, those private management districts may be a constructive partnership with government to better finance and manage selected urban services.

Private Foundations/Direct Giving Campaign: The uniqueness of Najaf's historical assets will attract international foundation support, if properly packaged, especially for management of the monument areas and the museum. Najaf's international visibility may also be the basis to establish its own international foundation for a direct giving campaign especially directed at Shi'i, Sunni and Ismaeli communities in Europe, North America and Asia. If the Program Working Groups decide that private foundation opportunities are worthy of expanded consideration, this element could be expanded into a private investment project. The religious sites are controlled by the Awqaf Ministry.

Focusing Opportunities: As can be discerned from the above descriptions of potential development opportunities for Najaf, there are diverse areas that can be considered. However, focusing its development program on improving the tourism potential of Najaf is the main priority. Initiating an effective Heritage Plan to improve the management and presentation of the historical assets of Najaf as a world-class tourist attraction, and developing investment projects to support that objective, would offer the most effective opportunity to improve the economy in Najaf and protect the antiquities from degradation.

Grant Opportunities: Investment Strategy will have been defined in the course of the work as the most critical elements that should be implemented, and

Sustainable Tourism, F. D. Pineda, C. A. Brebbia & M. Mugica (Editors)

a report for each project that identifies the scope, scale, cost, and effect of each project will be developed, with the aim of seeking sources of public and private investment. These projects could include the development of:

The development of a new resort area with adequate infrastructure

- Restoration of the Great Souk/ Bazaar.
- Development of the Open Museum and Heritage District in Najaf city-center

5 The Heritage Plan

The Heritage Plan must recognize that the city itself is historic and has an important context that goes beyond individual monument sites. The Plan should define measures to protect and enhance settings and districts which have integrity and can convey a larger sense of quality which is the context for each individual site. The city of Najaf itself, beyond its individual monuments, represents an important historical continuity that needs to be understood, thematically linked, and reinforced in order to take best advantage of its settings and resources.

- Visitors to the city find it difficult to appreciate the setting of the city, the importance of its monuments, and their inter-linkage:
- There is a general lack of interpretive programs for the city and its antiquities. There is no overall interpretive center, modest signage, and scant information regarding the evolution of the overall setting.
- The resources of the city are not well presented or communicated. No clear delineation of preservation districts is apparent and new development is often at odds with adjacent resources.
- Many new hotels have been scattered throughout the community and surrounding area rather than reinforcing the existing urban core and concentrating visitor activities.
- Land use and development at the edges of monument sites are encroaching on important historic settings; this will get worse if clear directions are not established for development.
- Increased visitation will require improved welcoming points of arrival to the city.

As in other locations in Iraq, population expansion pressures and the shortage of arable land create conflicts between settlement pressures and prudent land use. In Najaf, these pressures are felt with the added concern for historic and cultural sites of priceless value. What is required for the Heritage Plan is a clear understanding of the heritage of Najaf and a strategy for encouraging evolution, growth, and development which can reinforce that heritage.

The Heritage Plan for Najaf will include consideration of preservation, interpretation, economic development, visitor infrastructure, and management.

Preservation: Defines the resource and how it should be protected. Clearly, the key monuments and their settings must be preserved. In the case of Najaf, resources are within a larger cultural landscape -- sometimes a natural setting and in other times a man-made setting -- which needs to be understood and respected.

Sustainable Tourism, F. D. Pineda, C. A. Brebbia & M. Mugica (Editors)

The Plan should broadly define the attributes of these contextual landscapes in the vicinity of each monument and needs to propose actions to insure that these settings enhance and do not detract from them. Beyond that, the Plan should indicate districts of the city where contextual qualities should be maintained, as well as those where significant new development can be encouraged and sustained.

Figure 2: Shrine of Imam Ali, Najaf.

Interpretation: Tells the story of resources so visitors can appreciate them and understand how they relate to one another and to their context. The story of Najaf and its centuries of change and discovery has been compelling to potential visitors for generations and it should encompass not only key monuments but also the city which surrounds them. The Plan should indicate where this story should be told, the means to make it accessible and communicable, and how the stories of individual sites and settings relate to one another.

6 Conclusions

The trend in heritage management and tourism development tends to emphasize narrative and interpretation. The cities of Najaf and Kufa need these elements, however, they are in greater need of physical development. The end of the war will see greater numbers of pilgirms coming to visit the shrine, and like Mecca one can benefit from visiting during the year as well as during religious holidays.

The great number of pilgrims that have come to visist Najaf in 2003 are a clear indicator of the numbers to expect in the coming years and decades.

The cities need to understand where their needs are going to be in the short and long term. The planning must engage the municipal leadership as well as the clerics. The planning must be done in an iterative manner and with concensus among all the different parties. The planning must also engage the investment community. The investors in Najaf and the surround cities/countries are clearly able to see the benefits that can be had , however, the local government must create an enabling environment with appropriate controls.

Najaf is ideally suited for a development both in urbanization and its surrounding rural communities. These elements can be developed to complement one another, indeed to enhance each other. The city grows to accommodate growing numbers of pilgrims, while the farming communities thrive by producing agricultural produce for Najaf and the rest of the nation. In Najaf , understanding lessons learned from regional tourism/heritage centers is essential; the culture and heritage must continue to thrive and be cherished, while economic development continues. These elements are ultimately symbiotic.

References

[1] Killidar, R. Personal communication, 10, October 2003, Custodian of the Shrine of Imam Ali, Najaf Iraq.

[2] Egyptian Ministry of Tourism. Annual Report. Cairo Egypt, 2003.

[3] McDonald, H. Why Business Improvement Districts Work. Civic Bulletin No. 4 May 1996. http:/ /www.manhattan-institute.org/html/cb_4.htm.

Sustainable Tourism, F. D. Pineda, C. A. Brebbia & M. Mugica (Editors)
© 2004 WIT Press, www.witpress.com, ISBN 1-85312-724-8

Community based cultural tourism: Findings from the US

J. Herranz Jr., M.-R. Jackson, F. Kabwasa-Green & D. Swenson
The Urban Institute

Abstract

Community-based cultural tourism remains an unexamined aspect of urban cultural tourism which has grown in importance during the past several decades primarily as an economic development strategy but also as a key characteristic for improving and indicating urban quality of life. While prevalent in Europe and other parts of the world, such tourism has also grown in scope and size in the United States which has experienced a proliferation of informally and formally designated arts and cultural districts, entertainment districts, and historic districts. Despite the prevalence of such efforts, there has been relatively little research into community-based cultural tourism in comparison to the extent that urban cultural tourism is being developed in cities and towns across the United States. This paper contributes to addressing this knowledge gap by explaining how the dominant context of urban cultural tourism neglects local residents and community-based tourism. In doing so, this paper identifies several of the issues associated with understanding the complexity, identification, and analysis of urban cultural tourism at large.

1 Context

Community-based cultural tourism remains an unexamined aspect of urban cultural tourism which has grown in importance during the past several decades primarily as an economic development strategy but also as a key characteristic for improving and indicating urban quality of life. While prevalent in Europe and other parts of the world, urban cultural tourism has also grown in scope and size in the United States which has experienced a proliferation of informally and formally designated arts and cultural districts, entertainment districts, and historic districts. Despite the prevalence of such efforts, there has been relatively

Sustainable Tourism, F. D. Pineda, C. A. Brebbia & M. Mugica (Editors)
 ISBN 1-85312-724-8

little research in community-based cultural tourism in comparison to the extent that urban cultural tourism is being developed in cities and towns across the United States. Recent research (Jackson and Herranz [10]) in the United States reveals that while there are abundant examples of the relationship between cultural activities and community development, there is little corresponding analytical research on community-based cultural tourism. This paper contributes to addressing this knowledge gap by explaining how the dominant context of urban cultural tourism tends to neglect local residents and community-based tourism. In doing so, this paper identifies several of the issues associated with understanding the complexity, identification, and analysis of urban cultural tourism writ large.

Several factors contributed to the growing importance of tourism in general and urban cultural tourism in particular. Beginning in the 1950s, mass tourism developed as a result of the increase in leisure time of the growing middle class, commodification of leisure/recreation/culture, and the reduction in travel costs associated with automobiles and airlines (Shaw and Williams [23]). In the 1960s, many urban political and business leaders began developing tourism strategies in attempts to capture a piece of this growing market demand as well as a means to lure investment in downtowns that began showing signs of urban distress. Urban tourism-related activities increased in the 1970s and 1980s as a result of economic shifts from manufacturing to service industries when downtown land and buildings formerly associated with manufacturing industries decreased in value and became investment opportunities for growing service sectors such as hospitality, travel, and tourism. Several researchers have examined the relationship between tourism as a vehicle for downtown revitalization (Frieden and Sagalyn [7]; Zukin [26] and Judd and Fainstein [12]). While cities have invested in cultural amenities since the 19th Century, the recent patterns of local government entertainment investment are different from earlier periods in several ways: demographic and economic context is different; intended patron base has shifted from the city's residents to visitors; and the scale of entertainment construction is significantly greater (Eisinger [5]).

2 The business of culture

As noted by Zukin [26], "culture is more and more the business of cities." Indeed, increasingly over several decades, municipal governments and private developers worked together to create festival malls, riverfront walks, and urban entertainment districts. One of the early prototypes for the urban festival mall was Boston's Faneuil Hall–Quincy Market complex in the mid-1970s when the city and private investors combined architectural renovation, mixed retailing, and an array of restaurants and cafés to attract people into the center of the city. The economic and aesthetic success of Quincy Market prompted almost 250 communities to copy the model in one way or another over the following dozen years (Walters [24]).

In addition to downtown tourism development, many cities also extended such activities along urban riverfronts, often in decaying industrial districts.

Sustainable Tourism, F. D. Pineda, C. A. Brebbia & M. Mugica (Editors)

Cities such as Cleveland, Chattanooga, Columbia (South Carolina), and Louisville attempted to transform wasteland areas by combining parkland, mixed-use commercial and residential development, and entertainment venues to create a riverside version of the festival mall (Jordan [11]). One city considered to be among the most successful riverfront tourism development is Baltimore, where formerly decaying property was transformed into a convention and tourism space known as Harborplace. While Harborplace attracted tens of millions of visitors each year, it also functioned as an "economic island" that was unconnected to deteriorating neighborhoods around it (Levine [16, p. 118]). Such tourism sites that emphasize secure and consumption-themed environments have been described as "tourist bubbles" where the space is an artificial, segregated environment devoted to consumption and play, whereas substantial areas of the city outside the bubble are often not included in deriving benefits associated with the development (Judd and Fainstein [12]). For example, Atlanta has a downtown tourist space that is devoted to sports, consumption, and spectacle but encloses its visitors within a secured and protected environment in which business travelers and tourists are segregated from urban living (Newman [19]).

Some tourist bubbles include sports stadiums—often the most expensive components of a city's tourism infrastructure. Civic boosters often consider stadiums and sports arenas as essential for downtown regeneration, so despite their enormous costs, these facilities are an essential signifier of "big league" status. Indeed, the major benefit of professional sports teams to a city may be the intangible quality of the image they provide for civic boosters, as the stadiums and sports arenas are among the most expensive components of a city's tourism infrastructure (Newman [19]).

3 Tourism effects

The development of urban cultural tourism has been associated with large investment of public amounts to construct large entertainment projects, including stadiums, convention centers, entertainment districts, and festival malls. Their justification is that such projects will generate economic returns by attracting tourists to the city. Tourism was seen as a way to attract visitors, generating income and jobs, spurring investment in upgrading local facilities and infrastructure, and benefiting local residents and businesses. Overall, such studies have found positive economic impacts. There is an extensive literature on impacts of tourism and attractions (Goeldner and Brent [8]; Plaza [21]). The macroeconomic approach includes research into effects on arrivals and overnight stays, balance of payment, effects on income, and employment, principally using multiplier and input-output analysis, and cost-benefit analysis of projects in terms of fiscal impact. Microeconomic studies tend to reflect a more customer-oriented approach principally using interviews, survey methodologies, and urban market segmentation techniques. While economic analyses often provide the foundation for assessing the role and effects of tourism-related activities, many cities refer more generally to the quality of life aspects of cultural tourism. Such quality of life references may include tourist surveys but often rely on anecdotal

Sustainable Tourism, F. D. Pineda, C. A. Brebbia & M. Mugica (Editors)

information about the cultural claims and reputation of cities. To a large extent, data about arts and culture and other such tourism-related activities is not collected or integrated in urban quality of life information systems (Jackson and Herranz [10]).

According to Eisinger [5], most studies on the impacts of urban tourism focus on economic benefits and consequently even less is known about the political and social implications of building a city for visitors rather than local residents. Indeed, there is considerable literature showing that the economic effects of stadium investments, casino projects, convention centers, and other such entertainment amenities are generally negative from a public investment perspective, and that the few positive effects tend to be highly localized (Swindell and Rosentraub 1998). Eisinger [5] suggests that, in many cases, building the city for the "visitor class" may strain relations between local leaders and the citizenry and skew the civic agenda to the detriment of fundamental municipal services. Other researchers suggest that a region benefits most when cultural amenities cater to higher status groups. Richard Florida [6] argues that the "creative class" of the "new economy" is attracted to cultural amenities and that regions rich in such quality of life are associated with higher economic competitiveness. Relatedly, Kotkin [13] suggests that places are likely to thrive economically if they offer cultural amenities, recreational opportunities, and local qualities of life that appeal to social classes in the new economy. Kotkin elaborates a typology of places that correspond to the lifestyle distinctions and opportunities of specific social classes. "Nerdistans" offer the trappings of high-end suburban settings for upper-middle-class technology workers; rural "Valhallas" provide pristine environments and outdoor lifestyles for professionals and entrepreneurs who can work remotely from industry centers; and some older cities have been revitalized as "boutique cities" for dot-com bohemians or contemporary "casbahs" for entrepreneurial immigrants.

4 Cultural tourism and residents

However, such recent attention on the role of cultural amenities in regional economic competitiveness extends a pattern of underemphasizing the relationship of cultural tourism to all segments of local residents. Such approaches share a limitation associated with conventional cultural tourism development focused on entertainment districts and festival malls in that they neglect the complexity of culture within an urban context. From this perspective, urban tourism is more complex because it is multi-spatial, multi-functional, and multi-spatial. As noted by Burtenshaw et al. [3], even within a single city there is "tourist city," "shopping city," "culture city," and a "historic city." This complexity has made it difficult to describe and consequently has been underexamined by researchers. Indeed, one of the challenges of identifying and studying cultural phenomenon in an urban context is that conventional notions of arts and culture underemphasize and often neglect the breadth and depth of such activities as they are actually practiced and experienced by urban residents (Jackson and Herranz [10]).

Sustainable Tourism, F. D. Pineda, C. A. Brebbia & M. Mugica (Editors)

Some researchers suggest that the benefits of cultural tourism become more mixed when accounting for local residents. While there are few comparative studies of scale and importance of urban tourism, there has been a debate regarding assessing the benefits of urban cultural tourism in terms of economic and social sustainability (Shaw and Williams [23]). The main issue concerns the viability and implications specific cultural tourism policies and activities. Some researchers suggest that cultural tourism has shifted from the disadvantaged and working middle class to higher income groups as cities increasingly focused on image creation and "place marketing" (Mommass and van der Poel [17]). Rather than developing cultural amenities for local residents, place marketing is a way to sell to investors and tourists such as business and conference visitors who spend more money than local residents. However, such initiatives are seen as divisive in that they target affluent aesthetics and conspicuous consumption while ignoring or neutralizing local ways of life (Bramham et al. [2]). These types of initiatives are also problematic because such tourism is variable and dependent on new products and services in order to stay competitive, thereby requiring continual and expensive upgrading of facilities and infrastructure (Law [15]).

Large-scale investments in urban cultural tourism have also been questioned because the expected benefits to local residents have not been clearly apparent. Some researchers challenge the notion that tourism brings prosperity and jobs to inner city areas. Law [15] found little evidence of job creation, while Sawaki [22] found that "new" jobs associated with urban tourism were actually shifted from outside the central business district. In general, urban cultural tourism has been found to generate few clear spillover benefits to neighborhoods and residents that are not directly involved in tourism activities. Indeed, researchers have found most tourism benefits are very localized and bring improvement to a specific area (Shaw and Williams [23]). However, the concentrated effects of tourism raise issues related to the spatial polarization of mass tourism (Shaw and Williams [23]). That is, that local areas become dependent on particular market segments leading to saturation tourism and its attendant problems of similar products and services as well as environmental pressures on infrastructure, lodging, and traffic.

At the same time, the development of mass tourism may also be intrusive to local people, leading to "staged authenticity" where tourists experience culture through commercial and social filters, rendering uniform what was culturally diverse (Shaw and Williams [23]).

5 Cultural tourism and community development

However, while there are few studies documenting such effects, a tourism-based strategy for local economic development may show positive benefits. Researchers have noted the development impact of tourism on previously marginal areas (Williams [25]; Nels and Binns [18]). There is evidence that tourism may serve as a means for local economic development including providing services (electricity, housing, water, housing, jobs), racial

Sustainable Tourism, F. D. Pineda, C. A. Brebbia & M. Mugica (Editors)

reconciliation, and empowerment of historically disadvantage groups (Nels and Binns [18]). At the same time, place marketing can be regarded as a locality-based strategy to reimage and restructure local economies (Demaziere and Wilson [4]). According to Hall and Hubbard [9, p. 162],"The strategic manipulation of image and culture clearly provides a strong basis for coalition building." As coalition building is a main element of community building initiatives, cultural tourism may offer considerable potential to bring community stakeholders together.

There is growing evidence that art and culture activities contribute to community building and the development of social capital according to a six-year study conducted by The Urban Institute exploring the development of indicators of arts and culture in communities in United States (Jackson and Herranz [10]). In that study, field interviews and focus groups involving more than 300 people in seven cities (Los Angeles, Boston, Providence, Chicago, Oakland, Denver, Washington DC) revealed various examples of community-based cultural tourism. However, the study found little corresponding analytical research on the topic. Exceptions included notions of the "creative city" (Landry [14]) and "community cultural development" (Adams and Goldbard [1]) that suggested complex patterns of cultural-based development benefiting both local residents and visitors.

In order to better understand community-based cultural tourism, several questions remain to be explored. How does cultural tourism relate to community building processes? In addition to its role as an economic development generator, to what extent does cultural tourism contribute to social capital and civic engagement? In specific cases of community-based cultural tourism, in what ways do residents shape the identity of the community they want portrayed to the public, and how do local art-forms and practices get put forth as community assets? What is the role of community development and other social change organizations—nonprofits, NGO's—in establishing, planning, and creating cultural tourism agendas? Are these kinds of organizations equipped to enter that arena? How receptive is the tourism "industry" to this kind of involvement?

Specific methodological questions also require attention. How does tracking of the impact of cultural tourism align with indicator efforts to monitor quality of life? In communities where cultural tourism is a significant revenue generator, how is this tracked and how does it intersect with other kinds of community measures? In places where cultural tourism efforts are nascent, what kinds of systems are set up to capture impacts--economic and other?

In so far as such activities are elements of community-based cultural tourism specifically, then urban cultural tourism more generally may yield potential social benefits previously underestimated. However, the extent of such benefits is uncertain in circumstances where urban cultural tourism is primarily expressed through heavy commercialized forms and staged authenticity rather than community-based cultural tourism. The proliferation of informal and formal cultural, entertainment, and heritage districts suggests that there is breadth of

Sustainable Tourism, F. D. Pineda, C. A. Brebbia & M. Mugica (Editors)
© 2004 WIT Press, www.witpress.com, ISBN 1-85312-724-8

experiences that may yet offer lessons on better understanding the fuller range of drawbacks and benefits associated with community-based cultural tourism.

References

[1] Adams, Don and Arlene Goldbard. Creative Community: The Art of Cultural Development. New York: The Rockefeller Foundation. 2001.
[2] Bramham, P., I. Henry, H. Mommass, and H. van der Poel. (eds), Leisure and Urban Processes: Critical Studies of Leisure Policy in West European Cities. London: Routledge. 1989.
[3] Burtenshaw, D., Bateman, M. and Ashworth, G.J. The European City: A Western Perspective. London: David Fulton. 1991.
[4] Demaziere, C., and P.A. Wilson. Local Economic Development in Europe and the Americas. London: Mansell. 1996.
[5] Eisenger, Peter. The Politics of Bread and Circuses: Building the City for the Visitor Class. Urban Affairs Review. Vol. 35, No. 3, January. 316-333. 2000.
[6] Florida, Richard. The Rise of the Creative Class: and how it's transforming work, leisure, community and everyday life. New York: Basic Books. 2002.
[7] Frieden, B., and L. Sagalyn. 1989. Downtown, Inc. Cambridge: MIT Press.
[8] Goeldner, Charles R. and J.R. Brent Ritchie. Tourism: Principles, Practices, and Philosophies. Hoboken, N.J.: John Wiley and Sons. 2003.
[9] Hall, T., and P. Hubbard. The Entrepreneurial City: New Urban Politics, New Urban Geographies. Progress in Human Geography 20 (2): 153-74. 1996.
[10] Jackson, Maria-Rosario, and Joaquin Herranz, Jr. Culture Counts in Communities: A Framework for Measurement. Washington DC: The Urban Institute Press. 2002.
[11] Jordan, A. River of Dreams. Governing 10:26-30. 1997.
[12] Judd, D., and S. Fainstein, eds. The Tourist City. New Haven, CT: Yale University Press. 1999.
[13] Kotkin, Joel. The New Geography: How the Digital Revolution Is Re-shaping the American Landscape. New York: Random House. 2000.
[14] Landry, Charles. The Creative City: A Toolkit for Urban Innovators. London: Earthscan Publications. 2000.
[15] Law, C.M. Urban Tourism and its Contribution to Economic Regeneration. Urban Studies, vol. 29, pp. 597-616. 1992
[16] Levine, M. Downtown Redevelopment as an Urban Growth Strategy: A Critical Appraisal of the Baltimore Renaissance. Journal of Urban Affairs 9:103-23. 1987.
[17] Mommass, H., and van der Poel. "Changes in Economy, Politics, and Lifestyles: An Essay on the Restructuring of Urban Leisure," in P. Bramham, I. Henry, H. Mommass, and H. van der Poel. (eds), Leisure and

Sustainable Tourism, F. D. Pineda, C. A. Brebbia & M. Mugica (Editors)

Urban Processes: Critical Studies of Leisure Policy in West European Cities. London: Routledge. 1989.
[18] Nel, Etienne, and Binns, Tony. Place Marketing, Tourism Promotion, and Community Based Local Economic Development in Post-Apartheid South Africa. Urban Affairs Review. Vol. 38, No. 2, November. 184-208. 2002
[19] Newman, Harvey. Race and the Tourist Bubble in Downtown Atlanta. Urban Affairs Review, Vol. 37, No. 3, January. 301-321. 2002.
[20] Nevarez, Leonard. Competition and Culture in the New Geography. Urban Affairs Review. Vol. 37, No. 4, March. 596-599. 2002.
[21] Plaza, Beatriz. Evaluating the Influence of a Large Cultural Artifact in the Attraction of Tourism. Urban Affairs Review. Vol. 36, No. 2, November. 264-274. 2000.
[22] Sawicki, D.S. The Festival Marketplace as Public Policy. Journal of the American Planning Association, vol. 55, pp. 347-61. 1989.
[23] Shaw, Gareth, and Allan M. Williams. Critical Issues in Tourism: A Geographical Perspective. Oxford: Blackwell. 1994.
[24] Walters. J. After the Festival is Over. Governing 3:26-34. 1990.
[25] Williams, S. Tourism Geography. London: Routledge. 1998.
[26] Zukin, S. The Cultures of Cities. Cambridge, MA: Blackwell. 1995.

Sustainable Tourism, F. D. Pineda, C. A. Brebbia & M. Mugica (Editors)

Sustainable tourism initiatives in European saltscapes

K. H. Kortekaas
Environmental Consultant

Abstract

When we speak about salt landscapes, or saltscapes, eroded, polluted, lifeless flats come to our minds. Saltscapes, however, are rich in halophyllic fauna and flora. These life forms are well adapted to salty environments but are very sensitive to changes in their ecosystem. Many halophyllic species are included in the Habitats Directive and a number of their sites are within the Natura 2000 network. Saltscapes are also rich from the cultural and ethnological points of view. The industrialisation of the salt business, in combination with low transportation costs, however, have led to the abandonment of the smaller, traditional salt making sites everywhere. Many examples of agonizing or already abandoned solar evaporation salt making sites (salinas) can be found in the Mediterranean basin and in inland Iberia. Fortunately, a number of managers of these sites have changed the orientation of their businesses towards sustainable tourism and artisanal salt production. In this presentation, some examples of sustainable tourism in salinas will be discussed as well as the role of different saltscape conservation initiatives.
Keywords: saltscapes, salinas, salt making, sustainable tourism, cultural landscape conservation, protected areas, saline wetlands.

1 Saltscapes as wetlands

High salinity is associated with polluted soils and desertization. However, saltscapes are defined here as "a type of cultural landscape formed in salt making areas, combining saline semi-natural habitats and cultural values related to salt-making activity". Most saltscapes function as wetlands and are treated as such by policy makers, nature conservationists, visitors, etc.

Sustainable Tourism, F. D. Pineda, C. A. Brebbia & M. Mugica (Editors)

Wetlands are landscapes in which water is present either on a permanent or a temporary basis. They are highly valuable for the local population thanks to the high productivity of the ecosystems they host, as well as the services they provide (food, transportation, building materials). Also, wetlands are of important cultural and spiritual value [1].

The Ramsar Convention of Wetlands holds a wetland classification system in which salt lakes and marshes are included. Ramsar distinguishes between coastal and continental or inland saline wetlands, temporary or permament salinas and artificial saline wetlands (that is, salt making sites). The Ramsar List has included a number of them, which are about 15% of the total number of Ramsar sites. Most of these are coastal salinas or salt marshes, since the size of inland salinas is usually too small to be of major importance for birds [2].

As we know, wetlands are disappearing in Europe. In the UK, the surface of salt marshes has been reduced to half its size since they have been in use for salt production in the Middle Ages. Between 1950 and 1984, 20,000 hectares of salt marshes have disappeared in the Wadden Sea and only 40,000 are left. The Netherlands, France, Spain, Germany, Italy and Greece have lost more than half of their wetlands in the last century [3]. An inventory of Spanish lakes made by Pardo [4] in 1948 includes 80 salt lakes, which represents 3% of all Spanish lakes. It is not known how many are found today, since only partial inventories exist.

2 The natural values of saltscapes

In the light of Zonneveld's [5] definition of landscape, "the part of space on the surface of the Earth that consists of a complex of systems formed by the activity of rocks, water, air, plants, animals and man, and whose physiognomy make it a recognizable entity", saltscapes can be considered an easily recognizable entity due to the special saline conditions it imposes on the flora and fauna it hosts. The presence of salt forces biota to find survival strategies based on physiological adaptations that are energetically very demanding. Therefore, the biodiversity found in saline habitats is low, but highly specific and sensitive to changes in salt concentration. The most common fauna are halobacteria, crustaceans (especially *Artemia sp.*), insects and birds [6,7]. Most species can usually survive in a narrow range of salt concentration, occuring just where the right degree of salinity and salt composition is found [8]. Halophyllic flora and fauna communities are thus easily outcompeted by generalist species as soon as the saline conditions disappear. This narrowly occupied niche makes saltscapes easily recognizable as an entity.

There is a high diversity of saltscapes, from the arctic saltmarshes in Canada to hypersaline lakes in the high Andes or the rock salt making sites in the Mediterranean, many different types of saltscapes can be found. This diversity has been acknowledged by the EU and the Habitats Directive (Directive 92/43/CEE) includes a number of habitats of community interest related to saline environments (atlantic, mediterranean and continental saline pastures, halophyllic mediterranean bushes, mediterranean and pannonic salt steppes, etc.).

Sustainable Tourism, F. D. Pineda, C. A. Brebbia & M. Mugica (Editors)

Here we will only discuss coastal and inland salinas and ignore the high altitude salinas, which are found in America and Asia, out of the scope of this study. Most coastal salinas are found in the Mediterranean basin (Spain, France, Italy, Greece, Malta, Slovenia, Croatia, Tunis, Libya, Egypt, Turkey) as well as the southern European Atlantic shores (Canaries, Morocco, Spain, Portugal, France). Inland saltscapes, mainly found in the Iberian peninsula, are located in flat areas or more or less steep depressions in the middle of which there is a temporary or permanent body of salt water. Many athalassohaline lakes (inland salt lakes) and salt springs are found in arid and semiarid zones, usually in depressions of the Tertiary Era or in endorrheic areas [6,7].

3 The cultural heritage of saltscapes

Heritage is defined here by two main features. First, it has a sense of belonging, "a form of heritage that is inextricably linked to the area in question and has a clear association with it". Second, it involves a sense of time, "based on the history or geography of the place". Therefore, cultural heritage does not only refer to museums and monuments, but encompasses any cultural expression from the past that has been inherited by present society [9]. It can be divided into material and intangible heritage. The first type is the physical result of cultural expression, that is, objects of historical, archaeological, artistic or scientific interest as well as buildings or other constructions that cannot be moved from place. The second type, intangible heritage, are those activities, techniques, customs, traditions and beliefs that belong to a certain culture [1].

Salt making, in the context of saltscapes, takes place in so-called *solar evaporation salinas*. These are a type of facilities where brine is canducted via channels and spread in flat, shallow basins to facilitate evaporation of the brine's water content by effect of solar radiation and wind, leaving salt crystals ready for collection. This type of facilities can range in size between a few to a few thousand hectares. They are remarkably variable according to local history and culture, as well as the use of site-specific (pre-)industrial technology [1]. Therefore, salt making in Europe has left a considerable amount of cultural heritage behind, both material and intangible. To the first type belong all the buildings, facilities and tools used for this activity. Solar evaporation salinas usually have a series of channels, evaporation basins, crystallisation pools, pumps, windmills, storage buildings, salters' homes, building, maintenance, scraping and collection tools, etc. Worth mentioning are the wind mills used for pumping water in Trapani (Sicilia), Piran (Slovenia) and in different salinas in the Canary Islands [10,11]. Also, mule driven waterwheels were used to pump brine in Imón (Spain) and elsewhere in inland Spain [12]; man powered wells in Rio Maior (Portugal), Salinas de Añana and Poza de la Sal (Spain), etc. Particular salters' homes and special vessels for salt transport were used in Cádiz (Spain) [1,13,14].

Salt making also is full of traditions, beliefs and local knowledge of technology. Much of this knowledge is being lost due to the abandonment of traditional salt making activities everywhere in Europe, although exceptions

Sustainable Tourism, F. D. Pineda, C. A. Brebbia & M. Mugica (Editors)

occur, see case studies. Salt has been used for centuries as a food preserving material and as a food item. Therefore, salt has also a culinary heritage. Salted fish or meat, or vegetables in brine exist everywhere. Researchers work to preserve and recover recipes in which salt in the main ingredient. The *garum* (a salty fish paste) prepared by ancient Greeks and Romans is a good example of culinary heritage [15,16]. Salt water also has healthy properties and has therefore been used in spas since ancient times. Examples of salt spas can be found in numerous places in the Mediterranean and Atlantic coasts. Also inland spas can be found in Aragón, Castilla-La Mancha and Castilla-León, in continental Spain [15].

Many salt making sites, abandoned or not, have built salt museums, salt interpretation centres, ecomuseums, etc. with the purpose of “preserving and restoring within the restrictions of the feasible, everything that imprinted and still does the character of our landscape” [17]. In Europe, about 45 such facilities exist, some of which are related to salt mines [13,15,16,18,19,20,21]. Many others just allow visitors in, without having any specific facilities for them. For instance, it has been estimated that 5,000 people spontaneously visit the Salinas of Imón, in Guadalajara (Spain) every year, without being promoted by any body, private or public (Assoc. of Friends of Inland Salinas, unpublished data).

4 Tourism in salinas and saltscapes

Tourism is defined as the “activities performed by people when they travel and stay away from their places of residence, whether for business or leisure reasons” [22]. Tourists, as opposed to visitors, stay overnight between one night and one year. According to a Eurobarometer [23] survey, 50% of the Europeans choose their holiday destination according to the scenery. Climate, historical interest and environment are also good reasons for 25-45% of the surveyed Europeans. The types of tourism found in salinas and saltscapes can be considered sustainable tourism, which respond to the behaviour described above. It manages resources, fulfills economic, social and aesthetic needs and maintains cultural and natural heritage [9,22]. Within this broad category, many different types of specialised tourism can be found in salinas [15,16,24,25,26,27,28]:

-*Cultural tourism*: Rather heterogeneous group of tourists who are interested in culture, traditions, art, history, etc. in different degrees. Salt making is seen as a mixture of culture and history.

-*Agrotourism*: Tourists demand small sized, cosy accommodation. They seek a blend of culture and nature and travel in small groups (couples or families). Salinas offer both in one visit.

-*Ecotourism*: People who are interested in the biodiversity and the rare flora and fauna found in salinas, as well as in their landscape values. They demand well signed paths and travel alone or in small groups and usually stay outdoors in salinas. A specific type of ecotourism is bird watching, very common in larger coastal salinas.

Sustainable Tourism, F. D. Pineda, C. A. Brebbia & M. Mugica (Editors)
© 2004 WIT Press, www.witpress.com, ISBN 1-85312-724-8

-*Educational tourism*: Usually, groups of students who visit a specific salt making site or museum and study one or several aspects of it in different degrees of depth.

-*Health tourism*: Spa visitors are usually middle or older aged and focus their interest on the array of treatments offered by the facilities.

-*Gastronomical tourism*: visitors are interested in the culinary side of salt and, besides learning how it is obtained, hope to taste new recipes or salt types. In some areas, this type of tourism combines salt with other local specialities (wine, olive oil, fish, seafood). It usually attracts middle aged couples.

5 Case studies

5.1 Guérande

The salt marshes of Guérande lie in northwest France. Today, 250 salt workers produce yearly 10 to 12,000 tonnes of salt in its 2,000 hectares. However, Guérande was an artisanal salina and was bound to disappear early in the seventies, under the threat of urban sprawl and uncontrolled development. The local population realised that the salinas were an important part of their heritage and economy; slowly by slowly they reconstructed the abandoned facilities, made them productive again and trained young salters. In the nineties, the Guérande gray salt (*sel gris*) became the well known product that it is today, thanks to a good marketing campaign, favourable regulations and a feel of belonging of the French public. The *sel gris de Guérande* is sold to tourists with an added value of heritage, landscape, holiday feelings, nostalgia, etc. [29]. Guérande hosts a museum of salt marshes (*Musée des Marais salants*), which was founded already in 1887, and an eco-museum, devoted to the natural values of these salinas, mainly birdlife [30].

5.2 Piran

Slovenia has a very short coastline, most of which is used for touristic purposes. In the middle of it, lie the large Sečovlje salt pans. Still active in the seventies, a few people raised their voices to defend the cultural and natural heritage of these salinas. Two decades later, an open air museum was built and in 1990, the salinas of Piran were declared protected area. Large restoration works were needed for the buildings, channels and dykes, which were performed in politically unstable times. Already in use in 500 AD and essential for the Venetian power in the 16th century, preserving them is not only important for Slovenian heritage, but also for Europe's. Today, Piran salters follow specific training courses and show tourists and visitors how salt is being made – live [11].

5.3 Salinas de Añana

The salt valley of Añana lies in a deep V-shaped valley, in the Basque Country. Salt is produced on wooden platforms on stilts, set up in terraces [31,32]. The incredibly complex array of hanging channels and platforms had been

Sustainable Tourism, F. D. Pineda, C. A. Brebbia & M. Mugica (Editors)

progressively abandoned in the sixties and had fallen in bits and pieces. The provincial government of Álava have been working in their restoration since a few years, painstakingly drawing every piece of wood and every stone, in order to respect the original structure [31]. Before that, the ownership situation needed to be solved. After years of discussions, the 80 former owners created a company in order to be able to negotiate the terms of the renovation agreement with the authorities. Some of the restored platforms are now used to produce salt again, which is apparently very popular among Japanese tourists.

5.4 Læsø salt

In such a northern latitude, evaporating brine with sunshine is a Herculean task. Therefore, salt is obtained by boiling brine in large cast iron pans. Numerous archaeological studies have shown that salt had been produced in this small island. No one knew how exactly, so Poul Christensen went to Germany to study brine boiling techniques and went back to the island to set up his own salt making hut, with support from the local authorities and some sponsorship. After several failures, he finally succeeded in producing a soft, airy salt. Today, twelve years later, he uses the hut for educational purposes and visitors willingly pay his salt as if it were a piece of art. *Læsø Salt* has significantly contributed to put the island on the tourist map of Denmark [33].

6 Other efforts to save saltscapes

Efforts are being made from universities, authorities, NGOs, etc. to gather knowledge and recover the cultural and natural heritage related to salinas and salt making. Examples worth mentioning are the ALAS project, the MedWet salinas network and the Chemins du sel initiative. The ALAS project (2000-2002) coordinated efforts from four European regions with traditions in salt making (Lesvos in Greece, Figueira da Foz in Portugal, Piran in Slovenia and Pomorie in Bulgaria). ALAS aimed at the development of salt production by means of experience exchange, training of salt-workers, management of salt-works in harmony with the ecological requirements and the collection and preservation of material and intangible culture related with salt production. ALAS produced a wealth of technical and dissemination material related to salt and salinas [7,16,18,25,26,27,28,29]. As a result of the ALAS project final conference, the salinas network promoted by the Mediterranean Wetlands (MedWet) initiative was born [34]. The aim of this network is to promote the efforts for the development and the implementation of a pan-Mediterranean strategy for salinas, with the participation of all relevant stakeholders. So far, the network has been actively searching for funds to perform this task. Another interesting initiative is the Chemins du Sel tour. Gilles Desomme, a French biologist, will finish in September 2004 his bicycle tour around Mediterranean salinas. He will have visited over a hundred salinas in sixteen countries. The purpose of this trip is to raise awareness on the fragility of the natural and cultural heritage of saltscapes and promote their economic value [35]. The Association of Friends of Inland

Sustainable Tourism, F. D. Pineda, C. A. Brebbia & M. Mugica (Editors)

Salinas [36], a Spanish NGO, is collecting and disseminating the knowledge resulting from these efforts, as well as trying to defend the interests of inland traditional salinas, which are a rarity in Europe.

7 Conclusions

Tourism in salinas should not be based only in the option to visit the facilities or a small museum. It should not be forgotten that traditional salt works are a mixture of culture, nature, agriculture, industry, history, architecture, archaeology, geology, medicine... The touristic potential of salinas is high, if one can use these different approaches to it. Active tourism should be promoted, in which visitors can participate in salt production, enjoy a spa, taste traditional salt recipes or learn about the cultural and natural heritage in a proactive way. Tourism in salinas can certainly save their natural and cultural heritage from being lost, however, there should be other measures of support.

Salinas that are usually found in rural, less developed and populated areas, should be supported in their survival with measures related to rural development. Rural areas in western Europe have lost many of their traditional productive functions, but have acquired new ones, such as the production of high quality food items, nature conservation, protection of cultural heritage, landscape management through amelioration of degraded landscapes and renovation of traditional architecture, promotion of handicrafts and artisanal production in general, cultural, touristic and leisure services, etc. [37]. Small traditional salt production, sale of artisanal transformed products (soap, bath salts, vegetables in brine, gourmet salts, etc.), may economically support salinas. The buildings can be used for alternative purposes (education, restoration workshops, cultural events, concerts, etc.) and the outdoor facilities have many possible uses (ecology workshops, meditation, filming, etc.). There are numerous ideas that are economically viable and compatible with the necessary respect for the cultural and natural heritage of saltscapes.

References

[1] Viñals, M.J. (ed). Wetland cultural heritage, Ministerio de Medio Ambiente, Dirección General de Conservación de la Naturaleza: Madrid, 2002.

[2] Oficina de la Convención de Ramsar, Manual de la Convención de Ramsar, Organismo Autónomo de Parques Nacionales, Ministerio de Medio Ambiente: Madrid, 1996.

[3] Commission of the European Communities, Communication of the Commission to the Council and the European Parliament on wise use and conservation of wetlands, COM (95) 189 final: Brussels, 1995.

[4] Pardo, L., Catálogo de los lagos de España. Biología de las aguas continentales VI, Ministerio de Agricultura: Madrid (Spain), 522 pp., 1948.

Sustainable Tourism, F. D. Pineda, C. A. Brebbia & M. Mugica (Editors)
© 2004 WIT Press, www.witpress.com, ISBN 1-85312-724-8

[5] Zonneveld, I.S., Land evaluation and landscape science, International Training Centre: Enschede (The Netherlands), 1979.
[6] Comín, F. A. & Alonso, M., Spanish salt lakes: Their chemistry and biota. Hydrobiologia, 158, pp. 237-245, 1988.
[7] Petanidou, Th., Mediterranean salinas: tradition and sustainable use. ALAS Newsletter, 3, pp. 3-6, 2001.
[8] Arrieta, R. T. From the Atacama to Makalu. A journey to extreme environments on Earth and beyond, Coquí Press: Panama City, Florida (EEUU), 1997.
[9] European Commission, Using natural and cultural heritage to develop sustainable tourism in non-traditional tourist destinations, European Commission: Luxembourg, 2002.
[10] Luengo, A. & Marín, C. El jardín de la sal, UNESCO Insula Programme: Santa Cruz de Tenerife (Spain), 1994.
[11] Žagar, Z., Museum of salt-making, Maritime Museum 'Sergej Mašera': Piran (Slovenia), 1995.
[12] Cruz García, O., Norias de tradición mudéjar en Imón. Revista de Folklore, 107, pp. 147-166, 1989.
[13] Alonso Villalobos, C., Menanteau, L., Navarro Domínguez, M., Mille, S. & Gracia Prieto, F.J., Antropización histórica de un espacio natural. Las salinas en la bahía de Cádiz. http://www.iaph.junta-andalucia.es/infopha/05textose/boletn35villalobos.html, 2001.
[14] Suárez-Japón, J.M., Sobre la arquitecturas salineras de la Bahía de Cádiz. http://www.iaph.junta-andalucia.es/infopha/05textose/boletn35suarez.html, 2001.
[15] Sala Aniorte, F., Antropología de la sal en el arco Mediterráneo. Las ciudades salineras y su identidad cultural. Actas del curso Antropología del Mediterráneo, Universidad Internacional del Mar, Murcia, 2000.
[16] Petanidou, Th. & Vayanni, L., Saltworks, cultural heritage and local development: Arguments for decision-making, ALAS Technical Letter: Koper (Slovenia), 2002.
[17] Duclos, J.-C., Role of ethnomuseums in the development of the museologic thought, Museum Association of Slovenia, MUZEOFORUM, Assembly of Museologic Lectures 1995-1996: Ljubljana (Slovenia), pp. 5-25, 1996.
[18] Dahm, H., Salt museums. ALAS Newsletter, 2, pp. 2-4, 2002.
[19] Benčič Mohar, E. & Žagar, Z., Cultural heritage and salt museums, ALAS interregional study: Piran (Slovenia), 2002.
[20] Puche Riart, O., Mazadiego Martínez, L.F. & Ayarzagüena Sanz, M., Los museos y las minas museo de la sal en Europa. Manuscript, 2002.
[21] Wirth, H., Salz Denkmale und Salz Museen. Journal of Salt History, 8-9, pp. 373-388, 2001.
[22] Organización Mundial del Turismo, Guía para administraciones locales: Desarrollo turístico sostenible, WTO, Madrid, 1999.

Sustainable Tourism, F. D. Pineda, C. A. Brebbia & M. Mugica (Editors)

[23] European Commission, Facts and figures on the Europeans on holidays 1997-1998, Executive Summary, Enterprise Directorate General: Brussels, 1998.
[24] Ivars Baidal, J. A., Turismo y espacios rurales: Conceptos, filosofías y realidades. Investigaciones geográficas, 23, pp. 59-88, 2000.
[25] Mitkova-Todorova, R., Traditional salt-works and tourism: A practitioners guide, ALAS Technical Letter: Koper (Slovenia), 2002.
[26] Skumov, M., Sustainable regional development of salinas and salt production based tourism, ALAS Interregional study: Pomorie (Bulgaria), 2002.
[27] Skumov, M., Salinas and tourism: The ALAS experience. Proc. of the Final Conference of ALAS All About Salt, eds. Th. Petanidou, H. Dahm & L. Vayanni, University of the Aegean: Mytilini (Greece), pp. 53-56, 2002.
[28] Vodenska, M, Popova, N. & Mitkova-Todorova, R., Sustainable regional development of salinas and salt production based tourism, ALAS interregional study: Pomorie (Bulgaria), 2002.
[29] Perraud, Ch., Une stratégie de marketing pour le sel traditionnel: le cas de Guérande. Proc. of the Final Conference of ALAS All About Salt, eds. Th. Petanidou, H. Dahm & L. Vayanni, University of the Aegean: Mytilini, pp. 83-94, 2002.
[30] Jourdaa, F., La route du sel de la côte atlantique, Éditions Ouest-France: Rennes (France), 1999.
[31] Diputación Foral de Álava, Gatz Harana-Valle Salado, Diputación Foral de Álava: Vitoria (Spain), 2001.
[32] Torre Ochoa, J.M., La recogida de la sal en Salinas de Añana. Narria 53-54, pp. 23-29, 1991.
[33] Christensen, P. & Bak, F., Læsø salt i røg og damp, Læsø Produktionsskole: Læsø (Denmark), 2001.
[34] MedWet. http://www.medwet.org
[35] Desomme, G. http://www.cheminsdusel.com
[36] Association of Friends of Inland Salinas, Annual report 2003, Sigüenza (Spain), 2004.
[37] Márquez Domínguez, J.A., Empleo y nuevas tareas rurales para el desarrollo local. Investigaciones geográficas, 29, pp. 57-69, 2002.

Sustainable Tourism, F. D. Pineda, C. A. Brebbia & M. Mugica (Editors)

Section 6
Coastal issues

Sustainable tourism development and social carrying capacity: a case-study on the North-Western Adriatic Sea

S. Marzetti Dall'Aste Brandolini[1] & R. Mosetti[2]
[1]*Department of Economics, University of Bologna, Italy*
[2]*Istituto Nazionale di Oceanografia e Geofisica Sperimentale, OGS, Trieste, Italy*

Abstract

This essay focuses on social carrying capacity (SCC) as an indicator of tourism sustainable development, and establishes a practical definition of SCC based on the majority rule. In order to understand the main difficulties encountered in measuring SCC from the point of view of beach visitors and residents, data about the well developed tourist resort of Marina di Ravenna (Italy) on the North-Western Adriatic coast were used. We also highlight that, when crowded situations are very frequent and these two aspects of the SCC are in conflict, coastal policy-making should result in a compromise between the need to preserve residents' life style and to increase the economic benefits of the beach recreational use.
Keywords: sustainability, sustainable tourism development, social carrying capacity, majority rule, well developed tourist site, crowding, day-visitor.

1 Introduction

Sustainability is essentially a product of the human mind, and in deciding that it is good and a duty to protect environment the international community has given ethical judgements. Every process of development has to be sustainable in order to attain the integrity of the life-support system on the earth; so what has to be promoted is sustainable development, which means that human development has to be sustained by the environment and the ultimate carrying capacity of the earth. Biogeophysical foundations must be integrated with social aspects such as the economic, cultural and political aspects of natural resource management, and

Sustainable Tourism, F. D. Pineda, C. A. Brebbia & M. Mugica (Editors)

therefore 'sustainability is a necessary and sufficient condition for a population to be at or below any carrying capacity' (Seidl and Tisdell [13]).

As regards the management of coastal resources for tourism and recreational activities, tourism sustainable development generally requires the management of all resources in order to fulfill economic, social and aesthetic needs, and to maintain ecological processes, biological diversity and life support systems (Council of Europe [5]). In other terms, sustainable tourism should be pursued by means of 'a rational distribution of tourism activity...without exceeding the saturation limits of each area...according to its vulnerability and characteristics' (Decleris [6], p.86).

In the Recommendation No. R(97) 9, the Council of Europe [4] specifies some criteria to be satisfied by a 'sustainable environment-friendly tourism' applied to coastal sites. After the premises that 'coastal areas are systems of great biological, geophysical, landscape, cultural and economic richness,..., which should be preserved for present and future generations', it is recognized that 'coastal tourism may be a major instrument of economic development for many regions and countries'. Nevertheless, 'it can also, if implemented in an intensive manner, cause considerable and sometimes irreversible damage to the natural and socio-cultural environment'; therefore a 'balanced tourism development' has to be promoted. Amongst the general principles established in the recommendation, we highlight that tourism should be limited 'to a level compatible with the ecological and social *carrying capacity* of the site'.

In this article, after a brief description of the concept of tourism carrying capacity as indicator of sustainable tourism, the focus is on social carrying capacity (SCC). We will highlight that the practical measurement of the SCC requires the specification of a voting rule. In order to understand the main difficulties that can be met in measuring SCC, we use data about the Italian tourist resort of Marina di Ravenna on the North-western Adriatic coast.

2 A practical definition of SCC

Carrying capacity as indicator of the use intensity of an area is not a simple concept. Decleris ([6], pp.85–9) highlights that 'in its narrow scientific sense, carrying capacity is the number of species or units of a species which can be maintained indefinitely by an ecosystem without degradation of that system. ...[Nevertheless in] its broader content the principle of carrying capacity says that the construction and management of man-made systems must not transcend their own carrying capacity or that of the ecosystems (land or water based, or marine) influenced by them'. This means that 'the application of carrying capacity to human species requires the recognition that carrying capacity is foremost socially determined, rather than biologically fixed due to the important influence of human consumption patterns, technologies, infrastructure, and impacts on the environment or food availability'; in other words the optimal number of visitors sustained is established according to the welfare function of the community involved (Seidl and Tisdell [13]). In spite of this complexity, measures of carrying capacity and methods for determining them have to be

Sustainable Tourism, F. D. Pineda, C. A. Brebbia & M. Mugica (Editors)

established, mainly for those systems which tend 'to develop to excess', such as mass tourism systems.

In general, tourism carrying capacity can be considered as the maximum number of visitors (day-visitors and tourists) that can be contained in a tourist area (abundance carrying capacity). We highlight that in this article tourism is intended in the broad sense, i.e. as an economic sector whose demand is not only composed by tourists (people who stay at least one night) but also day-visitors (people who do not live on the site, but visit it and do not sleep there), because on many tourist sites, the high number of these influences public authority planning.

A tourist system is an integrated system constituted by at least three different sub-systems, i.e. the ecological, social and economic sub-systems; therefore tourism carrying capacity is the result of the carrying capacities of all those sub-systems (Seidl and Tisdell [13]). Nevertheless, the levels of these different carrying capacities may be in conflict; for example, mass tourism is desirable from the economic point of view because its consequence is an increase of the local aggregate income, but from the environmental and social point of view it can be damaging if dunes are destroyed and criminality increases. This means that, as regards the sustainable development of a tourist site, policy-makers have to mediate between the carrying capacities of the different sub-systems, also stimulating discussion about society values in order to change their planning and action if necessary.

In well developed tourist sites the natural environment has generally been heavily sacrificed to economic growth, and the attention is about the dimension and kind of social interaction between visitors and local population, and also amongst visitors themselves. On these sites the satisfaction of visitors' needs generally goes well beyond the mere minimum subsistence level, and their life style (use level of facilities, visitors' recreational activities and so on) must also be considered for defining and measuring carrying capacity. In literature the SCC of a tourist area is defined from two different point of views: a) from the point of view of visitors, SCC is the maximum level of crowding that coastal visitors are willing to accept from the other visitors without reducing the quality of the recreational experience; while b) from the point of view of residents, SCC is the maximum number of visitors tolerated by the host population (O'Reilly [11]). De Ruyck et al. [7] highlight that as regards visitors, the existence of facilities and economic innovation such as the organization of crowd-attracting activities can considerably increase SCC, which also changes according to the characteristics of visitors (sex, education, attitude, etc.). Therefore, SCC is a dynamic indicator whose measure is influenced by many factors which are specific to the site situation considered.

From a working point of view, nevertheless, the a) and b) definitions of SCC involve a practical difficulty. What is meant in operational terms by 'tolerated by the host population', and 'that coastal visitors are willing to accept from the other visitors'? Do these sentences mean that all the host population (unanimity) tolerate and all the coastal visitors are willing to accept, or that only the majority of them, or some other part of them? This specification is important because

Sustainable Tourism, F. D. Pineda, C. A. Brebbia & M. Mugica (Editors)

social deliberations can be taken according to different rules of voting. Since the majority rule is generally used for social choices, as practical definitions of SCC we consider: a') the maximum number of people at the time when the majority of visitors feel comfortable with the number of other visitors on the beach; and b') the maximum number of visitors tolerated by the majority of residents. The reference to the voting rule stresses the normative nature of SCC. In politics the majority rule is applied to results obtained with the universal suffrage; as regards SCC the universal suffrage would be very expensive, therefore this rule should be applied to the results of a survey based on a random sample.

These two aspects of the SCC may be in conflict, since the maximum number of visitors tolerated by the visitors themselves may be different from the maximum number tolerated by residents. In case of conflict, coastal policy making should be the result of a compromise between the need to preserve residents' life style and to increase the economic benefits of the beach recreational use.

3 Methods for measuring the SCC

Traditional indicators such as arrivals and night-stays, and the structure of tourist supply are inadequate indicators of the tourist carrying capacity, because they do not consider the consequences of tourism on the socio-cultural environment. Other indicators are needed (e.g. Seidl and Tisdell [13]).

A) From the point of view of beach visitors, overcrowding can reduce the enjoyment of the recreational experience and they could go to an alternative site or return home. As an indicator of overcrowding, the WTO recommends using the number of visitors per m^2 of beach (Consulting & Audit Canada [3]). Therefore, in order to compute the maximum number of visitors tolerated by the visitors themselves per 100 m^2 of beach (density SCC), De Ruyck *et al.* [7] suggest: i) carrying out a survey by questionnaire (visitor questionnaire) on the most crowded days of the year in order to obtain information about visitors' perception of crowding on the beach at the survey time; the questionnaire should consist of questions to measure how uncomfortable visitors feel about the number of beach visitors at the moment of the interview, and the visitor's reaction to crowding; ii) obtaining the number of visitors on the beach in the most crowded days of the year by counting the number of people in photographs taken on the same days (see also O'Reilly [11]). The beach density SCC is computed by dividing the abundance SCC (maximum number of visitors tolerated) by the beach surface (m2), and multiplying by 100.

B) From the point of view of residents, in the high season they may suffer the crowding due to the success of beach recreational activities. Traffic, noise and pollution by day and by night can be the main causes of residents' discomfort (in particular during the weekends), and can oblige them to modify their lifestyle in some measure. Qualitative indices of saturation or irritation were established by Cohen [2], Doxey [8] and Butler [1]. In addition, a number of quantitative indicators of social pressure and social carrying capacity exists in literature. Considering tourists and day-visitors, de Albuquerque and McElroy [10]

Sustainable Tourism, F. D. Pineda, C. A. Brebbia & M. Mugica (Editors)

compute a host-guest ratio given by the average daily visitor density per 1,000 residents. This ratio can also be computed per 100 residents. Saveriades [12], instead, computes a tourist-host contact ratio by dividing the number of residents by that of tourists, and multiplying by 100. The optimum tourist-host contact ratio is the maximum number of tourists tolerated by that population, and indicates the threshold beyond which undesirable social tensions between residents and visitors would occur. This optimum ratio is computed by considering the information obtained from a survey by questionnaire designed to ask residents if they prefer a number of visitors greater or lower than, or equal to, that present on the site without feeling irritation.

4 Marina di Ravenna SCC

Marina di Ravenna is a well developed tourist resort near Ravenna (Italy) on the Northern Adriatic coast. The beach of light fine sand, shown in photograph 1, is 4 Km long and on average 200 Mt wide; the developed part of the beach consists of 42 sunbathing buildings, while only a small part is completely free (undeveloped beach). In the past the dunes were almost completely destroyed, but a wide pinewood still exists behind the beach.

Photograph 1: The Marina di Ravenna beach.

Sustainable Tourism, F. D. Pineda, C. A. Brebbia & M. Mugica (Editors)

In this resort some sunbathing building managers have innovated their services for beach visitors by reorganizing the sunbathing area, and expanded the traditional services (such as bar, showers, and the renting of cabins, seating and sun umbrellas) with restaurant services, new sport activities, parties, cultural and music meetings (called 'happy hours'), also by night. This economic innovation, made possible by the width of the beach, has been attracting numerous visitors, mainly day-visitors aged 20-40, and has been revealed to be a profitable business. Consequently, crowding phenomena have been occurring mainly during week ends in the spring/summer season.

4.1 SCC about visitors

The data available about the Marina di Ravenna resort permit an estimate to be made of the SCC from the point of view of visitors. At this site a survey by questionnaire was carried out by Vitali [14] in order to collect information about visitors' reactions to crowding. The De Ruick et al. method was adapted for the Marina di Ravenna situation, and some modifications were made to it: i) as regards the questionnaire new questions were added about beach visitors' preferences regarding the new recreational activities, and to find out the proportion of day-visitors on the beach with respect to that of tourists; ii) in addition, the procedure of counting visitors on the beach and dividing the beach in zones in order to do interviews was simplified. In Italy people generally stay several hours on the beach; in particular, a study about the beach use in a resort very near Marina di Ravenna shows that visitors stay on the beach on average about 5 hours (Marzetti and Zanuttigh [9]). On the Marina di Ravenna beach, the most crowded hours of the day were from 2 to 7 p.m.. Visitors were interviewed in the afternoon and counted only once during those hours because their number was fairly stable.

A representative beach area of about 44,000 m2 was chosen for carrying out an experimental survey of 62 face-to-face interviews (random sample). In this area there are four sunbathing buildings, three of which best represent beach recreational innovation in Marina di Ravenna. The interviews were done on the last two Sundays of May 2002. On those two days the beach was just as crowded as it is on the most crowded days of midsummer. Almost all respondents (93.5%) visit the beach mainly at weekends. Visitors do not use public transport; the majority of interviewees reach Marina di Ravenna beach by car (66%), 21% by motor bicycle, 11% by bicycle and 2% by foot. 6.5% of the interviewed visitors complain about traffic congestion and parking difficulty .

We summarize the findings about sensitivity to crowding in tables 1 and 2. Table 1 shows that on both Sundays the great majority of respondents felt comfortable with the number of visitors on the beach at the time of the interview. In addition, table 2 shows that on both days the majority of respondents who feel comfortable at present declared that s/he would also feel comfortable with more people on the beach (53.33% and 54.84% respectively); in particular, over 40% of respondents would feel comfortable with double the number of people on the beach.

Sustainable Tourism, F. D. Pineda, C. A. Brebbia & M. Mugica (Editors)
© 2004 WIT Press, www.witpress.com, ISBN 1-85312-724-8

Table 1: Percentage of respondents who feel comfortable with the number of people on the beach.

Day of interview	18/05/03	25/05/03
Feel comfortable	70.00	77.42
Do not feel comfortable	30.00	22.58

Table 2: Number of visitors according to which respondents feel comfortable: % of respondents.

Day of interview	18/05/03	25/05/03
Less: half the people	30.00	22.58
Same	16.67	22.58
More: double	43.33	41.94
More: four times	10.00	12.90

Finally, as regards respondent's behaviour in a hypothetical situation of overcrowding, on both days the majority of respondents declared that they would remain in the same beach area, while only a few would go to another beach or return home. On both Sundays, there were about 2,200 visitors on the beach area considered, with the mean beach density about 5 visitors per 100 m2. In that situation the carrying capacity was not surpassed because in that beach area the great majority of respondents did not feel uncomfortable.

Photograph 2: A 'happy hour' near the bar, and the sunbathing area near the beach.

According to this data, we estimate that, since the majority of respondents would feel comfortable with at least double the number of visitors on the beach, the density SCC of the beach area is about 10 visitors per 100 m2. People on the beach show a strong aggregation need because they stay in large groups, mainly

Sustainable Tourism, F. D. Pineda, C. A. Brebbia & M. Mugica (Editors)

near the bar and restaurant buildings (in the beach area furthest from the sea) and the sunbathing areas (nearest the sea); in these beach sub-areas the density is higher than the overall beach density. This need of aggregation, as well as the existence of wide empty sub-areas as shown in photograph 2 seems to be why the majority of respondents would feel comfortable even with twice as many visitors on the beach.

These data, therefore, show that the Marina di Ravenna beach is mainly visited by people who enjoy being in groups. In particular, what these people value is not only the possibility of doing new recreational activities but also that these activities attract numerous people.

4.2 The Marina di Ravenna visitor-host ratio

In Marina di Ravenna, day-visitors are so numerous that they cannot be omitted from the estimate of a SCC index. We computed a visitor-host ratio by dividing the daily number of visitors (tourists and day-visitors) by the number of residents, and multiplying by 100. Official data are available only about residents and tourists (Vitali [14]). The number of tourists on a crowded day of the high season can be obtained by considering that in these days tourist accomodation is fully booked ; so the number of tourist beds is considered the measure of the number of tourists present at the site on the most crowded days.

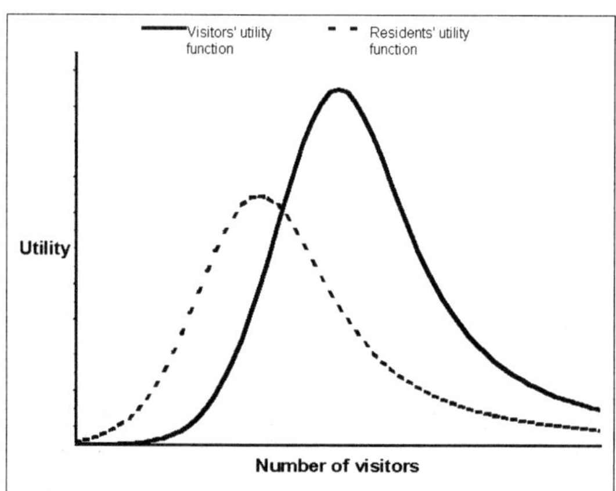

Figure 1: Residents' and visitors' utility curves.

As regards 2002, we estimate the number of day-visitors considering that on those two days of May day-visitors were on average 72.6% and tourists 27.4% (Vitali [14]). In that year and on those crowded days, given 5,612 tourist beds (presumed to be all fully booked), beach visitors would have been 20,482. If we also take into account 4,076 residents, the visitor-host ratio would have been about 502%. So, in Marina di Ravenna there would have been 5 visitors for one resident. We do not know if this number is the resident SCC, because a specific resident survey was not carried out. On the other hand, public petitions

Sustainable Tourism, F. D. Pineda, C. A. Brebbia & M. Mugica (Editors)
© 2004 WIT Press, www.witpress.com, ISBN 1-85312-724-8

(Vitali [14]) suggest that a certain number of residents feel discomfort as regards the number of visitors. Therefore we assume (fig. 1, in arbitrary units) that the maximum of the utility curve for residents is to the left of the maximum for visitors. The intersection of the two curves represents a Pareto equilibrium (an increase of utility for one player reduces the utility for the other player in a co-operative game). The number of visitors corresponding to this equilibrium could be a reasonable compromise for a policy-maker; it is located between 5 and 10 visitors per resident.

5 Conclusions

The attempt to estimate SCC highlights the need to specify a voting rule as criterion for establishing the maximum number of visitors tolerated by the visitors themselves and also by residents. This led us to define SCC with reference to the majority rule. As regards the SCC from the point of view of visitors, the data available about the Marina di Ravenna resort confirm that the number of visitors tolerated on the beach depends on the objectives of tourism management and visitors' value judgements. As regards the SCC from the point of view of residents, the computation of the visitor-host ratio is made more difficult by having to estimate the number of day-visitors due to the lack of official data. This difficulty can be overcome by using the information obtained from a visitor questionnaire.

Acknowledgements

We thank the Municipality of Ravenna and Giovanni Gabbianelli for photograph 1, and Emanuela Vitali for photograph 2.

References

[1] Butler R.W., The Concept of a Tourist Area Cycle of Evolution: Implications for Management of Resources, Canadian Geographer, 24, Part 1, pp. 5-12, 1980.

[2] Cohen E., Who is a Tourist? A Conceptual Clarification, Sociological Review, 22, pp. 527-555, 1974.

[3] Consulting & Audit Canada, What Tourism Managers Need to Know – A Practical Guide to the Development and Use of indicators of Sustainable Tourism", Report to the WTO, 1995.

[4] Council of Europe, Recommendation N. R (97) 9, of the Committee of Ministers to Member States on a Policy for the Development of Sustainable Environment-Friendly Tourism in Coastal Areas, 1997. http://www.coe.fr/cm/ta/rec/1997/97r9.html

[5] Council of Europe, Tourism and Environment, Questions and Answers, n.3, 1997.

Sustainable Tourism, F. D. Pineda, C. A. Brebbia & M. Mugica (Editors)

[6] Decleris M., The law of Sustainable Development, General Principles, European Commission, Luxemburg, 2003.

[7] De Ruyck, M.C., Soares & A.G., McLachlan, A), Social carrying capacity as a management tool for sandy beaches, Journal of Coastal Research, 13(3), pp. 822-830,1997.

[8] Doxey, G.V., A causation theory of visitor-resident irritants: methodology and research inferences, Proc. of the Travel Research Association 6th Annual Conf., San Diego, California, 1975.

[9] Marzetti Dall'Aste Brandolini S. & Zanuttigh B., Economic and Social Valuation of Beah Protection in Lido di Dante (Italy), Proc.of the 6th International Conf. on the Mediterranean Coastal Environment, MEDCOAST 03, ed. E. Ozham , Middle East Technological University, Ankara, Turkey, pp. 319-330, 2003.

[10] McElroy J.L. & Albuquerque (de) K, Tourism Penetration Index in Small Caribbean Islands, Annals of Tourism Research, 25(1), pp. 145-168, 1998.

[11] O'Reilly, A.M., Tourism carrying capacity. Concept and issues, Tourism Management, December, pp. 254-258, 1986.

[12] Saveriades A., Establishing the Social Carrying Capacity for the Tourist Resorts of the East Coast of the Republic of Cyprus, Tourism Management, 21, pp. 147-156, 2000.

[13] Seidl I. & Tisdell C.A., Carrying capacity reconsidered : from Malthus' population theory to cultural carrying capacity, Ecological Economics, 31, pp. 395-408, 1999.

[14] Vitali E., Turismo sostenibile: le conseguenze economiche dell'affollamento a Marina di Ravenna, Laurea thesis, co-ordinator Prof. Marzetti S., University of Bologna, 2003.

Sustainable Tourism, F. D. Pineda, C. A. Brebbia & M. Mugica (Editors)

Evaluation of the recreational use of Barcola beach in Trieste (Italy)

S. Marzetti Dall'Aste Brandolini[1] & A. Lamberti[2]
[1]*Department of Economics, University of Bologna, Italy*
[2]*DISTART, University of Bologna, Italy*

Abstract

This paper focuses on the economic evaluation of the recreational use of Barcola seafront in Trieste (Italy). Within the EU DELOS (2000) framework a contingent valuation survey in the value of enjoyment version was carried out in order to estimate the gain for a project of building a new artificial beach on the Barcola seafront. The project satisfies sustainable tourism development. Evaluation questions not only about the beach use in spring/summer but also in autumn/winter were included in the questionnaire. The survey results show that the beach use value changes for different seasons. In addition, the hypothetical new beach would attract new visitors.
Keywords: cost-benefit analysis, contingent valuation method, value of enjoyment, beach recreational activities, coastal sustainable development, integrated coastal management.

1 Introduction

This article presents results of the economic valuation of recreational benefits due to a project of beach expansion on the Barcola seafront in Trieste (Italy). The project is justified by the need to satisfy the demand for beach recreational activities of local residents within a sustainable development framework. This study deals with the economic valuation of informal recreational benefits due to this project. The European Union (DELOS 2000) and the City Council of Trieste supported this research.

Informal recreational activities such as sunbathing, swimming and walking are non-marketable values, and represent *use values*. Cost-benefit Analysis requires non-marketable values to be estimated. As regards recreational

Sustainable Tourism, F. D. Pineda, C. A. Brebbia & M. Mugica (Editors)

activities, the Travel Cost Method (TCM) and the Contingent Valuation Method (CVM) can be applied. They are based on the simple idea of asking beach visitors specific questions by means of a survey, and the practical difficulty of their application lies in obtaining rational and consistent expressions of value from the relevant population. In addition, because carrying out a valuation survey is time-consuming and very expensive, the procedure of the Benefit Function Transfer (BFT) is suggested, whereby the value of an improvement of beach quality, obtained from a set of study sites, is generalised to other empirical situations (policy sites). One of the main problems of the BFT is that benefit transfer studies do not always yield valid and reliable estimates. The use for a new site of benefits *transferred* from other studies regarding other sites must respect some basic criteria. We mention the following: i) non marketable goods need to be the same (for example coastal recreational activities depends on the characteristics of the beach – sand or stones, large or narrow – on the quality of the sea water, weather conditions, facilities on/near the beach, and so on); and ii) population characteristics should be similar for the policy and study sites (Boyle and Bergstrom [2]; Desvousges *et al.* [3]).

We found no application of evaluation methods to sites very similar to the case-study of Trieste, and therefore the transfer of benefits from other sites to this Italian site was not possible. In order to quantify non-marketable use values about the Barcola seafront before and after the implementation of the project, a specific interview survey was carried out. The main aims of this survey were: i) to evaluate the enjoyment of a daily use of the seafront in its current condition in spring/summer and in autumn/winter; ii) to evaluate the gain after the expansion of the beach in spring/summer and in autumn/winter; iii) to collect information on type, frequency and duration of use of the Barcola beach, and on the social characteristics of respondents. The distinction of the beach use according to seasons is justified by the fact that weather conditions are very different in Italy in autumn/winter and spring/summer, and this difference influences beach use and value.

2 Methodology

Given the need for a new survey, the TCM cannot be applied to this site. The Barcola seafront is used mainly by residents, and the cost of travelling may be very low or even zero. For this reason the cost of the distance travelled to visit Barcola cannot be considered the value of the recreational activities. The CVM was, instead, applied. This technique aims to create a hypothetical market which permits respondents to express non-marketable use value for the environmental change considered in that site by means of a survey. Each respondent expresses a value which is contingent to the hypothetical scenario created within the survey.

The CVM philosophy, generally known in the version of the willingness to pay (WTP), is: " If you want to know what something is worth, go to those who might value it and ask: 'what are you *willing to pay* for it?'" (Price [8]). This procedure can obviously also be used to evaluate damages. An other version of the CVM philosophy focuses on the *value of enjoyment* (VOE), and the question

Sustainable Tourism, F. D. Pineda, C. A. Brebbia & M. Mugica (Editors)

may be: "What value do you put on your enjoyment of a daily visit to …?" (Penning-Rowsell *et al.* [7]). A comparison between WTP and VOE, highlights that the former, unlike the latter, requires specification of a payment vehicle, such as tax, entry charge, rate, voluntary donation and so on. As regards Barcola seafront, the CVM in the WTP version was considered unsuitable because any payment vehicle about the recreational use of Barcola seafront would have been unpopular. Therefore, the VOE approach for beach management was applied. It allows estimation to be made for each individual of the value he/she attributes to the enjoyment obtained from a daily visit on the beach. Because the unit of measure for the valuation is the *recreation day* on the beach, the number of visits is considered as the quantity consumed of beach services.

According to whether the seafront change is considered an improvement or a worsening of the present state respectively, the gain or loss after the beach expansion can be computed. Penning-Rowsell *et al.* [7] distinguish beach visitors in those who continue to visit the site and those who would visit an alternative site. If people continue to visit the beach after the project implementation, the gain (loss) per visit (D) is the difference between the VOE of a visit after the implementation of the project (Vp) and the VOE of a visit in the current condition (Vs), i.e. for each individual

$$D = Vp - Vs \tag{1}$$

Nevertheless, after the implementation of a project, individuals may visit other sites because they dislike the change. When people visit an alternative site, the gain or loss per visit is the difference between the VOE at the site in the status quo and the VOE at the alternative site plus the possible increase in the cost of the visit to the new site, i.e. for each individual

$$Da = (Vs - Va) + (Ca - C) \tag{2}$$

where Da is the gain, or loss, Va the VOE in the other site, Ca the cost per visit in the alternative site, and C the cost per visit in the status quo. Finally, in order to test if after the project implementation the total benefit per year is increased, the aggregate gain (loss) is estimated:

$$B = N q_m D_m \tag{3}$$

where B is the total annual gain (loss), D_m the mean gain (loss) per adult visit, Nq_m the total annual number of beach use days obtained multiplying the total relevant population of the site N by the individual mean number of visits per annum q_m.

3 The project of building a new artificial beach on the Barcola seafront

Trieste is a town in the North-East of Italy of almost 235,000 inhabitants, located on the Northern Adriatic Sea and close to the border with Slovenia. The Barcola site involves a strip of the coast between Miramare castle and the town of

Trieste, 2400 mt long. Viale Miramare, the road that forms the inland boundary of the reinstatement area, was built following the profile of an old abrasion terrace formed by the action of the waves. The Barcola promenade is defended from the sea by an artificial wall that protects the road and pedestrian paths. The Barcola coastline is divided into two different areas: the first includes yacht and canoe clubs, a small pinewood, and the small harbour of Barcola; the second includes the area for sunbathing, consisting of concrete changing-rooms (topolini), a very small pebble beach and the small Cedas harbour.

Photograph 1: Barcola beach in the present state.

The second area may be changed to satisfy the increasing demand from residents for recreational activities because the Barcola beach is very crowded in spring/summer, as shown in photograph 1. The City Council of Trieste sent us a scientific report (2000) describing the characteristics that a project has to satisfy to avoid major damages to the Barcola environment and to the current use of the seafront for recreational activities (Brambati [1]). According to these guidelines, the project of beach expansion, selected by a public competition, consists of the building of two artificial beaches, each 400 m long and 40 m wide (see photomontage 1).

4 The CVM survey design

In October – November 2002 a CVM survey of 600 interviews (random sample of people aged 18 plus) was carried out in the town of Trieste. The Barcola seafront is exclusively visited by residents, therefore face-to-face interview were done at home in order to assess the recreational use of the beach; in this way, not

Sustainable Tourism, F. D. Pineda, C. A. Brebbia & M. Mugica (Editors)
© 2004 WIT Press, www.witpress.com, ISBN 1-85312-724-8

only the current use of the beach, but also the potential new use after the change to the coast was estimated.

Photomontage 1: Simulation of the Barcola seafront after the beach expansion.

Interviews were done by a market research firm. Anonymity was guaranteed in order to avoid strategic behaviour. Face-to-face interviews were justified by different reasons: the need to motivate respondents to cooperate fully; the need to provide a better explanation of the scenario described in photomontage 1; and the need to help the respondent to understand the unusual evaluation questions.

The standard resident questionnaire included in Penning-Rowsell *et al.* [7], Appendix 4.2 (b), was adapted to the Barcola seafront characteristics. The main innovation is the inclusion of evaluation questions about the beach use not only in spring/summer but also in autumn/winter. This is justified by the fact that weather conditions are very different in Italy in these seasons: very sunny and hot in spring/summer, and cold and windy in autumn/winter. In its final wording the questionnaire is divided into sections. The first section contains questions of a general nature regarding the respondent's general opinion about the quality of life in Trieste. The second section seeks information on attitudes toward the beach (daily visit), whilst the third section investigates the respondent's familiarity with the seafront including questions about the number and duration of visits to the Barcola beach, the type of recreational activity undertaken and

Sustainable Tourism, F. D. Pineda, C. A. Brebbia & M. Mugica (Editors)

means of transport. The fourth and fifth sections are the heart of the questionnaire since they include the evaluation questions. Respondents were first asked how much they evaluate the recreation activities of a daily visit to the Barcola seafront in the present conditions, then whether they would have an increase or a decrease in enjoyment from the expansion of the beach after the project implementation and then were finally asked to elicit the daily use value of the new artificial beach. These values were elicited for spring/summer use and also for autumn/ winter use of the seafront. Questions to identify protest answers are also included here. In the sixth section all respondents are asked to say whether or not they are in favour of the implementation of the new artificial beach. Those respondents who do not agree with the project are asked to evaluate the use of an alternative beach. The last two sections enquire about the respondents' socio-economic characteristics, and the interviewer's opinion on the respondents' comprehension of the questionnaire. Most of the biases that may occur in a CVM survey are related to the questionnaire structure, so a pilot survey of 50 interviews was carried out to test the questionnaire before conducting the main survey.

5 Empirical results

The majority of respondents, mainly young and middle-aged people, generally consider the Trieste seafront highly important. More specifically, 57% of respondents think that it is the right place for recreational activities; its mean rating is 7.6 on a scale from 1 to 10, with only 11% of respondents giving a rating lower than 6.

In spring/summer the majority of Trieste residents (63.8%) go to the Barcola seafront. The average number of days spent on the seafront is 23.5 days (Std. Deviation 23.2). Respondents stay on the seafront a mean time of 161.7 minutes (Std. Deviation= 79.4) per day; 76.2% of respondents usually go to the Barcola seafront in groups, and 40.8% of the groups include boys or girls under 15 years of age. The main activities done on the Barcola seafront in the present state are walking, sunbathing, jogging and swimming.

In autumn/winter the seafront is visited by a highest number of respondents (73.5%), and the mean number of days is 18.3 (Std. Deviation = 23.3). The main activities are walking and relaxing. Respondents spent a mean time of 105.8 minutes (Std. Deviation = 52.9) on the Barcola seafront.

As regards the hypothetical expansion of the beach, the great majority of respondents are in favour of the implementation of the project, and 81% of respondents would visit it; young residents are more in favour than older residents. A significant percentage (65.8%) of these people claim that, if the beach was actually extended, they would visit it more or much more, and 4.5% less or much less often. 19% of respondents would not go to the extended beach. Since the Barcola seafront has alternative beaches near Trieste, 3.83% of respondents would go to another beach if the new beach is built (see also Marzetti [4]).

Sustainable Tourism, F. D. Pineda, C. A. Brebbia & M. Mugica (Editors)
 ISBN 1-85312-724-8

5.1 Daily beach use values

As regards the present state (table 1), in spring/summer the mean daily use value of the Barcola seafront is 5.24 € (Std. Deviation 7.66, median 2.00 and mode 0.00), and in autumn/winter it is 5.25 € (Std. Deviation 7.97, median 2.00 and mode 0.00). In spring/summer 35.8% of respondents do not visit the Barcola beach and elicited 0.00 €, and in autumn/winter 26.5% of people elicited zero values. Extreme values (0.2% spring/summer, 0.5% autumn/winter) higher than 100.00 €, protest responses (3.5% both seasons) and non-responses (7.7% both seasons) were excluded from the mean computation.

Table 1: Mean use values (Euros) according to different seasons – Present state.

Mean value (median)	Present state
Spring/summer	5.24 (2.00)
Autumn/winter	5.25 (2.00)

80.2% of respondents declared their household income bracket, and people with the highest incomes elicited lower mean use values than people with lower income.

5.2 Gain and loss after the beach expansion

As regards the beach change, the great majority of respondents would get more enjoyment and only 2.9% of interviewees would have a reduction in the daily enjoyment. The mean gain for the project of building a new artificial beach on the Barcola seafront has been computed according to equations (1) and (2).

Table 2: Expanded beach: daily mean gain and loss (Euros).

Mean value (median)	Spring/ summer	Autumn/ winter
Whole sample	3.07 (1.00)	1.39 (0.00)
Alternative beach*	- 2.60	- 2.04
Same beach*	3.40	1.56
Potential visitors	6.04	3.60

[* 'Alternative beach' means that people would go to another beach, and 'same beach' that they would not go.]

Table 2 shows that, considering the whole sample, if the new beach project is implemented, respondents would have a mean gain in both seasons; while those who would go to an alternative beach in the vicinity of Barcola seafront (5.25% of respondents) would have a daily mean loss. The reason is that the majority of

Sustainable Tourism, F. D. Pineda, C. A. Brebbia & M. Mugica (Editors)

people who would not visit the new beach evaluate a daily visit to the alternative beach as equal to that of the Barcola seafront in the present state, but they would pay more for the transport. People who would continue to visit the Barcola beach, if the new beach is built, would have a mean gain of 3.40 € in spring/summer and 1.56 € in autumn/winter. In addition, potential visitors - respondents who do not visit the Barcola seafront in the status quo, but would visit it if the new beach is built – are 18.67% of the whole sample in spring/summer and 12.5% in autumn/winter, and they would have a mean gain of 6.04 € in spring/summer and 3.60 € in autumn/winter.

Finally, according to the equation (3), the aggregate annual recreational value of the beach change is of the order of 1 million Euros.

6 Conclusions

This research confirms that, in order to satisfy the need of recreational activities, an artificial beach expansion is considered an improvement of the Italian coast (see also Marzetti & Lamberti [5]; Marzetti & Zanuttigh [6]). The Barcola project would increase the number of beach visits and also would attract new visitors. The use value of a daily beach visit would also increase. In addition, this CVM survey show that it is useful to distinguish the mean gain of enjoyment according to seasons; as regards the expanded beach, in spring/summer the mean gain is more than 50% higher than in autumn/winter.

Acknowledgements

EU support through RTD project DELOS, contract EVK3-CT-2000-00041, is gratefully acknowledged. Thanks are also due to the City Council of Trieste for their support and the material provided, Paolo Wrabletz for information about the Barcola project, Alberto Cazzola and Romina Filippini for the questionnaire formatting, and Francesca Galassi for work with Excel and SPSS.

Authors' contribution

Marzetti Dall'Aste Brandolini S. dealt with the economic valuation of the beach use; Lamberti A. with the engineering aspects of the research.

References

[1] Brambati A., Studio di fattibilità dell'ampliamento del lungomare tra Barcola e il bivio di Miramare (Trieste), Regione Autonoma Friuli-Venezia Giulia, Direzione regionale viabilità e trasporti, 2000.

[2] Boyle K.J. & Bergstrom J.C., Benefit Transfer Studies: Myths, Pragmatism and Idealism, Water Resources Research, **28(3)**, pp. 657-663, 1992.

Sustainable Tourism, F. D. Pineda, C. A. Brebbia & M. Mugica (Editors)

[3] Desvousges W.H., M.C. Naughton & G.R. Parsons, Benefit Transfer: Conceptual Problems in Estimating Water Quality Benefits Using Existing Studies, Water Resources Research, **28(3)**, pp. 675-83, 1992.

[4] Marzetti Dall'Aste Brandolini S., D28A, 2003, www.DELOS.unibo.it

[5] Marzetti Dall'Aste Brandolini S. & Lamberti A., Economic and Social Valuation of the Defence System of Venice and its Lagoon (Italy), Proc. of the 6th International Conf. on the Mediterranean Coastal Environment, ed. E. Ozam, Middle East Technological University, Ankara, Turkey, pp.307-318, 2003.

[6] Marzetti Dall'Aste Brandolini S. & Zanuttigh B), Economic and Social Valuation of Beach Protection in Lido di Dante (Italy), Proc. of the 6th International Conf. on the Mediterranean Coastal Environment, ed. E. Ozam, Middle East Technological University, Ankara, Turkey, pp.319-330, 2003.

[7] Penning-Rowsell, Green C.H., Thompson P.M.,. Coker A.M, Tunstall S.M., Richards C. & Parker D.J., The Economics of Coastal Management: a Manual of Benefit Assessment Techniques (Yellow Manual), Belhaven Press: London, 1992.

[8] Price C., Valuing of Unpriced Products: Contingent Valuation, Cost-Benefit Analysis and Participatory Democracy, Land Use Policy, **17**, pp. 187-96, 2000.

Sustainable Tourism, F. D. Pineda, C. A. Brebbia & M. Mugica (Editors)

Beach visits in the UK: what influences choice and do environmental awards matter?

J. Butcher
Market Research Department, ENCAMS, UK

Abstract

ENCAMS, which administers the Blue Flag Awards in the UK, commissioned independent research to ascertain:

- Who visits the beach
- Why they visit
- Which factors influence their choice of beach
- What deters people from beach visits
- Levels of awareness and understanding of beach awards and flags for environmental quality

The research compares what visitors expect from a UK beach with what they actually get. It also contrasts the experience of visiting UK beaches with beaches abroad. The results will help seaside resorts market themselves, attract visitors and provide the standards and facilities that people really want.

The research examines the role of environmental standards and is being used to inform the future development of Blue Flag and other UK coastal awards.
Keywords: ENCAMS, beaches, awards, Blue Flag, Seaside Awards, cleanliness, flags.

1 Background information

ENCAMS [1] (Environmental Campaigns) is an independent national charity working to improve local environments through public campaigning and working with others such as local authorities, schools and other large scale land owners. In addition to this, ENCAMS also run the Blue Flag and Seaside Awards schemes for beaches throughout the UK.

Sustainable Tourism, F. D. Pineda, C. A. Brebbia & M. Mugica (Editors)

1.1 Seaside Awards and Blue Flag

The Seaside Awards [2] provide information about a wide range of beaches. In March each year, the distinctive yellow and blue flag is given to beaches that are clean, safe, well managed and have water quality that meets the minimum European legal standards [3]. Because beaches are all very different in character, the Seaside Awards are split into two categories, 'resort' and 'rural'. A Seaside Award 'resort' beach attracts many visitors with its facilities and activities. A Seaside Award 'rural' beach however, is quieter and usually enjoyed for its simplicity rather than its facilities.

The Blue Flag Campaign [4] is administered in the UK by ENCAMS on behalf of FEE (the Foundation for Environmental Education) [5] The Blue Flag for Beaches provides a comparison with coastal resorts across 24 participating European countries. The bathing water quality must exceed the legal minimum European standards and the beach must be clean, well managed and promote sound environmental management. In the UK the Blue Flag has previously been more synonymous with beaches, however, since 1999 marinas that meet strict environmental and management standards have also been allowed to enter the Blue Flag scheme.

2 Research outline

ENCAMS carries out market research on an ongoing basis to ensure that all its programmes and campaigns are developed to be relevant to the appropriate target audience. As part of this programme of research, ENCAMS commissioned a study into users of British beaches in 2002.

2.1 Research objectives

This study was carried out to establish who visits UK beaches and why they do so, to understand the factors which affect their choice of beach and what, if anything, people find offensive when visiting beaches. The research also addressed the awareness and level of understanding of the various award schemes for beaches.

2.2 Research methodology

The methodology consisted of a mix of qualitative and quantitative research techniques. A series of focus groups were carried out with members of the public (all who must have visited a beach in the last 12 months) and a number of depth interviews were conducted during the summer period on beaches with visitors. In addition to this, 500 telephone interviews were carried out, again with people who had visited a beach in the last 12 months.

Sustainable Tourism, F. D. Pineda, C. A. Brebbia & M. Mugica (Editors)
© 2004 WIT Press, www.witpress.com, ISBN 1-85312-724-8

3 Results

3.1 Positioning of UK beaches

Travelling to European beaches has affected the perception of UK beaches in particular with reference to cleanliness standards and awards. Foreign beaches are described as being places that are visited infrequently as a planned, main holiday and are expensive (relative to visiting a UK beach). Whilst on a foreign beach holiday, the main focus is to spend time on the beach, sun-bathing and swimming. Sunshine is a key motivator for visiting European beaches and high quality beaches are expected and often researched prior to the visit. In contrast, UK Beaches are seen as cheap, spontaneous trips which happen much more frequently than travelling abroad. Time spent at the seaside in the UK is much less focussed on the actual beach and a range of facilities is expected. There is a low awareness of beach standards and awards and lower standards are expected and accepted.

3.2 Profile of beach users

More women go to the beach than men and the most popular age range for visiting UK beaches is 35-64. Visiting beaches is more popular amongst couple than singles but interestingly there is no difference in frequency of visit between those couples with or without children. Visiting beaches is less common amongst social classes D and E and those who do not work and trips to the beach are generally family occasions with the majority of people visiting the beach with their partner and/or children rather than their friends.

The average number of visits to the beach is around 5 per year, however this ranges from single visits to those individuals who visit the beach more than 11 times a year. Frequent beach visitors (i.e. those who visit more than 5 times a year) tend to be over 35 years of age and visiting a nearby beach for a day trip. Not surprisingly, the majority of beach visits take place in the summer months, visitors in the colder months are more likely to be of slightly higher social classes (ABC1).

3.3 Beach destinations

Trips to resort beaches are much more common than trips to rural beaches with one in four beach visits being to a resort area. About one fifth of beach users, use both rural and resorts beaches throughout the year. Rural beaches are more popular with the higher social classes and are more likely to be day trips than longer trips or holidays. Resort beach users appreciate popular resorts with high levels of awareness and activity. Their needs include bars/cafes, amusements and shops and they expect to see boards outlining standards and safety procedures. Rural resort users, however, enjoy the quiet, untouched nature of rural beaches, these beaches are often found by chance or recommended by a friend. There is often an element of beach snobbery with rural beach users and

Sustainable Tourism, F. D. Pineda, C. A. Brebbia & M. Mugica (Editors)

they generally prefer not to have the natural environment spoiled by boards advertising standards and procedures.

Most beach users travel to the beach by car (84%), this is particularly high for families with children and visitors of rural beaches. Coaches are a more popular form of travel for longer journeys (more than 3 hours). Day trippers to the beach tend to limit their travel time to no more than one hour from their home. Longer journeys tend to be for those who are spending a few days or longer at their destination.

3.4 Beach activities

Following the introduction of the package holiday in the 1960's and more recently with decreasing costs of flights to European destinations, the British are increasing travelling abroad for their beach holidays with the focus being on good weather, sun-bathing and swimming in the sea.

Experiencing these types of beaches abroad has changed the expectations of visitors to beaches in the UK. As Walton [6] states the British resort begun in Victorian times being all about simple fun, including donkey rides, roundabouts, Punch and Judy, boat trips and informal food on the move. Today, British beaches are still used for more than just sun-bathing and swimming. Table 1 shows the activities undertaken by beach users in the UK.

Table 1: Activities on UK beaches.

On the Beach	% of visitors
Walking	86%
Sun-bathing	42%
Picnics	41% *
Swimming/paddling (sea)	33% *
Walking dog	17%
Swimming (pool)	16% *
Barbecues	10%
Water Sports	6%

Off the Beach	% of visitors
Café's/Restaurants	68%
Shops	63%
Places of Interest	58%
Pubs	49%

*Significantly higher where children are present.

Clearly, British beaches are not simply used for swimming and sun-bathing, with the majority of people enjoying walking on beach visits. Visiting a beach is perceived to be a different experience when children are part of the party, in particular more time is spend swimming and having picnics. Trips to the beach often involve visiting amenities in the surrounding area as well as enjoying the beach itself.

Sustainable Tourism, F. D. Pineda, C. A. Brebbia & M. Mugica (Editors)
© 2004 WIT Press, www.witpress.com, ISBN 1-85312-724-8

3.5 Choice of beach

Many people cannot recall when they first visited specific beaches as they had often visited the same ones for many years having being taken there as children. Other beach choices are made 'by accident', i.e. the beach is simply stumbled upon when out for the day. Very few people research beaches before visiting them, in particular when travelling to a local beach and beach awards have very minimal influence on choice of beach.

A clean beach is important for both day trippers and holiday makers, whereas safe and supervised swimming is more important for people travelling to the beach for a longer visit/holiday. The importance of flags and awards is also greater for holiday makers than day trippers.

The provision of toilets is the most important facility required for both day trippers and holiday makers whereas other facilities such as cafes/restaurants, attractions, night life and watersports are more appealing to holiday makers than those simply on a day out.

Beach usage/choice is also influenced by lifestage. Singles or couples without children tend to visit the beach for the adjacent town and social activities, they have low expectations of standards. Families with young children choose beaches where they can relax with little worry, e.g. clean, sandy beach away from roads. Families with older children choose resorts based on the surrounding activities rather than the beach, e.g. café's, shops and amusements. The more activity the better for these families to avoid having bored kids! Parents whose children have left home tend to visit with their partner and want to avoid arcades and greasy café's and want coffee shops and quietness.

3.6 Offensive areas

When people are asked what offends them when they visit beaches, few can recall anything. Dogs/dog fouling and litter are the most emotive, top of mind issues. This concludes with previous research carried out by ENCAMS [7] into offensiveness of litter and dog fouling in relation to other local environmental quality issues. When issues are probed, more detail emerges regarding relative offensiveness. Broken glass is felt to be the worst culprit being not only dangerous but relatively common and a fear for all parents. Finding sanitary products on the beach is the next worst item found, although found less frequently they are perceived as disgusting and provoke concerns over health and disease. Following this, overflowing bins are the next offensive problem which are not only visual off-putting and reflect badly on the management of the beach but attract huge numbers of wasps and bees which are unpleasant to be near. Even amongst dog owners, dog related problems were viewed as key offensive areas. 'No dogs' is a very motivating factor and would affect future choice of beach in some cases.

Toilets on beaches are hugely criticised with the majority of beach users having very low expectations of standards of toilets on beaches. Comments included poor cleanliness, poor maintenance, bad smells and safety issues relating to drugs related litter. Many visitors seek out alternative public toilets in

Sustainable Tourism, F. D. Pineda, C. A. Brebbia & M. Mugica (Editors)

pubs or restaurants nearby. People would be happy to pay for well maintained, clean toilet provisions.

3.7 Seeking information

Around a quarter of beach users seek out information before choosing/visiting a beach.

Table 2 shows the information sought by these people and where they look for it.

Table 2: Beach information sought.

What information	%
Facilities	26%
Places of interest	23%
Clean beaches	20%
Places to stay	20%
Places to eat	18%
Toilets	14%
Sandy beach	11%

Where from?	%
Tourist Information	47%
Friends/family	36%
Internet	23%
Guide book	10%
Newspapers	7%
Beach guides	7%

The majority of information sought about beaches is obtained from Tourist Information centres and refers to the area as a whole rather than simply the beach. People tend to research foreign beaches and resorts more heavily before booking holidays abroad than they do for British beach holidays.

3.8 Beach awards

The general public are much more aware of the Blue Flag Awards scheme than the Seaside Awards scheme. Spontaneously, 48% of beach user mentioned the Blue Flag scheme whereas only 5% mentioned Seaside Awards. After prompting, 78% of beach users were aware of Blue Flag compared to 27% with Seaside Awards. The impact of the awards on public decision making is very low, it was felt by users that promotion of the awards is very low key away from the beach and even at the beach the flags are very isolated and not very visible. Having two awards for beach standards is causing public confusion. Cleanliness and safe bathing are the main qualities expected from a beach that has achieved an award. The Blue Flag Award is associated with clean beaches significantly more than the Seaside Award. The Seaside Awards appears to be more associated with the provision of facilities than the Blue Flag Award.

4 Conclusions

There is a broad spectrum of consumers visiting the beach but visits are slightly higher amongst females, 35-64 year olds and working adults. Although core

Sustainable Tourism, F. D. Pineda, C. A. Brebbia & M. Mugica (Editors)
© 2004 WIT Press, www.witpress.com, ISBN 1-85312-724-8

issues of importance are fairly consistent, needs do vary in terms of lifestage and holiday type (day trip/longer holiday). Further communication is required to inform the public of beach standards and facilities available to enable more people to make an informed choice before travelling. Areas in which communication is required prior to arriving at the beach are: cleanliness of beach, toilet availability and condition, type of beach (sandy/ rocky), parking, dog status, lifeguards and awards. Although information provision is generally good at the beach, efforts need to be made to promote these issues to the public more widely, though everyday sources such as the Internet, motoring organisations and even supermarkets.

Although public interest and awareness in beach awards is relatively low, elements of the awards, such as beach cleanliness, are of significant public interest. Promotion of the criteria involved in achieving an award would vastly improve their perceived value to the public and therefore their influence on decision making. Finally, at the beach, flags should be positioned at regular points and there should be numerous signs highlighting awards and criteria to ensure maximum awareness in the future.

References

[1] ENCAMS, www.encams.org
[2] Seaside Awards, www.seasideawards.org.uk
[3] EURPOA. Bathing water quality, Directive 76/160/EEC www.europa.eu.int/water/water-bathing/directiv.html
[4] The Blue Flag Campaign, www.blueflag.org
[5] Foundation for Environmental Education (FEE) www.fee-international.org
[6] Walton, J.K, *The English Seaside Resort: A Social History*, Leicester University Press, 1983.
[7] ENCAMS, Public behavioural study into littering 2001. www.encams.org/publications/research/pubbehavstudylitter2001.pdf

Sustainable Tourism, F. D. Pineda, C. A. Brebbia & M. Mugica (Editors)

Artisanal fisheries in the SE Brazilian coast: using fisher information towards local management

A. Begossi
Nepam Unicamp, CP 6166, Campinas, S.P. 13081-970, Brazil

Abstract

Coastal artisanal fisheries in SE Brazil are located close to huge urban centers, such as Rio de Janeiro and São Paulo cities. Many of these fisheries are also adjacent to Atlantic Forest remnants. The growth of tourism, and associated recreational fishing, along with pollution in the coastal waters, increased the chances of impact on species and on artisanal fishing. Some fish species are located close to shore, such as species of Serranidae (groupers, such as *Epinephelus* and *Mycteroperca*) and seem vulnerable to the impact from fishing and from pollution. Other species, such as from the family Centropomidae (snooks, *Centropomus* spp.) are found in estuarine environments, and are also a target of recreational fishers, being subject to pollution coming from coastal rivers. In order to have more information on fishing for species of Serranidae and Centropomidae, I marked the fishing spots used by artisanal fisheries in different communities found in the SE Brazilian coast. The spots were marked using GPS Garmin III and V and Magellan. Maps of the fishing spots used to catch Serranidae and Centropomidae were drawn (103 fishing spots for groupers and 36 for snooks). Such maps are based on local fisher information, and they show the area used to fish the Serranidae and Centropomidae. Such data are important to designate areas for artisanal fisheries, and to evaluate the pressure on species of Serranidae and Centropomidae.
Keywords: Centropomus, Epinephelus, grouper, Mycteroperca, fishing, Brazil, snook.

Sustainable Tourism, F. D. Pineda, C. A. Brebbia & M. Mugica (Editors)

1 Introduction

Coastal artisanal fisheries in Brazil are an important source of employment and food for local communities, contributing to 40-60% of the marine fish production [1]. These communities, including the communities located in the SE Brazilian coast, between the cities of São Paulo and Rio de Janeiro, still maintain an artisanal technology for fishing. Fishing is mostly performed using paddled canoes or motor small woody or aluminium boats. The gear employed in these fisheries includes a variety of nets, traps and lines. There is information published for these fisheries, in particular for the communities mentioned in this study [2, 3, 4, 5]. In spite of the small-scale level of these communities, they receive influences and interferences from the outside, especially coming from activities associated with tourism. Tourists include recreational fishers that frequently fish using hook and line for different species. Some species are special targets of tourists, and they include primarily species of Serranidae. Centropomidae species are usually target of tourists in estuarine areas. In other countries, such as in Asia and in Africa, in special cases, artisanal fishing was considered to contribute to reduce fishing stocks of commercial fishes [1]. A higher impact may be expected for species targeted by both tourists and artisanal fishers, compared to other species. This could be the case of the Serranidae, represented in this study by species of *Epinephelus* and *Mycteroperca* (groupers) locally called *badejo, garoupa or cherne.* Among the 32 Brazilian marine fish species listed in IUCN red list, *Epinephelus itajara, E. nigritus* and *E. marginatus* are endangered or threatened [6]. Such species are used by local fishers of the SE coast of Brazil and are also target of tourists. Silvano [6] show that the estuarine snook *Centropomus* (*Centropomus parallelus and C. undecimalis*), locally called *robalo* is also a target of tourists, increasing the probability of concentrating catches on this species. A local demand, for studies on *Centropomus*, is a claim of fishers from Puruba Beach, an estuarine area that receives recreational tourists in weekends. The objective of this study is to locate the major fishing areas of the Serranidae and Centropomidae, mentioned by local fishers, in order to help the management of fishing in these coastal areas of Brazil.

1.1 Methods and study

This study is part of a major project that has the objective of marking the main fishing spots used by fishers of the SE Brazilian coast, funded by Fapesp, Brazil [grants # 97/16160-7, 01/00718-1, 01/05263-2]. For this objective, communities already studied in earlier projects were re-visited (Búzios I., Grande I., Itacuruçá I., Jaguanum I, Puruba and Picinguaba) and some new communities were included (Bertioga, Guarujá I., Comprida I., Gipóia I., Itaipu and São Sebastião I.). Full-time experienced fishers, 30 years up, including at least 10 years of residence and fishing in the area studied, were chosen as informants in order to mark the spots by boat, using GPS Garmin III and V plus, and Magellan –Field. The boats used, in order to mark the fishing spots, have 15ft with motors

Sustainable Tourism, F. D. Pineda, C. A. Brebbia & M. Mugica (Editors)
© 2004 WIT Press, www.witpress.com, ISBN 1-85312-724-8

of 75 and 115 HP, and 10.5 ft, with a motor of 25 HP. The spots were marked between 1997-2004, with the help of Eduardo Camargo in the fieldwork. These fishing spots are stable in time, and such stability was checked for ranges of 10-30 years, through other studies [7,8].

Table 1: Studied sites in São Paulo State and Rio de Janeiro coast, in order from the southern to the northern coast. H= high degree of urbanization and pollution; U=urbanized tourist sites, L= less urbanized sites receiving tourists, and I= isolated places.

Local	Island or Coast	Municipality	State	Number of fisher informants	Date of spot marking	Classification
Icapara	Comprida I.	Iguape	São Paulo	1	May 1998	U
Pereque Beach	Guarujá I.	Guaruja	São Paulo	1	January 2004	U
Indaiá	Coast	Bertioga	São Paulo	1	November 2003	U
Jabaquara	São Sebastião I.	Ilhabela	São Paulo	1	December 2003	L
Serraria	São Sebastião I.	Ilhabela	São Paulo	1	December 2003	L
Porto do Meio	Búzios I.	Ilhabela	São Paulo	1	May 1998	I
Puruba Beach	Coast	Ubatuba	São Paulo	1	May 2003	L
Picinguaba	Coast	Ubatuba	São Paulo	2	October, 2003	L
Proveta	Grande I.	Angra dos Reis	Rio de Janeiro	1	March 1998	L
Flechas Beach	Gipóia I.	Angra dos Reis	Rio de Janeiro	1	January and March 1998	L
Calhaus	Jaguanum I.	Sepetiba, Mangaratiba	Rio de Janeiro	1	April 1998	L
Gamboa	Itacuruçá I.	Sepetiba, Mangaratiba	Rio de Janeiro	1	December 1997	U
Pescaria Velha Beach	Marambaia I.	Sepetiba, Mangaratiba	Rio de Janeiro	1	December 2001	I
Praia do Sitio	Marambaia I.	Sepetiba, Mangaratiba	Rio de Janeiro	2	December 2001	I
Itaipu Beach	Coast	Niteroi	Rio de Janeiro	1	September 2002 and March 2003	H

2 Results

I show the results related to the spots used to fish groupers and snooks based on data collected through 17 informants from 9 islands and 4 coastal sites between São Paulo and Rio de Janeiro (Table 1). The most common species of Serranidadae found at SE Brazilian coast are in Table 2. The species of *Centropomus* found are two: *parallelus* and *undecimalis.* The sites studied

Sustainable Tourism, F. D. Pineda, C. A. Brebbia & M. Mugica (Editors)

include areas with a high degree of urbanization and pollution (Itaipu Beach, Niterói, Rio de Janeiro), or urbanized tourist sites (Guarujá, Comprida, São Sebastião and Itacuruçá Islands, as well as Bertioga, in the coast), less urbanized sites receiving tourists (Gipóia, Grande and Jaguanum Islands, and Puruba and Picinguaba in the coast), and relatively isolated places such as Marambaia and Búzios Islands.

Table 2: Species of Serranidae found in São Paulo coast and in the coast of Sepetiba Bay, Rio de Janeiro coast [6, 9].

Species	**Local Name**
Dules auriga	Cherne
Epinephelus itajara	Mero
Epinephelus marginatus	Garoupa, garoupa-verdadeira
Epinephelus morio	Garoupa-são-tomé
Epinephelus nigritus	Cherne
Epinephelus niveatus	Cherne
Mycteroperca acutirostris	Miracelo
Mycteroperca bonaci	Badejo, badejo-preto
Mycteroperca interstitialis	Água fria
Parathias furcifer	Namorado

2.1 Fishing for groupers

In these Brazilian SE coastal areas, groupers are often caught through hook and line fishing. In the southern part of Sao Paulo, I marked 13 spots used to catch groupers, among others, in the coast of Guarujá Island, and 8 in the coast of Bertioga. In the northern coast of São Paulo, at Ubatuba, I marked 13 spots at Picinguaba, and none at Puruba Beach, 20 spots at Jabaquara and 14 at Serraria, São Sebastião Island, Ilhabela. At Búzios Island 10 spots were marked for groupers. At Rio de Janeiro State, 14 spots were marked at Grande Island, 10 at Gipóia Island and only 1 at Jaguanum Island. No spots were marked for grouper at Itacuruçá Island. In the city of Niterói, 13 spots were marked at Itaipu Beach (Figure 1). The spots cited as used to catch groupers are found especially close to rocky substrates, and for this reason they are located close to the islands of Búzios, S. Sebastião, Grande, Gipóia and Guarujá. Rocky islands are especially Búzios, S. Sebastião, and Grande. However, rocky shores close to sandy beaches also permit to find groupers, such as in the rocky substrates of Itaipu beach. Considering the high level of urbanization of Itaipu Beach at Niterói, Rio de Janeiro, and the intense tourist activities at Gipóia, Guarujá and São Sebastião Islands, especial attention should be given to such sites. The information given by the spot coordinates permits to estimate the distance of the spot to the shore, as a tool to verify if the grouper spots are located far from the rocky shore. Such information could be an indicator of fishing pressure, if close fishing spots are substituted by distant spots, or if distant spots are being used more frequently, compared to spots located close to the coast.

Sustainable Tourism, F. D. Pineda, C. A. Brebbia & M. Mugica (Editors)
© 2004 WIT Press, www.witpress.com, ISBN 1-85312-724-8

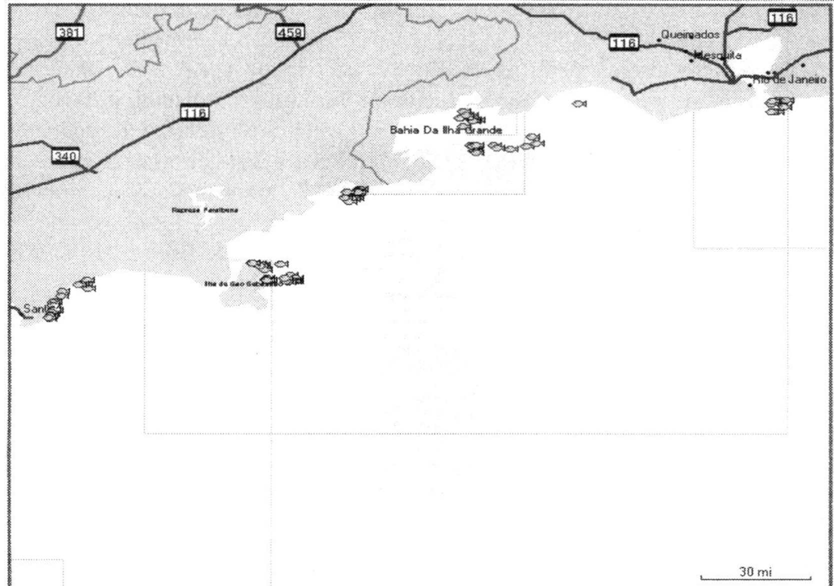

Figure 1: Map of the fishing spots cited by artisanal fishers to catch groupers. The map includes 103 fishing spots used to fish groupers, between the cities of São Paulo and Rio de Janeiro (Map using Garmin Ltd., 1995-2003 software).

2.2 Fishing for snooks

Snooks are caught in the coast of Sao Paulo and Rio de Janeiro, using in special different kind of nets. I marked 4 spots used to fish snooks, among others, at Guarujá Island, 12 at Bertioga, 1 at Picinguaba, 11 at Puruba Beach, 2 at Serraria, São Sebastião Island, Ilhabela, 5 at Marambaia Island and 1 at Comprida Island. Snooks occur in estuarine environments, and the fishing spots cited to catch snooks are located close to the many small rivers that come from the Atlantic Forest coast. The high predominance of a snook fishery in Puruba Beach is associated with the activity of fishers in the two rivers that occur in the community: the Puruba and the Quiririm rivers. Fishing occurs in spots located in these rivers or in the sea, in the mouth of such rivers. A communal fishing activity for snook, using beach seine at night is known in this community. I might consider that Bertioga and Puruba, both in the coast and receiving tourists all year round, should have special care for these species (Figure 2).

3 Conclusions

The high level of urbanization and of pollution in some areas, such as at Itaipu Beach and Guarujá-Bertioga areas, associated with the intense tourist activities found in these communities, through the presence of recreational fishers, make these areas vulnerable for the continuity of the local artisanal fisheries. The high

Sustainable Tourism, F. D. Pineda, C. A. Brebbia & M. Mugica (Editors)

speed in the growth of urbanization and tourism increases the urgency in having available data on local fishing. In this regard, fishers can be especially useful to science and to management, as shown by the method used in this study. In Brazil, there are examples of the exclusion of local artisanal fishing in favour of recreational fishing, such as in Araguaia river [10,11]. Considering the economic importance of artisanal fishing in the Brazilian coastal waters and the vulnerability of groupers and snooks, the necessity of management, probably through a local or a co-management [12] toward these fishes should be considered. Maybe, the reservation of areas for artisanal fishers, as already proposed by earlier studies [4,7,8], could be helpful for local fisheries.

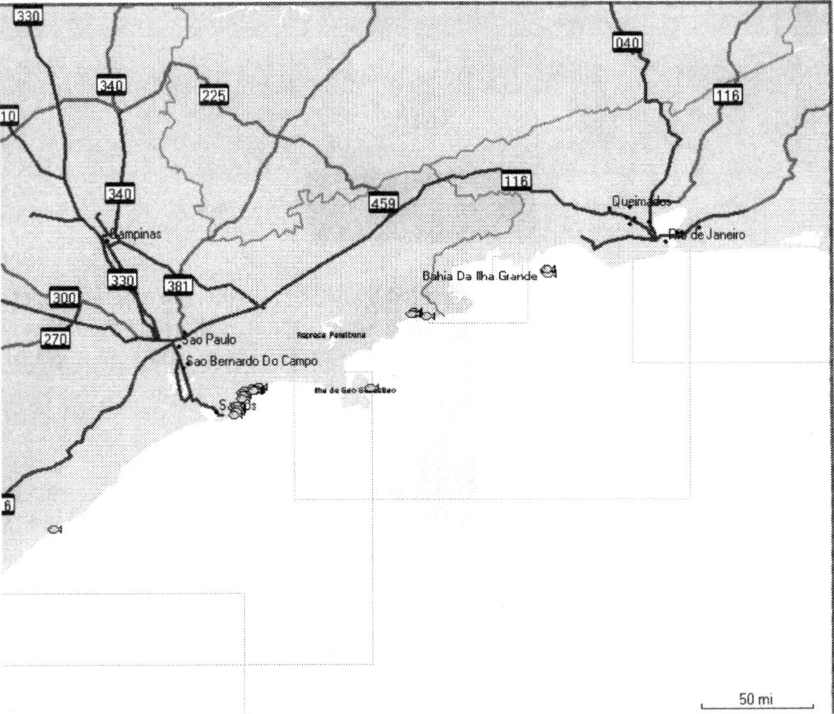

Figure 2: Map of the fishing spots cited by local artisanal fishers to catch snooks. The map includes 36 fishing spots used for snooks, located between the cities of São Paulo and Rio de Janeiro (Map using Garmin Ltd., 1995-2003 software).

Acknowledgments

I thank Eduardo Camargo for helping in the fieldwork, Fapesp for the grants 97/16160-7, 01/718-1, 01/05263-2 that supported the fieldwork, and Fapesp, CNPq, and Faep-Unicamp for traveling support to attend the Coastal Environment 2004.

Sustainable Tourism, F. D. Pineda, C. A. Brebbia & M. Mugica (Editors)

References

[1] Silvano, R. A. M. Pesca artesanal e etnoictiologia. *Ecologia de Pescadores da Mata Atlântica e da Amazônia,* A. Begossi (Org.), Editora Hucitec, São Paulo, pp., 2004.

[2] Begossi, A. The use of optimal foraging theory to understand fishing strategies: a case from Sepetiba Bay (State of Rio de Janeiro, Brazil). *Human Ecology*, 20 (4): 463-475, 1992.

[3] Begossi, A. Fishing activities and strategies at Búzios Island. *Proceedings of the World Fisheries Congress*, Theme 2, Atenas, Maio de 1992. *In:* R. Meyer, C. Zhang, M. L. Windsor, B. J. McCay, L. J. Hushak, R. M. Muth, *Fisheries Resources and utilization*, Calcutta: Oxford and IBH Pub. Co, pp.125-141, 1996.

[4] Begossi, A. Cooperative and territorial resources: Brazilian artisanal fisheries, *The Commons Revisited: na Americas Perspective*, J. Burger, R. Norgaard, E. Ostrom, D. Policansky and B. Goldstein (eds.), Island Press: Covelo, CA, pp. 109-130, 2001.

[5] Diegues, A.C. *Pescadores, Camponeses e Trabalhadores do Mar.* Editora Atica, São Paulo,1983.

[6] Silvano, R. A. M. Biodiversity, conservation and use of fishing at the Sao Paulo coast (Brazil). *Biodiversity and Conservation* (submitted), 2004.

[7] Begossi, A. Mapping spots: fishing areas and territories in the Atlantic Forest coast, Brazil. *Regional Environmental Change,* 2: 1-12, 2001.

[8] Begossi, A. Conservation and fishing territories in Coastal Brazil. Paper to be presented in the *XII Meeting of the Society for Human Ecology*, February 18-20, 2004, Quintana Roo, Cozumel, Mexico.

[9] Begossi, A. and Figueiredo, J. L. Ethnoichthyology of southern coastal fishermen: cases from Búzios Island and Sepetiba bay (Brazil). *Bulletin of Marine Science*, 56(2): 682-689, 1995.

[10] Ribeiro, M. C. L.B. and Petrere, M. Ecological integrity and fisheries ecology of the Araguaia-Tocantins river basin, Brazil. *Regulated Rivers: Research and Management* 11: 325-50, 1990.

[11] Begossi, A. Knowledge on the use of natural resources: contributions to local management. *In: Research in Human Ecology: na interdisciplinary overview*, L. Hens, R. J. Borden, S. Suzuki e G. Caravello (eds.), Proceedings of the Symposium organised at the VII International Congress of Ecology (INTECOL), Florença, Italia. Bruxelas: VUB Press, 1998.

[12] For definitions of co-management, see: Wilson, D. C., Nielsen, J. R. and Degnbol, P. (eds.). 2003. *The fisheries co- management experience: accomplishments, challenges and prospects.* Kluwer Academic Publishers, Fish and Fisheries Series 26, Dordrecht.

Sustainable Tourism, F. D. Pineda, C. A. Brebbia & M. Mugica (Editors)

Section 7
Tourism and protected areas

Sustainable tourism in Scotland's National Parks: the search for effective frameworks for planning, action and evaluation

L. R. MacLellan[1] & D Strang[2]
[1]*University of Strathclyde, Glasgow, Scotland*
[2]*Cairngorms National Park Authority, Scotland*

Abstract

The paper reviews the current situation facing the implementation of sustainable tourism in Scotland's recently constituted National Parks. It examines the background and unique characteristics of the national park model in Scotland and discusses alternative approaches to achieving sustainability through tourism. The paper argues that the European Charter for Sustainable Tourism provides a useful framework, in particular for The Cairngorms. The research is based on a combination of published literature, official reports and consultation with key National Park partners and interest groups. To reap the benefits of sustainable tourism development whilst ensuring that the natural and cultural heritage resources are enhanced and protected, the Cairngorms National Park Authority has sought an effective framework for planning, action and evaluation of sustainable tourism. It has sought to select a process that encompasses the many sustainable tourism initiatives and programmes that already exist in the area. As part of this process the park authority has established a private sector led Tourism Development Working Group that includes representatives from all key organisations with responsibility for tourism in the Cairngorms. The process of working towards Charter status raises several interesting issues, including sequencing, as it is hoped that the National Park Plan could be launched with the area having first achieved European Charter status.
Keywords: protected areas, National Parks, sustainable tourism, Scotland, European Charter for Sustainable Tourism.

Sustainable Tourism, F. D. Pineda, C. A. Brebbia & M. Mugica (Editors)

1 Introduction

The links between protected areas and tourism are long established but problems associated with increasing demands of tourism are testing park management to the limit. Reconciling the core environmental protection aim with social, cultural and economic pressures, often tourism related, becomes ever harder to achieve. Conflicts arise over contested space, issues of costs and benefits and increasingly who foots the bill. Transport congestion, regulations, controls and draconian pricing threaten to diminish the intrinsic qualities of protected areas and their enjoyment by the public. The sustainable development paradigm applied to tourism offers frameworks that may help. Scotland provides an interesting case study for three reasons: first, it has adopted a broad interpretation of the National Park designation, similar to the established UK model of multiple owned, 'lived in' parks; second, the parks are very recent and as such are still evolving; third, they purport, from the outset, to incorporate sustainable development objectives. This last point is demonstrated by the extent to which sustainable tourism lies at the core of park strategies.

2 Tourism, sustainability and National Parks

Sustainable development theory is based on the concept that environmental protection and economic growth can be compatible objectives [1]. Tourism has been gradually incorporated into this concept. The goal of sustainable tourism is to include all tourism activities, regardless of scale or location, in the sustainable development agenda. Many principles and guidelines have been developed for sustainable tourism in attempts to include environmental, cultural, economic and social goals within the context of tourism. For example, the acronym VICE represents four sustainable tourism aims: visitor satisfaction; industry profitability; community acceptance; and environmental protection [2]. Sustainable tourism has particular resonance for a National Park where nature is fragile and ecotourism or nature based tourism (NBT) relies on the long term well being of the environment [3]. Furthermore, the concept offers great utility in how parks may be planned and managed for tourism [4].

2.1 Sustainability and protected areas

Throughout history there have been examples of efforts made by governments and landowners to protect areas with special natural attributes for their intrinsic value and recreational qualities. Government involvement and responsibility for landscape protection has become the norm and government is now seen as the primary delivery vehicles of protected areas. Some argue that this involvement has gone too far in terms of complexity and number of protected area designations [5]. However it is the growth of National Parks over the last ten years that has been remarkable. Eagles [6] estimated there were 30,361 parks and protected areas in 1996 and in 2002 the number of National Parks alone had risen to 3386 worldwide. National Parks are viewed as the top tier designation

Sustainable Tourism, F. D. Pineda, C. A. Brebbia & M. Mugica (Editors)

and their scale and attractions have always acted as a magnet for tourism activities, resulting today in the search sustainable solutions to reconcile tourism and conservation demands.

The majority of National Parks follow the American model and come under category II of the IUCN classification where land is largely uninhabited, publicly owned and access is controlled. This model is representative of areas where 'human activities are prohibited or closely regulated in order to protect the natural environment' [7]. Despite this conservation priority, from an early stage National Parks had a clear connection with tourism and recent growth has tested category II parks to the limit [8]. Britain, on the other hand, is unusual in that areas designated as National Park come under category V of the IUCN classification mainly because areas are populated, privately owned and arguably require a holistic, or sustainable, approach based on social, environmental and economic issues. Category V is 'where the interaction of people and nature over time has produced an area of distinct character with significant aesthetic, ecological or cultural value, and often with high biological diversity' [9].

Although these parks share many tourism pressures experienced by their more 'pure' category II cousins it could be argued that they are better placed to deal with twenty first century pressures. Today everybody wants a piece of the park. Increasing visitor numbers and diversity of visitor expectations and behaviours exerts pressure on protected area management. The growth in emphasis on wider stakeholder involvement complicates policymaking: 'The management of protected areas must increasingly contend with the philosophical debate of use versus preservation, as urbanization, modernization, population mobility and international tourism growth continue to impact diminishing and fragmented green spaces' [10].

2.2 Nature Based Tourism: costs and benefits

The growth of specialist tourism segments, such as nature based tourism (NBT), often takes place in National Parks and despite its benign image, the volume and specialised activities still manage to exert environmental pressures [6, 8, 11]. This movement raises many questions relating to funding, access, transport, carrying capacity, visitor management and pricing [12]. The issues of willingness to pay for access to parks and community costs and benefits become acute with rapid growth and associated impacts. While measuring costs and benefits is more commonplace in the clearly delineated and closely controlled North American parks their structures are less adaptable to change. The category II model has multiple objectives built in and recent studies have adapted similar methodologies. Liston-Heyes and Heyes [13] use the travel cost method in Dartmoor, England to evaluate benefits users derive from access to the park.

Yet solving funding issues in current parks remains elusive as visitor numbers grow disproportionately to the levels of funding, visitor fees and user charges, creating a situation where increased maintenance and refurbishment requirements influence the quality of services [14, 15]. National park authorities need to review their pricing policy, which affects entrance fees and other charges, and reflects the true 'willingness-to-pay' [11]. Much of the literature

Sustainable Tourism, F. D. Pineda, C. A. Brebbia & M. Mugica (Editors)

also indicates the importance of implementing a pricing framework consisting of a mixture of regulation and incentives, 'sticks' and 'carrots' [6, 7, 14, 15]. The situation in Scotland presents an opportunity to examine a, perhaps, more holistic approach to resolving these issues.

3 Scotland's National Parks

As discussed, Britain's late adoption of National Parks in 1949 is attributed to the predominance of humanised landscapes so the model chosen lacks coherence with the IUCN category V. Parks are characterised by a high degree of privately owned land, living communities and neighbourhoods. The opportunity to exploit land for consumptive practices such as tourism is hence much greater. The majority of conflicts in British National Parks can thus be linked to this [16]. Success in attracting tourists, the majority in private cars, has led to problems of congestion, pollution, erosion, litter, and land use conflict leading to calls for more sustainable tourism development [17, 11].

Scotland shares similar land ownership characteristics with the rest of the UK however National Parks were rejected in 1949 due to a combination of opposition from landowners fearing land nationalisation and local authority concerns with further depopulation evoking memories of the 'highland clearances'. In addition, economic development through the in vogue hydro electric schemes was given top priority [18]. Finally, the need for public recreation was less urgent than in England [19]. So, despite having natural heritage characteristics more suited to IUCN category V National Parks, for fifty years Scotland remained one of the few countries without any form of National Park. By the late 1980s, the weak land management arrangements were straining under a series of highly publicised tourism related conflicts, resulting finally in recommendations for four National Parks to include 'independent planning boards comprising local and national members' [20].

Public support was overwhelming however the government of the day thought National Parks unsuitable, suggesting alternative voluntary partnership arrangements. Partnership boards for the two high profile areas were set up but arguably without the necessary powers or funding to cope with growing development pressures. The true sustainable development credentials of these policies may be judged against international criticism such as a World Conservation Union report which condemned Scotland for: 'operating one of the weakest management arrangements for vulnerable areas in Europe' [21].

Campaigns for National Parks continued however the change came abruptly with a new government in 1997. Two announcements came in quick succession from Donald Dewar, Secretary of State for Scotland: first devolution for Scotland; secondly the establishment of National Parks: 'I believe that National Parks are the right way forward for Scotland. The major gap we have identified in the current system of natural heritage designations relates to the management of a small number of relatively large areas of natural heritage importance.' [22].

The detail in the announcement is significant. After years of consultation and debate over alternative designated area models for Scotland, in one political gesture, the die was cast: 'Instead of proceeding logically from problem to diagnosis to prescription the political decision that Scotland must have National Parks came first, and only then was attention given to what their form and function should be.' [18].

The statutory agency responsible for implementation had to catch up fast. In 1998, Scottish Natural Heritage (SNH) launched the main consultation paper 'National Parks for Scotland' and the Government formally accepted this report in 1999. The Loch Lomond and the Trossachs National Park formally opened on 24 July 2002. The Cairngorms National Park followed on 1st September 2003.

The details of the enabling legislation are worth closer examination. Section 1 of the National Parks (Scotland) Act 2000 lists the core aims of Scotland's National Parks as:

a) to conserve and enhance the natural and cultural heritage of the area;
b) to promote sustainable use of the natural resources of the area,
c) to promote understanding and enjoyment (including enjoyment in the form of recreation) of the special qualities of the area by the public, and
d) to promote sustainable economic and social development of the area's communities [23].

It is clear that these aims go beyond traditional objectives for National Parks and are based on core sustainable development themes of social and economic aims in addition to environmental. Aims (c) and (d) illustrate two main differences with this model and explain why Scottish National Parks comes under category II of the IUCN protected area classification and not category V. The ability to promote National Parks is highly unusual and is not part of comparative English and Welsh legislation. The responsibility for the economic and social development of park communities is also unusual and linked to the British tradition of designating National Parks in populated areas.

The Government was heavily criticised for aim (d) and decided to include the Sandford Principle to strengthen the conservation aspect. Section 9, point (6), states: 'In exercising its functions a National Park Authority must act with a view to accomplishing the purpose set out in the subsection (1); but if, in relation to any matter, it appears to the authority that there is a conflict between the National Park aim set out in section 1 (a) and other National Park aims, the authority must give greater weight to the aim set out in section 1(a)' [23].

A pivotal issue in the debates in the Scottish Parliament related to the balance between conservation aims and social and economic development. Responses to consultation highlighted concerns that social and economic issues were to take second place to conservation. Drawing park boundaries to include populated rural communities exacerbated this. Consequently, the bill was amended to ensure that the National Park authorities accept an integrated approach in order to reconcile competing interests. It was established that a National Park Authority would only be required to give greater weight to conservation after failing to resolve a conflict. The emphasis placed on sustainable development indicates they: 'are not intended to be preserved areas in which all development is fossilized; instead, they are intended to be places that set an example of how to

Sustainable Tourism, F. D. Pineda, C. A. Brebbia & M. Mugica (Editors)

integrate the rural economy with the protection of the natural and cultural heritage' [20].

It is still too early to judge whether this represents a modern, innovative framework for National Parks or a watered down designation based on an already weak British interpretation of a National Park.

3.1 Linking sustainable tourism with the new model

Tourism has been identified as a critical factor in securing environmentally and socially sustainable development for areas within the two National Parks. The onus is therefore on park authorities, together with their partners and stakeholders, to avail themselves of good practice in sustainable tourism. Whilst it would appear that sustainable tourism should contribute most to the delivery of the all-important fourth aim 'to promote sustainable economic and social development of the area's communities', the development and management of sustainable tourism has the potential to contribute to all four primary aims. As noted earlier, Schedule 3 of the Act sets out specific powers for the National Park Authorities (NPAs) with respect to tourism. This includes the provision of information, education and interpretive facilities as well as services to promote the enjoyment of the parks' environments. Importantly and significantly, the NPAs are able to provide tourism facilities in the National Parks and encourage persons to visit the National Parks (paragraph 4, Schedule 3 of the Act). This ability to directly provide, manage and intervene creates interesting opportunities to be proactive, especially in partnership with other stakeholders, to provide sustainable tourism programmes. Unlike NPAs in England and Wales, the Scottish NPAs will be able to "encourage persons to visit the National Parks rather than service demand once within the parks. This additional power gives the Scottish NPAs the chance to engage in creative destination marketing to promote sustainable tourism.

In addition, SNH sets out a vision for parks that includes the following key elements relevant to sustainable tourism development:

- National Parks should engender trust between national and local interests in the delivery of conservation and community objectives; and
- National Parks should be pioneers of techniques for achieving sustainable development [24].

4 Combining sustainable tourism strategies within the Cairngorms National Park Authority

Partnership working and research into sustainable tourism strategies for Scotland's National Parks began before the parks themselves were established. Scotland was keen to devise unique models and draw on international best practice. For example, prior to the setting up of the Cairngorms National Park Authority (CNPA) a tourism forum, the Tourism Development Working Group (TDWG) was convened, comprising representatives from all tourism interests within the Cairngorms NP area. Two important and highly relevant pieces of

Sustainable Tourism, F. D. Pineda, C. A. Brebbia & M. Mugica (Editors)

research were drawn on: 'Sustainable Tourism in National Parks and Protected Areas' [25] and 'The European Charter for Sustainable Tourism in Protected Areas – A Prospectus for Action in Scotland's National Parks' [26].

4.1 Sustainable Tourism Development in Scotland's National Parks

The first of these reports [25] had three objectives: to identify the key principles for sustainable tourism in Scotland's National Parks; to illustrate these principles with a number of case studies; and to make recommendations on arrangements for collaborative working. It reviewed, analysed and evaluated best practice in respect of two aspects: the current guidelines for tourism in protected areas in Britain and elsewhere; and management best practice in terms of policy and planning; monitoring and review of impacts; use of facilities provided by managing bodies and the range of strategies, tools and techniques for promoting sustainable tourism.

The report provides both specific examples of sustainable tourism in action and highlights the importance of appropriate policies within the NPA to enable and facilitate sustainable tourism development. The various options (guidelines, tools, codes of conducts) to manage sustainable tourism were considered, and the TDWG felt that the Charter provided the most appropriate framework to the National Park Authority at that time. In particular, the principles and background information could provide valuable guidance to the relevant National Park Working Groups (for example, Access, Parks for All, Park Gateways and Information Provision) in advance of the strategy being developed and finalised.

4.2 The European Charter for Sustainable Tourism in Protected Areas – a prospectus for action in Scotland's National Parks

Thus, the second study [26] was jointly commissioned by Loch Lomond and The Trossachs National Park, the Cairngorms Partnership (responsible for management of the Cairngorms area prior to CNP) and SNH. All partners were familiar with the Charter and felt further research into the potential suitability for Scotland's future NPs was worthwhile. A joint approach would also build on existing collaborative Visitor Survey work. The Charter, part of the Europarc Federation, umbrella organisation of protected areas in Europe, reflects worldwide and European priorities as expressed in the recommendations of Agenda 21 adopted at the Earth Summit in Rio in 1992 and by the European Union in its 5th Environment Action Programme and Strategy for Sustainable Development. The underlying aims are:

- to increase and support Europe's protected areas as a fundamental part of our heritage, that should by preserved for and enjoyed by current and future generations;
- to improve the sustainable development and management for tourism in protected areas, which takes into account the needs of the environment, local residents, local businesses and visitors [26].

The Report [26] identifies the structures and activities relating to sustainable tourism at that time in each park area and looks at ways in which these might be strengthened in order to meet the requirements of the Charter. It identifies seven benefits for the parks including: raising the profile of the parks and sustainable tourism; providing an opportunity to align the policies to current international thinking and practice; networking with other Charter Parks; and helpful internal and external assessment. The Report notes the importance of not losing momentum for this area of work in the setting up of the NPAs.

The Charter is useful in that it outlines a process and provides guidance to ensure that a park authority is able to manage sustainable tourism effectively and innovatively through a set of principles. It provides a framework specifically for protected areas to create a structure and context for working in partnership on sustainable tourism so that a sustainable tourism strategy can be developed which includes a 5 year action plan. It also places a commitment on the park authority to undertake on-going consultation with the private sector; and to devise a means by which targets are set and progress is evaluated. Through core principles, the Charter covers all the key areas that should be considered for sustainable tourism development and linked activities in a protected area:

- protecting and enhancing the natural and cultural heritage;
- understanding and meeting visitor needs and ensuring quality;
- communicating the special qualities of the area;
- encouraging tourism products relating to the protected area;
- training relating to the protected area and sustainable tourism;
- maintaining the local quality of life;
- increasing benefits to the local economy;
- monitoring and influencing visitor flows.

5 Cairngorms National Park Authority

The CNPA was formally established on 25 March 2003 and took on full operational powers on 1st September 2003. As a statutory Non Departmental Public Body (NDPB) the CNPA is directly funded by the Scottish Executive. In the longer term, the CNPA objectives will be mainly determined by the National Park Plan, the statutory strategic plan for the whole National Park area. However, prior to the CNPA becoming fully operational, the first corporate plan outlined the National Park Board's early thinking in both operational and policy terms for the CNPA as an organisation, and the long and short term priorities for the Park.

Four policy themes encapsulate the statutory aims of the Park. These themes will be refined as the National Park Plan develops, but they represent current priorities to drive and guide the work of the CNPA. The four priority themes are: to foster a 'Park for All'; to encourage widespread enjoyment, understanding and appreciation of the special qualities of the area; to develop clear, cohesive strategies for stewardship of the natural resources in the Park; and to encourage and support balanced, thriving, stable communities. The last theme notes:

Sustainable Tourism, F. D. Pineda, C. A. Brebbia & M. Mugica (Editors)

"Tourism- the CNP is a large area with tremendous tourism potential. The CNPA aims to establish, working with tourist boards and local businesses, a co-ordinated park-wide approach to sustainable tourism through the preparation and implementation of a sustainable tourism strategy including a marketing strategy and brand for the whole Park, based on the special qualities and attractions of the area and the establishment of a hallmark of quality."

Tourism is a vital part of the economy in the new Park. Local employment relies heavily on tourism and the area benefits from the income that visitors to the area generate. As with all tourist areas however, potential conflict exists between environmental, socio economic and cultural interests and the Cairngorms area is no different. It therefore follows that the resource base on which present and future tourism and tourist activities in the CNP are based must be sustained, since if the resource base is destroyed the tourism that it is based on will surely follow suit.

5.1 Sustainable tourism in CNP

The development of a Sustainable Tourism Strategy is seen as a priority by the CNPA to provide an effective framework for planning, action and evaluation to ensure that tourism is developed in a sustainable and sympathetic manner, whilst ensuring that the heritage and resources are protected. To oversee the development and implementation of this a Sustainable Tourism Officer and Business and Marketing Officer were appointed.

As noted earlier, the ability of NPAs in Scotland to directly provide, manage and intervene in tourism promotion, creates interesting opportunities to be proactive, especially in partnership with other stakeholders to provide sustainable tourism products, initiatives and programmes. This power gives the Scottish NPAs the chance to engage in creative destination marketing and to encourage and co-ordinate the marketing of appropriate activities in order to promote sustainable tourism. A key element is the TDWG, an industry based group, comprising private sector businesses, Area Tourist Boards, VisitScotland and other relevant public sector organisations involved in tourism in the Cairngorms. The purpose of the Group is to identify priorities for establishing improved co-ordination of tourism related activity in the CNP and to develop and implement CNP wide initiatives as appropriate. The TDWG recognises that tourism is all encompassing. Its January 2004 report to the NP Board identified seven key interlinked issues for tourism in the Cairngorms:

- successful co-operation, integration and encouragement of cross-sectoral working for all those involved in tourism in the area;
- development of a Sustainable Tourism Strategy and the successful application for, and implementation of, the European Charter for Sustainable Tourism;
- development and implementation of a Marketing Strategy & Action Plan for the Cairngorms;
- delivery of quality standards that build on nationally recognised standards which are specific to the Cairngorms;

Sustainable Tourism, F. D. Pineda, C. A. Brebbia & M. Mugica (Editors)

- support for and continued development of quality assured products grown, made or available in the area;
- need for ongoing research, with easily accessible results, which assesses the needs, opinions and demands of visitors in order to be able to anticipate, meet and exceed visitor expectations;
- enhancement of visitors' experience while in the area, through improved information and interpretation provision.

This is clearly at an early stage, and further research, analysis and development of actions plans is the next step for the TDWG. Whilst recognising the linkages between the issues it is important that a coordinated approach with partners and other working groups is maintained. It is also recognised that although the TDWG has identified these key issues, they may be driven forward by other Working Groups.

5.2 Relevance of Charter to the Cairngorms National Park Area

For the Cairngorms the 'checklist' of principles is particularly significant as it should help include all key areas or actions required in the early stages of strategy development. The Charter process also involves an objective assessment of the strengths, weaknesses, opportunities and threats facing the Park and requires a review and evaluation mechanism. The TDWG recognises that it is the process contained within this framework that is as important, if not more so, than gaining the Charter itself. To be successful, it is important that all the key stakeholders are involved in its development and implementation. The private sector will ultimately be a key beneficiary, though individual businesses are unlikely to see the full benefits until later in the process when the action plan is implemented. It is important nonetheless to involve them from the start, and make particular efforts to engage them in the development of the strategy. The TDWG is aware that this approach can bear fruits as demonstrated in the other UK Charter park, Mourne Mountains AONB, Northern Ireland, awarded the Charter last year.

6 Conclusions

Scotland's approach to National Parks is firmly based on the principles of sustainable development, attempting to integrate the needs of local communities living and working in the park with the needs of heritage conservation and enhancement. The model seeks to avoid conflicts and reconcile competing interests through partnership working. The approach differs from the dominant international approach to National Parks, based on the primacy of protecting the natural environment. It could be argued that this is a modern model reflecting contemporary circumstances in a post industrial country. The robustness of this model will be closely examined in its ability to reconcile tensions between environmental protection and sustainable development for the benefit of communities within park boundaries. The TDWG emphasises the key role of the tourism sector in implementing sustainable tourism strategies and their role will

Sustainable Tourism, F. D. Pineda, C. A. Brebbia & M. Mugica (Editors)

be critical. The worth of the European Charter as a guiding framework and the ability of the park authority to incorporate this within the park plan will both be tested in coming months. It is too early to judge the success of the Scotland's National Park model or the specifics of sustainable tourism in the Cairngorms. However the uniqueness of the Scottish approach might offer some insights into issues of reconciling tourism growth with issues of park protection, stakeholder consultation and funding. Developments in the coming months should prove interesting for observers of National Parks in both Scotland and internationally.

References

[1] Hardy, A., Beeton, R.J.S., and Pearson, L., Sustainable Tourism: An Overview of the Concept and its Position in Relation to Conceptualisations of Tourism, Journal of Sustainable Tourism, Vol. 10, No. 6, pp.475-494, 2002.

[2] Stevens T., Sustainable Tourism in National Parks and Protected Areas: An Overview, Scottish Natural Heritage, 2002.

[3] MacLellan, L. R., Tourism and the Natural Environment, Scottish Environment Audits No. 5, Scottish Environment LINK, Perth, Scotland, 2001.

[4] Boyd, S. W., Tourism, National Parks and sustainability, in Butler, R.W. and Boyd, S.W. (eds), Tourism and National Parks: Issues and Implications, Chichester, John Wiley & Sons Ltd, pp 161-186, 2000.

[5] Bishop, K., Phillips, A. and Warren, L.M. Protected Areas for the Future: Models from the Past, Journal of Environmental Planning and Management, Vol. 40, No. 1, pp.81-110, 1997.

[6] Eagles, P.F.J., Trends in Park Tourism: Economics, Finance and Management, Journal of Sustainable Tourism, Vol. 10, No. 2, pp. 132-153, 2002.

[7] Leitmann, J., Options for Managing Protected Areas: Lessons from International Experience, Journal of Environmental Planning and Management, Vol. 41, No. 1, pp.129-143, 1998.

[8] Boyd, S.W. and Butler, R.W., Tourism and National Parks: the origin of the concept, in Butler, R.W. and Boyd, S.W. (eds), Tourism and National Parks: Issues and Implications, Chichester, John Wiley & Sons Ltd, pp. 13-27, 2000.

[9] International Union for Conservation of Nature and Natural Resources (IUCN), Guidelines for protected area management categories, Switzerland, Gland, 1994.

[10] Jamal, T. and Eyre, M., Legitimation Struggles in National Park Spaces: The Banff Bow Valley Round Table, Journal of Environmental Planning and Management, Vol. 46, no. 3, pp. 417-441, 2003.

[11] Laarman, J.G. and Gregersen, H.M., Pricing policy in nature-based tourism, Tourism Management, Vol. 17, No. 4, pp.247-254, 1996.

Sustainable Tourism, F. D. Pineda, C. A. Brebbia & M. Mugica (Editors)

[12] World Tourism Organisation (WTO) and United Nations Environment Programme (UNEP), Guidelines: Development of National Parks and Protected Areas for Tourism, Madrid, WTO, 1992.
[13] Liston-Heyes, C. and Heyes, A., Recreational benefits from the Dartmoor National Park, Journal of Environmental Management, vol. 55, no. 2, pp. 69-80, 1999.
[14] Van Sickle, K. and Eagles, F.J., Budgets, pricing policies and user fees in Canadian park's tourism, Tourism Management, Vol. 19, No. 3, pp.225-235, 1998.
[15] Buckley, R., Pay to Play in Parks: An Australian Policy Perspective on Visitor Fees in Public Protected Areas, Journal of Sustainable Tourism, vol. 11, no. 1, pp. 56-73, 2003.
[16] Parker, G. and Ravenscroft, N., Benevolence, nationalism and hegemony: fifty years of the National Parks and Access to the Countryside Act 1949, Leisure Studies, vol. 18, no. 4, pp. 297-313, 1999.
[17] Lovelock, B., Why It's Good to be Bad: The Role of Conflict in Contributing Towards Sustainable Tourism in Protected Areas, Journal of Sustainable Tourism, Vol. 10, No. 1, pp.5-30, 2002.
[18] Warren C., Managing Scotland's Environment, Edinburgh, EUP, 2002.
[19] Moir, J., The designation of valued landscapes in Scotland, in MacDonald, R. and Thomas, H. (eds.) Nationality and Planning in Scotland and Wales, University of Wales Press: Cardiff, pp. 203-242, 1997.
[20] McCarthy, J.; Lloyd, G. and Illsley, B., National Parks in Scotland: Balancing Environment and Economy, European Planning Studies, 1 July 2002, vol. 10, no. 5, pp. 665-670, 2002.
[21] Edwards, T., Pennington, N. and Starrett, M., The Scottish Parks System: A Strategy for Conservation and Enjoyment, in Fladmark J M (ed), Heritage, Donhead Publishing, London, pp 141-151, 1993.
[22] Scottish Office, Planning Bulletin, issue sixteenth December, 1997, National Parks for Scotland; www.scotland.gov.uk/library documents1/dd-pl16a.htm, 1997.
[23] HMSO, National Parks for Scotland, SNH, 2000.
[24] Scottish Natural Heritage, National Parks for Scotland: Advice to Government, SNH, Edinburgh, 1999.
[25] Stevens T., Sustainable Tourism in National Parks and Protected Areas: An Overview, Scottish Natural Heritage, 2002.
[26] EUROPARC Consulting The European Charter for Sustainable Tourism in Protected Areas – A Prospectus for Action in Scotland's National Parks; Germany: EUROPARC Consulting GmbH, 2003.

Sustainable Tourism, F. D. Pineda, C. A. Brebbia & M. Mugica (Editors)
© 2004 WIT Press, www.witpress.com, ISBN 1-85312-724-8

Sustainable tourism and visitor satisfaction: social carrying capacity in 'Sierra de Grazalema' Natural Park (Spain)

J. Navarrete[1], A. Lora[2] & J. González-Arenas[3]
[1]*EGMASA, División Planes y Servicios, Seville, Spain*
[2]*ETSIAM, University of Cordoba, Spain*
[3]*IFAPA, CIFA "Alameda del Obispo", Spain*

Abstract

The increasing recreational use of protected areas regarding leisure activities usually involves negative impacts, both in natural resources and visitor experience, which are to be identified and monitored in order to achieve a sustainable tourism system. A number of planning and management decision-making frameworks have been developed to cope with the challenge of balancing recreation use and preservation. Carrying Capacity, one of them, mainly includes ecological and social parameters, such as environmental quality and visitor experience, respectively. The present research focuses on Social Carrying Capacity, defined as the level of use beyond which the recreational experience is negatively perceived. A survey on 400 visitors has been carried out during two years in 'Sierra de Grazalema' Natural Park, one of the most emblematic sites in Andalusia. This area was declared as Biosphere Reserve by UNESCO in 1977. The results show deep visitor satisfaction and high environmental quality assessment. In addition, other interesting information has been obtained from the questionnaire such as visit profile, optimal interval between groups along pathways, valuation of existing visitor facilities, influence of encounters on recreational experience, etc. These data will allow a better understanding on user's perception and will provide a helpful tool for planning and management.
Keywords: social carrying capacity, sustainable tourism, visitor satisfaction, Grazalema.

Sustainable Tourism, F. D. Pineda, C. A. Brebbia & M. Mugica (Editors)

1 Introduction

At the dawn of the 21st century, the environment is conceived in a global, integrated way, which intends to approach natural resources management under the flag of sustainable development. The recent world summit conference in Johannesburg, ten years after Rio, proved so. The main goal of sustainable development consists of taking from natural resources as much profit as possible without impairing future generations.

'Sierra de Grazalema' Natural Park withstands one of the highest levels of tourist pressure compared to other wilderness sites in the south of Spain, because of its unique landscape and cultural appeals, along with fine access roads that connect it with nearby, big cities such as Seville. Consequently, a number of negative impacts take place throughout the Park, especially when carrying capacity is exceeded. Through a social carrying capacity assessment approach we try to identify those factors determining recreation experience and their influence on visitor satisfaction, as well as to evaluate how adequate visitor daily quotas existing for certain pathways actually are.

2 Site description

'Sierra de Grazalema' Natural Park covers an area of 51.695 hectares and is located in the south of Spain, in the western part of the Baetic Mountains. As a frontier land between Grenade Muslims and Castilian Catholics, a number of battles took place on this strategic site during the 13th and 14th centuries. As a result, a populated landscape gradually developed, where small scattered villages spread up the hills getting thoroughly integrated in the environment. This unique cultural framework still remains nowadays keeping its own identity despite modern times. Thirteen villages with approximately 76,000 inhabitants are either completely or partly within the protection limits of the park. The highest rainfall level of the Iberian Peninsula caused by moisture loaded clouds coming from the sea and condensing while moving over the hills (Foehn effect), has created over the years a magnificent karst landscape with hundreds of caverns and underground streams. In spite of human presence from ancient times, this natural site still maintains important native Mediterranean forests mainly composed by Holm oaks (*Quercus rotundifolia*), Cork oaks (*Quercus suber*) and Andalusian oaks (*Quercus faginea*), among others. However, the real jewel of vegetation is the Spanish fir forest (*Abies pinsapo*), a relictic conifer from Tertiary Era, which shelters in the shady, wet side of the mountains, and represents the best preserved stand of this endangered, endemic tree in the world.

3 Recreational use

The main tourist facilities in the park are visitor centres, information points, ecomuseums, viewpoints, botanic garden, camp-sites, picnic areas, youth hostels, hotels and rural accommodation. Moreover, a well developed footpath network across the park ensures a concentrated use of certain points in order to avoid

Sustainable Tourism, F. D. Pineda, C. A. Brebbia & M. Mugica (Editors)

negative impacts over sensitive ecosystems. There are two types of signed, hiking paths:

a) Restricted access footpaths: Only four paths run across the Reserve Area, the core of the park holding the most valuable natural resources. A special permit from the park's office is required to enter this zone.

b) Free access footpaths: They are situated outside the Reserve Area and no permit is necessary.

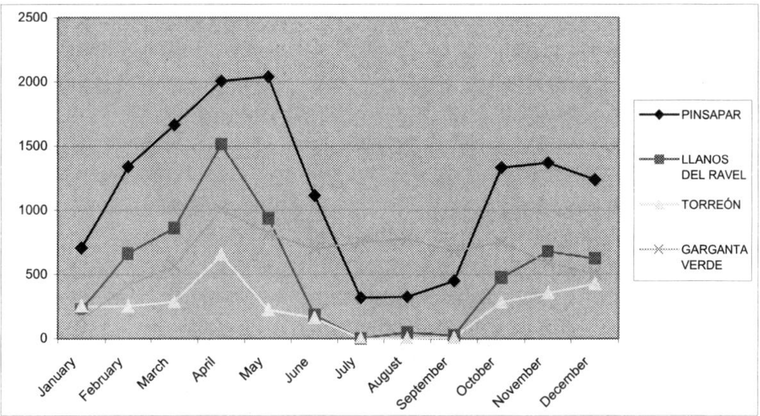

Figure 1: Seasonality of visitor flow in pathways of Reserve Area in 2001.

Tourist development has not yet reached its maximum, according to the potential capacity of the park. Distribution, quality and capacity of tourist facilities must be improved within the coming years. One of the major constraints tourist management has to cope with is seasonality of visitor flow (figure 1).

3.1 Visitor profile

The typical visitor of this Natural Park, according to data obtained from the present research, is between 20 and 39 years old, educated to university level and with a family income of between 1,500 and 2,000 € per month. He comes from large cities like Seville, Jerez or Cadiz, 100 km away from the park, with his own car, accompanied by up to four people and usually without children. Recreation predominately occurs during weekends and holiday times, with stays of more than one day and the visitors spend approximately 73€ during the visit.

3.2 Quota system

The high ecological value sheltered in the Reserve Area along with its extreme fragility made the managers establish, from the beginning of the Natural Park's life, access restrictions to four pathways going across that sensitive area: El Pinsapar, Llanos del Ravel, El Torreón and Garganta Verde. Thus, limited numbers of visitors' Daily Quota Permits, varying from 30 to 60 people, were set

Sustainable Tourism, F. D. Pineda, C. A. Brebbia & M. Mugica (Editors)

for each trail. Quota system regulates how many groups can enter the Reserve Area each day. The assumption of such a polemic measure was mainly based on preservation criteria, although no scientific research was ever made to support it, and hence, those numbers may no longer be appropriate at present. In fact, visitor flow has notably increased over the last years exceeding the number of quota permits available (figure 2). In other words, the demand is now much bigger than the offer. In consequence, a number of visitors get frustrated every year for not being able to acquire the necessary permit to enter the Reserve Area. A question then arises: Could daily quota be increased without impairing visitor satisfaction?

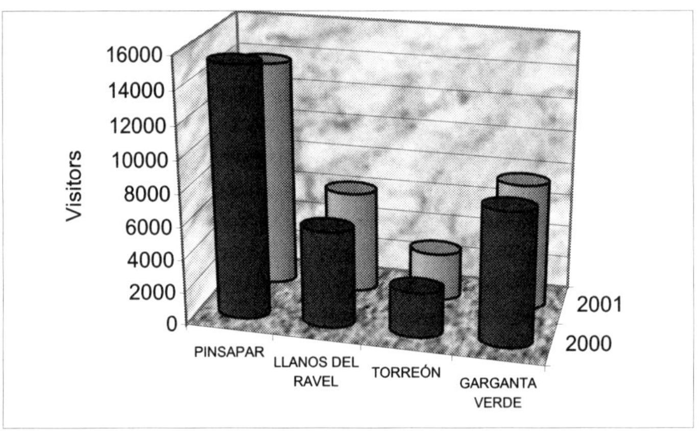

Figure 2: Number of permits delivered in 2000 and 2001 for each pathway of Reserve Area.

3.3 Recreational carrying capacity

Recreational Carrying Capacity is defined as the maximum use level a specified area can support without negatively impacting natural resources or visitor experience (Countryside Commission [1]). Another definition is the level of use that can be supported over a specified time by an area without causing excessive damage to either the physical environment or the experience of the visitor (Stankey and Manning [2]). Four dimensions can be considered:

a) Physical Carrying Capacity: the amount of recreational use that can physically occur in a defined space. It mainly depends on facilities, infrastructure and topology conditions (canyons, shorelines, marshes, swamps...)

b) Ecological Carrying Capacity: the amount of recreational use that can occur without producing unacceptable impacts on the ecosystem (Limit of Acceptable Change). This is difficult to measure and monitor but is of utmost importance especially if the ecosystem is sensitive.

c) Economic Carrying Capacity: this dimension deals with the ability to cope with new economic activities related to tourism without marginalizing traditional economic activities of the community.

Sustainable Tourism, F. D. Pineda, C. A. Brebbia & M. Mugica (Editors)

d) Social Carrying Capacity: the level of use beyond which the recreational experience is negatively perceived. Psychological aspects as well as the level of subjectivity implicit in this concept make it the most difficult parameter to determine (Manning *et al.* [3]). Furthermore there is little research on this topic, especially in Spain. In fact, Social Carrying Capacity is not a property of the site, but a property of the visitor, and so, it is more related to the type and the behaviour of users encountered during the visit than by the level of use itself.

The two principal dimensions of Recreational Carrying Capacity are ecological and social. Recently, negative impacts on soil conditions and vegetation derived from hikers' trampling have been evaluated through a research carried out by University of Cordoba in 'Sierra de Grazalema' Natural Park (Castro [4] and Almagro [5]). This is why we have decided to focus on Social Carrying Capacity assessment at the same time in order to complement the existing information and provide a helpful tool for planning and management decision-making in this particular natural site.

As a matter of fact, one of the conclusions of the recent study by Gonzalez-Capitel [6] about the Pinsapar pathway, which goes along the unique Spanish fir forest in the Reserve Area, affirms that, as physical environment does not seem to be close to its maximum (Physical Carrying Capacity), visitor satisfaction (Social Carrying Capacity) might become the limiting factor for the capacity of the pathway. Recreational experience monitoring and assessment is therefore suggested.

4 Methodology

A survey on 400 tourists was carried out by means of personal *in situ* interviews in order to determine visitor experience. To achieve the defined objectives a questionnaire was designed according to brevity and comprehension criteria. This design is of utmost importance in order to minimize bias and optimize data analysis (Navarrete [7]). Most interviews took place in high intensity, recreational spots, such as the visitor centre, information points, footpath network (especially the four ones within the Reserve Area), viewpoints, picnic areas and villages, under fine weather conditions (Navarrete and González-Arenas [8]).

5 Results

It is important to emphasize once again the fact that the subject of the present research are visitors' personal opinions regarding their own experience, and hence the subjectivity of such issues. Results are shown in the same order as the questionnaire was made.

5.1 Environment quality

Question: If you had to evaluate the general quality of this Natural Park's environment, which mark would you give it from 0 to 10?

Sustainable Tourism, F. D. Pineda, C. A. Brebbia & M. Mugica (Editors)

The average mark reached 8.17 over 10, which indicates firstly a fairly high opinion of the park's environment, and secondly, a high level of conservation of its resources. Therefore, tourists are sensitive enough to appreciate the values of the place they are visiting. Only 8 out of 400 of them assigned a mark below 5, whereas 167 (42%) gave 9 or 10.

5.2 Tolerance to other visitors

Question: What do you think about the amount of people currently visiting the park?

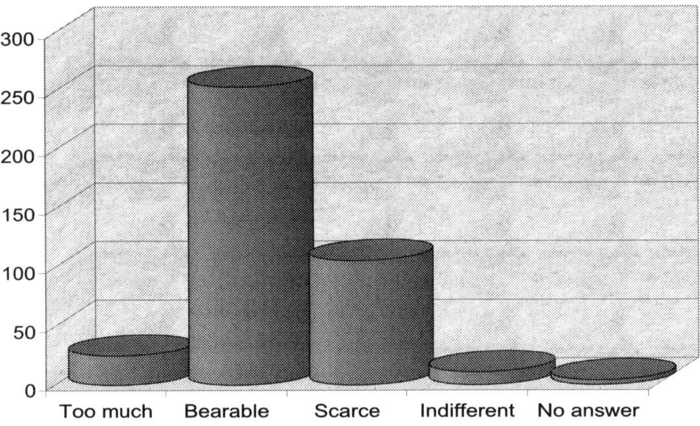

Figure 3: Tolerance to other visitors.

As figure 3 shows, for over 60% it was acceptable and only 6% said it was too high, identifying the most crowded places as the villages and the Reserve Area.

These results can be explained in two different ways:

a) Visitors have a high level of tolerance to the presence of others, since most interviews were made on holidays and at weekends (high season).

b) The particular conditions of park's topography allow for a large number of tourists without their disturbing one another.

We must remark that we are always considering instantaneous carrying capacity, that is, the number of people at a certain moment.

5.3 Tourist facilities

Question: How well do you think this park is provided with reception facilities?

Half of the interviewees considered that the park provided an acceptable number of public use infrastructure such as carparks, accommodation, viewpoints, pathways, etc. Some 27% agreed that it was very well endowed, whereas 18% thought it was insufficient. The recent effort made over the last years to implement new services and facilities, as well as to improve the ones already existing is therefore appreciated by the visitor. As a matter of fact, this

Sustainable Tourism, F. D. Pineda, C. A. Brebbia & M. Mugica (Editors)

park holds some of the fullest facilities on offer in the Andalusian Network of Protected Natural Areas (RENPA).

5.4 Visit purpose

Question: Choose the main purposes of your visit from the suggested list and order them according to your preference (assign 1, 2, 3 and so on)

'Contacting with nature' and 'visiting villages and meeting their people' occupy first places. Although the first reason was expected, the second one really constitutes a peculiarity of this site. The outstanding beauty of those small, bright white, typical villages has made them worthy of being included in the so called "White Villages Route", which represents a major tourist attraction. Practising sport and walking through the magnificent Spanish fir forest were other relevant reasons. However, both activities need certain requirements from users, such as fitness and youth, so not everyone can enjoy them. In addition, the required permit to enter the Reserve Area, where the Spanish fir grows, is often difficult to obtain. This is why these two purposes are placed lower in the ranking than the first ones. Getting rid of stress is placed at 5th position, since the standard visitor comes from large, populated cities, where this problem is increasingly common.

5.5 Encounters with other groups

Question: How is your recreational experience affected by encounters with other groups?

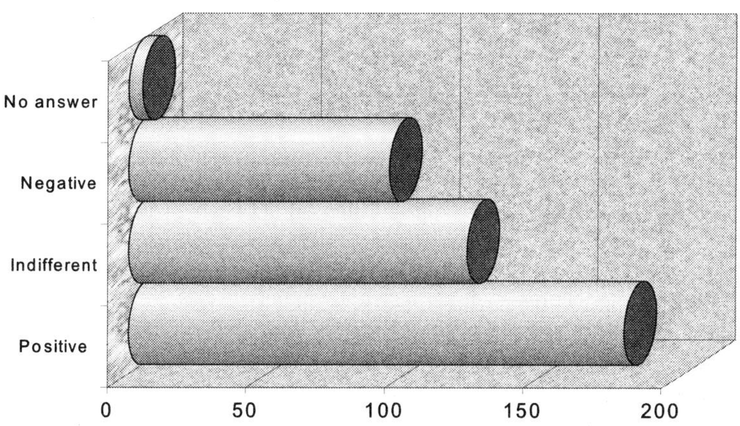

Figure 4: Influence of encounters with others.

About 45% of surveyed people found it a positive experience to encounter other visitors, whereas some 23% perceived it as something undesirable and negative. The total group of users then may be divided into two psychologically

Sustainable Tourism, F. D. Pineda, C. A. Brebbia & M. Mugica (Editors)
© 2004 WIT Press, www.witpress.com, ISBN 1-85312-724-8

different groups: those preferring to meet other people during their visit and those preferring few or none. In the middle of them, though, there is still a significant 30% who does not care about this issue (figure 4).

People considering the encounters as something positive were unexpectedly predominant in contrast to the common idea of going to the countryside so as to avoid the city worries. In this case, this is actually not an accurate assumption since the typical visitor is apparently used to living in large towns and so prefers a certain level of socialisation even in the wilderness. Furthermore, they are mainly southern young people accustomed to populated, noisy ambience and often gregarious behaviour, what definitely makes them especially tolerant to overcrowding. Coming to the park in groups instead of alone as well as perceiving the use level as bearable or scarce even in high season also explain this result.

5.6 Optimal timing between groups

Question: While hiking along a pathway, how often would you like to encounter other group so as your satisfaction is optimal?

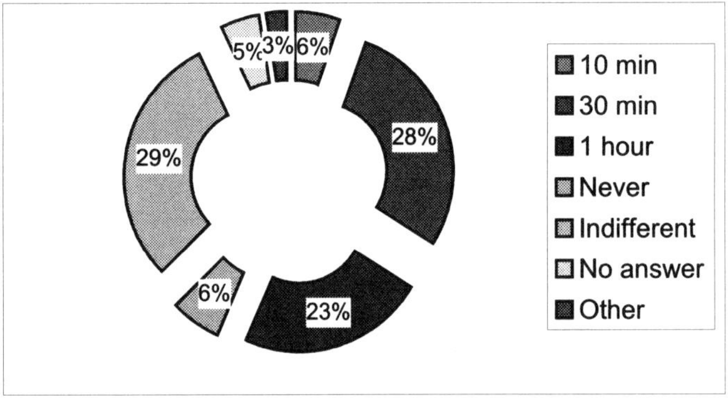

Figure 5: Optimal interval between groups.

The number of encounters a person has while recreating is the basic social recreation component for this carrying capacity assessment. This issue was thought indifferent by nearly 30% of surveyed people, which means they did not find any link between encounter frequency and satisfaction level, whereas for 57% such a relation did exist (figure 5). In order to provide a helpful tool for planning and management, the optimal interval between groups should be every 40 minutes approximately. Subsequently, two major goals could be achieved:

a) Regarding Ecological Carrying Capacity, negative impacts such as noise or trampling would be reduced along certain pathways by regulating the groups entrance, which is especially interesting in high sensitive areas. Tourist pressure on the environment would become more uniform and less intense.

b) Regarding Social Carrying Capacity, visitor satisfaction would increase (except for the minority preferring not to meet anyone along a pathway).

Sustainable Tourism, F. D. Pineda, C. A. Brebbia & M. Mugica (Editors)

Those who answered indifferent would not notice any change in their experience, neither positive nor negative.

5.7 Quota system

Question: To enter the four pathways of the Reserve Area Daily Quota Permits have been established going from 30 to 60 people. What is your opinion about them?

As shown in figure 6, over 60% agreed they are adequate. Most of interviews took place along those paths, and hence to visitors that succeeded in getting the required permit. Different results would certainly have been obtained with people whose permit was denied. To summarize, several conclusions can be extracted:

a) Visitors are aware of the necessity to put certain limits to enter high ecological value areas, although it is possible that the existing quotas are not the optimum.

b) People thinking that the existing quotas are too restrictive and more people should therefore be allowed to get in are much more than people considering them too permissive. Thus, increasing those limited quotas would eventually satisfy more people than reducing them.

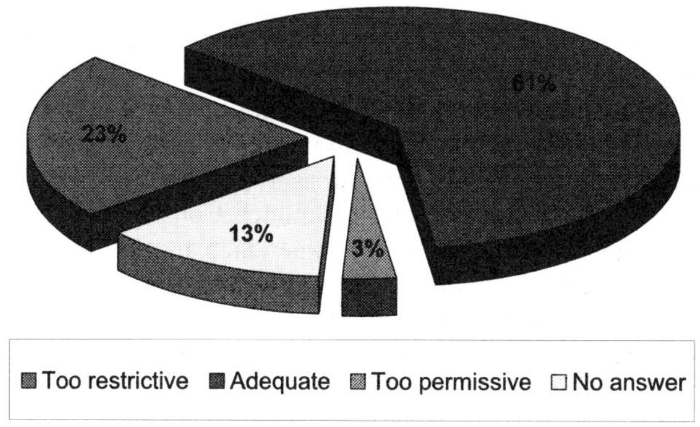

Figure 6: Opinion about visitors' daily quota.

5.8 Satisfaction level after the visit

Question: How much satisfied are you leaving the park after your visit?

Most of surveyed people (68%) affirmed they felt very satisfied and 29% moderately satisfied. No-one answered they were not satisfied at all and just 1.5% little satisfied mainly due to heat or frustration for not having a chance to get the permit for the Reserve Area. In other words, this park widely satisfies visitor expectations and so becomes an extraordinary recreation site.

Sustainable Tourism, F. D. Pineda, C. A. Brebbia & M. Mugica (Editors)

5.9 Tourist management

Question: What would you improve in this park?

This multiple choice question intends to identify those management issues needing improvement from the visitor's opinion. Directional and interpretative signs occupy the first steps. Cleanliness goes next. Unexpectedly, over 60 people answered that nothing should be changed, which is probably due to tiredness making them tick off the first box of the list proposed in the questionnaire.

5.10 Distinctive features

Question: In your opinion which features of this park are different from other nature sites you visited before?

Local villages are regarded as the principal issue that differentiate this park from the rest of the sites belonging to the RENPA. Therefore, the unique cultural heritage provides a complementing offer to the natural resources of the park, enhancing the visitor satisfaction. As expected, *Abies pinsapo*, the real park's emblem, is seen as the second distinctive feature.

6 Conclusion

Social Carrying Capacity at 'Sierra de Grazalema' Natural Park is still far away from its limit. Thus, increasing the number of people allowed in the Reserve Area could be possible from the visitors' point of view without impairing their satisfaction. However, from a preservation perspective, the visitors' flow should be diversified both in time and space so as to reduce tourist impact on sensitive areas and achieve a sustainable tourism model. Consequently, in order to cope with the challenge of balancing visitor experience and resource preservation we strongly recommend the implementation of a measure consisting of regulating the time interval between groups so that encounters along pathways take place every 40 minutes approximately, as the majority of users would eventually get a benefit.

References

[1] Countryside Commission. *Environmental assessment: The Treatment of Landscape and Countryside Recreation Issues*. English Tourist Board, U.K., 1970.

[2] Stankey, G. and R. Manning. *Carrying capacity of recreation settings. A Literature Review: The President's Commission on Americans Outdoors*. Washington, D. C.: U. S. Government Printing Office, M-47-M-57, 1986.

[3] Manning, R., D. Lime and M. Hof. *Social carrying capacity of natural areas: theory and application in the U.S. National Parks*. Natural areas journal 16:118-27, 1996.

Sustainable Tourism, F. D. Pineda, C. A. Brebbia & M. Mugica (Editors)

[4] Castro, R. *Research of the ecological impact derived from recreational use in Sierra de Grazalema Natural Park.* Forestry engineering final-year project. E.T.S.I.A.M. University of Córdoba, Córdoba, 2003
[5] Almagro, C. *Methodology approach for the evaluation of vegetable diversity in a Protected Natural Area. Implementation to Sierra de Grazalema Natural Park (Cádiz-Málaga).* Forestry engineering final-year project. E.T.S.I.A.M. University of Córdoba, Córdoba, 2002.
[6] González-Capitel, E. *Recreation carrying capacity in the Andalusian Network of Protected Natural Areas.* Junta de Andalucía. Consejería de Medio Ambiente, Sevilla, 2001.
[7] Navarrete, E. *Economic and recreational valuation of Sierra de Hornachuelos Natural Park (Spain).* Forestry engineering final-year project. E.T.S.I.A.M. University of Córdoba, Córdoba, pp. 86-87, 1999.
[8] Navarrete, J. and J. González-Arenas. *Valorando las áreas protegidas.* Vision net, pp.117-118, 2003.

Sustainable Tourism, F. D. Pineda, C. A. Brebbia & M. Mugica (Editors)

Section 8
Tourism, infrastructure, transport and hotels

Tourist satisfaction: airline service performance as a satisfaction determinant

J. W. de Jager & L. de W Fourie
Tshwane University of Technology, South Africa

Abstract

The problem under investigation in this paper is to investigate to what extent airline management has sufficient knowledge about the perceived perception of tourists or passengers with regard to the services rendered to them. This becomes increasingly important resulting from the financial difficulties airlines are experiencing since the terrorist attacks of 11 September 2001 in the United States of America. The need for the study results from a worldwide tendency of economic downturn and the public caution on air travel, which is caused by the capacity of the airline industry to exceed demand substantially. The purpose of this study is to investigate selective service quality elements that contribute to the satisfaction of tourists when making use of domestic airlines in South Africa. The perceptions of consumers on service recovery is vital in understanding areas of success and areas of failure within three major airline passengers in South Africa on specific performance areas, *inter alia* South African Airways, Comair and Kulula.Com.

1 Introduction

The rapid increasing rate of tourism to developing countries needs to be synergised with good planning of all necessary services and facilities, of which transport is vital, but often a neglected area. Since the democratic election in South Africa in 1994, tourism has increased at a progressive pace. After the upliftment of sanctions the country became a global competitive tourist attraction. For this reason it is important to ensure that tourists are amongst others satisfied with the services provided by domestic airlines. This can be achieved by managing service quality to maintain a sustainable tourism environment. The study attempts to identify the service dimensions that matter

Sustainable Tourism, F. D. Pineda, C. A. Brebbia & M. Mugica (Editors)
 ISBN 1-85312-724-8

most to airline passengers as well as the rate of satisfaction with regards to pre-selected service elements.

2 Tourism and the service experience

Tourism is essentially a service industry or perhaps more accurately an amalgam of service industries. Its management practices are typically concerned with issues as service quality and productivity (Otto & Ritchie [19]; Yoon & Uysel [24]; Kozak [13]; Haber & Lerner [9]; Nield et al. [18] and Weiermair & Fuchs [23] as they fall within the aegis of services marketing. Although Otto & Ritchie [19] refer to these aspects as critical concerns, it refers to technical issues that may only tell part of the management story. The other critical side, according to the author, is the subjective personal reactions and feelings experienced by consumers when they consume a service. This phenomenon has been termed the service experience and has recently been found to be an important part of consumer evaluation of satisfaction with services. He concludes that understanding experiential phenomena in tourism is particularly important as emotional reactions and decisions often prevail amongst consumers. Bearing in mind the abovementioned it is evident that airlines and to a lesser extent tour operators should understand the needs and perceptions of passengers in order to satisfy their needs and consequently to try and capture the biggest market share.

3 Tourism transport and need satisfaction

Transport is an integral part of tourism that facilitates the movement of e.g. holidaymakers and business travelers. Transport can be regarded as the key element of the tourist "experience" and is an integral part of the tourism industry. Transport provides the essential link between tourism origin and destination areas (Page [20], p.1). Prideaux ([21], p.53) states that air transport has made a significant contribution to the growth of tourism in many parts of the world including destinations in Asia, Spain, Africa and the Pacific Islands. For this reason it can be argued that tour operators should be concerned with various issues facing the tourism industry. This includes aspects like customer care and the tourist's experience while traveling as well as the preparation process before traveling. Page ([20], p.3) states that owing to the choice of transport available and the competitive environment for tourist travel in free market economies, transport operators recognize the importance of ensuring that the travel experience is both pleasurable and fulfills consumers' expectations. Clearly an investigation should include aspects that originate from the pre booking stage through to the completion of the journey. Gursoy et al. [8] point out that several studies suggested that airline service quality is one of the most critical factors that is likely to influence travelers airline selection decision and significant relationships exist among reputation, service and retained preference. Attributes that are related to service quality that are perceived as important by airline customers are price, safety, timelines, luggage transportation, quality of food and beverage, comfort of the seat, check in process, and inboard service. Chang and

Sustainable Tourism, F. D. Pineda, C. A. Brebbia & M. Mugica (Editors)

Yeh ([3], p.166) however point out that aspects like price, was initially regarded as primary competition weapon. According to the author, airline industries soon realized that competition on price alone represent a no win situation on the long run. Empirical studies of demand for airlines, show that service quality is central to the choice of airlines for both business and leisure travelers.

4 Tourism marketing strategies – swift towards customer care

According to Tsaur et al. ([22], p.107) airlines are offering amongst others more convenient routes, more promotional incentives like mileage rewards, frequent flyer membership program and sweepstakes in an attempt to consolidate their market share and to enhance profitability. However, they point out that the marginal benefits of marketing strategies gradually reduce because most of the airlines act similarly. Due to the recognition of the limitation of marketing strategies, some air carriers rather tend to focus on the commitment of improving customer service quality. Like any other industry, the airline industry's understanding of what passengers expect is essential to providing superior service quality. Gilbert and Wong ([7], p.519) suggest that delivering superior service quality is a prerequisite for success and survival in today's competitive business environment. Gursoy et al. ([8], p.1) points out that an essential component of a successful positioning strategy is gaining a better understanding of customers' perception of quality of services provided by airlines. Dube and Renaghan ([5], p.90) emphasize that a positioning strategy should wove together promises of distinct experiences, benefits, and personal values with the actual production of the service experience. The tourist should experience the feeling of power when he/she for example experiences a bigger seat compared to the normal economic class seat.

According to Gilbert and Wong ([7], p.519) the airline industry is undergoing a very difficult time and many companies are in search of service segmentation strategies that will satisfy different target market segments. Some of these segmentation strategies may include choices like low cost versus traditional airlines and business class versus a combination of economic and business class travelers. Eccles ([6], p.20) point out the need for social marketing strategies – in essence tourism marketing will increasingly focus on the customer. This includes investigating the needs, expectations and satisfaction rates of consumers regarding the service rendered on airlines. Gilbert and Wong ([7], p.519) came to the conclusion that the lessons that have been learned over the last decade from service quality proves that there is a strong indication that improvement in service provides improved profit due to increasing customer base through new and repeat purchases from more loyal customers. The improvement in performance quality and satisfaction will result in retention and expansion of tourist numbers, more vociferous and active tourism support, and ultimately enhanced profitability and political support. As a result it seems logical that there should be a causal link between quality of tourism supplier's performance, level of consumer satisfaction, and the organizations success.

Sustainable Tourism, F. D. Pineda, C. A. Brebbia & M. Mugica (Editors)

Higher performance quality and satisfaction levels are perceived to result in increased loyalty and future visitation, greater tolerance of price increases, and an enhanced reputation. This is important to attract new tourists through positive word-of-mouth and media acclaim [1, p.786].

5 Research problem

It is assumed that tour operators and airline management are planning their business with sufficient knowledge about the perceived perception of tourists or passengers with regard to the services rendered to them. The problem under investigation in this paper is to investigate to what extent the services are being satisfied. This should provide some extent of direction in order to satisfy client's need and consequently be profitable and to increase their market share. Gilbert and Wong ([7], 520) states that in the airline industry context, the problem is whether management can perceive correctly what passengers want and expect. This becomes increasingly important resulting from the financial difficulties airlines are experiencing since the terrorist attacks of 11 September 2001 in the United States of America. The need for the study results from a worldwide tendency of economic downturn and the public caution on air travel, which is caused by the capacity of the airline industry to exceed demand substantially (Gursoy et al. [8], p.1).

6 Purpose of the study

The purpose of this study is to investigate selective service quality elements that contribute to the satisfaction of tourists when making use of domestic airlines in South Africa. This will offer future research directions. The paper consists of an empirical study measuring selective service quality issues on board three different domestic airlines. The outcomes of the research will result in the sustainable management of service quality associated with the airline industry with specific reference to tourists. This is preceded by a literature study addressing service quality and the application of some strategies to ensure satisfied tourists on board domestic airlines.

7 Research design and methodology

The primary objective of the study is to identify the perceived perception and resultant issues of importance with regard to pre selected service quality variables to tourists when making use of domestic airlines in South Africa.

A distinction is made between travelers for private purposes and travelers for business purposes. Both groups are regarded as tourists in this study as their visits included some extent of leisure that exceeded one night's stay in another destination.

Persons who have traveled by domestic airline during the last 12 months were screened and approached for their willingness to participate to the survey.

Sustainable Tourism, F. D. Pineda, C. A. Brebbia & M. Mugica (Editors)

Three hundred and forty one respondents agreed to be interviewed in the Tshwane region. Travelers mainly flying South African Airways, Comair (British Airways) and Kulula. Com (British Airways) were eventually included in the survey, while only a few travelers flying on Nationwide and Sun Air could be traced. Personal interviews were conducted with the respondents by means of a self –completion questionnaire that was set up in English. The fieldworkers were capable to assist in translating some of the issues to especially African languages.

The marketing literature suggests several customer satisfaction measurement approaches. This includes expectation – performance, importance – performance, pure satisfaction ratings and performance only ratings. Both the performance and the satisfaction ratings method avoid the use of expectation within the measurement of customer satisfaction due to the limitations of the disconfirmation approach and its variants. Millan & Esteban [17] confirms and point out that when dealing with frequently used services, the average client is capable of creating normal expectations of a service. If these services are sporadically used and previous experiences of use exist, the expectation information is not very reliable and can consequently not be used. It is proposed that regardless of the existence of any prior expectations, the customer is likely to be satisfied when a product or service performs at a desired level (Kozak, [13], p.392 and Yoon & Uysal [24]). Crompton and Love [4] points out that there is empirical support for the idea that the performance only approach had higher reliability and validity values than other approaches. This has been put to the test by several researchers in order to measure tourist satisfaction (Kozak [13] and Millan & Esteban [17]).

The questionnaire was constructed by various inputs from both primary and secondary sources. Primary inputs were generated by focus groups that had prior experience of domestic airlines. Secondary inputs were collected from brochures and publications (Johnston [11] and Otto & Ritchie [19]). The questionnaire dealt with aspects like demographic information, preferred airlines and perceived perception of pre selected service quality variables. The latter was measured on a five point scale ranging from not acceptable at all (1), unacceptable (2), neither satisfied nor unsatisfied (3), satisfied (4) and excellent (5). After the questionnaire was pilot tested, it was tested on 341 travelers on domestic airlines living in the Tshwane region.

8 Analysis and findings of study

For the purposes of this study the findings are discussed by means of tables that reflect the respondents' reactions to questions and/or statements in the questionnaire.

The largest group, or 52.5 percent of the respondents, were flying mainly for business reasons, as opposed to 47.5 percent flying for private reasons. The majority of the respondents (52.5 percent) have flown in the last three months.

As to be expected the business travelers flew more regularly that the private travelers. The majority of business passengers (36.3 percent) flew between 1 and 5 times in the past twelve months, as opposed to 43.4 percent of private passengers. Conversely, only 0.6 percent of private passengers flew more than 11 times, as opposed to 8.2 percent of the business passengers.

South African Airways (SAA) is used most frequently by both private (24.9 percent) and business (43.4 percent) passengers. The fact that the majority of the business passengers fly with South African Airways could be attributed to well-established name of SAA and the prestige associated with this airline. Alternatively, it could be attributed to SAA having more operating aircraft that its competitors.

Table 1: Most recent flight with an airline.

	Business travellers		Private travellers	
	Frequency	Percentage	Frequency	Percentage
Within the last month	69	20.2	19	5.6
Within the last three months	50	14.7	41	12.0
Within the last six months	35	10.3	29	8.5
Within the last twelve months	17	5.0	30	8.8
More than a year ago	8	2.3	43	12.6

Statistical significant dependency on a 5% level of significance $p< 0.05$ between the two groups.

Table 2: Frequency of air travelling during last twelve months.

	Business travellers		Private travellers	
	Frequency	Percentage	Frequency	Percentage
Once	38	11.2	83	24.5
2 – 5 times	85	25.1	64	18.9
6 – 10 times	28	8.3	11	3.2
11 –15 times	12	3.5	0	0
More than 15 times	16	4.7	2	0.6

Statistical significant dependency on a 5% level of significance $p< 0.05$ between the two groups.

The vast majority of respondents flying with SAA (81.5 percent) indicated that the airways' services were above average. The majority of Kulula.Com

Sustainable Tourism, F. D. Pineda, C. A. Brebbia & M. Mugica (Editors)

travellers (45.6 percent) rated the satisfaction as average, followed by Comairs' travellers (45.8 percent) who equally indicated the service as average.

More than 74 percent of respondents that fly first class, do so for business reasons, indicating that they fly on a company's business account and not their own expenses. The majority therefore have to take economic factors in consideration and therefore fly economy class.

Table 3: Airlines travelled most frequent.

	Business travellers		Private travellers	
	Frequency	Percentage	Frequency	Percentage
Comair	8	2.3	12	13.5
Kulula.Com	13	3.8	9	2.6
South African Airways	148	43.4	119	24.9
Private	8	2.3	3	0.9
Other	2	0.6	19	5.6

Statistical significant dependency on a 5% level of significance $p< 0.05$ between the two groups.

Table 4: Rate of satisfaction pertaining to the respective airlines.

	Above average		Average		Below average	
	Business travellers	Private travellers	Business travellers	Private travellers	Business travellers	Private travellers
Comair	33 26.4	23 18.4	31 24.8	28 21	6 4.05	4 2.7
Kulula. Com	26 20.5%	20 15.7%	30 23.6%	28 22%	14 11%	9 7.09%
South African Airways	139 45.9%	108 35.6%	28 9.2%	22 7.3%	1 0.3%	5 1.7%
Other	13 17.8%	19 26%	13 17.8%	13 17.8%	7 9.6%	8 11%

The previous table (table 12) measured the rate of satisfaction on a five point scale where 1 indicated an excellent experience and 5 an unacceptable experience. In this regard the business travelers indicated the following variables as the five most satisfied services: the audio announcements in the departure hall, information display billboard, the information desk, parking in general, and the restaurants. The private travelers have indicated that the five most satisfied

Sustainable Tourism, F. D. Pineda, C. A. Brebbia & M. Mugica (Editors)

services were the restaurant, the information desk, audio announcements in the departure hall, flights available and ticket offices. The three most dissatisfied variables for both business and private travelers were medium term parking facilities, amenities and lock up facilities.

Custom dictates, and therefore the majority of travellers (51.2 percent) prefer to book by means of a travel agent. As technology develops it can be expected that more passengers will make use of the Internet to book for flights.

The rate of satisfaction regarding variables on board the aircraft that contribute to good service delivery were measured among the respondents. In this regard the business travellers indicated the following variables as the five most satisfied variables: Language proficiency of the flight announcements on board, quality of the refreshments, the conduct/courtesy of the air hostesses, the language proficiency of the air hostesses and the quantity of the refreshments. Private travellers indicated the language proficiency of flight announcements on board, the language proficiency of the air hostesses, the conduct/courtesy of air hostesses, the quality of refreshments and the quantity of the refreshments as the top five variables. The worst performers for both groups were the flight rates.

Table 5: Class preferred to fly.

	Business travellers		Private travellers	
	Frequency	Percentage	Frequency	Percentage
Business class	63	18.5	35	10.3
Economy class	114	33.5	116	34.1
Other	2	0.6	11	3.2

Statistical significant dependency on a 5% level of significance $p< 0.05$ between the two groups.

Interestingly, safety, convenient departure days and hours, and direct flights to destinations were regarded as the most important issues when selecting an airline by both business and private travellers.

The majority of the respondents (57.4 percent) have indicated that the events of September 11, when passenger aircrafts were hijacked and flown into prominent American landmarks, did not influence their personal usage air travel. However, that means that 42.6 percent of respondents do feel affected by the events of September 11. Passengers will therefore have to be ensured that every possible measure has been taken to ensure the safety of customers.

9 Conclusions

The perceptions of consumers on service recovery is vital in understanding areas of success and areas of failure within a particular industry. This study measured the responses of airline passengers in South Africa on specific performance areas. The three major national airlines were compared, *inter alia* South African

Sustainable Tourism, F. D. Pineda, C. A. Brebbia & M. Mugica (Editors)

Airways, Comair and Kulula.Com. In general the respondents were satisfied with the quality and quantity of services rendered, although specific areas of concern were highlighted. Attention to these specific areas of concern by the different airlines will ensure an increase in service quality and quantity.

References

[1] Baker, A.D. and Crompton, J.L. 2000. "Quality satisfaction and behavioral intentions", Annals of Tourism Research, 27(3):785 – 804.

[2] Butcher, K. Sparks, B. and O'Callaghan, F. 2001. "Evaluative and relational influences on service loyalty" International Journal of Service Industry management, 12(4): 310-327.

[3] Chang, Y. and Yeh, C. 2002. "A survey analysis of service quality for domestic airlines", European Journal of Operational Research, 139(1):166-177.

[4] Crompton, J.L. and Love, L.L. 1995 "The predictive validity of alternative approaches to evaluating quality of festival. Journal of Travel Research 34 (1): 11-24.

[5] Dubè, L. and Renaghan, L.M. 1999. "How hotel attributes deliver the promised benefits", Guests' Perspectives on the Lodging Industry's Functional Best Practices (Part II), 89-95

[6] Eccles, G. 1995. "Marketing, sustainable development and international tourism", Contemporary Hospitality Management, 07(7): 20-26.

[7] Gilbert, D. and Wong, R.K.C. 2003. "Passenger expectations and airline services: a Hong Kong based study", Tourism Management, 24(5):519 – 532.

[8] Gursoy, D. Chen, M. and Kim, H.J. 2003. "The US airlines relative positioning based on attributes of service quality", Tourism Management, Article in press.

[9] Haber, S. and Lerner, M. 1998. "Correlates of Tourist Satisfaction", Annals of Tourism research, 25(4):197-000.

[10] Hays, B.E. 1998. Measuring customer satisfaction survey design, use, and statistical analysis methods, Wisconsin: American Society for Quality (ASQ).

[11] Johnston, R. 1995. "The determinants of service quality: satisfiers and dissatisfies", International Journal of Service Industry Management, 6(5): 53-71.

[12] Kasper, H. van Helsdingen, P. and de Vries, W. 1999. Service marketing Management, an international perspective. Chichester: Wiley.

[13] Kozak, M. 2001. "Comparative assessment of tourist satisfaction with destinations across two nationalities", Tourism Management, 22: 391 - 401.

[14] Lemer, A.C. 1992. "Measuring performance of airport passenger terminals", Transport Research Part A: Policy and Practice, 26(1): 37-45.

[15] Mason, KJ. 2000. "The propensity of business travelers to use low cost airlines", Transport Geography, 08(2):107-119.

Sustainable Tourism, F. D. Pineda, C. A. Brebbia & M. Mugica (Editors)

[16] Mason, KJ. 2001. "Marketing low-cost airline services to business travelers", Air Transport Management, 7(2):103-109.
[17] Millan, A. and Esteban, A. 2003. "Development of a multiple-item scale for measuring customer satisfaction in travel agencies services", Tourism Management, Article in press.
[18] Nield, K. Kozak, M. and LeGrys, G. 2000. "The role of food service in tourist satisfaction", Hospitality Management, 19: 375 – 384.
[19] Otto, E. and Brent Ritchie, J.R. 1996. "The service experience in tourism", Tourism Management, 17(3):165 – 174.
[20] Page, S.J. 1994 Transport for Tourism. London:Routledge.
[21] Prideaux, B. 2000. "The role of the transport system in destination development", Tourism Management, 21(2000): 53-63.
[22] Tsaur, S., Chang, T. and Yen, C. 2002 "The evaluation of airline service quality by fuzzy MCDM", Tourism Management, 23(2): 107-115.
[23] Weiermair, K. and Fuchs, M. 1999. "Measuring tourist judgment on service quality", Annals of Tourism research, 26(4):1004-1021.
[24] Yoon, Y. and Uysal, M. 2003. "An examination of the effects of motivation and satisfaction on destination loyalty: a structural model", Tourism management, Article in press.

Sustainable Tourism, F. D. Pineda, C. A. Brebbia & M. Mugica (Editors)

From sustainable mobility to sustainable tourism

K. G. Høyer
Head of Research, Western Norway Research Institute,
N-6851 Sogndal, Norway

Abstract

The paper consists of four main parts. The first part gives an analysis of the sustainable tourism discourse. Two main axes of understanding are presented; intensity problems versus volume problems on one axis, and stationary activities versus mobile activities on the other. The prevailing understanding of the concept of sustainable tourism mostly as a matter of *stationary activities* and *intensity problems* raises several issues for further analysis and discussion. One is that there is no tourism without travel and transport - or mobility and mobile activities as are the terms applied. This of course also requires a focus on the mobile activities in tourism, not least as transport is a major cause of the most serious *environmental problems*, both as intensity and volume problems. The second part of the paper elucidates – with Norway as a case – how transport on the one hand and leisure time activities and tourism on the other have grown like Siamese twins all through modern history. The main aspects in the European discourse on *sustainable mobility* are presented in the third part. Some of the aspects highlighted are the needs to develop public transport in general and *rail transport* in particular, thus also tourism based on these transport systems. The last part gives a *typology* of how sustainable transport may become a road to sustainable tourism, and some examples of how this has been carried out in some European countries.
Keywords: sustainable mobility, sustainable tourism, transport and tourism, transport and sustainability, volume problems, intensity problems, mobile activities, stationary activities.

Sustainable Tourism, F. D. Pineda, C. A. Brebbia & M. Mugica (Editors)

1 The sustainable tourism discourse

In 2000 I published in the *Journal of Sustainable Tourism* an article titled *SustainableTourism or Sustainable Mobility?* [1]. It was mainly conceptually oriented, and gave an analysis of several theoretical articles about the concept of *Sustainable Tourism* published in the journal during the 1990`s.

The dominating use of the concept *sustainable tourism* was found to be somewhat of a paradox, in several ways. Sustainable tourism of course originates in the discourse on sustainable development, basically a global concept, and not the least a concept that puts into focus the need to solve environmental problems in the global commons. But the articles mostly conveyed a purely local understanding, applying terms like local carrying capacity.

According to a work by Butler [2] for instance, sustainable tourism is tourism of a type that makes it sustain its viability in *one area* for an indefinite period of time. A similar definition was given by Squire [3]. In several of these former studies attempts were made at applying the concept of *carrying capacity*. This refers to the maximum number of people who can use *an area* without an unacceptable reduction in the quality of the experiences that visitors may gain [4]. Conditions for sustainable tourism were very much the same as the core indicators of such tourism developed by *WTO* in the first half of the 1990`s [5]. All these works in addition excluded transport-related problems from their analytical framework.

These are perspectives which however were met with criticism by some. Hunter notably [6], underlined the fact that sustainable tourism must primarily be developed in the point of intersection between tourism as a global phenomenon and sustainable development as a global task. In his opinion, the focusing on defined destination areas by trying to implement policies and measures for a sustainable tourism implies a danger by ignoring the further connections the area is a part of.

In my article I particularly emphasised the basic links between tourism and transport, but then also found that most of the conceptually oriented contributions about sustainable tourism were written as if transport was a non-topic, as if one could have tourism without travels. Surprisingly enough not even tourism-related transport locally - for instance in major tourism-cities - were included in the analytical framework, even though it is known to be the cause of substantial local environmental problems connected to air-pollution, noise, and traffic jams. It should then not come as a surprise that I found no mentioning of any relations to the concept of *sustainable mobility*, a highly focused topic both in politics and science during the same period. A conclusion drawn from my analysis was that the two concepts – sustainable tourism and sustainable mobility – needed to be united. This was considered a larger challenge for the tourism side, as tourism and leisure time issues already were integrated in the sustainable mobility discourse.

In connection with the writing of an article to a forthcoming international book [7] I carried out a renewed analysis of the more conceptually oriented

Sustainable Tourism, F. D. Pineda, C. A. Brebbia & M. Mugica (Editors)

contributions published in the same journal (Journal of Sustainable Tourism) after my first article. Included in this analysis were newer contributions by Sharpley [8], Hardy and Beeton [9], Teo [10], and Hardy et al [11]. It was surprising to find that the above conclusions largely still were valid. Several articles have of course put into focus the sustainability issues related to transport - also global transport - as a crucial part of tourism, and then of the issue of sustainable tourism But only to a minor extent were such perspectives included in the more theoretical and conceptually oriented contributions.

2 A sustainable tourism typology

The limited application of the concept of sustainable tourism of course appears particularly paradoxical in view of the understanding of *sustainable development* expressed in the *Brundtland Commission report* [12]. After all it was this UN-report - and the follow-up global conferences in Rio (1992) and Johannesburg (2002) - which really launched and highlighted the sustainability concept. The major conventions from this process - in particular related to climate change and biological diversity - consider these to be global issues and a matter of global agreements. Key characteristics of the sustainable development concept applied are ecological sustainability, globality, and fair distribution over time and in space. The distribution aspect is linked both to benefits and burdens.

In a historical perspective, there is nothing new in the fact that limits of ecological sustainability are exceeded, locally and even regionally. The crucial challenge drawn up by the UN-report and processes is that this now also needs to be considered as *a global phenomenon*. The sum of the man-made encroachments has become too big, even when what happens locally - within the local context - is not. This may be referred to as "the sum-tyranny of the small decisions" and expressed as a *volume problem*. And it emphasises the need to consider local decisions - also in tourism - within such global contexts.

We may then talk of volume problems and a *volume perspective* when our prime focus is on the danger of exceeding global sustainability limits. In the other end we may talk of *problems of intensity* and an *intensity perspective* when it is the local/regional limits we focus on. Above they were mentioned as problems within *one area*, and also connected to the concept of *local carrying capacity*. This - volume problems on the one side and intensity problems on the other - is one of two axes in my typology, as it is illustrated in Figure 1. And as already outlined the intensity perspective forms the basis of an internationally prevailing understanding of the concept of *sustainable tourism*.

But even if we have an intensity perspective we may consider problems caused by transport to be important. After all transport is the cause of serious local/regional environmental problems, and is not only related to problems of global reach and importance. We apply the term mobility - or *mobile activities* - as an expression of transport in this context. In the other end we may talk of *stationary activities*. They are for instance the hotels and destinations use of energy and natural resources for their ordinary daily activities, including the loads put on these resources by various tourist activities. Even though golfers

Sustainable Tourism, F. D. Pineda, C. A. Brebbia & M. Mugica (Editors)

move around on the golfing fields, they represent a stationary activity. The stationary activities thus comprise all the other activities that are not covering how tourists transport themselves or are transported to, from and between destinations. In Figure 1 this is represented by the second axis with mobile activities in the one end and stationary activities in the other. I have outlined that stationary activities - as the intensity perspective - are focused in the prevailing understanding of the concept of sustainable tourism, at least as it has been addressed in the more conceptually oriented works.

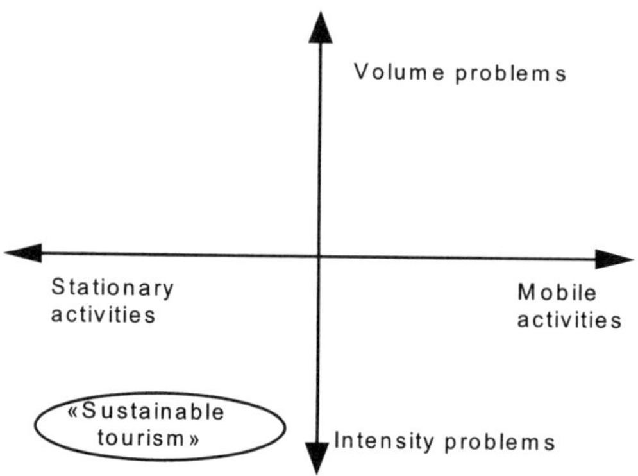

Figure 1: The internationally prevailing understanding of sustainable tourism (from [1]).

The prevailing understanding of the concept of *Sustainable Tourism* mostly as a matter of *stationary activities* and *problems of intensity* raises several issues for further analysis and discussion. With Norway as a case I shall below in particular elucidate the fundamental relations between transport development on the one hand and leisure time and tourism development on the other.

3 Transport and tourism - the Siamese twins

The first automobiles – in Norway in the early 1900`s – were met by large opposition, both among politicians and common people. In order to increase its use extensive marketing efforts were needed. Most people did not need cars in their daily lives; they walked or bicycled to work and nearby shops. New urban rail systems gave the opportunities for longer travels. Thus, cars were neither needed for *production* nor *reproduction* related mobilities. Close links were on the other hand made between the car and a third category of mobility: *leisure time mobility*. Car use so to speak started as a purely leisure time activity, and this link has later been fairly prominent during the whole car-age history. Early advertisements presented cars as means to come out in the fresh country air and landscapes, and away from the industrialised and polluted cities.

Sustainable Tourism, F. D. Pineda, C. A. Brebbia & M. Mugica (Editors)
© 2004 WIT Press, www.witpress.com, ISBN 1-85312-724-8

Similar emphases on the links between cars and leisure time are given in historical works from many countries and continents [13,14].

The car has ever since kept its firm grip on leisure time, and vice-versa. Not the least is this due to the development of car-based tourism. The first cars with *caravans* popped up on Norwegian roads in the 1960`s. Later this type of tourism has vastly expanded, and taken a variety of new forms; caravans with ever increasing sizes, camping sites with caravans as permanent summer houses, and the later large motor-caravans which travel everywhere, domestic as abroad. And as these are examples of tourism completely formed by the car, other types of tourism have changed with the car and become totally dependent on it in their current form and size.

Also through their whole history Norwegian *airways* have been tightly connected to leisure time. Just as for automobiles this is actually where the airplanes started. Sports played a particularly important role. Through several decades airplanes were almost completely a matter of breaking speed limits, breathtaking air acrobatics and adventurous travels across seas and continents.

As they became collective transport means airplanes have in an incredible way managed to keep their association to unlimited individual freedom and mobility. It is for airways as for highways, but very much in contrast to railways. The *institutional system* developed to foster the individual mobilities is an impressing story.

Not the least is tourism an integral part of this system. Already in the 1960`s the first charter flights started to transport Norwegians to the sun and warm beaches in Southern Europe. The growth has been exceptional all the years since, not only in numbers but also through a continuous increase in distances. This has made really long distance travels an opportunity for all social groups, a type of travels which to day takes a large share of the total mobilities for many households. As it in countries like Greece, Spain and Portugal has caused fundamental changes in thousands of local communities and their populations, the changes in Norwegians` mobility patterns and extents have been no less. One of the changes is the development of a new form of *dwelling-tourism*; where Norwegians settle in Southern Europe for large parts of the year to travel to and fro with plane, in some cases in the form of sheer plane-commuting. This has now become the largest settlements of Norwegians abroad since the large migration to America some hundred years ago.

Norway has thus become a society of *aeromobility*, just as it is a society of automobility. This is a global mobility which in extent and type has the aeroplane as a fundamental precondition. Aeromobility – as automobility - plays a major role in structuring the late-modern societies, where leisure time and tourism are particularly important components [14].

Norwegian *railways* have never played a similar role in forming tourism. This is somewhat different from the situation in England where railways were built to bring people from main industrial cities to beach areas along the coasts. Whole new towns – as Blackpool – were developed solely to serve this *railway-tourism*. It is actually one of the major forms of mass-tourism through history.

Sustainable Tourism, F. D. Pineda, C. A. Brebbia & M. Mugica (Editors)
© 2004 WIT Press, www.witpress.com, ISBN 1-85312-724-8

Trains – the *iron horses* - were first of all transport means for the earlier forms of modernization, the industrial production society. Railways were primarily a matter of developing the national economy, actually of building the whole nation. They did not as automobiles inspire to individual mobility. Connections were to work and not to sports and leisure time. When car-use really took off in the 1970`s railways should soon become a symbol of a sunset-society. Cars and airplanes were the symbols of the new modern times with expectations of unlimited individual mobilities.

4 The sustainable mobility discourse

In a report from the EU joint research centre in Seville the importance of a sustainable mobility is emphasised in this way:

"No road toward a sustainable society can avoid a redesign of the entire mobility sector, involving both the installation of a transport system following the dictates of ecological considerations and a modification of our overall mobility behaviour".

Two things are emphasised in this citation. Firstly, the crucial role of transport - for good and for bad - in a sustainable development. Secondly, that not only is it a matter of restructuring of transport systems, but also a modification of our overall mobility behaviour.

The concept of *Sustainable Transport* was launched already in 1990. Two years later - in 1992 and the same year as the Rio-conference - EU for the first time applied the concept *Sustainable Mobility* as an overriding term for its common transport policy [14]. Later both concepts have been used extensively not only in Europe, but in many parts of the world. When the basic term is *transport*, focus is on changes required in transport means and the wider transport systems they are part of. With *mobility* as the basic term, it is movement patterns and movement volumes that are put on the agenda. For our purpose here we consider the two - sustainable transport and sustainable mobility - to be parts of the same overall discourse on relations between sustainability and transport.

Regarding policies to achieve sustainable transport and mobility, they are of three different types as illustrated in table 1: *Efficiency - Pattern - Volume.* To put it simply: we can either *travel more efficiently*, that is with less energy used and with less polluting emissions per kilometre. Or: we can *travel differently*, especially change to transport means that are more ecologically sustainable. Or: we can *travel less*, that is reduce our total number of kilometres travelled. All three are included in the overall discourse, and all three are necessary to achieve a sufficient degree of sustainability.

From Table 1 I shall in particular draw attention to the importance given to public transport, other than airways. Sustainable mobility is in this context seen as *synonymous* with *buses and rail*, and just as much for urban as for long distance transport. *Modal shift* is then mainly about enforcing substantial

Sustainable Tourism, F. D. Pineda, C. A. Brebbia & M. Mugica (Editors)
© 2004 WIT Press, www.witpress.com, ISBN 1-85312-724-8

transfers from cars and planes to buses and rail. *Intermodality* is about creating efficient interconnections so that buses and rail can take much larger shares of the total distances travelled, and similarly to reduce the distances covered by cars and planes. A measure along this line is to place the cars on trains, and let them take the large part of the total distance travelled.

Table 1: Sustainable transport and mobility. A typology of policies in passenger transport.

Efficiency	**Pattern**	**Volume**
- Energy efficiency - Alternative energy - Emission efficiency - Load factor efficiency, increased load factors	Modal shifts; - From cars to walking/cycling - From cars to public transport, buses and rail - From cars to urban rail transport - From cars and planes to long distance rail transport Intermodality; - Larger share of buses and rail transport of total transport chains - Better interconnections between walking/cycling, buses and rail transport	- Sustainable Urban Development with public transport as a core - Car-free city areas - Spatial localising and restructuring to reduce mobility demands - Coordinated land-use and transport planning to reduce mobility demands

The change in understanding of the role of long distance rail transport is remarkable. I have formerly emphasised that this type of rail transport in the 1970`s and 80`s to a large extent was considered as a transport system for the sunset-society. This was subject to a radical change in the early 1990`s. Railways in general were then presented as transport systems for the future *sustainable society* and crucial means to reduce climate-gas emissions from transport. But to the extent that there have been any real changes railways have strengthened their role as transport means for urban and inter-city commuting. This has served to further cement rail transport to the production society, as was very much the original history of rail development. It is my thesis that it never will become a real tool for sustainable mobility before it takes on a completely new role to serve *leisure time mobilities*. And one of the main problems in this context is that railways never have been able to form their own tourism to the same degree as highways and airways.

Sustainable Tourism, F. D. Pineda, C. A. Brebbia & M. Mugica (Editors)

5 With sustainable mobility to sustainable tourism

Even though the hegemonic discourse on sustainable tourism is not related to the sustainable mobility discourse, there are several examples where sustainable transport and mobility constitute crucial parts of tourism. Table 2 below presents *a typology* of such current examples. Some of them have long historical links, but it is still reasonable to place them within an overall context of sustainable transport.

Table 2: Sustainable transport and sustainable tourism connections. A typology of current examples

Sustainable Transport as Aims in Tourism	Sustainable Transport as Means in Tourism	Sustainable Transport as Means to Sustainable Tourism
- Soft Mobility Destinations - Sustainable Transport means as Destinations - Soft Transport Tourism	- Public Transport for Tourism travels - Public Transport in Event tourism - Intermodal Transport for Tourism travels	- Spectacular Rail Tourism - Sustainable Cities as Sustainable Tourism - Sustainable travels as parts of Sustainable Tourism

Category I – Sustainable Transport as Aims. In *soft mobility destinations* soft forms of mobility are the prime or very important attractions of the destinations. Examples are car-free towns in Switzerland (GAST-network) and some Greek islands, notably Hydra where all forms of motorized transport is prohibited. Networks of car-free towns and areas are also found in Austria and Bavaria. *Sustainable transport means* may be the *destinations* in themselves. Examples from my own country are a very spectacular railway line from sea level and high up into the mountains. It is actually one of the largest tourism destinations in Norway. Other examples, also known from many other countries, are steam boat travels on canals and lakes. The most important aspect is the transport mean itself and its connections to the natural landscape and not the length of the travel. Cycle tourism is the most common example of *soft transport tourism*. It is a form of tourism that one will find in most European countries today.

Category II – Sustainable Transport as Means. Examples of *public transport as tourism travels* are charter bus transport for long distance travels and not the least *inter-rail*. The later years however inter-air travels have become more popular among youngsters than inter-rail. This represents a rather dramatic change from sustainable to unsustainable tourism travels. There are many examples of systematic use of *public transport* – buses and rail – in *event tourism*. During the winter Olympics in Norway in 1994 for one such transport systems were an integrated part of the event, and was highlighted as an important

Sustainable Tourism, F. D. Pineda, C. A. Brebbia & M. Mugica (Editors)

part of something they called "Environmental Olympics". An important example of *intermodal transport for tourism travels* is the German system whereby private cars are placed on trains and transported for long distances, even to the extent that most of the total transport distance is covered by rail. Other examples are combining cycle tourism with rail, where particular rail routes and wagons are set up to transport the cycles on trains for the longer parts of the travels.

Category III – Sustainable Transport as Means to Sustainable Tourism. *Spectacular long distance rail travels* may be placed within this category. The most known examples are travels with the Transsiberian railway and the Orient-express railway. In these cases the rail system is both the attraction and may take a very large part of the total transport distance for the individual tourists. There are many European examples of *sustainable city development* and where sustainable transport in particular is an important part. There are also some – but much fewer – examples where this also has been linked to sustainable tourism within the city context. I do not however know of any examples where the sustainable city relation is used as a superior context for marketing of the sustainable tourism attractions. The NAP – the Netherlands Alpine Platform –is an example of an initiative where *a sustainable way of travelling to and fro destinations* is an integral part of a complete sustainable tourism package for Dutch tourists travelling to the Swiss and Austrian Alps.

I have earlier presented the sustainable transport typology – *efficiency, pattern, volume*. A limitation in the above examples is that they only to a minor extent address the serious volume-issues in car and plane transport; they are mostly about efficiency and pattern. It would however demand too much of sustainable tourism if we in every singular case expect them to address the volume issues. But it is not too much to demand that even such issues should be an integral part of the *discourse and concept* of sustainable tourism. Not the least do the above examples illustrate the need to include the other transport issues in the sustainable tourism discourse. Sustainable transport – and soft mobility – may in themselves form crucial parts of sustainable tourism attractions, in addition to strengthening such attractions. There is thus the evident need to interconnect the two concepts: *sustainable mobility and sustainable tourism*.

References

[1] Høyer, K.G. (2000) Sustainable Tourism or Sustainable Mobility? The Norwegian Case. Journal of Sustainable Tourism 8 (2), 147-161.

[2] Butler, R.W. (1993) Tourism: An evolutionary perspective. In: Nelson, J.G., Butler, R.W. & Wall, G. (eds) Tourism and Sustainable Development: Monitoring, Planning, Managing. Waterloo, Ontario: Heritage Resources Centre, University of Waterloo

[3] Squire, S.J. (1996) Literary Tourism and Sustainable Tourism: Promoting "Anne of Green Gables" in Prince Edward Island. Journal of Sustainable Tourism 4 (3), 119-134

Sustainable Tourism, F. D. Pineda, C. A. Brebbia & M. Mugica (Editors)

[4] Williams, P.W. & Gill, A. (1994) Tourism carrying capacity management issues. In: Theobald, W. (ed) Global Tourism. The next decade. Oxford: Butterworth-Heinemann

[5] World Tourism Organisation (WTO) (1995) What Tourism Managers Need to Know : A Practical Guide to the Development and Use of Indicators of Sustainable Tourism. Ottawa : Consulting and Audit Canada

[6] Hunter, C.J. (1995) On the Need to Re-Conceptualise Sustainable Tourism Development. Journal of Sustainable Tourism 3 (3), 155-165

[7] Høyer, K.G. & Aall, C. (2004) Sustainable Mobility and Sustainable Tourism. In: Hall, M.C. & Higham, J. (eds) Tourism, Recreation and Climate Change: International Perspectives. London: Routledge (forthcoming)

[8] Sharpley, R. (2000) Tourism and Sustainable Development: Exploring the Theoretical Divide. Journal of Sustainable Tourism 8 (1), 1-20.

[9] Hardy, A.L. & Beeton, R.J.S. (2001) Sustainable Tourism or Maintainable Tourism: Managing Resources for More than Average Outcomes. Journal of Sustainable Tourism 9 (3), 168-193.

[10] Teo, P. (2002) Striking a Balance for Sustainable Tourism: Implications of the Discourse on Globalisation. Journal of Sustainable Tourism 10 (6), 459-475.

[11] Hardy, A.L., Beeton, R.J.S. & Pearson, L. (2002) Sustainable Tourism: An Overview of the Concept and its Position in Relation to Conceptualisations of Tourism. Journal of Sustainable Tourism 10 (6), 475-497.

[12] WCED (1987) Our Common Future. World Commission on Environment and Development. Oslo: Tiden (Norwegian edition)

[13] Belasco, W. (1984) Commercialized Nostalgia: the Origins of the Roadside Strip. In: Lewis, B.L. & Goldstein, L. (eds). The Automobile and American Culture. USA: Ann Arbor

[14] Høyer, K.G. (1999) Sustainable Mobility – the Concept and its Implications. Ph.D. thesis. Roskilde, Denmark: Roskilde University, Department of Environment, Technology and Social Studies.

Sustainable Tourism, F. D. Pineda, C. A. Brebbia & M. Mugica (Editors)

Environmental management in hotels: mitigation of impacts and strategies for eco-efficiency

J. Demajorovic & F. Z. Antunes
Faculty SENAC of Environmental Education, São Paulo, Brazil

Abstract

The tourism sector plays a fundamental role in creating jobs, income and economic growth in both developing and developed countries. However, little attention is given to the environment, which implies a poor knowledge of the problems of environmental degradation associated with, e.g., the hotel industry, both in terms of construction and operation. This paper presents some of the principal initiatives at the global level and in Brazil in the hotel industry, focusing on the strategies of a hotel operation located in Brazil. The research shows the huge potential for cost reductions in water and energy consumption and solid waste disposal, through investments in technologies and new management procedures. It also shows the importance of the cultural dimension in the internalization of environmental issues, not only for management and employees, but also for guests who may or may not accept the new environmentally friendly practices in the hotel industry.
Keywords: eco-efficiency, environmental impact, solid waste, effluents, reducing water consumption.

1 Introduction

According to data from the World Tourism Organization, revenues from the tourism sector, whose activities range from transport (planes, buses and automobiles), visits to national parks, and ecotourism (climbing, diving, etc.) to accommodations (*pousadas*, bed and breakfasts, hotels and resorts), increased 35% faster than the average for the global economy, totaling $US 469 billion in 2000. The World Travel and Tourism Council reports that with the indirect effects of tourism activities such as increased agricultural income and job creation in the construction sector, travel and tourism activities accounted for

Sustainable Tourism, F. D. Pineda, C. A. Brebbia & M. Mugica (Editors)

around $US 3.6 trillion in 2000, or around 11% of global GDP, making it a leading economic sector. All these activities require a huge labor force, estimated at around 200 million jobs and representing 8% of the global labor market (Mastny [1]).

Brazil's tourism sector has a huge growth potential, and it could be one of the greatest beneficiaries of the sector's global expansion. In 1998, according to Carvalho [2], 32 million Brazilians and 4.8 million foreigners undertook tourism activities in Brazil, compared to 1994 when the latter figure was less than 2 million. As a result, Brazil jumped from 43rd to 24th place in the global ranking of the most popular destinations in the world between 1995 and 1999. The country is expected to move further up this ranking, with an estimated 6.5 million foreign tourists visiting the country in 2003, joining 57 million domestic tourists (Dias [3]).

These figures, however, don't address the environmental impacts associated with increased tourism activity and especially the hotel industry, which is assuming an increasingly important role. Hotel projects in new tourism centers, along with generating jobs and income, often result in damage to local communities from deforestation and pollution in waterways and soils, through poor planning for the management of wastes and effluents. The objective of this paper is to identify the principal environmental impacts associated with the hotel sector, as well as the economic and environmental benefits resulting from implementing eco-efficiency strategies. To achieve this objective, in addition to a review of the relevant literature, it was decided to carry out a case study of an operating hotel, to show the benefits and pitfalls involved in adoption of eco-efficiency strategies and mitigation of impacts.

2 The hotel sector: economic importance and potential for environmental impacts

According to Mastny [1], the number of rooms available in hotels in the world increased by 25% between 1990 and 1998, reaching a total of 15 million. In the United States alone, the accommodations sector, including hotels, motels and bed and breakfasts, totaled 51,000 establishments with 3.1 million rooms, employing more than 1.6 million persons and accounting for 1.3% of the GDP, or around US$ 130 billion. Hotel chains are assuming an increasingly dominant role, with direct control over the establishments, replacing the previous wave of franchising. There is also an increasing growth in small establishments such as bed and breakfasts (Davies and Cahill [4]).

The hotel sector and its clients directly consume a huge amount of resources such as energy for heating and cooling, electricity, and water for recreation, washing and gardening. These resources are an increasingly important part of the cost of operating hotels, and have a negative environmental impact when poorly managed. According to Davies and Cahill [4], in 1995 energy consumption in the U.S. hotel sector represented around 9.5% of the total consumed in all commercial buildings, and consumption per square meter in hotels is 38% higher than the average in other commercial buildings. The sector today has the fifth highest energy consumption in the U.S. economy. Even though since 1970

Sustainable Tourism, F. D. Pineda, C. A. Brebbia & M. Mugica (Editors)
 ISBN 1-85312-724-8

energy consumption has been dropping, this area remains one of the sector's great challenges.

The uses of water are very diverse, and include drinking, cleaning, recreation, firefighting, bathing and sanitary functions. Water use depends on the size and type of hotel. Large hotels use large amounts of water to maintain facilities such as swimming pools and watering of lawns. Stipanuk *et al.*, 1996 (cited in Stipanuk and Ninemeier [5]) estimates a consumption of 384 liters/room/day in hotels with less than 75 rooms, and reaching 790 liters/room/day in hotels with 500 or more rooms. This results in an average of 585 liters/day or 213.598 liters of water/room/year. Since the 1990s there has been an effort to rationalize water use in industrialized countries because of increasing water use fees.

Also, high water consumption means greater amounts of effluents to be treated. The problem worsens in the peak season, since the amount of sewage is proportional to the number of tourists. The impacts tend to be much greater in developing countries because of the less restrictive legislation and/or lack of enforcement. A 1994 study carried out by the Caribbean Tourism Organization, showed that 80 to 90% of effluents generated by hotels in the region were released without any type of treatment along the coast near hotels, beaches and coral reefs (Mastny [1]).

The generation of solid wastes also depends on the size and type of hotel. A study carried out in Florida showed that solid waste generation could range from 2.5 kg/room/day in a Comfort Inn to 4 kg/room/day in a Hilton. This average is much higher than the average for household waste, estimated at 2 kg/person/day in developed countries. Sharply rising costs for solid waste disposal in sanitary landfills in developed countries since the 1980s have helped make this area one of the sector's leading environmental concerns (Davies and Cahill [4]).

In this context, the great challenge is how to stimulate the hotel industry and the tourism sector as a whole to incorporate environmental factors into their decision-making process. For Mastny [1], the fragmented nature of the sector is an obstacle to the development of legislation covering all aspects of the industry. The lack of regulations has made it easier for international chains to establish operations, especially in developing countries interested in attracting these investments as a way to generate jobs and income, while ignoring the potential long-term environmental impacts of the new projects.

Davies *et al.* [4] report that in sectors with poorly developed regulations, such as in the tourism sector, educational programs aimed at encouraging environmentally responsible behavior are the more promising management instrument. The target public also plays an important role: while "*tourists may be more receptive to educational efforts that focus on the environmental benefits of altering their behavior than to regulatory prohibitions (...) educational efforts geared toward industry sectors seem more effective when cost savings and the marketing benefits of "being green" are emphasized*" (p. 9).

Thus for the hotel industry, it is not regulatory requirements but the perception of costs and benefits of environmental investments, along with the return in terms of institutional image, that are responsible for the sector's new interest in eco-efficiency programs. In fact, a study carried out with 13 hotel

Sustainable Tourism, F. D. Pineda, C. A. Brebbia & M. Mugica (Editors)

chain executives showed that rising fees for solid waste disposal and the positive effects of initiatives on public image are the determining factors in the implementation of new solid waste management programs (Davies and Cahill [4]). Also, a study in Jamaica showed that cost savings is the principal motivating factor for hotels in addressing environmental issues, with government pressure resulting from environmental regulations being secondary (Meade and Monaco [6]).

3 Hotel sector strategies for eco-efficiency

Especially since the 1990s, the hotel sector has seen some coordinated efforts to address environmental issues, such as the International Hotels Environmental Initiative (IHEI) and the Green Hotels Association (GHA), which disseminate information about cleaner products and eco-efficiency initiatives. The IHEI is a non-governmental organization created in 1992 that represents around 11,200 hotels in 111 countries (Mastny [1]). Its activities include promoting the concept of eco-efficiency among its members and influencing their relationships with suppliers through the "supplier program". This program works towards establishment and publication of environmental specifications for products or groups of products and provides CD-ROM with a list of supply industries whose products meet the best environmental standards (Davies and Cahill [4]).

Brazil has recently seen related initiatives such as the new system for classification of hotels by EMBRATUR in partnership with the Brazilian Hotel Industry Association (ABIH). The new classification incorporated environmental criteria for awarding the number of stars to hotels. Environmental criteria considered include solid waste management, adoption of programs to reduce water and energy consumption, the use of less environmentally damaging products, and the implementation of an environmental management system, certified by a specialized body (EMBRATUR [7]). To promote this new classification system, ABIH has implemented a program for environmental responsibility called "Guests of Nature". The objectives of this program are to integrate the environmental management activities in the hotel sector, develop a critical environmental awareness in executives of the sector, and achieve economies in resources and costs.

Along with these initiatives of hotel associations, non-governmental organizations and the public sector, hotels are also implementing a range of projects individually. One good example was a project of the Accor chain in Sydney for the Olympic Games. To issue the license for the hotel construction, the Australian authorities imposed environmental requirements requested by the International Olympic Committee. Thus the project addressed sewage treatment and the treatment and reuse of water for secondary purposes, such as in toilets, watering of lawns and washing of patios, as well as a system for collection and use of rainwater. The hotel also installed solar water heating systems, which generate 80% of their hot water needs for the rooms. The air conditioning system turns off automatically when the windows are open. According to the hotel, these measures reduced electricity costs by 40%. The chain also established a partnership with the NGO WWF, contributing US$ 1 for each room occupied.

Sustainable Tourism, F. D. Pineda, C. A. Brebbia & M. Mugica (Editors)

A study was carried out with guests and collaborators of Accor's project in Sydney on their willingness to support environmentally sustainable practices in the hotel operations. This study showed that 95% were willing to separate their garbage for recycling; 90% prefer to stay in a hotel that is committed to environmental preservation policies; 83% agree with replacing individual soap by a collective liquid soap dispenser; 57% agree to reuse towels; and 35% agree to sleep with the same sheets for more than one night (Davies and Cahill [4]).

This case study provides some important lessons for the incorporation of environmental factors into hotel management. First, regulations can play a fundamental role, since some procedures were clearly set out for the construction of the project. Second, the initial higher costs for solar energy collectors and water reuse, for example, can provide significant payback in terms of operating costs in the medium term. Third, the study confirms the value that clients place on hotels committed to environmental responsibility. However, it should be noted that guests value these changes in services less if they are perceived as a reduction in the quality of services. For example, a much greater percentage of guests agree to separate their wastes than to sleep in the same sheets.

Thus, the incorporation of environmental factors by the hotel sector cannot be restricted to technological aspects – behavioral change in workers and clients are essential. Many hotels encourage voluntary behavioral changes in their clients. The Green Hotels Association offers clients in member hotels a card through which the user defines whether towels and sheets will be changed on a daily basis or not. This initiative can reduce operating costs by 5% (Green Hotels Association [8]). Employees are also key actors, because they work directly in areas with a great potential for reduction of inputs and environmental impacts such as the laundry, kitchen, governance and maintenance.

Despite the progress made, there is still a long way to go in implementing eco-efficiency strategies in the hotel sector. For example, in the United States, 77% of hotels use flow regulators for showers and 33% use low-flow toilets. However, only 4% of hotels reuse their laundry effluents and only 2% use greywater for irrigation (Davies and Cahill [4]). In Brazil, discussions of eco-efficiency strategies are very recent, and there is a need for relevant information for the country's rapidly growing hotel sector. In line with trends in the global hotel sector, the expansion of the sector in Brazil is linked to the entry of large international groups, resorts and theme parks, which could have severe environmental impacts.

The next section presents a case study of an environmental management system being implemented in a hotel in the State of São Paulo, focusing on eco-efficiency strategies and showing their principal benefits and challenges.

4 Case study: Grande Hotel Campos do Jordão

4.1 Characterization of the Grande Hotel Campos do Jordão

The Grande Hotel Campos do Jordão (GHJ) is located in the city of Campos do Jordão (SP), in a state Environmental Preservation Area (APA). The hotel covers a total area of 400,000 m², with more than 300,000 m² of green space covered by lawns and forests of araucarias and pines. The buildings have 19,000 m^2 of floor space, with a capacity for around 320 guests in an infrastructure that includes 95 suites, bars, restaurants, kitchens, laundry services, convention center, swimming pools, saunas, gymnasium, games rooms, tennis and squash courts, and a large number of trails though the forests.

Given the scale of the hotel operations, in 2002 GHJ's senior managers decided to implement an environmental management system following the environmental standard NBR ISO 14001:1996, with an emphasis on eco-efficiency strategies. The reasons for this decision included a management decision to make the hotel a reference in the area of management of quality and the environment. Also, the hotel's business strategy took into account EMBRATUR's new hotel classification process, in which the implementation of an environmental management system is essential to achieve the highest level. Finally, this strategy is understood by management as an opportunity to reduce costs in the short and long terms, through optimization of consumption of resources such as water and energy, and improving management of solid wastes.

The implementation of the environmental management system (EMS) started with an environmental assessment of the activities, products and/or services that can have a direct or indirect influence on the environment, with emphasis on water consumption and solid waste generation and disposal. Other important areas considered in this phase were the LPG and diesel storage tanks, because of the potential dangers of explosions and fires, which thus requiring proper controls and maintenance procedures.

After this work, aspects with adverse and beneficial environmental impacts were identified and assessed and eco-efficiency strategies were outlined for all the adverse aspects where there was a potential for reducting consumption of resources, such as water. For the other aspects, the controls needed and opportunites for mitigating impacts were identified, as in the case of effluents, which in the past were not treated. Below are the strategies for eco-efficiency and mitigation of impacts adopted by GHJ.

4.2 Principle strategies for environmental management

Water consumption in the GHJ is one of the most interesting areas, with a wide range of uses and opportunities to reduce consumption. Water consumption has significant cost implications for the hotel, because it pays fees to the local utility based on the amount of water it uses. The hotel consumes an average of 5000 m^3 of water/month, of which around 2000 m^3 is used for watering the 10,000 m^2 of lawns and for washing of patios. The remainder is consumed in bathrooms, kitchens (food preparation and dishwashing), the laundry and pools and sauna. Through this project, a range of actions are being planned and implemented over the short and medium terms to reduce GHJ's water consumption.

In the short term, the focus is on reduction of water consumption in showers and bathroom sinks. Showers are estimated to use more than 1000 m^3 of water/month, or 20% of the hotel's monthly water consumption, while bathroom taps account for around 400 m^3 of water/month. The strategy adopted was installation of flow regulators in order to reduce the amount consumed without

Sustainable Tourism, F. D. Pineda, C. A. Brebbia & M. Mugica (Editors)

compromising the comfort of the users. This aspect is crucial, because any discomfort caused to the guests will undermine strategies for rationalizing resource consumption. A pilot program was begun in some suites and other installations, showing the great potential for reducing water consumption through the use of this technology, as presented in the tables below.

Table 1: Preliminary results of the installation of flow regulators in showers.

Floor / Location	Water use without flow regulators (l/s)	Water use with flow regulators (l/s)	Estimated savings (%)
3rd floor / Suite	0.25 l/s	0.21 l/s	16%
1st floor / Suite	0.35 l/s	0.21 l/s	40%
Ground /	0.90 l/s	0.18 l/s	80%

Table 2: Preliminary results of the installation of flow regulators in sinks.

Toilet in Convention Center	Water use without flow regulators (l/s)	Water use with flow regulators (l/s)	Estimated savings (%)
Cold water taps	0.2 l/s	0.07 l/s	65%
Hot water taps	0.4 l/s	0.08 l/s	80%
Total for two taps	0.6 l/s	0.1 l/s	84%

Despite the great potential for reducing water consumption, the senior administration chose to extend the tests for 7 months in order to be sure that guests would not perceive the changes as a reduction in quality of services. Potential savings of 15% to 20% of water consumption are estimated for installation of flow regulators in all the showers and taps in suites, common bathrooms, changing rooms and dormitories. Difference in estimated savings for different locations resulted from variations in water pressure, which means reduction is not uniform.

Also, short-term strategies for water reduction were implemented in irrigation and laundry activities. A computerized control system was implemented for irrigation, which represents around 35% of all water consumed by the hotel. This system can control the timing of watering activities, thereby avoiding waste. However, the amount of water used in watering is not controlled or even monitored, which prevents an exact measurement of the economic and environmental gains of acquiring this system. Other simple practices, such as consulting weather forecasts to identify the possibility of rainfall, could contribute to reduction of water consumption in this activity.

In the laundry, which consumes around 350 to 400 m³ of water/month, simple short-term actions can significantly reduce water use. The hotel has sought to optimize washing process, by establishing a procedure through which the following information is taken into consideration: the type of material (sheets, tablecloths, towels, uniforms for employees and guests), the type of material (light or heavy), the weight of material (kg), and the washing machine to be used. It was also sought to reduce the amount of water used in the pre-wash process, which also contributed to reducing the amount of chemical products

Sustainable Tourism, F. D. Pineda, C. A. Brebbia & M. Mugica (Editors)

used. In addition, the hotel placed a display in the bathrooms of the suites requesting that the guest reuse to the extent possible the sheets and towels before sending them to the laundry.

For effluent treatment, the initiatives involved medium term strategies. The implementation of the EMS turned out to be an important source of learning, and one result was that an aspect that had been practically ignored became one of the hotel's principal activities in terms of environmental commitments. All the effluent generated in the GHJ is released directly into the municipal sewage utility's system. Since the establishment never had problems with the environmental agency, this strategy had never been questioned. However, to fulfill its environmental commitments, which emphasized pollution prevention and continuous improvement and compliance with the legislation, the senior administration decided to build a treatment station for its effluents. A longer-term strategy involves installation of a system that allows reuse of this water for secondary purposes, such as watering of lawns and washing of patios. The cost of implementing these two systems is around US$ 100,000.

Another priority of the environmental management system is solid waste management. Before its implementation, the hotel relied on the municipal solid waste collection system for waste disposal. With the start of implementation of a recycling system, the recyclable materials were sent to a non-governmental organization in another municipality. However, in early 2002, the recyclable materials were no longer collected by this NGO and the program was suspended.

In January of 2003, with the objective of ensuring that the solid wastes generated are disposed of properly, mitigating possible environmental impacts in terms of soil and water table contamination, the hotel signed a contract with a waste collection company to haul away the wastes to a sanitary landfill licensed by the regulatory agency of the state of São Paulo, CETESB [9]. This landfill received the highest rating in CETESB's classification of the quality of waste disposal facilities. The company provided a compacting container, which facilitated the storage and weekly removal of this waste. Currently the GHJ generates an average of 15 tonnes of non-recyclable wastes per month.

GHJ also reactivated the recycling program, with pre-separation of materials in the areas generated them, and provides them to a local NGO. Light bulbs are also being separated and sent to a company specializing in and licensed for the work of appropriate treatment and final disposal of these materials.

The implementation of separation systems also meets two conditions of the environmental program being implemented. First, the separation of materials contributes to reducing environmental impact, to the extent that it diverts part of the waste generated away from the sanitary landfill and contributes to its useful lifetime, while at the same time it stimulates recycling and reuse of recyclable materials in the municipality. Second, there is an economic reason. At a cost of US$ 20 per tonne for disposal of wastes in the landfill, added to transport costs, the hotel spends around US$ 2000,00 monthly to dispose of the 15 tonnes generated. The hotel generates an estimated 10 tonnes of recycled materials per month, which effectively cuts transport and disposal costs almost in half.

Sustainable Tourism, F. D. Pineda, C. A. Brebbia & M. Mugica (Editors)

Another important element of the waste management program was the renegotiation of the hotel's contracts with some of its suppliers. Before the environmental management system started, the drums for cleaning products were not collected by the supplier, and the hotel was responsible for disposing of them. As waste reduction began to be integrated into decision-making in negotiations with suppliers, the hotel required the supplier to remove the drums. Although there was some initial resistance from the supplier of cleaning products to accepting responsibility for disposal of packaging, the possibility presented by the hotel of switching suppliers brought about a change in position, which demonstrates the hotel's power to influence the behavior of some of their stakeholders (downstream impacts).

In terms of energy consumption, the hotel has adopted strategies for it's different energy sources – electricity, LPG and diesel fuel. The hotel introduced some changes and maintenance in electrical equipment, such as replacement of conventional light bulbs by fluorescent lighting, and turning off lights when areas are not being used. A technical and economic feasibility study is now underway for changes to the current lighting system. This study includes retrofits such as adding reflectors to lighting fixtures to improve lighting quality.

Finally, the learning from implementation of the environmental management system has revealed the potential for synergistic effects providing multiple gains. A good example of this is the reduction of water consumption, which should also reduce consumption of LPG used hot water heating by up to 50%.

5 Final remarks

The study presented here shows some of the forces contributing to the adoption of environmental management in the hotel industry. Rising operating costs in the hotel sector, especially for solid waste management and water consumption, combined with the growing number of clients concerned about hotel's social and environmental commitments, has translated into concrete actions on the part of the sector in many countries. The case study shows that the principal motivating factor was the pursuit of a management tool which in the short and medium term would allow optimization of management of natural resources through eco-efficiency strategies, and the construction of an image of excellence for the hotel in terms of quality and environmental commitment, backed up by a future certification under NBR ISO 14001:1996 and by new criteria in EMBRATUR's classification.

Although the environmental management system analyzed is still in the implementation phase, some conclusions can be drawn. First, the study shows the huge potential for cost reductions in water and energy consumption and solid wastes, both through investments in technologies and changing procedures as a result of learning driven by an environmental management system. Leading areas in this regard are the flow regulators for showers and taps as well as new laundry procedures. Also important was the recycling program and creation of new relations with suppliers which required them to haul away the drums which contained products, in order to reduce the amount of solid wastes going to the

sanitary landfill. On the other hand, a significant gap in the environmental management system of the GHJ is the lack of effective monitoring systems for certain management strategies, as in the case of water consumption. This presents an obstacle to a more specific assessment of the environmental performance of the company.

The case study also shows the great concern on the part of hotel management that the measures implemented not be perceived by guests as a decline in the quality of services provided. A result of this was the long period of time spent on the pilot plan for reduction of water consumption through the installation of flow reduction devices, even after their huge potential for reducing consumption was demonstrated. This indicates the great importance given to the opinion of guests in the decision-making process.

Thus, along with the technological and economic dimensions, the cultural dimension also plays a fundamental role in the incorporation of environmental variables. Changes in the hotel sector depend not only on the internalization of environmental issues by management and employees, but also on the acceptance by guests of the new practices that can lead to a reduction of environmental impact from activities carried out daily in the hotel industry.

References

[1] Mastny, Lisa. “Redirecting international tourism” in: State of the World 2002. Worldwatch Institute, 2003.

[2] Carvalho, Caio Luiz de. “A revolução silenciosa”. Brasília, DF: [s.n.], undated. Available at: www.brasil.embratur.gov.br Access on: 11 Feb. 2003.

[3] Dias, Marlene. “Aplicação de Tecnologias Limpas na Indústria Hoteleira para um Turismo Sustentável”. Faculdade Senac de Educação Ambiental, 2002 (Monograph for completion of program).

[4] Davies, Terry; Cahill, Sarah. “Environmental Implications of the Tourism Industry”. Discussion Paper 00-14. Washington: Resources for the Future, 2000. Available at: <http://www.rff.org>. Access on: 15 Fev. 2003.

[5] Stipanuk, David; Ninemeier, Jack “The future of the U.S. lodging industry and the environment: Cornell hotel and restaurant administration quarterly”. [S.l.: s.n.], 1996, cited in Davies, Terry; Cahill, Sarah. 2000, op.cit.

[6] Meade, Bill, Monaco, Antonio del. “Environmental management: the key to successful operation”. First Pan-American Conference, Latin American Tourism in Next Millenium: Education, Investment and Sustainability, Panama City, 1999. Available at: <www.hotel-online.com/Trends/PanAmerProceedingsMay99> Access on: 21 Fev. 2003.

[7] Embratur (Instituto Brasileiro de Turismo). “Deliberação Normativa n° 429, de 23 de abril de 2002. Brasília, DF, 2002. Available at: <www.embratur.gov.br> Access on: 20 Mar. 2003.

[8] Green Hotels Association (GHA). “Green ideas”. Available at: <www.greenhotels.com> Access on: 15 Fev. 2003.

[9] CETESB. “Inventário Estadual de Resíduos Sólidos Domiciliares; Relatório 2002.” São Paulo: CETESB, 2002.

Sustainable Tourism, F. D. Pineda, C. A. Brebbia & M. Mugica (Editors)

Section 9
Surveys and analysis

Visitors' valuation of natural and cultural landscapes: space-preferences coincidence analysis

M. F. Schmitz[1], P. Fernández-Sañudo[2], I. de Aranzabal[1], & F. D. Pineda[1]
[1]*Department of Ecology, Complutense University, Madrid, Spain*
[2]*Centro de Investigaciones Ambientales de la Comunidad de Madrid "Fernando González Bernáldez", Madrid, Spain*

Abstract

Many Mediterranean territories contain traditional rural systems in which very high naturalistic and environmental values are recognized. Currently the resource 'landscape' is becoming increasingly attractive, and recreational activities and tourism therefore constitute new uses which lend cultural and economic interest to the territory. Indeed, the traditional activities indicate a valuable use of the natural resources of some marginal areas, whether these are protected or not, which add cultural interest to the tourist attraction they constitute.

In this paper, we have characterized certain territories in Central Spain, using variables indicating both the structure of the landscape and its natural and cultural characteristics. Furthermore, we have typified the visiting tourists using surveys on their preferences. We have carried out analyses of the two sets of data, and expressed one through the other by means of products of matrices. We have also characterized the types of landscape perceived by the tourists and certified their preferences, as well as potential spatial distribution – "outdoor recreational niche" – and the degree of coincidence between their preferences and the characteristics of the space. Thematic maps are obtained which constitute very useful tools for applying planning and environmental management strategies.
Keywords: cultural landscape, landscape preferences maps, outdoor recreational niche, visitors' preferences, landscape ecology, landscape planning.

Sustainable Tourism, F. D. Pineda, C. A. Brebbia & M. Mugica (Editors)

1 Introduction

In the Mediterranean basin, ancestral cultural landscapes persist which are controlled in a secular manner by man (Bunce et al. [1]). These landscapes are being subjected to a growing demand for tourism. The recognized quality of the territory and of its different components, along with its rare products, are a strong attraction to visitors (FIDA [2]). Tourism in these territories ought to be a priority objective with regard to planning, as this activity tends to be carried out in areas which are clearly fragile in the socio-environmental sense (German Federal Agency for Nature Conservation [3], Schmitz et al. [4]).

Sensible development of tourism may very well constitute a good use of the natural resources in protected areas and in many marginal territories with particularly sensitive natural and cultural values. Tourism in areas which are of interest with regard to landscape and culture provide extra income which can raise the standard of living of the local populations and can affect the management and protection of the habitats, and it is important to establish close links between the recreational use of nature and conservation. This would help to maintain traditional uses and landscapes.

This study characterizes cultural landscapes in Central Spain and typifies the visitors to them. We considered both the natural and cultural (rural) characteristics of the territory with a potential power to attract tourists. We also obtained a typology of landscape in accordance with how they were perceived by the visitors, and we established the correspondence between the spatial distribution of the characteristics of the landscape and the preferences of the visitors. The results are expressed cartographically, and can be used as a tool for planning tourism.

2 Study area

We considered the province of Madrid (Central Spain), which covers an area of around 8,000 km^2. From early times, this territory has been used for different human activities, some of which have been very well integrated and dependent on the characteristics of the natural environment –traditional mixed rural systems based on agriculture, forestry and pastoralism–. Although there have been big changes in the landscape over the last few decades, which have depended on the intense socioeconomic change that has taken place, there are still regions of great naturalistic, agricultural and aesthetic-cultural value, which offer interesting possibilities for leisure, recreation and cultural tourism (Díaz Pineda [5]).

3 Landscape typology

An automatic sectorization of the territory was applied, taking into consideration variables that account for its structure and functioning in accordance with the available data on climate, topography (altitude and slope), lithology, edaphic typology, current vegetation and rural uses of the land. The data referred to 1x1

Sustainable Tourism, F. D. Pineda, C. A. Brebbia & M. Mugica (Editors)

km grids –the municipality of Madrid was excluded, due to the distortion which its particular characteristics introduced into the analyses of the territorial structure–. The resulting matrix, made up of 7,836 grids described by 115 variables, was treated by analysis of principal components (PCA) and by the agglomerative hierarchical classification of the ten main axes of the analysis (De Pablo et al. [6]). Thus we obtained eight types of cultural landscapes (Table 1), represented cartographically.

Table 1: Description of the types of cultural landscapes in Madrid according to the variables of greatest discriminant value in the numerical analyses carried out.

Type 1. Alternation of dry farming crops, shrubland and urban areas. Olive groves. Water divides with mountainside and river valleys, hills and countryside. Agricultural use of the territory. Clear tendency towards housing development.
Type 2. Predominance of holm oak groves, some in *dehesas,* included in a matrix of dry farming crops and urban areas. Water divides with mountainside with the presence of river valleys. Altitude from 440 to 835 m. Agricultural and urban use of the territory.
Type 3. Mosaic of crops and forest, predominantly pines and holm oaks (some in 'dehesas'). Area of piedemont. Water divides and mountainside. Altitude from 440 to 1032 m. Forestry, livestock farming and subsistence farming uses. Urban areas.
Type 4. Pastures with representation of shrubland, holm oak groves and 'dehesas' with holm oak, ash and other oaks. Areas with a mosaic of dry farming crops and urban areas. Areas mainly with piedemont. Altitude from 440 to 1427 m. Forestry and livestock farming use. Tendency to substitute uses for urban development.
Type 5. Eminently agricultural landscape with a mosaic of dry farming and irrigated crops. Presence of shrubland with moorlands, barren plateaus and countryside. Altitude from 440 to 1032 m.
Type 6. Mediterranean 'monte' (complex mosaic of shrubland, holm oak groves and pine forest) and pastures at medium altitudes. 'Dehesas' with holm oak, ash and other oaks. Hillsides, mountainside, and piedemont. Altitude from 637 to 2414 m. Forestry and livestock farming use. Presence of urban areas and housing development.
Type 7. Mediterranean 'monte' (complex mosaic of shrubland, oak and pine forest) and pastures at high altitudes. 'Dehesas' with oaks Area of mountaintops and summits, mountainside and piedemont of the depression-corridor type. Altitude from 637 to 2414 m. Forestry and livestock farming use.
Type 8. Mediterranean 'monte' and pastures undergoing a process of abandonment and degradation. Abundant shrubland. Mountainside and piedemont. Altitude from 637 to 1427 m. Forestry and livestock farming use.

The map obtained facilitates study of the relationships between the characteristics of the territory and the demand for tourism-recreation.

4 Classification of the visitors

We characterized the theoretical demand for tourism by providing the visitors to the area with questionnaires. These contained aspects related to the expectations

Sustainable Tourism, F. D. Pineda, C. A. Brebbia & M. Mugica (Editors)

and experiences of the visitors in the territory, along with their sociological and cultural profile (Múgica & De Lucio [7], Fernández *et al.* [8], De Aranzabal et al. [9]).

We selected areas considered to be of particular interest for tourism, recreation areas, campsites, and the Environmental Education Centers of the protected areas. We availed of 1,549 questionnaires. A matrix of qualitative data on this number of observations, described by 157 variables constituted the analysis material. We identified different groups of visitors by means of factorial analysis of correspondences and agglomerative classification of the ten main factors extracted from this analysis.

With the use of the variables with the greatest discriminant value, we described four types of visitors with different attitudes and perception of the territory: i) indifferent (45,84% of the total), whose only interest is to enjoy their free time in the open air; they showed no preference for any particular type of landscape or activity related to the natural or rural environment; ii) generalist (6,71%), who are characterized by a low level of appreciation of the variables representing the natural and cultural offer of the territory. The reasons for their visit are mainly related to leisure time activities and, to a lesser degree, to their family or job; they value the proximity of nature to their place of residence; iii) naturalist-sports (28,3%) and iv) naturalist-rural (19,17%), both types show great interest and knowledge regarding nature and the rural environment. The main aspects that differentiate them are, respectively, a preference for sports and for cultural landscapes, especially related to agriculture and livestock farming.

5 Valuation and perception of the attraction of the territory with regard to tourism

The questionnaires enabled us to value and quantify the appreciation by the typology of visitors of the different characteristics of the territory. Some of these characteristics can be referenced geographically, so that the territory can be expressed according to them. These ecological components of the landscape, which can be perceived sensorially, contribute to the perception of its typology and environmental state and significantly influence the preferences and appraisal of the observers with regard to the landscape. The spatial analysis of the interaction between both quantifications identifies the degree to which the zones of the territory adjust to the preferences of the tourists.

Based on the questions asked in the survey, we selected 32 territorial variables that satisfy the requirements of the analysis. The procedure is based on two sets of data (Fig. 1): 1) matrix of valuation of the natural characteristics of the territory (32 variables x 4 observations) (Fig. 1 [A]); its elements, a_{ij}, quantify the answers by the types of tourists identified to the questions asked about the 32 spatial variables; 2) matrix of territorial representation of the factors attracting tourism (32 variables x 8 observations) (Fig. 1 [B]); its elements, b_{ij}, quantify the presence of the 32 territorial characteristics in the types of landscape considered.

Sustainable Tourism, F. D. Pineda, C. A. Brebbia & M. Mugica (Editors)

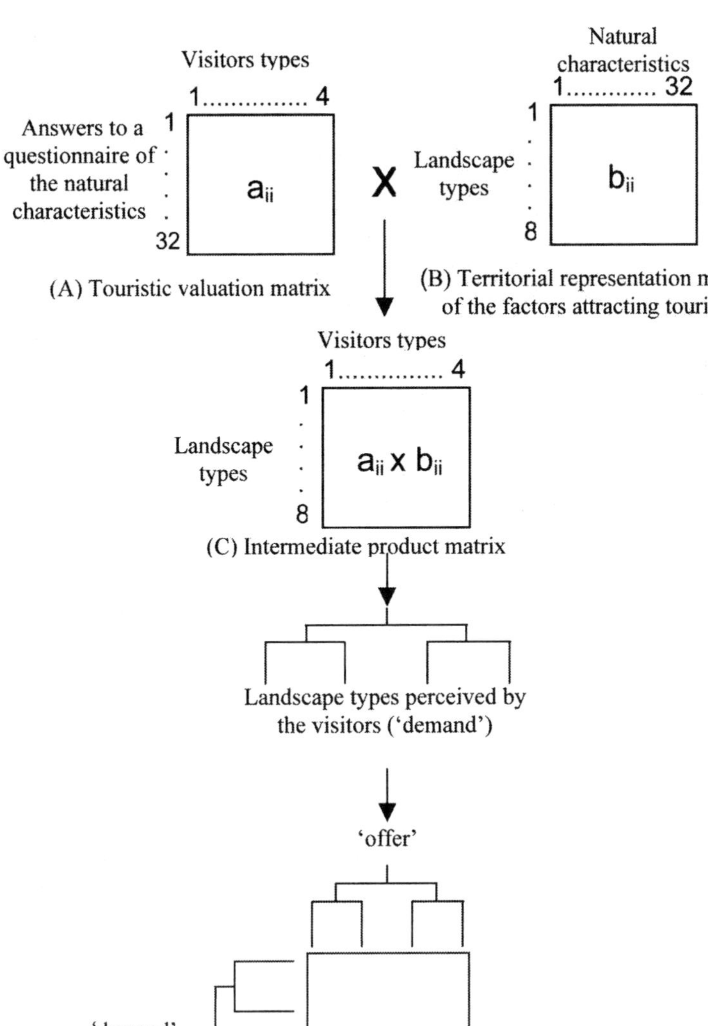

Figure 1: Methodological development. The procedure is based on a multiplication of matrices [A] x [B]. The resulting produced matrix, [C], quantifies the demand by the tourists for the territorial variables. A classification analysis of this intermediate product matrix indicates that the visitors only perceive 4 types of landscapes in the territory. The correspondence of the groups of landscapes that represent the territorial offer and the demand by the visitors was calculated with the use of a matrix of coincidences (Fig. 2).

Sustainable Tourism, F. D. Pineda, C. A. Brebbia & M. Mugica (Editors)

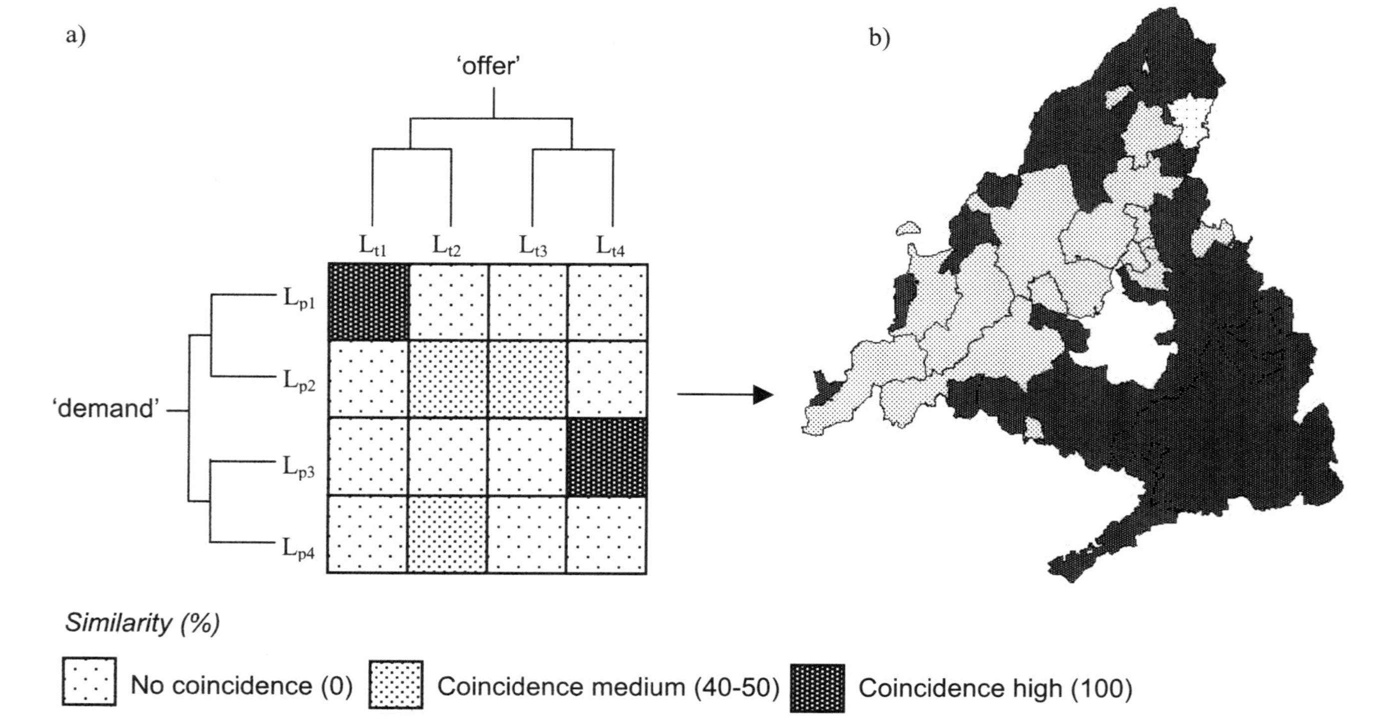

Figure 2: Matrix image (a) and cartographic representation (b) of the comparison of groups obtained in the analysis of the territorial offer and the visitors' preferences. The coincidence of the two forms of description of the territory is maximum (similarity 100%) between Lt_1-Lp_1 –mountain landscapes– and Lt_4-Lp_4 –agricultural landscapes–.

Sustainable Tourism, F. D. Pineda, C. A. Brebbia & M. Mugica (Editors)
© 2004 WIT Press, www.witpress.com, ISBN 1-85312-724-8

5.1 Characterization of the natural and rural offer of the territory for tourism

A classification analysis of the matrix [B] shows that, according to the natural variables selected, the territory is divided into 4 landscape groups representing the types of potential 'offer' for tourism in the area:

Lt_1: Mountain tops and slopes. Formations of broadleaf species and complex mosaics of shrubland, holm oak groves, oak and pine forests. Pastures at the highest elevations. Forestry and livestock farming use. Possibility for activities related to the mountain, hunting and fishing;

Lt_2: Mountain gradients and slopes and water divides with a presence of river valleys. Pastures with shrubland and holm oak groves, oak and ash. Areas with mosaics of dry farming crops. Forestry, livestock farming and marginal agricultural uses. Presence of urban areas. Tendency towards substitution of uses by urban development. The main potential recreational activities are hunting and watching fauna;

Lt_3: Mountain gradients and slopes. Mediterranean 'monte' and pastures undergoing a process of abandonment and degradation. Abundance of shrubland. The main possibilities for recreation are hunting, watching land vertebrates, particularly birds, hiking, cycling and nature routes, potholing, fishing and water sports;

Lt_4: Hillsides, countryside, and river valleys. Agricultural landscape with dry farming and irrigated crops. Shrublands and urban areas. Recreation potentiality related to hunting, observing the aquatic vegetation and fauna, hiking, cycling and other types of nature routes.

5.2 Perception of the territory and landscape preferences of the visitors

In order to learn of the perception of the territory by the visitors, we carried out matrix product of [A] x [B]. The result is a product matrix [C] of 8 observations (ecological sectors) x 4 variables (types of tourists) (Fig. 1), the elements of which, a_{ij} x b_{ij}, quantify the demand by the tourists for the spatial variables studied. A classification analysis of this intermediate product matrix indicates that the visitors only perceive 4 types of landscape in the territory, which differ to a greater or lesser degree from the typology of landscapes obtained in the analysis of the territorial offer:

Lp_1: Mountain tops and slopes. Broadleaf species, pine forest, shrubland and high altitude pastures. The areas and geographic location of these coincides exactly with the Landscape type 1 (Lt_1) obtained by means of the characterization of the territorial offer;

Lp_2: Mountain gradient and slopes. Mediterranean 'monte', pastures with trees ('dehesas'). Tendency towards shrublands ('matorralización');

Sustainable Tourism, F. D. Pineda, C. A. Brebbia & M. Mugica (Editors)
© 2004 WIT Press, www.witpress.com, ISBN 1-85312-724-8

Lp_3: Piedemont. Water divides and mountainsides with river valleys. Mosaic of crops, pine forest, Holm oak groves and ('dehesas'). Urban areas;

Lp_4: Moorlands, countryside and valley bottoms. Mosaic of crops. Urban areas. The territorial limits of this landscape unit overlap with those of Landscape type 4 (Lt_4) from the previous analysis.

6 Correspondence between the offer of the territory and the perception of this by tourists

The joint consideration of the landscape groups represented by the types of potential offer for tourism in the area and the preferences of the visitors enabled us to analyze the correspondence between the two forms of description of the landscape.

Conceptually speaking, a matrix of interaction between offer and demand with maximum values of fit between both of them would indicate a total coincidence of the two interpretations of the territory. The area would be made up of as many spatial units as there were types of visitors, whose preferences would be aimed at a specific sector of the territory which would have the optimum composition of landscape variables preferred by a given type of tourist. A high level of correspondence indicates that the typology of the territory shows a good acceptance of the demand it is subjected to, and its spatial variation can be described by considering both the natural characteristics and the preferences of the visitors –one same map could be interpreted through two alternative legends–.

In this case, in order to establish the fit between the characteristics of the territory and how the different types of visitors perceive it, we made a comparison of the clusters obtained from the matrices [B] –groups of landscapes according to their natural and rural characteristics ('offer')– and [C] –groups of landscapes preferred by the tourists –('demand')–. The correspondence between them is obtained from a table of contingencies of the respective groups (Fig. 2a). The similitude (%) between the groups of classifications was calculated as the quotient between the number of common observations in the groups of one or another classification and the total number of different observations in each group. The coincidence of the two forms of description of the territory is total in the case of mountainous areas and of the eminently agricultural landscapes (Lt_1-Lp_1 y Lt_4-Lp_4, respectively), whereas the sectors representing formations of Mediterranean 'monte', with greater or lesser degrees of abandonment of the traditional uses, present a medium or zero coincidence.

This spatial analysis of coincidences can be expressed cartographically, in order to obtain maps based on the fit between the set of demands and the potential capacity of the territory to satisfy them (Fig. 2b).

7 Analysis of satisfaction of the demand

The results of the analysis of the perception and demands of the visitors were

Sustainable Tourism, F. D. Pineda, C. A. Brebbia & M. Mugica (Editors)

used to make a new matrix of preferences of the tourists for the landscapes that they perceive (4 observations x 4 variables) (Fig. 1 [D]). It comprises elements, c_{ij}, which represent the mean values of the discriminant variables in the types of landscape appreciated by the visitors. The division into three categories –high, medium and low (natural break method)– of the vectors of the matrix that value the preferences of the tourists for the different types of landscapes (Table 2), facilitates the interpretation of the territorial preferences of each class of visitors, and serves to draw up maps which spatially express the relative degree of satisfaction they obtain (Table 2). This maps can be interpreted as the 'outdoor recreation niche' of the visitors. We observed a gradient of increase in satisfaction, from the medium and low values that predominate in the indifferent and generalist visitors, to high-level appraisals characterizing the naturalist-rural visitors. All of these show a clear preference for high-mountain landscapes.

Table 2: Relative satisfaction obtained by the visitors in the landscapes they perceive (Lp_n). We classified the values of the matrix of the tourists' preferences and divided them into three categories using the natural break method: low satisfaction level (L) –variation range from -1.01 to -0.66–, medium satisfaction level (M) –values of between -0.65 and 0.04– and high satisfaction level (H) –from, 0.05 to 2.52–.

Visitors	*Landscape types*	*Satisfaction*		*Visitors*	*Landscape types*	*Satisfaction*	
'indifferents'	L_{p1}	-0.27	M	*'naturalists -sports'*	L_{p1}	1.30	H
	L_{p2}	-0.85	L		L_{p2}	-0.14	M
	L_{p3}	-1.01	L		L_{p3}	-0.66	L
	L_{p4}	-0.94	L		L_{p4}	-0.43	M
'generalists'	L_{p1}	0.61	H	*'naturalists -rural'*	L_{p1}	2.52	H
	L_{p2}	-0.46	M		L_{p2}	0.58	H
	L_{p3}	-0.85	L		L_{p3}	0.04	M
	L_{p4}	-0.69	L		L_{p4}	1.23	H

8 Conclusions

We developed a method of classification and analysis of the interaction between visitors and landscape: their potential distribution, perception, preferences and degrees of satisfaction with regard to the natural and rural characteristics of the territory, and the degree of coincidence between both.

The results show that all the visitors to the area studied highlight the importance of nature as an element of reference of the tourism they practice. There are different types of tourists with greater or lesser degrees of specialization. Among the most specialized are visitors motivated by nature and the rural environment, conditioned by nature and by the traditional cultural landscape, and sports-orientated visitors, also associated with aspects of nature and the rural environment.

Sustainable Tourism, F. D. Pineda, C. A. Brebbia & M. Mugica (Editors)

Spatial analysis of coincidences indicates a maximum correspondence between the natural and cultural offer of the territory and the demand by the visitors in the high mountain landscapes and in those clearly dedicated to agriculture. Although the characteristics of the area provide a variation in the degree of satisfaction which tallies with the increase in the level of specialization and knowledge of nature of the visitors, they all show a clear preference for the high mountain landscapes.

The process followed enabled us to draw up maps showing the distribution of the preferences and possible areas to be visited of the different types of tourists, the degree of satisfaction of their current and potential preferences, the degree of correspondence or adjustment between the set of demands and the potential capacity of the territory to satisfy these. This doubtlessly provides a useful reference for the design of a rational planning of tourism in the study area.

References

[1] Bunce, R.G.H., Pérez, M., Elbersen, B.S., Prados, M.J., Andersen, E., Bell, M. & Smeets, P.J.A.M., *Examples of agri-environment schemes and livestock systems and their influence on Spanish cultural landscapes*. Alterra, Wageningen, 2001.

[2] FIDA, *Turismo y desarrollo sostenible.* Papeles para la sostenibilidad. Fundación para la Investigación y el desarrollo Sostenible, Madrid, 2004.

[3] German Federal Agency for Nature Conservation (ed.). *Biodiversity and Tourism. Conflicts on the World's Seacosts and Strategies for Their Solution*. Springer-Verlag, Berlin, Heidelberg and New York, 1997.

[4] Schmitz, M.F., Aranzabal, I., Aguilera, P., Rescia, A. & Pineda, F.D., Relationship between landscape typology and socioeconomic structure. Scenarios of change in Spanish cultural landscapes. *Ecol. Modelling* **168**, pp. 343-356, 2003.

[5] Díaz Pineda, F., Espacio y tramas de funcionamiento en el paisaje mediterráneo. *El hombre y el paisaje: evaluación y conservación del paisaje natural, rural y urbano*, eds: M. Morey, & J. Mayol, UIMP, Santander, pp. 37-54, 2000.

[6] De Pablo, C.L., Gómez Sal, A. & Pineda, F.D., Elaboration automatique d'une cartographie ecologique et son evaluation avec des parametres de la theorie de l'information. *L'Espace Geographique* **2**, pp. 115-128, 1987.

[7] Múgica, M & De Lucio, J.V., The role of on-site experience on landscape preferences. A case study Doñana National Park (Spain). *Journal of Environmental Management* **47**, pp. 229-239, 1996.

[8] Fernández, E., Rescia, A., Aguilera, P., Castro, H., Schmitz, M.F. & Pineda, F.D., The natural offer of the landscape and the demand for tourism: a spatial analysis of visitors' preferences. *Management Information Systems 2000. GIS and Remote Sensing*, ed. C.A. Brebbia & P. Pascolo. Wessex Institute of Technology, Southampton, Boston, pp. 75-89, 2000.

Sustainable Tourism, F. D. Pineda, C. A. Brebbia & M. Mugica (Editors)

[9] De Aranzabal, I., Schmitz, M.F. & Pineda, F.D., Análisis de la relación paisaje-uso turístico en un paisaje cultural mediterráneo. Asociación Española de Ecología Terrestre. *España ante los compromisos del Protocolo de Kioto: Sistemas Naturales y Cambio Climático*. AEET, Barcelona, pp. 1171-1185, 2003.

Sustainable Tourism, F. D. Pineda, C. A. Brebbia & M. Mugica (Editors)

Segmenting and targeting European package travellers

G. Siomkos[1], Ch. Vassiliadis[2] & Th. Fotiadis[2]
[1]*Athens University of Economic and Business*
[2]*University of Macedonia*

Abstract

This article analyses the profile of the two fundamental foreign traveller market segments. Specifically, German and British visitors of tourism destinations of Northern Greece are analysed. The analysis results contribute toward a better understanding of the preferences and behaviour of these two market segments. In addition, based on the results of the study, the development of a special database at an international level regarding information on the preferences and behaviour of the two groups is also possible.
Keywords: market segments, German and British visitors, targeting, destination management.

1 Introduction

Specifically, the study researches the perceptions that agents of imported tourism hold about their customers whose destination is the prefecture of Chalkidiki. A cluster analysis of German and British tourists who reach Northern Greece destinations by charter Flights, is also conducted. The profile of German and British visitors of Chalkidiki who prefer high quality lodging is finally studied.

1.1 Research objectives

More specifically, the purpose of this paper is to propose a systematic boundary of strategic segmentation and targeting actions that helps a marketing researcher and a tourism planner to position the total product offers of the specific tourist destination in profitable German and UK market segments.

Sustainable Tourism, F. D. Pineda, C. A. Brebbia & M. Mugica (Editors)

2 Customer analysis of the German and UK travellers

In order to investigate whether observed customer characteristics are related with the development of profitable sustainable strategies for the specific destination area, it is necessary to review some related customer profile description studies and data regarding demand characteristics. The definition and description of market (consumer) characteristics is the basis for the identification of target markets and the development of positioning strategies [11, 19, 26].

Many countries develop strategies targeting the same markets of consumers - tourists. Mediterranean countries target primarily the German and the UK market segments [12, 24, 25]. According to Eurostat data, overnight and arrival proportions of German and UK travellers to countries such as Italy, France and Portugal, range from 30% to 50%. The corresponding proportion for Spain is around 60%, and for Greece, arrivals proportion ranges between 35%-40%. For Northern Greece destinations in particular, the overnights proportion is about 70%.

Syriopoulos and Sinclair [31] using the AIDS model (a consumer expenditure model) concluded that: "major tourism-generating countries exhibit different preferences in their demand for tourism in the Mediterranean". Specifically, they found that the most expenditure elastic demand for tourism is related with tourists from Sweden and France. German and UK travellers exhibited the lowest expenditure elasticity for Mediterranean destinations. In particular, the Germans' elasticity values seem to be higher for the following destinations: Turkey, Greece, Italy and Portugal. By contrast with the above countries, German travellers have the lowest elasticity value for Spain (as their selected destination). The UK traveller's elasticity values seem to be higher for Turkey, Portugal and Greece. Spain and Italy are associated with the lowest elasticity values for UK travellers. Syriopoulos and Sinclair [31] also note that ".. price increases in Greece have large negative effects on demand from the UK, West Germany and Sweden. Pairs of destinations which were substitutes for most origins were Greece and Spain, Greece and Portugal, Spain and Portugal, and Italy and Turkey". In segmentation studies the income and expenditures are two basic explanatory variables, but in the '90s the competitiveness and sustainability of destinations also requires more quality tourism tactics in order to attract different nationalities or different consumer targets.

According to Aquilo [4], the integral Development Plan for Tourism in Andalucia, aims to provide quality through destination user satisfaction guarantees rather than providing products for very limited groups from a high-income bracket (i.e., quality tourism is not tourism for millionaires).

It should be noted that targeting tactics help tourism service providers to be more effective in satisfying customer needs [8, 21, 35]. Carey et al. [6] note that countries like Greece, Spain, Turkey "sell" the 3's (sea-sun- sand) which are considered complex commodities, with a virtually substitute core tourist product. That kind of destinations gradually become more of a mass tourism industry standardized product. The "majority of the consumer of such destinations organizes their travel through the tour operator. However, tour operators are also

Sustainable Tourism, F. D. Pineda, C. A. Brebbia & M. Mugica (Editors)

dependent on customer needs because the customers decide where to go". Customer-oriented tactics can help the destination (tourism) product supplier to create a better long-term relationship with tour operators and therefore to retain their customers. Also foreign mass tour operators (up to 80% of holiday activity is organized by tour operators) can help the destinations to offer total products of satisfactory quality with the sole aim of satisfying the tourist [6].

Bakkal [5] identifies eleven studies that have analyzed the demand characteristics of international tourism. Another research paper also analyses the determinants of individual choice among destinations and vacation activities of 5283 German tourists [13]. Of the above respondents, 15% had spent more than one spell of leisure-related vacation in 1985. More specifically, Table 1 presents the basic determinants of individual German behavior for six subsegments. In addition, the same study reports the following:

•German tourists adjust the level of consumption to the regional price level instead of choosing inexpensive vacation resorts,

•the sunnier the climate at a destination, the larger the frequency of visitors who choose the destination ,

•the less sites are plagued by ecological problems, the higher the frequency of visitors who choose 'untouched' nature destinations, and

•first-time visitors frequent more newly developed vacation areas (such as Portugal) yet they also visit destinations favored by the very young.

Smeral [27] identified important eurostyles of British and German visitors of Austria. The classification of the visitors into winter and spring visitors constitutes a useful basis for profile comparison of visitors of other destinations during winter. During winter, mainly German employees and pensioners visit Austria. They usually complain about the high cost of living and the rainy weather. Visitors collect information about Austrian destinations personally (48.5%), from relatives (27.8%) and from promotional leaflets (15.8%). Their basic motives include: landscape, common language, cultural sites, comfort and sports. Their activities are usually sleep, excursions and shopping. They mainly arrive to Austria by car (74.8%) and bus (13.8%). As far as British winter visitors of Austria are concerned, they are classified mainly into the category of "experience seekers" who are more than 40 years old, and the category of "culture seekers" who are about 39 years old. Their favourite activities are shopping and good weather for touring. The "culture seekers" avoid sports activities.

3 Methodology

The methodology makes use of three field studies. In the first and second study, German and UK traveler responses are studied. This selection was made on the basis that these two categories of travelers are the most traditional "heavy - users" of the destination (GNTO, arrivals and expenditures data 1960-2001).

Sustainable Tourism, F. D. Pineda, C. A. Brebbia & M. Mugica (Editors)

Table 1: German segments: The determinants of individual behavior of German tourists.

SEGMENTS:				
The young German	The retired persons	The low schooling- little income Germans	The German parents	The urbanised and non-urbanised German residents
Less inclined to spend a vacation in 1985	Larger incomes; more inclined to travel and to spend on more expensive vacations	They prove to have reduced the respondents willingness to travel	Less inclined to travel	Urbanized Germans favored relaxing vacations at a small distance from home-preferably at vacation resorts with German tourists and a good knowledge of the German language
Have chosen more cost-intensive vacation activities at more distant destinations with typically warm and sunny climates		Have increased their willingness to spend relaxing or relatively inactive vacations	Prefer to travel with children; to spend vacations either with relatives or spend inactive vacations at traditional resorts within a small distance from home (preferably at beaches)	Non-urbanized Germans seem to be willing to travel and incur high vacation expenditure
Larger incomes; evidently increased the shadow price of time and thus reduced willingness of young persons to spend a vacation		Have reduced their willingness to visit destinations where German is neither spoken nor easily understood		
Spend a vacation at a place different from home; choose more expensive vacation activities and are more willing to accept higher travel cost.				
Source: SFB 178 Internationalisation of the Economy -University of Kostanz [29], Eymann and Ronning [13].				

These two foreign segments also reflect the largest proportion of the total arrivals in Greece [12]. The sun-lust German and UK package tourists seem to

Sustainable Tourism, F. D. Pineda, C. A. Brebbia & M. Mugica (Editors)

be the basic customers of the Northern Greece lodgings and especially of the summer resort Chalkidiki (GNTO data). Even in crisis periods, like the Golf War and the Yugoslavian Crisis [12], the two segments showed an increasing trend in their arrival-proportion with charter flights in the Macedonia Airport of Thessaloniki.

In the first study, the data were obtained from the field research database of the University of Macedonia, "Macedonia Airport (low season study) - Profiling German and UK package travelers". After a Cluster Analysis on 4105 German - UK respondents and the specification of the segments, the study focused the analysis to the offering factors that determine a high level of tourist satisfaction. To analyze the relations, unsaturated logit models were created. These simplified models show the relationship between each of the independent variables and the dependent variable (i.e., tourist satisfaction). At this level of analysis, the relationship between travelers' motivation and tourist satisfaction is also obtained.

At the next step, the second study analyses the perceptions of 236 quality lodging tourists about the total product that has been offered. To analyze the perceptions, frequency tables with the respondents - customers profile and weaknesses of the destination are presented. Finally, the perceptions of the six local organizers are analyzed, using the same technique. Furthermore, some main factors for the development of sustainable strategic actions which are related to the German and UK package travelers are extracted.

The questionnaire was designed to investigate in greater depth, the motivation and customer satisfaction determining factors. A total of 4105 German and UK charter flight travelers responded to all questions. This database was the foundation for the clustering-segmentation study. The sample was representative of the tourist population that had Northern Greece as their final destination.

4 Analysis and results of the field studies

The cluster analysis provided 10 clusters (Table 2). The average behavior of the travelers for each of the ten clusters was not the same with the respective ANOVA results for the descriptive variables. The respondents profiles, based on the cluster analysis, are presented in Table 3.

The segments of Northern Greece i.e., low season and charter flight German and UK travelers, differ among them in age and travel motivations. There are several "older" segments, namely, (Germans): 5, 1,3,2,7 and (UK): 3, 5, 4, 6. The young segments are 8 (Germans), 10,1,9 (UK). Sea, sun and sand seekers are all in the German segments, and the 3s are especially important for the high population segments 9 (90%) and 2 (82%). Lowest importance is assigned by German segments 1, 8, and 3. All UK segments consider 3s highly important, especially segment 7 (84%). Touring seekers are concentrated in German segment 8 and UK segments 4 and 6. Sports seekers belong primarily to German segments 8 and 10, and UK segment 6. Religion-culture seekers can be located mostly at German segment 1. Agricultural seekers are mostly concentrated in German segment 8, and the UK segments 4 and 6. Finally, education-culture

Sustainable Tourism, F. D. Pineda, C. A. Brebbia & M. Mugica (Editors)
© 2004 WIT Press, www.witpress.com, ISBN 1-85312-724-8

seekers frequent German segments 4 and 1, and UK segment 4. Winter and health travel seekers are not an active German or UK low season traveler category for Northern Greece.

Table 2: Cluster analysis results.

Cluster	Number of Cases	%
1	89	2,17
2	599	14,6
3	50	1,22
4	223	5,43
5	139	3,39
6	35	0,85
7	2003	48,8
8	154	3,75
9	688	16,8
10	125	3,04
Total cases	4105	100

Table 3: Respondents profile.

Segments	German	UK travelers
1 (2,17%)	Mixed - age group. Young and older, students, clerks and pensioners. Part of a travel group. Basic destination attractiveness: educational vacation and religion vacation experiences.	
2 (14,6%)	Mostly middle-aged travelers and older. Clerk, pensioners, workers, and administrative personnel. Many of them (22%) visited N.G. for the second time. Pairs or pairs of friends, relatives. Important destination attractions: sea, sun and sand, educational and touring objectives. Top destinations are: the east beach sites of Chalkidiki.	Mostly middle-aged travelers and older. Clerk, pensioners, workers, and administrative personnel. Many of them (22%) visited N.G. for the second time. Pairs or pairs of friends, relatives. Important destination attractions: sea, sun and sand, educational and touring objectives.
3 (under 1,22%)	Older and middle-aged travelers, clerks, administrative personnel. Arrivals in N.G. with relatives and friends. Sea, sun and sand are not their very important destination attractions.	Older and middle-aged travelers, clerks, administrative personnel. Arrivals in N.G. with relatives and friends. Sea, sun and sand are not their very important destination attractions.
4 (under 5,43%)	Older, pensioners, not singles, clerks, administrative personnel and workers. Arrivals with over two more older people. Basic destination attractions: sea site vacation and educational vacation experiences.	Older, pensioners, not singles, clerks, administrative personnel and workers. Arrivals with over two more older people. Basic destination attractions: sea site vacation and educational vacation experiences.

Sustainable Tourism, F. D. Pineda, C. A. Brebbia & M. Mugica (Editors)

5 (under 3,39%)	Middle - aged and older, pensioners, clerks, workers. Arrivals with over two more older people of the family.	Middle - aged and older, pensioners, clerks, workers. Arrivals with over two more older people of the family.
6 (0,85%)		Older, pensioners, and some learned professional men and housekeepers. They come in N.G. with others. They visit friends and relatives. Basic destination attractions: sea site vacations, touring, agricultural, religion and sports vacation experiences.
7 (48,8%)	Middle-aged travelers and older, clerks, administrative personnel and workers. Arrivals with relatives and friends. Important destination attractions: sea, sun and sand touring and educational travel objectives. Top destination areas are the west beach sites of Chalkidiki.	Middle-aged travelers and older, clerks, administrative personnel and workers. Arrivals in N.G. with relatives and friends. Important destination attractions: sea, sun and sand touring and educational travel objectives.
8 (3,73%)	Young or middle-aged visitors, clerks, administration personnel and workers. Most of them are traveling alone. Several of them have come more than once in N.G. Basic destination attractions: the sea site vacations, touring, sport and agricultural vacation experiences.	
9 (16,8%)	Young people, mainly less than 29 years old, clerks, workers and administration personnel with friends, relatives and other older people. Basic destination attractions: mainly the sea site-sunny vacations, and educational, touring vacation experiences in all Chalkidiki destinations.	
10 (3,04%)	Young people, mainly less than 29 years old, clerks and students with friends and relatives. Basic destination attractions: the sea site vacations, and sports vacation experiences.	

The factors which influence visitor satisfaction were identified with the use of unsaturated logit models. These models indicate the degree to which the independent variables (i.e., the 21 offering variables of the destination) affect the dependent variable, i.e., the customer satisfaction variable (Agresti [1,2]). The basic results from the Pearsons X20,10 statistic for independence logit models (ln (F11/F12)=2xλ11) are reported in Table 4.

Table 4: Results of X^2 statistic for independence logit models.

Variables of unsaturated logit models Traveler Satisfaction (TS) with offer and motivation variables **ln (F_{11}/F_{12})=2 $\lambda^{\text{satisfied visitors}}$** TS with ...	X^2**, df, p**
Environment and landscape	344, 4, 0.000
Climate and weather	311, 4, 0.000
Image and beauty of place	333, 4, 0.000
Quietness at the place of stay	214, 4, 0.000
Transportation conditions	179, 4, 0.000
Design inside the place of staying and staying conditions	358, 4, 0.000
Service inside and outside of the staying place	335, 4, 0.000
Food quality	472, 4, 0.000
People familiarity, hospitality	588, 4, 0.000
Cultural offers	238, 4, 0.000
Getting information at the local travel agencies or information offices	209, 4, 0.000
More benefits from the whole tourist offer in Northern Greece	231, 4, 0.000
Sports and hobby offers	142, 4, 1 *
Quality of athletic establishments	91, 4, 7 *
Streets for walking and touring	132, 4, 2 *
Entertainment possibilities	303, 4, 0.000
Shops timetable	101, 4, 6 *
Tidiness/ cleanliness in the environment	111, 4, 5 *
Origin	44, 2, 2 *
Religious reasons/ Pilgrimage	0, 1, 1.000
Quality of service	4, 1, 0.046

Sustainable Tourism, F. D. Pineda, C. A. Brebbia & M. Mugica (Editors)
© 2004 WIT Press, www.witpress.com, ISBN 1-85312-724-8

The offering factors which determine German and UK visitors' satisfaction, are the following (listed in order of importance):
1. People familiarity, hospitality
2. Food quality
3. Design in the place of staying and staying conditions
4. Environment and landscape
5. Service inside and outside the staying place
6. Image and beauty of place
7. Climate and weather
8. Entertainment possibilities
9. Cultural offers
10. More benefits from the whole tourist offer in Northern Greece
11. Quietness at the place of stay
12. Getting information at the local travel agencies or information offices
13. Transportation conditions
14. Motivation factor: Quality of service

The analysis of the second field study data showed positive relationship between traveler satisfaction and service quality. Table 5 reports the results of the field study of 236 German and UK travelers, who were interviewed in seven high quality lodgings (4 and 5 star hotels) in tourism destinations of Chalkidiki.

Table 5: German and UK Travelers: Profile Characteristics and Negative Responses to Offering Factors (tourism destinations at Chalkidiki).

1. Profile characteristics of low season German and UK lodging travelers	Frequency results (%) of the sample
Demographics:	
50-64	37,7
30-49	33,5
19-29	15,3
over 65	13,1
Clerks	38,1
Pensioners	19,5
Workers	16,9
Married	76,3
Unmarried	13,6
Had children	69,9
Had children over 20 years old	46,6
Had children between 13-29 years old	11,9
Behavior:	
Select double rooms	85,6
Had travel with charter flights	65,7
Had travel with regular flights	32,6
Had organized the trip in a travel office	91,5
Had organized the trip individually	6,8

Sustainable Tourism, F. D. Pineda, C. A. Brebbia & M. Mugica (Editors)
© 2004 WIT Press, www.witpress.com, ISBN 1-85312-724-8

2. Negative customer answers: offering factors for 4 and 5 star hotels (15% and over)	
4&5 star hotels:	
Expensive drinks at the bars	40
Music, TV, video in the room	35
Furniture in the room	35
Means of transportation	22
Umbrellas at the beach	21
Bar in the room	19
Shopping center	17
Cinema room	15
Night club	15
3. Negative customer answers: offering factors for Destinations (15% and over)	
Destinations:	
Theatrical performances	23
Classic antique Greek art	23
Clean and organized beaches	20
Information tables	20
Private helicopter- airport	19
Rent a ship	19
Library with classic antique Greek writers	18
Noise	18
Accessibility	18
Disco clubs, bars	18
Cultural shows	16
Entertainment in Greek traditional taverns with Greek dances	16
Rent a private airplane or helicopter	16
Shops with traditional Greek handwork's	15
Greek kitchen	15
European kitchen	15
Travel programs with monuments and activity variety	15
Ecosystem, lake and water area travels	15
Rent sports equipment	15
Well knowing of destinations local area	15
Cleanliness of the roads	45
Cleanliness of the towns and villages	41
Cleanliness of arrival and departure gates	32
Cleanliness at the beach	30
Aesthetics at arrival and departure gates	29
Architectural - cultural aesthetics at towns, villages	28
Notes: n=236>30, N=1166 Germans and UK 4 & 5 star hotels travelers, Z^2=1,96 with significance level α=0,05 and rate π=0,5 the sample error is e=~5,7 (for significance level 0,05) sample error is between 5% and 6%.	

Finally, another study investigated the major local tour organizers' opinion about and perceptions of the tourism offers of Northern Greece, as well as the typical foreign travelers to Northern Greece destinations. Table 6 presents the highlights of that study's results.

Table 6: Local tour organisers' opinion and perceptions regarding foreign travelers to N. Greece and negative offering factors.

<table>
<tr><td colspan="3">Foreign travelers to N. Greece are...
<u>income</u>: At most middle income travelers (83%); sometimes high income travelers (33%)
<u>heavy users</u>: Heavy users (50%); not heavy users (33%) of the destinations
<u>return (come back)</u>: They return because of low cost (66%) and Tradition-Greek culture and friendly people (50%)</td></tr>
<tr><td colspan="3">The negative factors are...</td></tr>
<tr><td>100% negative perception</td><td>80% negative perception</td><td>60% negative perception</td></tr>
<tr><td>The quality of sports establishments
Conference facilities</td><td>Facilities in and out of the lodgings
Health and spa resorts
Facilities for horse riding and bird watching
Facilities in the staying places for children
Transportation conditions
Situation in the Airport and related services</td><td>Aesthetics at the visitor places
Quality of the food in and out of the staying places
Friendly local people
Infrastructure for sport and hobby activities
Value and benefit relations
Cleanliness of the environment
Quietness at the staying places</td></tr>
</table>

5 Major findings and discussion

Three points analysis (see final conclusion in tables 4 and 6), has shown that the factors which are directly related to the achieved level of satisfaction among the English and German visitors, are:

- Environment and landscape
- Image and beauty of place
- Quietness at the place of stay

The aforementioned factors are approached in a higher level of analysis in table 4. Furthermore, these factors seem to be negatively grade by the English and German visitors, who select lodgings of an upper category. The same point of view seems to be prevalent among the 4 local tour operators. Those factors where negatively evaluated by the 60% of the local tour operators..

Sustainable Tourism, F. D. Pineda, C. A. Brebbia & M. Mugica (Editors)
© 2004 WIT Press, www.witpress.com, ISBN 1-85312-724-8

Based on the above, the viewpoints of the selected local tour operators and the English and German visitors coincide. The relationship between the degree of satisfaction gained by the visitors and the 3 factors lying on the supply side (that is environment, landscape, image and beauty, and quietness of the place) seems to be confirmed, not only as a result of the analysis of the negative perspectives of the tour agents, but also based on the analysis of the German and English visitors who have chosen to stay in a lodge of higher category

6 Conclusions and recommendations

The above results focus mainly on the basic offering factors. The analysis of those factors can give to the Supplier a better chance to provide strategically clear customer satisfaction tactics. As implied above, the design of the second field study drew on two main results of the first study. The analysis of quality of service and 13 offering factors in basic travel destinations of Chalkidiki can help the community strategic planners to build a sustainable customer oriented tourism industry.

References

[1] Agresti A. (1984), Analysis of Ordinal Categorical Data, John Wiley & Sons, USA.

[2] Agresti A. (1990), Categorical Data Analysis, John Wiley & Sons, USA.

[3] Ahmed Z.U. (1996), The need for the identification of the constituents of a Destination's Tourist Image: A promotional segmentation perspective, Revue de Tourisme - The Tourist Review - Zeitschrift fur Fremdenverkehr 2/1996, 44-57.

[4] Aquilo E. (1996), Research into Policies on Tourism, Revue de Tourism 1/1996.

[5] Bakkal I. (1991), Characteristics of West German demand for international tourism in the northern Mediterranean region, Applied Economics 23.

[6] Carey S., Gountas Y. and Gilbert D. (1997), Tour operators and destination sustainability, Tourism Management, 18, 7.

[7] Clements M. (1998), Planning to Tourism Capacity in a Crisis, Journal of Travel Research, August 1998.

[8] Crompton J. L., Fakeye P. C., and Lue C.-C., Positioning: The example of the Long Rio Grande Valley in the Winter Long Stay Destination Market, Journal of Travel Research, FALL 1992.

[9] Crompton J.L. (1979), Motivations for Pleasure Vacation, Annals of Tourism Research 6: 408-424.

[10] Goodall B. (1995), The Opportunity set concept - An application to Tourist Destination Areas, in: Ashworth G. And Goodall B. (edit.) Marketing Tourism places, Routledge, London 1995 (5th Edit.), 63-84.

Sustainable Tourism, F. D. Pineda, C. A. Brebbia & M. Mugica (Editors)

[11] Day G. S., Shocker A. D., Srivastrava R. K. (1979), Customer Oriented Approaches to identifying Product-Markets, Journal of Marketing 43 FALL.
[12] Derek R. Hall (1995) Tourism change in Central and Eastern Europe, in: Montanari A. and Williams A.M., European Tourism: Regions, Spaces and Restructuring, John Wiley & Sons Ltd. pp. 221-244.
[13] Eymann A. and Ronning G. (1997), Microeconomic models of tourists destination choice, Regional Science & Urban Economics 27.
[14] Ferner F. K., Muller R. and Zolles H. (1989), Marketing practice in Tourism (D.), 3 edit. Orac Verlag, Wien.
[15] GNTO – Kontogiannopoulos G. (1992), The characteristics of the German Market (GR.), Direction of GNTO – Germany, Frankfurt 11.11.1992.
[16] GNTO – Direction of England (1994), Research project for the English Market, March.
[17] Hackl P., Scharitzer D. And Zuba R., The Austrian Customer Satisfaction Barometer, der markt 1996/2, 35 Jahrgang, Nr. 137, s.86-94.
[18] Hofner (1987), Industrialmagazin (D.), May.
[19] Hopkins D. S. (1981). The Marketing Plan, Conference Board Inc., New York, in: Siomkos I. G. (1995), Introduction in Strategic Marketing (GR.), Stamoulis A., Athens-Pireaus.
[20] IGF (1988), Institut fur Grundlagenforschung, Salzburg 1988, in: Ferner F.K., Muller R. and Zolles H. (1989), Marketing practice in Tourism (D.), 3 edit. Orac Verlag, Wien.
[21] Lehmann D.R. and Winer R.S. (1997), Analysis for Marketing Planning, fourth edit. IRWIN, USA.
[22] Mazursky D. (1989), Past Experience and Future Tourism Decisions, Annals of Tourism Research, 16 (3): 333-344.
[23] Moutinho L. (1995), Strategies for Tourism Destination Development: An investigation of the role of Small Businesses, in: Ashworth G. And Goodall B. (edit.) Marketing Tourism Places, Routledge, London 1995 (5th Edit.), 104-122.
[24] Owens D. J. (1994), The All-season opportunity for Canada's Resorts, The Cornell HRA Quarterly, October.
[25] Petkova I., (u.a) (1995), Die kleinen und mittelstandischen privaten Unternehmen in der bulgarischen Tourismusindustrie (D), Sudosteuropa 44, Jhg. 3-4.
[26] Siomkos G. I. (1994), Consumer Behavior & Marketing Strategy – part a, (GR.) Stamoulis A., Athens-Piraeus.
[27] Smeral E. (1994), Tourismus 2005: Entwicklungsaspekte und Szenarien fur die Tourismus und Freizeitwirtschaft (D.), Ueberreuter Wien.
[28] Sonmez S.F. and Graefe A. R. (1998), Determining Future Travel Behavior from Past Travel Experience and perceptions of Risk and Safety, Journal of Travel Research Vol. 37, Nov. 1998, 171-177.
[29] SFB (1985) Internationalisation of the Economy no.178-University of Kostanz
[30] STERN Magazine (1987), Gruner + Jahr: Markenprofile research 2.

Sustainable Tourism, F. D. Pineda, C. A. Brebbia & M. Mugica (Editors)

[31] Syriopoylos Th. C. and Sinclair M. T. (1993). An econometric study of tourism demand: the AIDS model of US and European tourism in Mediterranean countries. Applied Economics, Vol. 25, No.12, December, 1541-1552.
[32] THE ECONOMIST (1991), Package holidays – crash landing, February 16.
[33] Unternehmer (1987), Research Project for West Germany, 12/87.
[34] Vasiliadis C. a/o (1994), Improvement of quality in tourism services-proposals and expected benefits (GR.), SETE/PLOTIN A.E., October.
[35] Vavrik U. and Mazanec J.A. (1990), A priori and posteriori Travel Market Segmentation: Tailoring Automatic Interaction Detection and Cluster Analysis for Tourism Marketing, Cahiers du Tourisme, serie c, Nr. 62 / June.
[36] Weiermair K. and Maser B. (1996), Information and information search behavior of tourists: A cursory review of the literature, preliminary empirical tests and further research questions, Revue de Tourisme - The Tourist Review - Zeitschrift fur Fremdenverkehr 3/1996, 5-23

Sustainable Tourism, F. D. Pineda, C. A. Brebbia & M. Mugica (Editors)

Characterization of visitors to natural areas in the southeast of Spain

P. Aguilera[1], M. F. Schmitz[2], I. de Aranzabal[2], H. Castro[1] & F. D. Pineda[2]
[1]*Department of Ecology, Complutense University, Madrid, Spain*
[2]*Departamento de Ecología. Universidad Complutense, Madrid, Spain*

Abstract

The management of natural areas requires a knowledge of what tourists demand in order that these resources can be optimized. A survey was carried out in an area in the southeast of Spain, which contains three protected natural spaces, with the aim of finding out the types and characteristics of visitors. The data were treated using an agglomerative multivariate classification technique. The results allowed differentiation of two main types of visitors: generalists and specialists. Both showed a high interest in contemplation of the landscape and contact with nature. The generalist tourists place a low value on the wildlife and rural properties of the landscape, with their motives for visiting being related to leisure activities. The specialist tourists are highly interested in nature and wildlife, observation of birds and other fauna; they know the emblematic species of the area and appreciate the rural culture. Within this specialist tourist group, three subtypes can be identified: the rural specialist – who likes and knows about the agricultural landscape, such as the matorral, rivers, springs and the mountain landscape; the cultural specialist – who values the historical monuments, the local folklore and fiestas; and the adventure specialist – who typically undertakes sporting activities in the fields and open land.
Keywords: natural areas, visitor typology, cultural tourism, cultural landscape.

1 Introduction

In response to the demands of a new and growing cultural tourism, new forms of tourism have emerged based on the environmental resources of the landscape: the attraction of various ecological features in themselves, or the quality of the

Sustainable Tourism, F. D. Pineda, C. A. Brebbia & M. Mugica (Editors)

fauna or vegetation, etc., the natural landscape, the integration of the rural population within the environment – the cultural landscape, etc. This type of tourism does not provide an alternative to mass tourism, rather it is complementary to it and could, conceivably, soon become as important. In any of its guises, the greatest potential environmental risk of this tourism is its dependence on the quality of the natural environment, and the active search for places endowed with outstanding ecological characteristics.

Cultural tourism, considered as a recreational use, could represent the best use of natural resources for certain areas that are protected, or are especially sensitive from an ecological point of view. Moreover, it represents a means by which the money generated from tourism can be reinvested in the management and protection of the habitats and of the biological diversity, which are being affected by intensification of agriculture, abandonment of rural areas and the expansion of tourism.

In terms of managing this new type of cultural tourism, it is necessary to know the environmental characteristics of the landscape that form the principal 'attractors' for tourists, and the relationship these have with the number of visitors of various types. Knowing the profile of visitors is important in terms of being able to optimize resources for use by these visitors. In other words, management of the recreational use can be done according to the characteristics of the site and the possibility of developing a particular type of activities, according to the carrying capacity of the territory. In addition, in the case of protected natural spaces, one of the objectives that must be considered is to satisfy the needs and expectations of potential visitors.

Studies about visitors to natural spaces are a relatively recent idea –in the eighties, social parameters were related to environmental characteristics (Gómez Limón et al. [1]). Hammit and Cole [2] wrote a comprehensive review of these studies. In Spain, one of the pioneering studies was done by De Lucio and Múgica [3]. The relationship between recreational use and environmental perception has been carefully analyzed (Múgica [4]). These studies establish an experimental method that allows typology of visitors according to the activities they undertook during their visit, and the environmental attitudes and expectations they demonstrate. Such a typology could be related to the perception of landscape as a useful tool when establishing management strategies for the territory.

In this study the various types of visitor to natural areas in the southeast of Spain are characterized.

2 Study area

The survey of visitor types was done over an area of 1,987 km^2, covering 33 municipalities in the province of Almería. The area spanned the valleys of the Rivers Andarax and Nacimiento and the Desert of Tabernas (Figure 1). Three Protected Natural Spaces have been declared within this zone: the National Park of Sierra Nevada, the Natural Park of Sierra Nevada and the Natural Space of the Desert of Tabernas.

Sustainable Tourism, F. D. Pineda, C. A. Brebbia & M. Mugica (Editors)

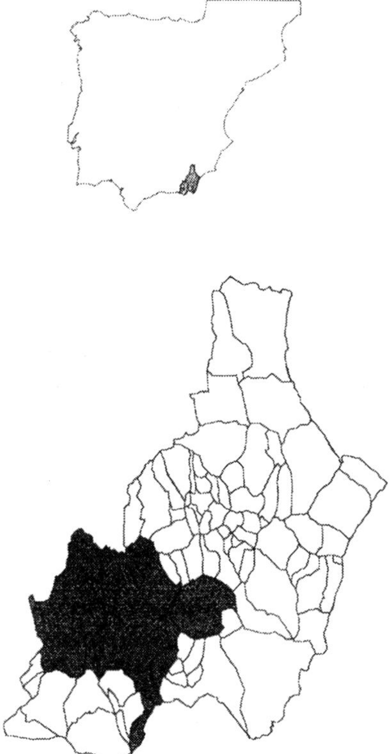

Figure 1: Study area.

This area is an example of Mediterranean territory with highly contrasting situations, where there is heterogeneous behaviour over both space and time and where abandonment of the rural areas is clearly visible. In addition to this abandonment the rarity of the natural landscape must also be considered, and the speed with which the rural world is developing new ways to use the land.

Within the study area there is a wide variety of agrarian land uses: non-irrigated crops, traditional vines on the hill slopes, citrus orchards, as well as wild areas on the steeper, higher slopes. The Desert of Tabernas is a unique space due to its particular combination of climate, geomorphology, biological diversity and human use. The coastal strip, contained within the municipality of Roquetas de Mar, has been highly modified by "sun and beach" type tourism, which is so common along the Spanish coastline. This municipality, with its mass tourism, provides a contrast with the land within the study area.

New land uses are exemplified by a new, highly lucrative method of intensive greenhouse agriculture, which is seen all over the municipality of Roquetas de Mar and which extends into other municipalities within the study area.

Sustainable Tourism, F. D. Pineda, C. A. Brebbia & M. Mugica (Editors)

3 Methods

Surveys were undertaken to classify the different types of tourists and determine their specific preferences. The surveys were based on a series of questions that dealt with expectations of visitors to the area, their sociological and cultural profile (Gómez Limón & De Lucio [5], Múgica and De Lucio [6]). Each questionnaire included 28 questions, divided into three groups according to the variables that: i) identified the tourists sociologically, ii) described their territorial preferences, and iii) identified various aspects of the landscape.

The survey was done using direct and indirect methods. Direct sampling involved asking visitors face to face, while indirect sampling was achieved by leaving questionnaires in information centres, hotels and hostels, rural accommodation and restaurants in the study zone. Direct interviews were carried out in accessible sites and also in steep areas with difficult access, such as the mountain refuges, recreational areas and camping zones. 430 questionnaires were filled in all, 74.2% from direct sampling and the remainder received by post.

Selection of the people interviewed was done at random for the direct surveys, either using a method of walking a route within the selected area, or by waiting for visitors to pass a particular survey post. No more than two people from the same group were interviewed, so as to avoid redundancy in the replies given. The surveys took place over a holiday period during 1998. Two days were spent at each sampling site. The people undertaking the survey were previously trained in order to obtain unity of criteria.

The questionnaires were used to construct a matrix of qualitative data, composed of 430 observations and 99 variables. Some sociological variables were used as external variables to help identify the different groups of visitors and so these were not included in the matrix. Classification of the visitors was done using a multivariate agglomerative classification, using the *UPGMA* algorithm. In the raw matrix, the similarity between pairs of observations was calculated using the Kulcinsky index, whose 'robustness' is suited to the type of data collected in this study (PATN [7]).

4 Results and discussion

The classification obtained allowed two groups of tourist to be distinguished, at a level of the similarity index of 1.20. These groups are denominated 'generalist' and 'specialist'. The two groups share some common indicators, namely a high level of interest in contemplation of the landscape (mountain, desert, river valley, wooded areas and pine or holm oak forests), and contact with nature. They are looking for recreation and leisure within the study area and like to undertake photographic itineraries during their visit. On the other hand, each visitor has his own perception of the landscape.

4.1 'Generalist' visitors

This group makes up 54.9% of the people interviewed. They typically put a low value on the variables representing the natural and rural resources of the area and its cultural activities. Their motive for visiting the area is principally for leisure and, to a lesser extent, to visit family or for professional reasons (Table 1).

Sociologically, 63.4% of the 'generalists' visitors fall into the 25 to 39 year-old age class (Figure 2), 56% have studied to university level (Figure 3) and 60% are visiting the area for the first time. They do not travel alone, they stay in hotels, and plan to spend two or three nights in the area. The car is the main means of transport, and their level of satisfaction with their visit was high.

Table 1: Discriminant variables for the 'generalist' group of visitors. The constancy value is given for each variable. The selection criteria for the variables is based on a constancy of ≥ 30%. In brackets it is indicated the medium (M) or low (B) evaluation given for these variables.

Variable	*Constancy (%)*
Visit to family or friends (B)	68
Professional reasons (B)	85
Climate in the area (B)	42
Rural landscape (B); (M)	33; 37
Sights and monuments (B)	41
Cultural activities (B); (M)	32; 58
Sports activities (B)	61
Health and treatments (B)	83
Attendance of courses (B)	95
Festivals and folk activities (B)	55
Craft works (B)	62
Gastronomy (B); (M)	33; 36
Proximity to place of residence (B)	62
Price (B); (M)	36; 41
Routes and footpaths	32

4.2 'Specialist' visitors

The second group in the classification (comprising 45.1% of the visitors) show a high level of interest in a specific group of nature and wildlife-related variables. The reasons for their visits include wildlife observation, particularly of birds. The rural landscape (field terraces, dry-stone walls, fences and hedges) is highly appreciated by these tourists, who know the emblematic species of the areas (Table 2).

This group is dominated by people aged 25 to 39 (Figure 2). Nearly 40% have studied to university level and 30% have primary education (Figure 3). They are not visiting the area for the first time and 34.2% would not stay the night in the area. Those who do stay overnight opt for hotels and camping areas.

Sustainable Tourism, F. D. Pineda, C. A. Brebbia & M. Mugica (Editors)

They travel by car and, to a lesser extent, on foot. Their level of satisfaction of their visit is high.

Table 2: Discriminant variables of the 'specialist' group of visitors. Constancy values are given for each variable. The selection criteria for the variables is based on a constancy of ≥ 30%.

Variable	*Constancy (%)*
Rural landscape	30
Birds	30
Wildlife	30
Emblematic species	30

This specialist visitor group has a lower index of similarity in the classification (1.06), and so it was subdivided into three subtypes for which the indicator variables are more specific: i) 'rural specialist', ii) 'cultural specialist', and iii) 'adventure specialist'. The generalist visitor group could not be split at this new level of the similarity index.

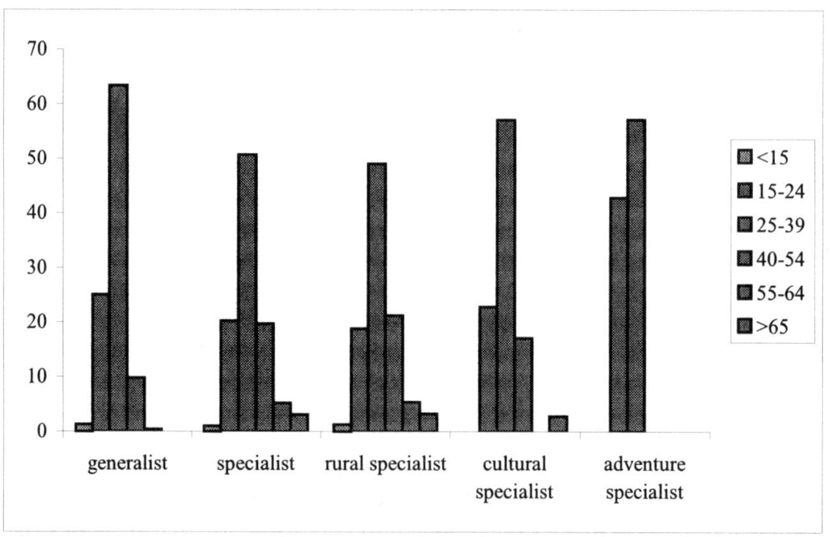

Figure 2: Age distribution of various visitor types. Values expressed as percentages.

4.2.1 'Rural specialist'

This type of tourist appreciates the gastronomy, contact with wildlife and the rural scene in general. They are particularly attracted by the agricultural landscape, matorral, pine forests, birds, wild animals, rivers and springs,

Sustainable Tourism, F. D. Pineda, C. A. Brebbia & M. Mugica (Editors)

mountain scenery, the valleys and the field terracing. This type of landscape is typical of the mountainous part of the study area called the Alpujarra. The principal activity was walking.

The 'rural specialists' mainly come from Andalusia, they are between 25 and 39 years old (Figure 2). 42% have studied at university and 29% have primary education (Figure 3). Half of them had visited the area more than three times, and come to the area on foot (the other half come by car). They do not usually stay the night, but those who do spend more than one day mainly stay in hotels. The level of satisfaction is high.

4.2.2 'Cultural specialist'

The second subtype of specialists comprises 8% of the people interviewed. They are attracted by contact with nature and wildlife, are interested in the sights of the area (churches, farmsteads, etc.) and by festivals and folklore. During their visit they watch birds and undertake aquatic activities. 70% of this group are men. 34% have university degrees, 29% primary education and 23% secondary (Figure 3). 65% have visited the area more than three times. They usually stay with family or in hotels. They arrive, basically, by car, and the level of satisfaction with their visit is high.

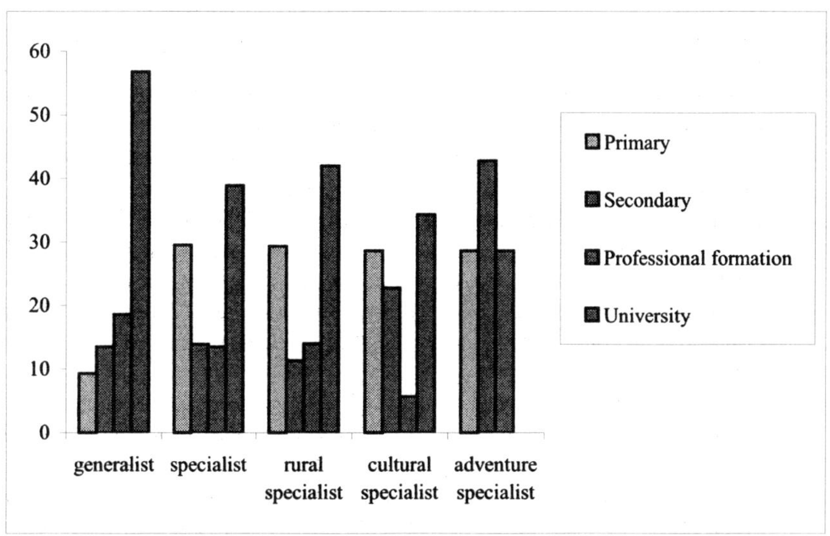

Figure 3: Educational profile of various visitor types. Values expressed as percentages.

4.2.3 'Adventure specialist'

The third subtype is made up of only 2% of the people interviewed. They like the grassland and open spaces in the study area and the main activity undertaken is adventure sport. The age of this type of visitors ranges from the 15 to 24 year age group, though the 25 to 39 year old group form the majority (Figure 2). They

Sustainable Tourism, F. D. Pineda, C. A. Brebbia & M. Mugica (Editors)
© 2004 WIT Press, www.witpress.com, ISBN 1-85312-724-8

have not studied to university level (Figure 3). 60% are not visiting the area for the first time. They camp in the open air, getting about mainly on foot. In contrast to the other people interviewed, they chose the area on the recommendation of family or friends. Their level of satisfaction is high.

5 Conclusions

The analysis results show that the visitors of the study area behave in a tourism stereotype way: there were generalist and specialist tourists. All of them reveal a great interest for the nature and express a high level of satisfaction about their visit to the study area.

We can recognize three types of specialist visitors: with 'rural' motivations –determined by the agrarian landscape–, 'cultural' specialists, attracted by the culture and the traditional landscapes, and, 'adventure' specialists, with preferences on nature and wildlife.

References

[1] Gómez Limón, F.J., Múgica, M., Muñoz, C., De Lucio, J.V., *Uso recreativo de los espacios naturales de Madrid. Frecuentación, caracterización de visitantes e impactos ambientales.* Serie Documentos N° 19. Centro de Investigación de Espacios Naturales Protegidos "Fernando González Bernáldez"-Consejería de Medio Ambiente y Desarrollo Regional. Comunidad de Madrid, 1996.

[2] Hammit, W.E., & Cole, D.N., *Wildland recreation. Ecology and Management.* John Wiley & Sons, New York, 1987.

[3] De Lucio, J.V, Múgica, M., *Percepción ambiental en los Parques Nacionales. Interpretación y gestión para la conservación.* ICONA, Madrid, 1990.

[4] Múgica, M., *Modelos de demanda paisajística y uso recreativo de los espacios naturales.* Doctoral Thesis. Facultad de Ciencias. Universidad Autónoma de Madrid, 1993.

[5] Gómez Limón, F.J. & De Lucio, J.V., Recreational use model in a wilderness area. *Journal of Environmental Management* **40**, pp. 161-171, 1994.

[6] Múgica, M. & De Lucio, J.V. The role of on-site experience on landscape preferences. A case study Doñana National Park (Spain). *Journal of Environmental Management* **47**, pp. 229-239, 1996.

[7] PATN. Pattern Analysis Package. *Reference Manual.* CSIRO Division of Wildlife and Rangelands Research, Canberra, 1990.

Sustainable Tourism, F. D. Pineda, C. A. Brebbia & M. Mugica (Editors)

Section 10
IT in tourism

A low cost reliable forecasting model of tourism data

A. Panagopoulos[1], Z. Psillakis[2] & D. Kanellopoulos[1]
[1]*Department of Tourism Management,*
Technological Educational Institute of Patras, Greece
[2]*Department of Physics, University of Patras, Greece*

Abstract

A new inferential model that allows low cost reliable time series forecasts is established. The model provides a new unique computationally straightforward approach based on widely used additive models. An application of the model referring to monthly percentages of occupancy in Greece is presented. The results are compared to those of the well know Box-Jenkins method. This study reveals the performance of the model and confirms its reliability.
Keywords: time series, forecasting models.

1 Introduction

The construction of time series models is an important aspect of business and economic analyses, because time series [1, 2] are many of the variables of most interest to business and economic researchers. Forecasting is about predicting the behavior of future events. Time series forecasts are extrapolations in future times of the available time series values. A good projection should provide a forecaster with a sense of the reliability of the forecast. A convenient way to capture this sense is the prediction interval, which provides a measure of the reliability of the forecast. Further, by varying the desired level of confidence the length of the prediction interval varies.

In this paper, an operational inferential model that allows low cost reliable time series forecasting, is presented. The proposed methodology (is described in section 2) refers to the decomposition of every time series value in three components namely: the trend component, the cyclical-seasonal component and the residual effect one. The first two components are considered, as random

Sustainable Tourism, F. D. Pineda, C. A. Brebbia & M. Mugica (Editors)

variables taking predefined probabilities (weights). By compounding these two random variables, a new random variable is established, as a linear combination of the two pre-referred ones. The coefficients (weights) used in this linear combination obey a selected fibonacci ratio. In this way, first a forecast (an estimate) of the future value of the time series is given by the expected value of the previously defined random variable, second a prediction interval is evaluated based on the standard deviation of this random variable. A properly selected length of the latter prediction interval can be used as an estimation of the residual effect. It is worthwhile noticing that the forecast and the accompanied prediction interval of the model require only seven existing time series values, so it is computationally straightforward.

In support of the proposed model, an application study of accommodation industry in Greece is presented in section 3. The data refers to the monthly percentages of occupancy of all types of tourist accommodation (except camping sites) of both foreign and domestic tourists. The data were derived from the official records of the Greek Statistical Office. The model is applied to these data and its results are compared to those of the well known Box-Jenkins method.

1.1 Notation

$\equiv$	implies an identity or definition
$\approx$	implies approximately – equal
$\Pr\{A\}$	probability of the event A
s-	implies "statistical (ly)"
r.v.	random variable(s)
$E(X)$	s-Expected value (mean, average) of the r.v. X
$\sigma(X)$	Standard deviation of the r.v. X
$f_n = O(g_n)$	implies $f_n \in O(g_n) \equiv \{h_n$: there exist positive constants c and n_0 such that $0 \le h_n \le c\, g_n$ for all $n \ge n_0\}$
$f_n = \Omega(g_n)$	implies $f_n \in \Omega(g_n) \equiv \{h_n$: there exist positive constants c and n_0 such that $0 \le c\, g_n \le h_n$ for all $n \ge n_0\}$

1.2 Definitions - assumptions

1. A *time series* is a collection of data obtained by observing a response variable sequentially at periodic points in time (e.g. on weekly, monthly, quarterly, or annually basis).
2. It is common practice to consider as *a reference cycle* or *period* p, a year for monthly (p=12) or quarterly data (p=4) and a five or ten years period for annually recorded data.
3. The repeated observations on a variable produce a time series, the variable is called *a time series variable*. We use w_m, to denote the values of the variable at time m. The data consists of N equally spaced values $w_1, w_2, \ldots, w_N$.
4. In practical applications, the main objective of times series, is to *forecast* (predict or estimate) some future value or values w_m, $m \ge N+1$ of the series. Forecasting based on existing values $w_{m_1}, \ldots, w_{m_2}$, $(1 \le m_1 < m_2 < N)$ and

Sustainable Tourism, F. D. Pineda, C. A. Brebbia & M. Mugica (Editors)

checked against existing values $w_{m_3},\ldots,w_{m_4}$, ($m_2<m_3<m_4\leq N$) of time series, to evaluate some measure of the forecasting accuracy, is called *ex-post* forecasting. *Ex-ante* forecasts predict future value (values) w_m , m> N of a time series beyond the time period of the existing data values w_m, m=1,2...,N. In such cases, there are not available data for comparison. Usually ex-ante forecasts are done for one reference period ahead.

5. *Forecast error* is defined as the *actual value* w_m minus the *forecasted value* (or fitted), f_m of the time series variable at time m, namely: $e_m = w_m - f_m$.
6. To analyze the relative performance of several consecutive ex-post forecasts in the time window m_1 to m ($1\leq m_1<m\leq N$), the popular *root mean squared error* (RMSE) criterion, is used. The RMSE r_m, for a such time-window is calculated as :

$$r_m = \left\{ \frac{1}{m - m_1 + 1} \sum_{n=m_1}^{m} e_n^{\,2} \right\}^{1/2}$$

2 The proposed model

Researchers, often approach the problem of describing the nature of a time series w_m by identifying three kinds of change, or variation of the time series values. These three components are commonly known as : (1) trend component, t_m, (2) cyclical-seasonal component s_m, and (3) residual effect, h_m. To obtain forecasts, some type of model that can be projected into the future must be used to describe the time series. One of the must widely used models is the additive model:

$$w_m = t_m + s_m + h_m \tag{1}$$

or alternatively the log-additive (or multiplicative) model:

$$\ln(w_m) = \ln(t_m) + \ln(s_m) + \ln(h_m) \tag{1'}$$

depending on the scale of the variation of the values of the underlying time series variable. Since business and economic cycles last usually 5 years, and seasonal data are usually related to their predecessor and successor ones, to simulate (1) the following methodology is used.

Let X_m denotes a r.v. simulating the "random" behavior of the trend component of a time series at time m $\geq 1 + 5$ p. Suppose that X_m, takes the value $x_{m,i}$ with probability (weight) f_i, i=1,2,3,4,5 given by the following table:

i	1	2	3	4	5
$x_{m,i}$	w_{m-5p}	w_{m-4p}	w_{m-3p}	w_{m-2p}	w_{m-p}
f_i	1/12	1/12	2/12	3/12	5/12

Sustainable Tourism, F. D. Pineda, C. A. Brebbia & M. Mugica (Editors)

This scheme, which obeys a Fibonacci-type memory rule, uses values of the time series of the same periodicity (lag) and gives more weight (memory) in the most recent used time series value.

To simulate the "random" behavior of the cyclical-seasonal component of a time series at time $m \geq 1 + p$, we define the r.v. Y_m {or alternatively Y'_m} with probability (weight) g_j, j=1,2,3 given by the following table:

j	1	2	3
$y_{m,j}$	w_{m-p-1}	w_{m-p}	w_{m-p+1}
$y'_{m,j}$	w_{m-1}	w_{m-p}	w_{m-p+1}
g_j	1/4	2/4	¼

This scheme which obeys a Fibonacci-type memory rule, takes account data with the same periodicity or cyclicality of m and two neighbor values of it with correlated seasonality. This means that we use: (a) for the definition of r.v. Y_m, the values w_{m-p}, w_{m-p+1}, and w_{m-p-1} if we are interested for one-step ahead forecasting (one time series value ahead) or for one-period ahead forecasting (per whole reference cycle p) and (b) for the definition of r.v. Y'_m the values w_{m-p}, w_{m-p+1}, and w_{m-1} if we have available the value w_{m-1} and we interested for one-step ahead forecasting.

Based on r.v. X_m and Y_m {or Y'_m}, a r.v. F_m can be defined as a Fibonacci weighed average of these.

Let the r.v.

$$F_m = 0.618\ X_m + 0.382\ Y_m \tag{2}$$

or alternatively

$$F_m = 0.618\ X_m + 0.382\ Y'_m \tag{2'}$$

simulate the "random" behavior of the time series value w_m except the residual effect h_m, for every $m \geq 1 + 5p$. Based on r.v. F_m we have the following results:

$$f_m \equiv E(F_m) \approx w_m \tag{3}$$

$$E(F_m) = 0.618\ E(X_m) + 0.382\ E(Y_m) \tag{4}$$

or alternatively

$$E(F_m) = 0.618\ E(X_m) + 0.382\ E(Y'_m), \tag{4'}$$

and

$$\Pr(|F_m - f_m| < k\ \sigma(F_m)) \geq 1 - \frac{1}{k^2}, \tag{5}$$

$$l_m = f_m - k\ \sigma(F_m),\quad u_m = f_m + k\ \sigma(F_m) \tag{6}$$

$$k\ \sigma(F_m) \approx |e_m| \approx |h_m| \tag{7}$$

where k is a positive number larger than or equal to 1.

It is worthwhile noticing that for every $m \geq 1 + 5p$ the forecast and the accompanied prediction interval with confidence at least $\left(1 - 1/k^2\right)\%$ of the

Sustainable Tourism, F. D. Pineda, C. A. Brebbia & M. Mugica (Editors)

model require only seven existing time series values. The computation of $\sigma(F_m)$, (not presented here but available on request) is based on an estimation of the correlation between r.v. X_m and Y_m {or Y'_m}. The overall scheme is computationally straightforward and can be computed simply by the use of a normal hand calculator.

The quantity $k\sigma(F_m)$ gives by its definition an estimate of the absolute value of the unknown error e_m or in other words gives an estimate of the order of magnitude of the absolute value of the random factor in the time series, namely of the residual effect. Let $k^* = \sqrt{2}$ be a threshold value of k, so that a prediction interval (l^*_m, u^*_m) with 50% at least confidence that it will contain the unknown value w_m. The quantities $k\sigma(F_m)$ and (l^*_m, u^*_m) do not give accurate estimate and prediction interval respectively for the "random" residual effect component of w_m, but rather give estimates about the order of its magnitude. To get more accurate estimates we ought to use larger values of $k > k^*$.

3 An application study

The importance of tourism industry in World and in Greece especially is indisputable. It constitutes very crucial economic activities and a valuable source of earnings, such as an increase of employment, gross domestic product and multiplier effect investments [3]. One factor of tourism industry is the ability to host visitors in various places. Therefore, the forecast of monthly and/or annually percentages of occupancy in Greece and in various regions is a desirable task. This potentially makes more effective use of the available sources for the Greece visitors.

In support of the proposed model, we present an application study in tourism data that refer to the monthly percentages of occupancy of all types of tourism accommodation (expect camping sites) in Greece. The data were derived from the official records of the Greek Statistical Office and involve the monthly occupancy of all the tourist accommodation both foreign and domestic tourists for the time period January 1990 {or 1990(1)} until December 1999 {or 1999(12)}. At this point, we underline that the Greek National Tourism Organization (GNTO) has not released any similar data for the period 2000-Nowadays. The model is applied to these data and its results are compared to those of the well known Box-Jenkins method, which is one of the newest methods in the time series domain. This study reveals the simplicity and the potential significant use of the model and verifies its high reliability.

3.1 The data and their coding

The monthly percentages of occupancy for Greece are presented in Table 1 [4]. The data were coded from w_1(1990(1)) to w_N(1999(12)) with N = 120, so that a time series w_1, w_2, …, w_N was derived for further processing. Figure 1 is an illustration of the time plot of our data.

Sustainable Tourism, F. D. Pineda, C. A. Brebbia & M. Mugica (Editors)
© 2004 WIT Press, www.witpress.com, ISBN 1-85312-724-8

Table 1: Greece - monthly percentage of occupancy.

	(1) Jan	(2) Feb	(3) Mar	(4) Apr	(5) May	(6) Jun
1990	29.67	33.42	33.81	43.51	55.93	66.37
1991	27.47	28.90	30.54	31.94	48.88	55.93
1992	30.13	33.57	32.07	41.55	53.83	62.73
1993	28.92	33.67	32.85	42.14	49.68	56.79
1994	29.26	32.47	32.76	41.64	58.44	66.02
1995	28.59	32.89	33.04	41.95	53.19	61.54
1996	28.35	31.46	30.00	38.94	50.55	56.28
1997	29.63	32.02	30.37	37.86	52.33	61.24
1998	30.41	32.88	31.20	39.40	56.08	65.60
1999	31.28	33.81	31.08	38.58	59.05	70.24
	(7) Jul	**(8) Aug**	**(9) Sep**	**(10) Oct**	**(11) Nov**	**(12) Dec**
1990	75.94	87.43	70.37	47.78	32.29	31.94
1991	70.41	84.13	68.54	47.92	32.04	31.39
1992	73.96	82.65	68.22	46.16	31.26	30.56
1993	71.96	82.16	68.38	47.88	31.30	29.86
1994	76.83	86.51	71.43	52.68	29.50	29.62
1995	68.90	77.14	66.45	46.39	29.46	30.81
1996	66.74	78.97	63.76	45.00	28.71	26.83
1997	73.99	88.05	69.38	47.62	30.80	31.15
1998	80.94	90.47	71.07	48.25	33.55	31.02
1999	82.73	91.11	73.73	52.93	32.75	31.89

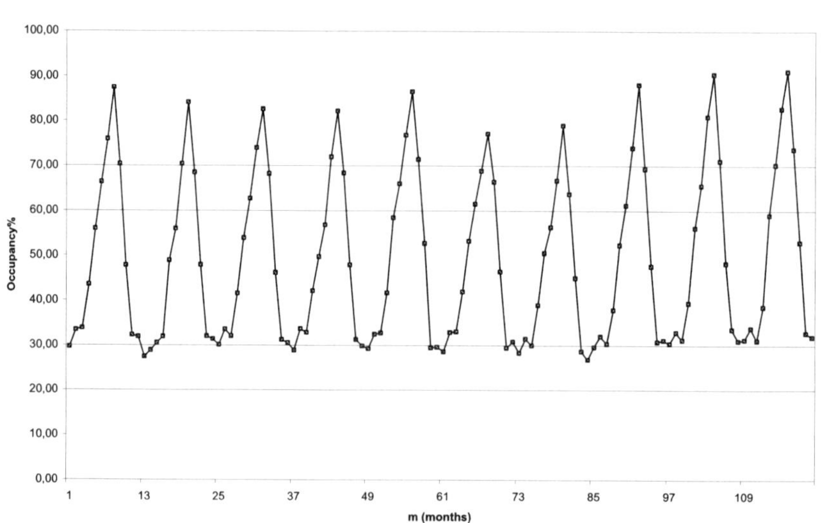

Figure 1: Greece –Timeplot 1990(1)-1999(12).

3.2 Results and discussion

Notation

Method 1{2}: implies the usage of the r.v. Y_m $\{Y'_m\}$

Sustainable Tourism, F. D. Pineda, C. A. Brebbia & M. Mugica (Editors)

We used our model and the Box–Jenkins method in order to forecast (predict) the monthly percentage (p = 12) of occupancy of accommodation in Greece for the year 2000 – that is to make 12 ex-ante forecasts. In order to have the ability to check the forecasts and the prediction intervals accuracy using real data, we made ex-post forecasts via our model (method 1 and 2). These forecasts correspond to time series values: w_{61} (1995(1)) to w_{120} (1999(12)). This means that the values which are going to be forecasted were excluded from our data set. Thus, our model is used without these observations of the time series values and then we made the forecasts. After that, these forecasts were compared with the real data that we kept outside from this procedure.

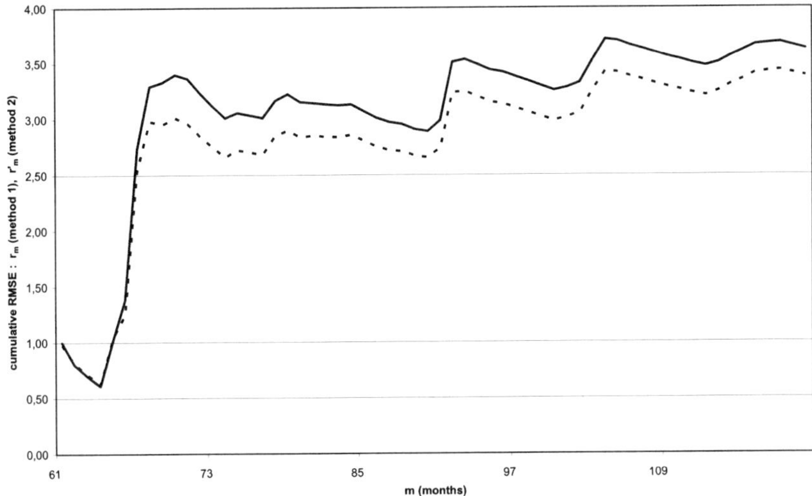

Figure 2: Greece 1995(1)- 1999(12).

Figure 2 displays the cumulative (running or moving) RMSE, r_m (method 1, solid line) and r'_m (method 2, dotted line) for m=61 to 120. Method 2 gives in the most cases smaller RMSE - thus more accurate forecast – owing that is used value w_{m-1} instead of value w_{m-p-1} (used in method 1). From the curves of Fig. 2 there is an evidence that $r'_m = O(r_m)$.

Figure 3 presents for $k = k^* = \sqrt{2}$ the cumulative percentages c_m (method 1, solid line) and c'_m (method 2, dotted line) of the number of times that a real time series value w_m is containing into the corresponding prediction interval – with confidence at least $\left(1 - \frac{1}{k^2}\right)\%$ =50%. The plots of Figure 3 depict that our model (methods 1 and 2) always fulfill the probability criterion of eq.(5), when the used sample for test has large enough size. Similar results (not presented here but available from the authors on request) for values $k > k^*$ confirm the same token. Furthermore as it can easily seen $c'_m = \Omega(c_m)$. The same comments as in the case of RMSE - Figure 2- are also true for c_m and c'_m.

Sustainable Tourism, F. D. Pineda, C. A. Brebbia & M. Mugica (Editors)
© 2004 WIT Press, www.witpress.com, ISBN 1-85312-724-8

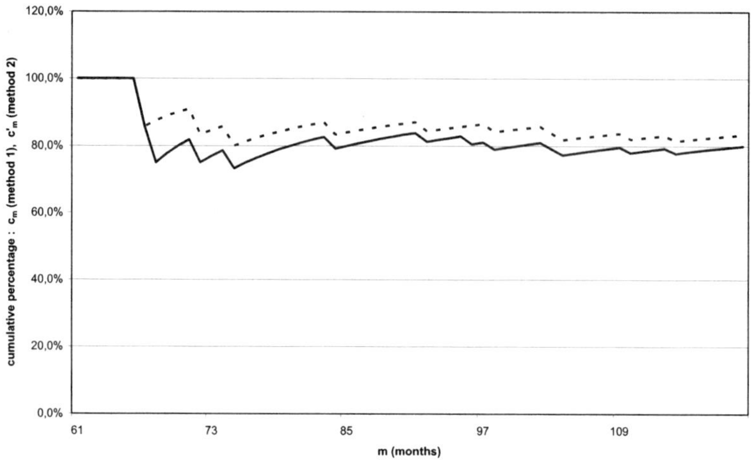

Figure 3: Greece 1995(1) - 1999(12), k=1.4142.

Tables 2 (a: method 1, b: method 2) present results of the application of our model to ex-post forecasts and give prediction intervals for monthly percentages of occupancy for the year 1999 from month 1(Jan) to 12(Dec). To take these results the last 12 observations namely w_{109}, w_{110}, ...,w_{120}, were excluded - as usually- from the time series values. We forecast values without these observations and then take forecasts for this latter interval 1999(1-12). Finally we compare these forecasts with the data that we kept outside of this procedure. The data of Tables are quite self-explained and confirm the comments on Figures 2 and 3.

Table 2(a): Year 1999 – Greece, method 1.

				(k, (1-1/k²)%)					
				(√2, 50%)			**(3, 88.89%)**		
m	**w_m**	**f_m**	**r_m**	**l_m**	**u_m**	**c_m %**	**l_m**	**u_m**	**c_m%**
1	31.28	30.23	1.05	29.02	31.45	100.00	27.65	32.81	100.00
2	33.81	32.18	1.37	31.14	33.22	50.00	29.98	34.39	100.00
3	31.08	32.07	1.26	29.90	34.23	66.67	27.48	36.66	100.00
4	38.58	40.17	1.35	34.56	45.78	75.00	28.28	52.07	100.00
5	59.05	54.22	2.47	47.90	60.54	80.00	40.81	67.63	100.00
6	70.24	64.33	3.30	58.57	70.10	66.67	52.10	76.57	100.00
7	82.73	77.02	3.74	67.84	86.20	71.43	57.54	96.49	100.00
8	91.11	85.26	4.07	77.15	93.37	75.00	68.06	102.46	100.00
9	73.73	69.51	4.08	60.71	78.31	77.78	50.84	88.18	100.00
10	52.93	48.73	4.10	40.31	57.14	80.00	30.88	66.57	100.00
11	32.75	33.37	3.91	28.47	38.27	81.82	22.98	43.76	100.00
12	31.89	30.79	3.76	29.10	32.48	83.33	27.21	34.37	100.00

Sustainable Tourism, F. D. Pineda, C. A. Brebbia & M. Mugica (Editors)

Table 2(b): Year 1999 – Greece, method 2.

				(k, (1-1/k²)%)					
				(√2, 50%)			(3, 88.89%)		
m	w_m	f_m	r_m	l_m	u_m	c_m %	l_m	u_m	c_m %
1	31.28	30.22	1.06	29.01	31.43	100.00	27.65	32.79	100.00
2	33.81	32.27	1.32	31.35	33.19	50.00	30.31	34.22	100.00
3	31.08	32.16	1.25	30.04	34.27	66.67	27.66	36.65	100.00
4	38.58	40.16	1.34	34.53	45.79	75.00	28.23	52.09	100.00
5	59.05	54.14	2.50	47.65	60.63	80.00	40.37	67.91	100.00
6	70.24	64.62	3.24	59.27	69.97	66.67	53.27	75.96	100.00
7	82.73	77.46	3.60	69.16	85.76	71.43	59.86	95.06	100.00
8	91.11	85.43	3.92	77.33	93.53	75.00	68.24	102.62	100.00
9	73.73	69.57	3.95	60.65	78.49	77.78	50.66	88.49	100.00
10	52.93	48.98	3.95	40.02	57.94	80.00	29.96	68.00	100.00
11	32.75	33.82	3.78	27.84	39.79	81.82	21.14	46.49	100.00
12	31.89	30.72	3.63	29.09	32.35	83.33	27.26	34.17	100.00

To compare our results, the Box-Jenkins model was used and its results are presented in Table 3. The implementation of the Box-Jenkins method is a very hard programming task or alternatively requires the usage of a high sophisticated computer package. For this task, we used Minitab12 package with properly selected Box-Jenkins parameters (do not presented here but available from the authors on request). A simple comparison of the results presented in Tables 2 and 3 reveals the potential performance of our model and confirms its reliability.

Table 3: Year 1999 – Greece, Box – Jenkins.

				95% limits		
m	w_m	f_m	r_m	l_m	u_m	c_m %
1	31.28	30.30	0.98	27.71	33.13	100.00
2	33.81	33.56	0.72	30.20	37.28	100.00
3	31.08	32.75	1.13	29.26	36.66	100.00
4	38.58	40.98	1.55	36.43	46.10	100.00
5	59.05	55.37	2.15	49.04	62.53	100.00
6	70.24	63.94	3.24	56.42	72.45	100.00
7	82.73	76.31	3.85	67.13	86.75	100.00
8	91.11	87.33	3.85	76.58	99.58	100.00
9	73.73	71.05	3.73	62.12	81.26	100.00
10	52.93	49.55	3.70	43.20	56.84	100.00
11	32.75	32.13	3.53	27.93	36.96	100.00
12	31.89	31.27	3.39	27.11	36.07	100.00

Finally, Table 4 presents ex-ante forecasts and accompanied prediction intervals for the monthly percentages for the year 2000. The results of our model (method 1 and method 2) and those of the Box–Jenkins method are of the same order of magnitude. However, it is noticing that the results of our method can be derived by the potential use of a normal hand calculator, whereas those referred to Box-Jenkins method require the usage of a computer.

Sustainable Tourism, F. D. Pineda, C. A. Brebbia & M. Mugica (Editors)

Table 4: Year 2000 – Greece.

	Box-Jenkins model			**Our model**				
		95% limits			**($\sqrt{2}$, 50%)**		**(3, 88.89%)**	
m	f_m	l_m	u_m	f_m	l_m	u_m	l_m	u_m
1	31.31	28.63	34.23	30.90	29.42	32.39	27.75	34.06
2	34.56	31.11	38.40	32.81	31.43	34.19	29.89	35.73
3	33.46	29.89	37.45	32.05	30.21	33.89	28.14	35.96
4	41.81	37.17	47.03	40.06	33.97	46.16	27.13	53.00
5	57.48	50.90	64.91	56.27	47.64	64.91	37.95	74.60
6	66.64	58.81	75.52	67.55	59.13	75.98	49.68	85.43
7	79.38	69.83	90.24	79.63	70.72	88.53	60.72	98.53
8	90.35	79.23	103.03	86.89	79.12	94.66	70.40	103.38
9	73.46	64.23	84.02	71.66	61.86	81.45	50.88	92.43
10	51.45	44.86	59.02	50.97	40.96	60.99	29.73	72.22
11	33.15	28.82	38.14	34.14	28.31	39.97	21.77	46.51
12	32.27	27.97	37.22	28.40	20.24	36.56	11.09	45.71

4 Conclusions

A new inferential and computationally straightforward model was introduced. The proposed model refers to the decomposition of every time series value in "random" components. These components are compounded to constitute a new weighted random variable. The expected value of this random variable gives a forecast of a future time series value. Its standard deviation serves to construct a prediction interval at a predefined confidence level. A case study of the proposed model, referring to data taking from tourism accommodation industry, verifies its usefulness and its high reliability.

References

[1] Mendenhall, W., Sincich, T., *A Second course in Statistics – Regression Analysis*, Prentice Hall, 1996.
[2] Frees, E., *Data Analysis Using Regression Models - The Business Perspective*, Prentice Hall, 1996.
[3] Piou, Greek Tourism Towards 2000, *Tourism and Economy*. 1993.
[4] Greek National Tourism Organization, *Annual Report* 1990-1999.

Sustainable Tourism, F. D. Pineda, C. A. Brebbia & M. Mugica (Editors)

Design of a novel management system of web multimedia travel plans

D. Kanellopoulos & A. Panagopoulos
Department of Tourism Management,
Technological Educational Institute of Patras, Greece

Abstract

The use of Internet based applications as an instructional tool in e-tourism is rapidly expanding. Nowadays, there is an increase in the development of attraction and accommodation websites with huge amounts of tourist material embedded within them. However, there is not a generic, dynamic and flexible architecture regarding the management of web attractions and accommodations by tourist agents. This occurs due to the lack of any type of standardization. Moreover, there is little empirical evidence regarding the actual use of the above mentioned web contents by e-tourists. We designed a novel web management system of multimedia travel plans, in order for web multimedia travel plans to become manageable, effective and adaptive to the e-tourists' needs. The new system is based on a best-effort architecture and includes a web log analysis module to evaluate how online contents are being consumed and to identify the individual differences among e-tourists in terms of content usage and the amount of content that are presented in a web-supported multimedia travel plan. The proposed web management system provides services such as: creation, presentation, modification, deletion and indirect evaluation of multimedia travel plans. In addition, it supports e-tourist patterns interpretation regarding their navigation habits to web travel plans.
Keywords: information technology, multimedia travel plans, multimedia attractions and accommodations, content usage, web log analysis.

1 Introduction

The World Wide Web (WWW) has emerged as the fastest growing area of the Internet, enabling distribution of multimedia information. As textual data,

Sustainable Tourism, F. D. Pineda, C. A. Brebbia & M. Mugica (Editors)

graphics, pictures, video, sounds are easily accessible through the WWW, it soon became the flagship of the Information Communications Technologies' (ICT's) revolution and instituted an innovative platform for efficient, live and timely exchange of both ideas and products. The WWW provides extremely vital service by incorporating similarly structured information and enables the packaging of a wide range of diverse tourism products and services. It also provides the infrastructure for inexpensive delivery of multimedia information, promotion and distribution [1]. Multimedia networks developments seem to have sharpened the traveler's appetite for travel information. Internet technologies are complementing the role of personal travel. For example, E-tourism is a field where web-based technology was very quickly adopted and used for e-travel delivery. Virtual reality (VR) offers numerous distinct advantages over the actual visitation of a tourist site: *a)* it affords access into a controlled environment, as all variables in the VR can be modified to create the perfect virtual experience and *b)* a virtual vacation dispenses many of the hassles that accompany an actual vacation. However, VR can never become a tourist experience complete substitute, because it is unable to replace the feeling of being in nature and seeing, hearing, feeling, and breathing an environment that is real [2].

From another perspective, Internet created the conditions for the emergence of new electronic tourism intermediaries (*eMediaries*) based on three *ePlatforms* named: the Internet, Interactive Digital Television and mobile devices relating to mobile Commerce [3]. The mCommerce will follow the Internet e-platform, as a number of Internet-based operators will offer services through different platforms. Tourism providers already use WAP and SMS for distributing information, for allowing consumers to check flight arrivals and departures and for checking in [3].

Hereafter, two core questions emerge: first, how can ICTs foster new web management services of multimedia travel plans? And second, how might this is related to multimedia communication networks [4]? Inevitably, a new web management system of multimedia travel plans must be proposed, that will adopt a generic, dynamic and flexible architecture regarding the management of content by tourist agents. Nevertheless, several issues need to be addressed, namely: security of transmissions, credibility of information; intellectual property and copyrights; bandwidth and multimedia network requirements; user confusion and dissatisfaction; lack of adequate trained specialists; equal access and pricing. Moreover, an analytical human engineering must be acting out regarding the actual use of the web contents by e-tourists.

The rest of the paper is organized as follows. Three notions: *multimedia travel plan, accommodation and attraction* are introduced in Section 2, while our system is described in Section 3. Finally, conclusions are given in Section 4.

2 Multimedia travel plans: A theoretical approach

Qualitative research demonstrated that great potential exists for the utilization of multimedia to convey graphic information and animation of tourist products [5]. This can include video, maps, interactive presentations etc. At this point, we

Sustainable Tourism, F. D. Pineda, C. A. Brebbia & M. Mugica (Editors)

introduce the notion of *multimedia travel plan*, which consists of a sequence of attractions and accommodations *time intervals*, which may be in turn:

```
Travel_plan_id={tourist_agency_id,
T_interval1, T_interval_2,.., T_interval_n)
```

where, `tourist_agency_id`: the owner of the multimedia travel plan and
`T_interval={attraction, accommodation)`

A `T_interval` is stated as an attraction's or an accommodation's time interval, as an e-tourist could be either to an attraction or to an accommodation state. Multimedia attractions and accommodations contain multimedia data as text, pictures, graphic, sound and video. They offer increased modularity, which is a very important aspect in the development and maintenance of travel plans.

2.1 Multimedia attractions and accommodations

The meaning of attraction is multidimensional depending on timing and territorial parameters. For example, an attraction (e.g. an exhibition) may have a limited periodical lifetime and different meaning in various countries. However, any multimedia attraction can be defined as a set of our proposed text parameters, accompanying with optional video, pictures, graphics and sound parts.

```
Attr_id={attr_name, attr_category, location, duration,
      transport, dangerous, visitors, cost,
      language, cicerone, visitor's permission}
```

where,

`Attr_name:` The attraction's name.

`Attr_category:` The category in which the attraction belongs.
`={cave, church, monastery, castle, archaeological place, museum, village, gallery, library, bridge, theatre, etc}`

`Attr_location:` The exact location of the attraction.

`Duration:` The time that the exhibition of the attraction is fulfilled.

`Transportation:` The means of transportation.

`Dangerous:` The level of exposure in danger.

`Visitors:` The number of visitors that visit the attraction.

`Cost:` The cost per visitor such as to visit the attraction.

`Language:` The presentation language of the conducted tour.

`Cicerone:` Required (yes/no).

`Permissions:` The permissions of the visitor to photograph or to make video recording.

A multimedia attraction includes not only the above text items, but also graphics, video and audio concerning the attraction. Fig. 1 illustrates these items in a windows relating to a multimedia attraction.

Sustainable Tourism, F. D. Pineda, C. A. Brebbia & M. Mugica (Editors)

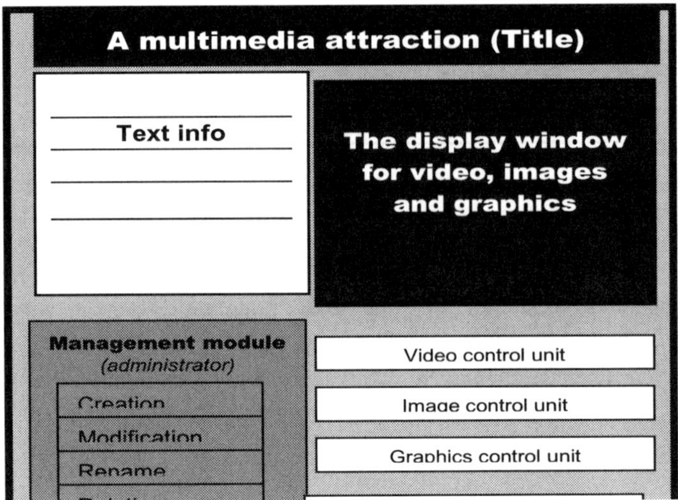

Figure 1: A multimedia attraction.

In our framework, any accommodation is defined as a set of proposed parameters:

```
Accom_id={accom_nane, accom_category, accom_location,
duration, transport, dangerous, visitors, cost, language,
visitor's permission}
```

where,

`Duration`: The proposed time interval for the residence.

`Visitors`: The number of visitors that will stay to the accommodation.

`Cost`: The cost per visitor in order to stay at the accommodation.

2.2 Managing and adapting multimedia travel plans

WTO argues that "the key to success lies in the quick identification of consumer needs and in reaching potential clients with comprehensive personalized and up-to-date information" [6]. ICTs enable travelers to access reliable and accurate information as well as to undertake reservations in a fraction of the time, cost and inconvenience required by conventional methods. Customer's satisfaction depends highly on the *accuracy* and *comprehensiveness* of specific information on destinations' accessibility, facilities, attractions and activities [7]. According to this approach, our system improves the QoS (*quality of service*) and contributes to higher e-tourist's satisfaction. This can be obtained by managing properly multimedia travel plans and adapting them to the e-tourists demands. In our framework, we overstate the tourist's demand as:

```
Tourist's demand= {travel_plan id, accuracy level,
comprehensiveness level, date&time of departure, reservation cost,
point locations of departures, language, evaluation}
```

The analysis of these parameters is out of the scope of this paper.

3 MMTP: The web management system of multimedia travel plans

The new web **M**anagement system of **M**ultimedia **T**ravel **P**lans (MMTP) is based on a proposed integrated architecture. This architecture, called *peer-to-peer (P2P) multimedia travel plans distribution architecture*, can support a large number of e-tourists at a low overall system cost. The key idea of the proposed architecture is that the multimedia travel plans web servers share some of their resources (e.g. multimedia attractions and accommodations). As web servers contribute resources to the MMTP, the overall system capacity increases and more e-tourists can be served. Most of the requesting web servers will be served using resources contributed by others. The (*super peer*) web servers apply well known cluster-based searching algorithms [8].

The MMTP supports *multilingual databases*, in order to inform e-tourists who speak different languages. Besides, MMTP provides multimedia systems techniques, in order to combine audio-visual information and basic services such as: *administration, information* and *indirect evaluation* of the distributed multimedia travel plans. An authorized e-tourist can be informed about a provided multimedia travel plan. During e-tourist's navigation, the attractions and accommodations components of a multimedia travel plan are *indirectly* evaluated.

3.1 Payment

Besides, a special payment service is provided to the e-tourists, which relies on an authorization service (e.g. Kerberos) and supports the credit-debit model. According to this model, e-tourists will maintain small accounts on a payment server and will authorize charges against those accounts. Supporting this model, the CMU's NetBill payment system [9] can be used, as it has low transaction cost and is suitable for small payments (*micropayments*). Another approach is the use of a merchant-initiated payment system such as PayPal® (www.paypal.com).

3.2 Intellectual Property Protection

MMTP's providers are concerned that once they make multimedia travel plans available electronically, copies will propagate and they will lose the ability to collect royalties. Though some researchers have proposed elaborate technical mechanisms to prevent illegitimate copying, it is our view that such attempts are bound to fail (consider the failure of S/W copy–protection mechanisms). Much of the technology needed to protect MMTP's network infrastructure already exist, while cryptographic techniques can be applied in support of authentication, authorization, integrity, confidentiality, assurance and payment [10].

3.3 Administrating multimedia travel plans

Discrete services are provided to the MMTP's administrator:

Sustainable Tourism, F. D. Pineda, C. A. Brebbia & M. Mugica (Editors)
© 2004 WIT Press, www.witpress.com, ISBN 1-85312-724-8

a) Creation of a multimedia travel plan by creating component attractions and accommodations, based on: (1) prototypes (attraction and accommodation) and (2) an information structure [11]. During creation, the MMTP facilitates the acquisition of pictures, videos, and presentations from important objects (e.g. objects d'art).
b) Modification of the content of an attraction or accommodation (e.g. modification of a video clip that presents a certain hotel-accommodation-after reconstructing).
c) Classification of multimedia attractions and accommodations according to selected criteria (*category* and *characteristics*) in order to facilitate retrieval.
d) Deletion, modification, presentation, listening and printing the whole data content (or a part) of a multimedia travel plan. Some printing facilities may be provided combining both magnification and reduction possibilities.

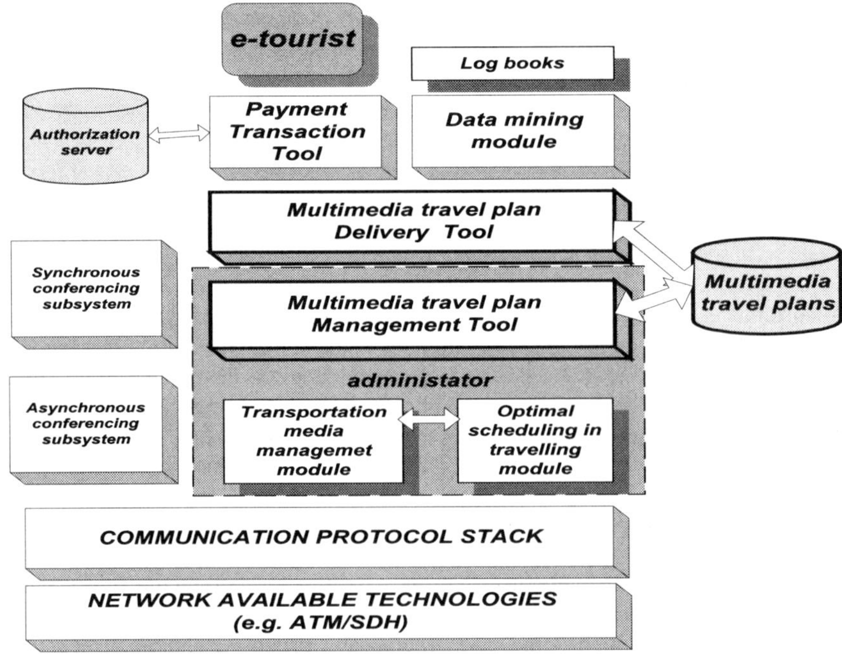

Figure 2: The MMTP system based on the OSI RM.

The MMTP (depicted in Fig. 2) includes: 1) the synchronous and asynchronous conferencing subsystems, 2) the multimedia travel plan management subsystem, 3) the multimedia travel plans delivery subsystem, 4) the payment transaction subsystem, 5) the data mining module and 6) the optimal scheduling in traveling, even in the presence of different transportation means. The MMTP was based on web [12], in order to avoid the implementation of

Sustainable Tourism, F. D. Pineda, C. A. Brebbia & M. Mugica (Editors)

different user interfaces (UIs) for each new platform or operating system. Any authorized e-tourist can be connected to the MMTP, while the system's administrator can manage existing multimedia travel plans. The administrator is able to send to the web server upgraded libraries of multimedia attractions or accommodations and manage them remotely. Separate web servers can be used for storing multimedia attractions and accommodations. For example, a distinct web server may be used for data concerning accommodations referring to class A hotels. Besides, various storing media must be considered for interim and final storage, including the necessary optimal compression strategies. Furthermore, in MMTP, a capability-based authorization model for the web [13] must be applied, since multimedia travel plans are hyperlinked documents and contents and may be stored in different web servers. The MMTP enables e-tourists (at home or at their offices) to receive multimedia attractions and accommodations at any time at their own convenience. A key feature of MMTP is that it can support up to several ten of multimedia terminals per server for the delivery of MPEG-3 encoded video materials.

3.4 Restrictions

At the e-tourist's side, we propose the use of ADSL technology [14], since large amounts of web pages direct from the web servers to the e-tourist. The e-tourist's client program returns back a small number of data packets. In addition, Asynchronous Transfer Mode (ATM) network technology [15] can be used in order to satisfy the required functionality of real time multimedia conferencing communications.

3.5 Indirect evaluation of the multimedia travel plans

Web usage mining in the tourism sector refers to non-trivial extraction of potentially useful tourism patterns and trends from large web access logs. The analysis of e-tourist patterns from navigation history by web usage mining can shed light on e-tourist navigation behaviour and the efficiency of the models used in the on-line tourist marketing process etc. In the literature, one can find several reasons why analysis of computer log files may be of enormous value for agents, managers and especially for educators [16]. Generally, web usage mining can be applied to all leading web sites of the tourism sector such as: a) travel agents and tour operators, b) specialist service providers, c) computer reservation systems (CRS) and d) public tourism agencies.

At MMTP the multimedia travel plans use is evaluated analysing the computer log derived, while e-tourists access multimedia travel plans. Precisely, in MMTP every single request, that a web server receives is recorded in an access log mainly registering the origin of the request, a time stamp and the resource requested, whether the request is for a web page containing for example a multimedia attraction or an accommodation. The evaluation of a multimedia travel plan (and so it's attractions and accommodations) by analysis of computer logs has two methological advantages: a) it does not suffer from biases due to self-report methods, b) the information regarding e-tourist's activities is

Sustainable Tourism, F. D. Pineda, C. A. Brebbia & M. Mugica (Editors)
© 2004 WIT Press, www.witpress.com, ISBN 1-85312-724-8

accumulated automatically in a way that does not interfere with everyday e-travelling activities and is stored in digital format. This is easy for future processing and analysis.

The data-mining module of the MMTP will perform the three consecutive procedures:

1) *Data gathering and pre-processing* for filtering and formatting the log entries: The administrator picks filters in the pre-processing phase to select desired e-tourist, or e-tourist group, the desired time period and/or the relevant subset of web pages in order to zero-in the travel plans, the attractions and the accommodations to evaluate. In addition, we can define the interpretation of "*session*" and sequence of e-tourist's clicks, concepts important in the web log data transformation. A *session* can be defined as the sequence of clicks on one e-tourist, which happen each time from "log in" and "log out" to a web multimedia travel plan. Also, we can define a session as a series of clicks of one e-tourist happening in the specified period after the certain specified action. Thereafter, data mining algorithms can use these sessions as the basic units for searching patterns.

2) *Pattern discovery* which consists of the use of a variety of algorithms, such as association rule mining, sequential pattern analysis, clustering and classification on the transformed data in order to discover relevant and potentially useful patterns, and finally

3) *Pattern analysis* during which the administrator retrieves and interprets the patterns discovered. The discovered patterns will not be easy to interpret, so we must implement intuitive graphic charts and tables for *pattern visualization and understanding*. We must implement an ad-hoc query language that would allow the weeding-out of irrelevant patterns and the focus on knowledge discovered to use for the evaluation of e-tourists on-line. Currently there is a variety of web log analysis tools available. However, the most of them like NetTracker, Webtrends, Analog and SurfAid provide limited statistical analysis of web log data [17, 18].

3.6 Future prospects

Following the need to know more about multimedia travel plans usage patterns, in addition to the potential of computer log analysis, four research questions of a further study should be addressed:

RQ1: *To what extent are multimedia travel plans presented in MMTP's websites?*

The data regarding this extent will enable us to understand how to utilize the web potential for multimedia travel plans providing and it's components (e.g. attractions, hotels).

RQ2: *What is the usage rate of content item in an MMTP website?*

Answering this question will help us understand whether there is a threshold for the amounts of items viewed by e-tourists. Do e-tourists concentrate on a very small number of content items, or, on the contrary, is their content consumption distributed equally over all items presented in the MMTP?

Sustainable Tourism, F. D. Pineda, C. A. Brebbia & M. Mugica (Editors)

RQ3: *What are the individual differences among e-tourists regarding content consumption?*
Whereas the second question deals with the content, this third question focuses on e-tourists. Understanding the individual differences between e-tourists will shed light on the ways in which implementation of the Internet affects patterns of e-tourist's content usage and on individual variance in e-travelling habits.

RQ4: *How do attractions and accommodations characteristics affect the presentation and consumption of content in MMTP website?*

It is imperative for us to direct the algorithms that will search for the rules answering the above questions. Therefore, a further study will be conducted on a pilot web site of MMTP during a future time period.

4 Conclusions

The continued growth and success of the WWW as a global delivery mechanism for multimedia tourist content (e.g. multimedia travel plans) will ride on technical issues as much as on economic, social, and political ones. Some questions that we can only raise include the following self questioning considerations: Will there be ways to pay for quality tourist content (e.g. travel plans)? Will jurisdictions force leading Internet service providers of the tourism sector to restrict access to parts of the Web considered in violation of local criminal statutes? Answers to these questions will be given, as integrated web management architectures evolve. As analyzed before, our web management system of multimedia travel plans (MMTP) is based on a peer-to-peer (P2P) architecture, in which multimedia travel plans web servers (peers) share some of their resources. The MMTP was analyzed, focusing especially on its "data mining" module that evaluates indirectly multimedia travel plans. Web usage mining in the tourism sector represents an increasingly burgeoning technology, which should be approached favourably, but with awareness about the positive and negative features accompanying it. Data mining techniques entail to better integrating of evaluating data into tourism sector, enhanced evaluation reliability and validity, and the saving of e-tourist's agent time. The implementation and installation of MMTP in European pilot sites will result in a substantial increase of the tourist flows, as this improves the QoS provided to the e-tourists.

Acknowledgments

The authors acknowledge Mr. Benetatos Theodore for his support and time in reading this paper.

References

[1] Hoffman, J., Emerging technologies and their impact on travel distribution. Journal of Vacation Marketing, 1(1), pp. 95-103, 1994.

Sustainable Tourism, F. D. Pineda, C. A. Brebbia & M. Mugica (Editors)

[2] Williams P, Hobson J. S. P., Virtual reality and tourism: fact or fantasy? Tourism Management, 6(6), pp. 423-427, 1995.

[3] Buhalis, D., Licata M.C., The future eTourism intermediaries. Tourism Management, 23, pp. 207-220. 2002.

[4] Tatipamula, M., Khasnabish B., Multimedia Communications Networks. Artech House: Boston-London, 1998.

[5] Buhalis, D., Strategic use of information technologies in the tourism industry. Tourism Management, 19(5), pp. 409-421, 1998.

[6] WTO, Guidelines for the Transfer of New Technologies in the Field of Tourism. World Tourism Organisation, Madrid, 1998.

[7] Buhalis, D., Information and telecommunications technologies as a strategic tool for small and medium tourism enterprises in the contemporary business environment. In Tourism – The state of the Art: The Strathclyde Symposium, Eds. A. Seaton et al. J. Wiley, London, pp. 254-275, 1994.

[8] Heffeda, M., et al., A hybrid architecture for cost-effective on-demand media streaming. Computer Networks, 44, pp. 353-382, 2004

[9] Sirbu, M., Tygar, J.D., NetBill: An electronic commerce system optimized for network delivered information and services. Proc. IEEE Compcon '95, Eds. IEEE, pp. 20-25, 1995.

[10] Neuman, B., Security, Payment, and Privacy for Network Commerce. IEEE JSAC, 13(8), pp. 1523-1531, 1995.

[11] Kanellopoulos, D., et al., Design issues for Dynamic Multimedia Applications in the field of advertisement using WWW technology. Technika Chronika, Scientific Journal of the Technical Chamber of Greece, 18(1-2), pp. 7-17, 1998.

[12] Schulzrinne, H., World Wide Web: Whether, Whither, What Next?. IEEE Network Magazine, pp. 10-17, March/April, 1996.

[13] Kahan J., A capability-based authorization model for the world-wide web. Computer Networks and ISDN Systems, 27, pp. 1055-1064, 1995.

[14] Standard ANSI T1.413., Network and Customer Installation Interfaces-Asymmetric Digital Subscriber Line (ADSL) Metallic Interface, 1995.

[15] Handel, R., Huber, M., and Schrober, S., ATM Networks - Concepts, Protocols, Applications. In Addison-Wesley (Eds), 1994.

[16] Pahl, C., Donnellan, D., Data mining technology for the evaluation of web based teaching and learning systems. Proc. of the AACE E-Learn Conference, Montreal, Canada, 2002.

[17] Zaiane, O.R., & Luo, J., Towards evaluating learners' behaviour in a web-based distance learning environment. 2001. Online available at: http://www.cs.ualberta.ca/~zaiane/postscript/icalt.pdf.

[18] Zaiane, O.R., Xin, XM., Han, J., Discovering Web Access Patterns and Trends by Applying OLAP and Data Mining Technology on Web Logs. Proc. of the ADL'98-Advances in Digital Libraries, Santa Barbara, 1998.

Sustainable Tourism, F. D. Pineda, C. A. Brebbia & M. Mugica (Editors)

Author Index